# Sins of the Flesh

## A History of
## Ethical Vegetarian Thought

ROD PREECE

UBC Press • Vancouver • Toronto

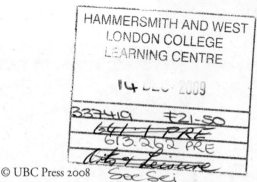
© UBC Press 2008

16 15 14 13 12 11 10 09 08    5 4 3 2 1

Printed in Canada with vegetable-based inks on ancient-forest-free paper (100%
post-consumer recycled) that is processed chlorine- and acid-free.

---

**Library and Archives Canada Cataloguing in Publication Data**

Preece, Rod, 1939-
Sins of the flesh : a history of ethical vegetarian thought / Rod Preece.

Includes bibliographical references and index.
ISBN 978-0-7748-1509-3 (bound); ISBN 978-0-7748-1510-9 (pbk.)

1. Vegetarianism–Moral and ethical aspects–History. 2. Vegetarianism–History.
I. Title.

TX392.P74 2008    179'.3    C2008-902835-X

---

Canadä

UBC Press gratefully acknowledges the financial support for our publishing program
of the Government of Canada through the Book Publishing Industry Development
Program (BPIDP), and of the Canada Council for the Arts, and the British
Columbia Arts Council.

This book has been published with the help of a grant from the Canadian Federation
for the Humanities and Social Sciences, through the Aid to Scholarly Publications
Programme, using funds provided by the Social Sciences and Humanities Research
Council of Canada.

UBC Press
The University of British Columbia
2029 West Mall
Vancouver, BC V6T 1Z2
604-822-5959 / Fax: 604-822-6083
www.ubcpress.ca

FSC
Mixed Sources
Cert no. SW-COC-001271
www.fsc.org
© 1996 Forest Stewardship Council

# Sins of the Flesh

For my fellows on the path

The sinful lusts of the flesh.

*– The Catechism,* in *The Book of Common Prayer* (1549)

For they that are after the flesh [of animals] do mind the things of the flesh.

– Tertullian (c. 160-220)

... the lust of the belly.

– St. Basil of Caesarea (329-379)

... that humour that lusteth after flesh and blood.

– Roger Crab (1655)

... 'tis no easy task to preach to the Belly that has no ears.

– Alexander Pope, paraphrasing Cato (1713)

... blood lusts ... brutalize the person and harden the instincts of the heart.

– Alphonse de Lamartine (1848)

# Contents

# Acknowledgments

Two books have been especially influential in my preparation of this volume: *Deep Vegetarianism,* by Michael Allen Fox, and *Vegetarianism: A History* (the second edition of *The Heretic's Feast*), by Colin Spencer. Much as is my admiration for the authors of these two books and the works they have produced, and much as I shall, unavoidably, repeat some of their messages and analyses in these pages, although in very different words and with very different emphases, my justification for *Sins of the Flesh* is that I believe I have something to offer that takes us a little further along the adventurous road Fox and Spencer have trod.[1] And whereas I now and again reject specific interpretations of Spencer and Fox, I must stress that such disputes are often a matter of interpretation of available evidence, not simple matters of fact. I do not insist that my interpretations are right and theirs erroneous – where we differ – but on the basis of probabilities, I do find some interpretations more appropriate than others, and my interpretations do not always coincide with those of my forerunners. Perhaps I deviate from Spencer the most in that I find his book almost as much a fascinating history of food – which I would be quite incapable of writing – as a history of vegetarianism and almost as much a history of philosophical and historical-cultural attitudes in general as of attitudes that relate to vegetarianism and animal ethics in particular. My interest lies primarily in the ethical dimensions of vegetarianism, and it is on this aspect of vegetarianism that I concentrate in this book. Moreover, I view neither our prehistorical past, nor the experience of the East, nor the wisdom of Pythagoras, nor the asceticism of early Christianity in anything like the same manner as Spencer.

And there is considerably more disagreement besides. Still, I have benefited a good deal from Spencer's erudition and am grateful for it, although I regret that none of his copious notes are referenced with page numbers. In fact, notes without a page reference are of almost no value. I deviate from Fox in that his work relates more to the philosophy than to the history of vegetarianism, as I am sure he intended and would be the first to acknowledge with justifiable pride. Despite *Deep Vegetarianism*'s major orientation, however, there is also much of interest to the philosophical historian in its pages, even if, again, I do not always concur with his interpretations.

Although Daniel Dombrowski's *The Philosophy of Vegetarianism* played only a modest role in directly influencing the preparation of this book, other than for Chapter 4, when I first read the book a number of years ago, it had a significant impact on my thinking. It is an impact that I am sure still lingers and will have had an important subliminal effect on my approach. Moreover, despite the title of Dombrowski's book, there is much of significant historical merit, especially on pre-Socratic, classical, and Hellenistic Greece. A fourth book, Tristram Stuart's *Bloodless Revolution: A Cultural History of Vegetarianism from 1600 to the Present Time* appeared when the research for this volume was essentially complete and all but the final words of the text had been written. It treats mainly the period and events covered in some of the later chapters of this volume. Although it was a most enjoyable read, was most informative, and is superbly composed and researched, especially for the period from the mid-seventeenth to early nineteenth centuries, the book proved only tangentially relevant to my theme and approach. It is certainly a most valuable addition to the literature on vegetarian history and absolutely essential for serious scholars interested predominantly in the European (and primarily British) seventeenth to early nineteenth centuries. Nonetheless, Stuart and I have very different – even competing – stories to tell.

I am indebted to the research of Keith Thomas that he used in his groundbreaking *Man and the Natural World: Changing Attitudes in England, 1500-1800*. It was especially valuable for the third section of my eighth chapter. Although I taught the *philosophy* of Rousseau for over thirty years, my biographical comments on Rousseau's *history* in Chapter 9 have been informed largely by Maurice Cranston's superb three-volume biography on the life of the Franco-Swiss philosopher. I am also grateful to Karen and Michael Iacobbo, whose *Vegetarian America: A History* helped to fill significant lacunae in my knowledge of the American vegetarian experience that I needed for Chapter 13. I deemed it important for the sake of a measure of completeness to include a chapter on American vegetarian history in this book. However, for those who require a more comprehensive examination, I can do no better than suggest they read the very informative and comprehensive book by the Iacobbos. My relatively few pages are no substitute for the detail of their nearly three hundred.

Long before I read Barbara Ehrenreich's *Blood Rites: Origins and History of the Passions of War*, I had accepted the hypothesis promoted by Ehrenreich that early humans were much more prey than predator, a hypothesis now confirmed in abundant detail by the meticulous researches of Donna Hart and Robert W. Sussman in *Man the Hunted: Primates, Predators and Human Evolution*. Nonetheless, Ehrenreich's book stimulated me to recognize the importance of animal sacrifice in relation to predation and the significance of animal worship. I have learned much from her evidence and argument but have applied it in a field in which she had no interest per se (her concern was with the origins of warfare), and I have reached conclusions that I am confident she would not share. Nonetheless, I am indebted to her analysis, albeit indirectly.

Just as I had accepted the view of the human as prey long before I read Ehrenreich, so I had some reservations about the extent of vegetarianism and the ethical treatment of animals in Eastern religious traditions long before I had read the work of D.N. Jha, professor of history at the University of Delhi. Indeed, I mentioned at some length in my *Animals and Nature: Cultural Myths, Cultural Realities*, written some years before Jha's major work on the subject of Eastern animal worship was published, the manner in which I consider the religions of the Orient to have been misinterpreted, especially by Western scholars. Nonetheless, the abundant evidence provided by Professor Jha in *The Myth of the Holy Cow* gave me access to detailed material of which I was previously unaware. I have relied on this material in part for Chapter 2 of this book. Of course, my sources for that chapter are quite varied, but without Jha's meticulous research, I would have lacked the rigorous evidence to draw the conclusions that my previous research had prepared me to expect on further investigation. I could not have unearthed independently the myriad sources he brings to bear.

For my understanding of Pythagoras, I am indebted in considerable measure to Charles H. Kahn, whose book on *Pythagoras and the Pythagorean Way of Life* was as invaluable to me for my third chapter as it was in my preparation of a chapter of *Brute Souls, Happy Beasts, and Evolution: The Historical Status of Animals*. Even where my conclusions on Pythagoras and the Pythagoreans may sometimes differ markedly from those of

Kahn, they are inspired by him. For the same chapter, I have been very fortunate to have Jonathan Barnes's *Early Greek Philosophy* as a source book of some of the most significant statements of the pre-Socratics.

In *The Ethics of Diet* (1883), Howard Williams provided a remarkable account of a very large proportion of material relevant to the history of vegetarianism, as previous researchers have found, some acknowledging their indebtedness to Williams, others pretending it to have been a great deal less significant than it really was. The book is in fact a boon to all those interested in the historical record. I have availed myself of that material as appropriate in the preparation of this book. For the convenience of the reader, I have made reference to the readily available 2004 Illinois reprint edition, edited by Carol J. Adams (I have referred to the 1883 edition in some of my previous work), both where I have profited from Williams's compilations, including the large number of citations from the original contributors, and where I have reason to believe the reader will not have access to some of the scarcer historical material. Elsewhere, I have also sometimes referred the reader to readily available sources rather than the more obscure originals.

My greatest debt is owed to those who were role models on the vegetarian journey. There were several, but foremost among these was Stephanie Brown of Toronto. If it was watching a documentary film in Calgary in 1992 on "downer" animals in stockyards that proved the immediate occasion of my wife and myself pursuing the vegetarian course, it was Stephanie who was the most persuasive personal catalyst. Her gracious and considerate, yet unwavering, advocacy by example and word both pointed the path and facilitated the choice.

The constant commitment of my wife, Lorna Chamberlain, to the animal cause helped to make the vegetarian path far easier, more enjoyable, and smoother than it otherwise might have been. I am especially pleased to acknowledge my indebtedness to Steve Sapontzis, Daniel Dombrowski, and Jodey Castricano for their erudite and sympathetic appraisals of the manuscript. Their insightful critiques helped me to avoid some inadequacies in the original manuscript. Yet, at the same time, their reviews persuaded the publishers that the manuscript was worthy of publication. They agreed to the release of their names so that their exceptional assistance could be duly acknowledged. Valuable as their assistance was, any remaining inadequacies are, of course, entirely my own. As always, my editor at UBC Press, Randy Schmidt, has been very helpful, indulgent of my idiosyncrasies, and supportive of my efforts.

# Sins of the Flesh

# Introduction

On an early page of her celebrated 1963 novel, *The Group,* Mary McCarthy introduced her readers to "Pokey" Prothero, a young woman who was "interested only in animals and hunt dances" and whose ambition "was to become a vet." Nor was it only the dances following the hunt that enthralled her, for, on the following page, we read that "she had been away hunting for the weekend."[1] To many, there would appear to be an incongruence, a cognitive dissonance, between desiring a career as someone devoted to the health and care of animals, on the one hand, and participation in the wilful destruction of animal life, on the other. Mary McCarthy does not consider the dissonance worthy of a mention, any more than does the early utilitarian philosopher Jeremy Bentham, who maintained competing propositions about animal suffering and the inferior value of animal life simultaneously.[2] Similarly, the veterinarians William Karkeek and William Youatt, nineteenth-century authors on animal immortality and animal wellbeing respectively, were also avid proponents of, and occasional participants in, the hunt.[3] For the ethical vegetarian, there is an equal contradiction in the lives of those who claim to abominate cruelty to animals but who still go home to a roast-beef supper. Many say they love animals. But all that the evidence suggests is that they love to eat them. Indeed, for most vegetarians, the eschewing of animal flesh is a natural extension of the accordance to animals of the most elementary of rights, just as we would consider human rights necessarily to include respect for human life. Nonetheless, there is a 1965 book by Robin Borwick about donkeys entitled *People with Long Ears* that makes an equation between human and nonhuman animals that drives the less radical animal-welfare scientists and

others into apoplectic fits – metaphorically speaking at least. There seems
to be a perception of glaring contradictions in such persons both between
their protection of life and their causing of death, on the one side, and
between the value they accord human animals and their lesser valuation of
nonhuman animals, on the other, that requires a careful analysis. I propose
to address in this book how this question of value has been approached historically and to investigate the path of ethical vegetarianism in human history.

## Where Are Vegetarians to Be Found?

Initially, one must ask: "what is vegetarianism and how numerous are its
adherents?" Reliable figures are hard to come by, and the existing data is
subject to conflicting interpretations. But probably not much more than 3
or perhaps 4 percent of North Americans – some say 5, whereas others,
such as the Vegetarian Resource Group, after having conducted a poll in
1994, suggest less than 1 percent – are moderately strict vegetarians, with a
slightly higher proportion in Europe. It is perhaps more instructive and
impressive to note that, already as of 1992, "as the *New York Times* reported, there are well over 10 million vegetarians in [the United States].
New York alone is supporting 35 vegetarian restaurants for about 100,000
strict vegetarians, and there are perhaps half a million who are part-time
vegetarians."[4] Hilda Kean has stated that as of 1994, "at least 5 per cent of
all Britons were vegetarian and 5,000 people a week were estimated to be
moving to a meat-free diet."[5] If this was true then – and some even estimate
the number to be as high as 7 percent – we would have good reason to
believe that the figures would be slightly higher today. But we might also
be inclined to wonder whether the higher figures are at least in part a product of wishful thinking.

The proportion of vegetarians who are vegan in the West is decidedly on
the rise, and an at least quasi vegetarianism appeals to many more than in
the past. And, of course, there are some omnivorous members of humane
societies and other animal organizations who practise vegetarianism from
shame when they are in the company of their more radical colleagues from
the same organizations but return to a flesh diet when they are at home.
There are also many vegetarians who are vegans manqués – wannabe vegans, if you will, or vegan "flexitarians" (see page 15) – those who are steadfastly vegetarian but vegan only when circumstances readily allow. Certainly, there are far fewer vegetarians in the Orient, including India, where
animal sacrifice is still practised, than is commonly believed, especially by

vegetarians themselves. A majority of those who are vegetarian in India (vegetarians constitute around one-third of the total population) are female, although certain areas of the country, predominantly the south, but also Gujarat in the northwest, are historically vegetarian as a whole. According to Sushil Mittal and Gene Thursby in *The Hindu World,* "the men of an estimated half of twentieth-century Hindu families (including those of several Brahman jatis) favor the eating of fish, chicken and mutton."[6] In fact, Indian men often claim the arduousness of their employment requires the strength purportedly derived from a flesh diet, a claim given encouragement by the young Gandhi, an encouragement he came later to regret. He thought initially that Indians could overcome their British masters by acquiring equivalent strength by eating the diet they ate. Later, on reading vegetarian advocacy literature in an English vegetarian restaurant, he was awakened to the ethical appeal of the fleshless diet. As James Gaffney has expressed it appositely: "Gandhi, who had renounced vegetarianism out of hostility to English colonialism, was restored to it by English liberalism."[7] As India becomes wealthier, we can expect, based on our experience of economic development elsewhere, that the proportion of vegetarians will decline, although not as rapidly as would be the case if there were no strong vegetarian cultural traditions.

In China, almost all vegetarians – excluding a few Buddhist monks (most Chinese Buddhist monks are not vegetarian) – are inhabitants of rural areas, and they are often vegetarians not by choice but by poverty, the vast majority of the rural population consuming 10 percent animal protein in their diet (in the United States it is about 50 percent). The figures for South Korea are very similar to those for China. With its ethic of unity and conformity, deviations from the dietary norm in South Korea are said to be frowned upon. On the other hand, it is reported that there are fifteen so-called "vegetarian" restaurants in Seoul alone, some of which offer more varied fare than purely vegetarian. But at least the availability of vegetarian dishes can be assured in those establishments. Westerners who arrive in Chinese cities as students and who are already vegetarian usually find it very difficult to remain true to their preferred diet. Even Chinese sleeper trains do not offer vegetarian meals. One fares little better in Japan, it would appear. According to Jan Dodd, "vegetarianism isn't widely practised, or a fully understood concept in Japan. You might ask for a vegetarian (saishoku) meal in a restaurant and still be served something with meat or fish."[8] Such is the ubiquity in urban China, Korea, and Japan of flesh and sauces derived therefrom, other than sometimes in the temples and the occasional vegetarian establishment. Nor are other Buddhist temples always secure for a plant-based diet. Even the Dalai Lama, the exiled head of Tibetan Buddhism, apparently having unsuccessfully tried vegetarianism once before, claimed in April 2005 to have recently begun to try a vegetarian diet again. Buddhists, particularly Buddhist priests, may have the reputation of being vegetarian. Only sometimes are they so in fact.

## WHAT IS A VEGETARIAN?

The question of what constitutes a vegetarian receives a host of conflicting answers. An employee of the Vegetarian Society in England once told me that they would count as a vegetarian anyone who does not eat anything with a face. While not having a face may be an initial pointer to the uninitiated in determining what is acceptable and what is not, being faceless is not ipso facto an infallible indicator of what is ethically appropriate. What of clams, mussels, oysters, scallops, and the like? Are they not animal? Are they not sentient beings? The scientific jury is in general still out about their sentience, while admitting serious doubts. It was once common for at least some to doubt the sentience of many more complex (and faced) creatures, although Scottish animal scientists have now concluded that the expressionless fish feel pain and quite substantially so. Recent investigations have convinced Duke University researchers that "bird-brained" birds have well-developed, feeling mental systems. Furthermore, a study by British scientists published in the *Proceedings of the National Academy of Sciences* casts serious doubt on the anthropocentric assumption of numerous philosophers that thought is dependent on language. "We are kicking against the claim that it is language which allows you to do other high order intellectual functions," said Rosemary Varley, lead researcher from the University of Sheffield.[9] Assuming such scientists are right – for, to misrepresent Euripides slightly, one scientist's newly discovered meat soon becomes another scientist's atrophied poison – the time-honoured sports of shooting and angling are decidedly cruel pastimes, even if the fish, after being tormented with a hook in its mouth, is returned alive to the water. Nonetheless, much to the chagrin of vegetarians, a Norwegian 2005 study suggests that lobsters, and by implication less complex crustaceans, do not feel pain. The animal advocate remains dubious. No questions on vegetarianism and the principles behind its practice are ever as simple as they at first appear.

What of the consumption of eggs and dairy products? Although eggs, milk, and cheese are not flesh, they are derived from the confinement, and some would argue the perennial mistreatment, of animals, even if they are

so-called "free-run" or "free-range" animals – intentionally deceptive mis-
nomers if ever there were any, at least in much of North America! For
example, in the United States the Department of Agriculture designates
"free-range" to mean that a bird has some, even if limited, access to the out-
doors, however confined and in whatever proximity to others, while practices of beak trimming and other invasive procedures continue unabated.
The life of a "free-range" turkey is four to six months. In the wild the bird
can live for up to twenty years. What if they are raised according to the five
freedoms that the more compassionate of omnivores regard as essential for
what they call cruelty-free farming? These freedoms are: (1) animals should
have freedom from thirst, hunger, and malnutrition through ready access
to fresh water and a diet to maintain full health and vigour; (2) animals
should have freedom from thermal and physical discomfort through the
provision of an appropriate environment, including shelter and a comfortable resting area; (3) animals should have freedom from pain, injury, and
disease by prevention or rapid diagnosis and treatment; (4) animals should
have freedom to express normal behaviour by the provision of sufficient
space, proper facilities, and company of their own kind; (5) animals should
have freedom from fear and distress by ensuring conditions and treatment
that avoid mental suffering.[10] Most vegetarians welcome these "five freedoms" for food animals enthusiastically but wonder, if the animals are entitled to such benevolent treatment, why they are not also entitled to their
lives and to the elimination of their inordinately early death pangs. If there
is a propensity to consider farm animals "stupid beasts," research conducted at the Babraham Institute of Cambridge should serve to dispel the
myth. In fact, not only pigs, long renowned for their intelligence, but other
food animals, too, are among the most perceptive and inquisitive of animals. Cattle, sheep, and the like are as worthy of protection as pets.

The proponents of the freedoms argue that a conversion of significant
proportions of the population to vegetarianism in the near future is highly
unlikely and that the "five freedoms" will ensure the animals a satisfactory
life prior to their becoming food. It will also ensure that animal wellbeing
will be a permanent feature of the minds of many. Nonetheless, any consequent success may encourage acceptance of the new status quo. One must
not forget, as George Bernard Shaw wrote in the "Epistle Dedicatory" to
*Man and Superman*, "the man whose consciousness does not correspond to
that of the majority is a madman."[11] Still, the vegetarian and socialist
Shaw's own life and values showed that although one must not venture too
far from prevailing views in order to be regarded as worthy of being heard,
one must also be something, if not too much, of a madman if one wishes

to effect changes in the values of society. Abstract ethics, however rational, can succeed only to the extent that they deviate not too greatly from society's deeply embraced norms. Yet the societal dietary norms are repugnant to ethical vegetarians. Vegetarians are thus forced to be both "man" and "superman" simultaneously. That is, they must play the wise madman and the mad wise man interchangeably, eccentric and *magus* together. And if one still wishes to proclaim the ethical principle unadorned, it is worthy to recall that numerous renowned luminaries – Pope, Gay, Mandeville, Goldsmith, Rousseau, Voltaire, Lamartine, Wagner, and Tennyson among them – have proclaimed the virtue of being vegetarian, while failing, by various degrees, or so it would appear, to practise what they preached. This principle without practice is reminiscent of several acquaintances who have said, "I *ought* to be a vegetarian," but who, despite the abstention from veal perhaps, continue in their omnivorous habits.

What, then, of animal by-products, such as skins that are transformed into leather? A case can be made, and often is by the opponents of vegetarianism, that animals raised for their hides to be used as leather are among the most cruelly treated of creatures. Such opponents insist that if vegetarians are to be consistent – and they are sometimes derided by the same voices for not being so – they must also reject the killing of animals for the use of their skins. And so they must. And very many do, a fact usually ignored by the cavillers. What the purveyors of such arguments also usually fail to recognize is that the argument applies to themselves just as strongly. If the way leather-producing animals are kept is manifestly cruel (and the cavillers are right to point out that it is, perhaps most notably for the production of specialty items such as doeskin gloves, crocodile shoes, alligator purses, or sealskin handbags), then, unless the opponents of vegetarianism wish to confess to fostering the abject cruelty they have correctly identified, they, too, must eschew the use of animal skins, including leather – for example, in certain clothing, belts, shoes, seats, briefcases, and the like. That anti-vegetarian omnivores do not recognize that the argument applies equally to themselves is a recognition that at least in some degree they hold the vegetarian to a higher degree of morality than they hold the flesh eater. Implicitly, they recognize the worthiness of the vegetarian's case and look for a ground on which they can claim that there are some limitations to the vegetarian's acknowledged moral superiority. As it is, the notion of the vegetarian who is not completely pure serves to provide a ready rationalization for the flesh eater. If it is satisfactory for the vegetarian to be a little less than perfect, so it seems to imply, then it is equally satisfactory for the flesh eater to be wholly imperfect. Omnivores must at the very least confess to the cruelty even if they excuse the cruelty as what they consider a "necessary" and justifiable cruelty. And in the above-proclaimed moral infraction, the omnivore has conceded the practice of using animal hides for human ends is unnecessary.

The vegetarian is initially at a social disadvantage. The special dinner at family gatherings, on first dates, at communal festivities, at weddings and funerals, on anniversaries, at church and employer barbecues, and on religious occasions, or occasions that had an initial religious or pagan impetus, such as Easter or Christmas (and still do for many), performs a vital societal function. It is no less significant in seemingly quite secular rituals with a religious origin such as Thanksgiving, where even the festive food, the animal to be slaughtered, is prescribed. The ritual promotes the solidarity, the belongingness, of the group or pair. Even the founder of the Vegan Society in England, Donald Watson, on being asked what were his greatest difficulties, replied: "Well, I suppose it is the social – excommunicating myself from that part of life where people meet to eat." To be sure, some vegetarians insist they prefer their ethical principles over the value of communal gathering, but they do so at the expense of the social bond.

The ritual meal tells the recipients of the bounty that they are welcome, appreciated, respected, and desired people. In early society, a man's wealth and prestige were determined by how many cattle he owned. In the words of Mary Midgley: "meat-eating indicates success and prosperity, therefore hospitality."[12] Discussions about cuisine, recipes, and cooking constitute a major point of human contact and revolve, in the first instance, around flesh dishes. The vegetarian member of an omnivorous family, church, business, or even society may thereby become an outsider, failing to participate fully in the communal process. Among several other purposes, the meal reflects the generosity, the good taste, the wealth, and the prowess of the provider – even male sexual prowess, for there seems to be some correlation between meat and virility in the public mind. Moreover, in early human societies, meat was used by males as a part of self-display in sexual selection, with the implication of: "Look at me! I am especially brave. I am a great hunter and therefore a good provider. I have good genes and will provide the seed of good offspring." The vegetarian appears to be the weak cousin. Perhaps, because of such evolutionary impetus, it will always be supremely difficult to persuade pubescent males to abandon flesh. The grander the meal, the more luxurious the offering from the hunt, the more impressive is the gift. And this usually involves the provision of flesh – the most expensive and exorbitant food item, such specialty items as truffles excluded. And even the provision of such specialty items will lack the bravery, strength, or status associated with the provision of flesh. Ineluctably, vegetarians will seem inadequately generous with their nonflesh offering or inadequately grateful for the donor's gift of flesh – and, in either case, inadequately attractive to potential partners. The vegetarian is likely to be viewed as an outsider. Moreover, the hero and the adventurer are unlikely to be depicted as vegetarians. Valour and the fleshless diet are not associated in the public perception.

The British philosopher Roger Scruton has argued very ably the importance of the human dining ritual and the vital civilizing distinction between feeding and eating, between *fressen* and *essen,* from the flesh eater's perspective.[13] If the vegetarian is to overcome the potential loss of the art of communal eating, on which so many aspects of societal life depend, it is of the greatest importance to maintain a concentrated emphasis on the social and integrative aspects of culinary events. Only then will vegetarians be able to escape the impending alienation of failing to participate in the communal dining process.

We may note also that the conventional conception of being "a man," of being "manly" or "masculine," involves the ideas of being courageous, robust, valorous, and warrior-like, of being "rational" rather than "emotional." By contrast, the popular "masculine" conception of a vegetarian is of one who is soft, unduly compassionate, and tender. These notions are all inherently incompatible with the traditional notion of "manliness." The male vegetarian is in considerable danger of being viewed by his fellows as unmanly, even cowardly and effete, perhaps somewhat effeminate. The relatively easy *moral* decision to become a vegetarian faces several, seemingly sometimes insuperable, *psychological* barriers. It is scarcely surprising that vegetarians are predominantly, if far from exclusively, female. Of course, many renowned male (as well as female) athletes and other celebrities are vegetarian or vegan, and many in the past have been so. But, strangely, this has had little effect on changing the public consciousness with regard to the masculinity of flesh eating.

By contrast, as early as 1885 in George Salmon's *Introduction to the New Testament,* referring to the early Christian era, we read that "even those who used animal food themselves came to think of the vegetarian as one who lived a higher form of life."[14] It is as true in the twenty-first century as in biblical times. Even those who have no inclination toward vegetarianism often share a mild sense of guilt that the vegetarian takes the high ground that they themselves have relinquished.

Nonetheless, especially when arrogantly, aggressively, pompously, or self-assertively expressed, vegetarian attitudes may make omnivores uncomfortable, oppositional, and defensive. At its worst, the vegetarian mentality is paraded mournfully in the self-congratulatory terms of "woe is me. I am so misjudged and maligned by people who ought to know better and who ought to understand what I so readily understand." The expected response is found in the attitudes of numerous animal welfare scientists. More often than not, they deride the vegetarians' unusual practices and their paucity in numbers, as though the numerous millennia of the customary consumption of flesh and the numerical majority of the omnivores counted as some kind of moral argument in their own favour.[15] Of course, the greatest opposition to vegetarianism comes from those engaged in, or vicariously maintained by, the flesh industry. They often condemn vegetarian advocates on the grounds of the vegetarians' opposition to their very right to their livelihood while ignoring, for example, that the abolition of capital punishment in certain states deprived the public executioner of his employment in that capacity – rightly so, many imagine – and that legislation against drugs once legal and readily available over the counter, such as laudanum (opium), has rendered certain related occupations untenable. No one regrets that unprotected asbestos workers, gas lamplighters, and child chimney sweeps can no longer find employment in these capacities. Indeed, opposition to tobacco use has deprived many farmers of a decent livelihood. And although most would express great sympathy for such farmers, and believe it appropriate to provide financial compensation in their search for a new and viable crop or for a new form of employment, few would consider the farmers' financial woes a sufficient ground to make tobacco use once again acceptable. No one has a lawful right to a position whose practice the society condemns. Of course, no such condemnation exists at the present in the case of flesh consumption, but many vegetarians believe that it should exist and that its arrival is only a matter of time.

## HUMAN-ANIMAL HIERARCHY

It is in fact not at all unusual for the omnivore simply to bypass the vegetarian ethical appeal on the assumption that humans are in some special manner "superior" to other animals and hence entitled to ethical preference over animals. Often, a refusal to become a vegetarian arises not from a rejection of the claimed moral imperative but from its avoidance in the assumption of some kind of exclusive status. As Pangloss says in Voltaire's *Candide:* "Swine were intended to be eaten, therefore we eat pork all the year round."[16] And most of us give the matter no more rational consideration than did Dr.

Pangloss. If this was "the best of all possible worlds," as Pangloss naively imagines in apparent but misguided imitation of Leibniz, it was certainly not so for the pigs. The idea that animals "were intended" for human use stretches in philosophical discourse back to Xenophon and Aristotle. The ethical question is obviated by the parroting of the unfounded and irrelevant "intended" dictum. Many Christians and Jews – and their opponents – misinterpret the doctrine of "dominion" over animals as one that allows them to use animals for their own ends at will, when, in fact, the relevant biblical passage imposes a modest obligation toward animals upon them.[17] Nonetheless, human claims to preferential treatment are implicit in all such dicta – whether a matter of the "intended" or "dominion" justification.

Have centuries of habit reduced the potential persuasiveness of the vegetarian appeal in the same way that male and white supremacy once reigned unquestioned because they were considered normal? Today, at least among the educated in the West, sexism and racism are almost universally condemned. Frequent and strident opposition is now the norm. Will the same perhaps happen to vegetarianism? Is the necessary step simply the constant raising of the issue on the animals' behalf in many minds over long periods of time? Have we reached the potential for a greater era of benevolence? Much as we may consider such progress a forlorn hope, we should not forget that in the eighteenth century it was not unusual to encounter the view expressed in Henry Fielding's *Tom Jones* by Mrs. Deborah Wilkins about Tom Jones's wayward mother that she was "one of those misbegotten wretches, whom I don't look upon as my fellow creatures."[18] Miss Bridget went further and described the unfortunate Jenny as "an impudent slut, a wanton harlot, a wicked jade, a vile strumpet."[19] If we acknowledge other animals as our fellow creatures, might we perhaps be on the road to consideration of the rights of all sentient beings just as we have learned to disparage the attitudes of a Deborah Wilkins or a Miss Bridget? Nonetheless, we frequently encounter the idea expressed by Émile Zola in *Nana* (1880) of the human "animal nature,"[20] acknowledging humans as animals but at the same time implying that while there are instinctive, unreflective, even lustful aspects of the human psyche, humans are not to be judged by the same criteria as other animals, for we also possess rational and ethical characteristics of which nonhuman animals are said to be incapable. In fact, quite in contrast to the disparagement of "animal nature," we find Zola three chapters later in *Nana* having Clarisse say of La Faloise that she was tempted to throw him out: "The idiot didn't like animals, and that put the finishing touch to him."[21] If the path to ethical consideration of animal interests has been eased, the human is still treated as a being entitled to be judged by quite different ethical criteria from other animals. Despite Clarisse's care for animals and dismissal of those inconsiderate of animal interests, she continues to eat the animals! Indeed, paradoxically and quizzically, liking or loving or respecting animals seems for many people to bear very little relationship to not eating them. What other entity than an animal can be commonly thought an object of affection, even admiration, by an admirer who then duly goes home to eat one of his or her fellows – indeed, one of *our* fellow animals? Can anything other than evolutionary impulse, lust, habit, and now convenience have brought about such a state of affairs?

In *Logic: Inductive and Deductive* (1909), William Minto of the University of Aberdeen argued that practical wisdom would be acquired by the rigorous pursuit of logical argument. He included a "chain of being" diagram, about which he said: "A table of higher and lower classes arranged in order has been known from of old as a *tree* of division or classification."[22] This was how he prefaced the chain of being diagram, which included categories of "Sensible" and "Insensible" leading upward to "Animal," which in turn lead to "Irrational" and "Rational," which then takes us on to "Man." Habit encourages us to treat the diagram as logically persuasive, perhaps even compelling. "Man" is at the helm, and therefore "sacred," in a secular way. But it is the centuries-long practice, not logic, that allows us to arrange the chain of being diagram as we customarily do, at least implicitly, and to regard animals as sensible but lacking substantial reason, as we are inclined, and thus to accept the validity of the logical procedure that allows us to use animals for human dietary ends, although it is one with dubious premises. What should be clear is that even if the model were logically satisfactory, it would not follow that animals provided suitable food for humans any more than that the purported greater sensibility and rationality of the classical Greeks over their neighbours justified their enslavement of many of them. Nor did the cannibalistic pride of the North West Coast Kwakiutl, based on their sense of superiority over others, justify the imperative of the lyrics of their Cannibal Dancer's song:

> I went all around the world to find food.
> I went all around the world to find human flesh.
> I went all around the world to find human heads.
> I went all around the world to find human corpses.[23]

Tradition may be persuasive but it is never morally compelling. And if the proclaimed superiority does not justify the enslavement and the cannibalism, on what basis can human rational superiority over animals entitle the just person to use animals for food? Most of us grant animals certain minimal rights – the right to protection from unnecessary cruelty, for example. On what basis does depriving the animals of their lives constitute a part of "necessity"?

## The Origins of the Term "Vegetarian"

Some, notably and initially Francis William Newman (an early member and later president of the Vegetarian Society, founded toward the end of the 1840s), argue the word "vegetarian" is not derived from "vegetable" but from the Latin word "vegetus," meaning "lively, vigorous, and active," factors that are proclaimed benefits of the abstention from flesh foods. It is a highly improbable, far-fetched conjecture. Yet the myth was at one time continued on the English Vegetarian Society's own website, even though there is no even moderately persuasive evidence for it. The term "vegetarian" was apparently first used in the late 1830s. The *Oxford English Dictionary* states that "the general use of the word appears to have been largely due to the formation of the Vegetarian Society at Ramsgate in 1847," although this begs the question of its origins, for one has to wonder under what terms the about-to-be-formed society appealed to potential participants and how it came to name itself the Vegetarian Society. The *Oxford English Dictionary* records a usage of the term already in 1842 when *The Healthian* for April of that year referred to the inutility to "tell a healthy vegetarian that his diet is very uncongenial to the wants of his nature." Such usage suggests that the term "vegetarian" was already in use, that it was well enough understood, and that the practice of vegetarianism was sufficiently widespread that at least those who were interested in health would require no explanation of its meaning. Certainly, by 1848 the magazine *Punch* was using the term "vegetarian" as though it were a commonly understood concept. Still, there was no general agreement on the appropriate term, complaints about the misleading name – misleading in that a vegetarian diet is not restricted to vegetables – being common until well into the twentieth century.

As early as some time around late 1813 we find the radical poet Percy Bysshe Shelley writing a pamphlet unpublished during his lifetime that is now known as *On the Vegetable System of Diet*. However, this piece was untitled before rediscovery and publication in the early twentieth century. It was the editors of his pamphlet who gave it the title by which it is now known, a pamphlet he had written earlier in the same year being entitled by Shelley himself *A Vindication of Natural Diet.* Nonetheless, even earlier, in 1811, John Frank Newton, who perhaps first introduced Shelley to vegetarianism, had written *Return to Nature, or a Defence of the Vegetable Regimen,* indicating quite clearly that the denial of flesh was already known by reference to vegetables. Earlier still, in *The Primeval Diet of Man* (1801) George Nicholson referred to the "superior effects of a vegetable diet."[24] Indeed, in 1762 Rousseau had already counted pastry and fruits as being a part of the vegetable regimen.[25] The move toward the term "vegetarian" was well under way long before the formation of the Vegetarian Society and long before Francis Newman invented the improbable notion of the "vegetus" origin. The puzzle remains, however. Vegetarians are so called despite the fact, as noted, that they eat a great deal more than just vegetable matter – fruit, grain, and nuts, for example. Certainly, for a very long time those who ate what is now called a vegetarian diet were said to partake of a Pythagorean diet, after the early Ionian Greek philosopher who is said by some to have introduced (or reintroduced, if prehistoric humans did not eat flesh) the practice to the West of declining to eat animal flesh. In the early twentieth century, dissatisfied with the use of the term "vegetarian," as were many others – it was a common topic of debate – George Bernard Shaw, who, as we have noted, was himself an avowed abominator of the consumption of flesh, recommended the adoption of the term "Shelleyism," but it did not take. We are left with the term "vegetarian," although the essence of being a vegetarian is of course not the practice of eating vegetables but the avoidance of consuming the flesh of sentient beings. The details of the origins of the term appear, as yet, to be lost in the mists of time. Perhaps the explanation is quite simply that there was no suitable term available and that, while "vegetarian" was inadequate, it seemed preferable to any alternative. Today, the term is so well recognized it would be inopportune to seek a more accurate alternative.

The *Oxford English Dictionary* defines a vegetarian as: "One who lives wholly or principally upon vegetable foods; a person who on principle abstains from any form of animal food, or at least such as is obtained by the direct destruction of [sentient, animal] life." I have introduced the words "sentient" and "animal" into the sentence both because it is usually not life itself, but sentient animal life, that is at issue – except among those such as "fruitarians" (and some Jaina and Buddhists), who will not kill a living plant for their diet but will eat the fruits of the plant, as that does not harm the plant itself – and because few vegetarians would really have much concern about the destruction of, say, microbic animals, despite Shaw's quip in

*Too True to Be Good* about the rights of "a poor innocent microbe" and the practices of the Jaina, which we will discuss later. It is primarily sentient animals that are not to be harmed and hence not eaten. I restrict the term "sentience" to conscious beings. (To be conscious is to respond to one's surroundings in awareness of them; plants respond to their surroundings but have no awareness of them.) The word "vegetarian" has a variety of applications not *entirely* consistent with the implications of the *Oxford English Dictionary's* definition, at least if the words "on principle" in the definition have ethical content. For example, Roman gladiators, it is said, lived on a vegetarian diet of barley and leeks. Moreover, "Roman legions," historians have it, "had conquered the world" on "coarse wheaten porridge."[26] They were vegetarians. We can be confident they did not adopt this nonflesh regimen as a matter of ethical principle to prevent the destruction of animal life. It is unlikely they acquired their diet from principle at all. Indeed, today, and historically, a proportion of vegetarians deny themselves flesh for none other than health reasons and many more for nothing other than economy.

## Types of Vegetarians

We read, even in books by vegetarians about vegetarianism, of "ova-lacto vegetarians," "pollo-vegetarians," and "pesco-vegetarians." "Ova-lacto vegetarian" is a cumbersome name for what are the most common form of vegetarians, those who eschew the flesh of animals but still consume such products as eggs, milk, and cheese. There seems little point in calling them anything other than vegetarians, pure and simple. ("Lacto-vegetarians" eat dairy products but no eggs or flesh; "ova-vegetarians" eat eggs but no dairy or flesh.) "Pollo-vegetarians" are those who refrain from mammals but are willing to eat the flesh of birds, notably chickens. It is difficult to find any justification for such people being called vegetarians at all, not even quasi vegetarians, even if they do decline all red meat. Are we to acknowledge equally their beefo-porko-lambo vegetarian colleagues? The absurdity of the question proclaims its appropriate answer. "Pesco-vegetarians" are those who refuse the flesh of birds and mammals but continue to consume fish and other seafood. There is no real sense in which they are vegetarians if we consider that one of the primary purposes of vegetarianism is to recognize the value of animals' lives and to avoid animal suffering – according to the old saw that "a semivegetarian" makes as much sense as "a semivirgin." Mary Tyler Moore describes herself as "a vegetarian but not a vegan" because she eats plenty of fish, reflecting a common confusion about vegetarian terminology.[27] She is plainly in error about the meanings of vegetarianism and veganism. At best, she could be described as "pesco-vegetarian."

Nonetheless, despite these quibbles, any form of "quasi vegetarianism" can be a useful starting point for those who acknowledge the justice of the vegetarian cause but need time to fully adjust to its stringent requirements. Today, vegetarian advocates are inclined to regard vegetarianism as a process whereby over time one comes to infringe increasingly less on the rights and wellbeing of animals. It is a process of which I am acutely aware. I must confess myself guilty that I was a flesh eater many years ago when I became chair of the Ontario Society for the Prevention of Cruelty to Animals (SPCA), renouncing flesh only two years after assuming the post and, even then, at first, continuing to consume some seafood on occasion. Thus, partial vegetarianism is treated by some vegetarian advocates as a sometimes appropriate initial step. The American Dialect Society deemed "flexitarian" the most useful new word of 2003, describing the term as applicable to "a vegetarian who occasionally eats meat." If we regard vegetarianism as a process, we should be wary of being too critical of such impurity. As the then twenty-six-year-old classical singer and actor Emily Klassen expressed her "flexitarian" mode: "I hope that one day I can be a bit more virtuous and not eat meat at all."[28] The vegetarian ethic is duly asserted while falling short of vegetarian practice. The path is proclaimed. Nonetheless, we should be concerned lest those who practise half-measures should become accustomed to the shortfall.

To refer to flesh eaters such as "pollo-vegetarians" and "pesco-vegetarians" as vegetarians at all seems, however, little different from regarding traditional Catholics who deny themselves meat on Fridays or Eastern Orthodox Christians who partake of vegan feast days on occasion (Orthodox monastics are often vegans ) as some kind of vegetarian. Indeed, the traditional Catholic and Orthodox practices of such self-denial seem in part at least to justify vegetarians' beliefs, although the religious would explain the reason for such absence as penitence rather than avoidance of harm. If there are grounds for the denial of flesh on occasion, then there would appear to be some ground for considering the denial of flesh as in some manner in principle preferable to flesh consumption, even though it may not be thought a practicable regular habit because the spirit and flesh of humankind are weak. It would appear Saint Paul opposed the requirement of vegetarianism in the early Christian church not because it was not admirable but because, if it were stringently required, many potential converts to the new faith would be driven from Christianity by the hardship of its practice. A good case can be made that the acceptance of flesh consumption in the Jewish biblical tradition arose as a concession to human frailty in environmentally deleterious circumstances following the flood.[29] Today, it is notable that many proudly proclaim they are vegetarians in part, even though they eat chicken or fish. This is an implicit acknowledgment of the virtue of the vegetarian case. Such people want to proclaim they approximate what they feel implicitly is the virtuous path. Moreover, to think of fish and poultry as of a very different order from the flesh of large animals is not without some cultural foundation. Thus, a case can be made that early Christian vegetarians would partake of fish, considering it a non-animal item because of its (apparent) lack of blood. Sometimes, supermarkets will have one section labelled "poultry" and another labelled "meat." And if one reads a contemporary Italian restaurant menu, one is likely to encounter, beyond "pasta," a section on "pollo" (chicken and maybe other poultry items) and one on "pesce" (fish and other seafood items, such as shrimp and scallops) before one reaches "carne" (flesh, meat proper, such as beef, veal, and pork), an item seen as of a quite different nature from "pollo" and "pesce."

Veganism came into formal name and practice in the English Midlands in the 1940s to identify those who not only reject all flesh and animal by-products from their diet, including honey, but also refuse to wear or use any products made from animals or involving harm to animals. Of these, many are vegan at home but find it impossible to procure a vegan diet when eating out; and sometimes a less rigid vegetarianism may be found to be necessary. Most vegans, of course, would frequent a restaurant only where they knew a vegan meal could be obtained. Today, it is often possible to find a restaurant with vegetarian options but far more difficult to find a vegan meal in many places. This is already a significant improvement, for not too long ago it was almost impossible to find a vegetarian meal when travelling or when a change of venue from home cooking was desired. Normal everyday celebrations outside the home provided insurmountable problems for the vegetarian, as is now sometimes the case for the vegan.

In addition to vegans, we encounter: vegetarian "raw fooders," who eat only uncooked nonflesh items, believing this to replicate the condition of original humanity (a few "raw fooders" also eat uncooked fish); "fruitarians," who refuse to kill either animals or plants and live from fruits, nuts, seeds, and a few vegetables, which are derived from plants but whose consumption, as we have noted, does not require the death of the host plant itself; "macrobiotic vegetarians," who live on whole grains, vegetation, and miso (a paste concocted from fermented grain and soybeans); and "natural hygienists," who combine plant foods in a certain manner and who frequently fast. These latter groups each tend to think of themselves as the most complete vegetarians, endeavouring to ensure that their dietary practices do not exploit any member of the sentient realm in any manner and/or to replicate what they see as the pure and pristine human of some very early period in prehistory. There are also "locavores," who, in addition to being vegetarian or vegan, and sometimes neither, try to eat local, seasonal foods whenever possible.

## Grounds for Vegetarianism

There are at least eight possible grounds for adopting a fleshless diet: (1) one is not able to afford the price of flesh – historically a common condition and in some parts of the world today a contemporary condition, facts that hint at the lie of those who claim flesh eating to be a precondition of human health, for those who cannot afford flesh but enjoy fruit and vegetables do not generally seem to suffer from the composition of their diet, although they may sometimes suffer from the paucity of it; (2) one refuses for religious or spiritual reasons to participate in any self-indulgence and practises instead self-denial and self-purity – a course pursued by some early ancients, Christians, Hindus, Buddhists, and Jaina alike; (3) one's habit-determining religion teaches that animal sacrifice is not a just means of appeasing the gods – an occasional, but sometimes contradicted, precept of the Hebrew Bible (Old Testament) and a more rigorous and customary precept by New Testament times; (4) one may have determined that a plant-based diet constitutes a healthy regimen and a significantly healthier one than that enjoyed by animal eaters; (5) one may have reached the conclusion that the conditions under which animals are reared and fed are environmentally harmful and that one should eschew the eating of animal products for environmental protection; (6) one may not be opposed to the eating of animals per se, but animals are so ill-treated under modern farming conditions that their consumption is unacceptable; (7) one may be born into a religion or caste that practises vegetarianism and may continue this dietary habit merely because it is a part of one's denomination or caste identification – "cultural vegetarianism," if you will; and (8) one may be persuaded that the eating of animals is unethical in and of itself. Although all of these instances will find an occasional mention in this book, it is with those who have been convinced to live a vegetarian or vegan life on the eighth ground that I am primarily concerned. The reason given for the rejection of flesh by 72 percent of vegetarians in a US 2005 poll was an ethical reason; four out of the first five reasons given by polled British vegetarians were ethical reasons. Vegetarianism has become predominantly a matter of ethical concern. To give the reader the flavour of arguments for vegetarianism as they have changed over time, wherever possible – and it is increasingly possible for some of the periods covered in the later chapters – I have included representative statements of their creed from the primary exponents of vegetarianism themselves.

## FLESH

The reader may wonder why I have chosen to write frequently of "flesh" rather than "meat." The word "meat" in origin refers to anything used as nourishment, whether from animals or not, usually solid foods, although in principle including liquids. "Green meat" refers to grass as fodder or appropriate vegetables as food. "Meat" was also, and occasionally still is, used to refer to the edible part of fruits, eggs, nuts, and the like. There was certainly no indication in its usage that exclusively the flesh of animals was or is meant. It can be positively misleading when someone may say that they eat fish but no meat, for one may rightly talk of the meaty part of the fish. And fish are of course animals as much as are cows, at least according to the scientific criteria of Western culture. "Viand," too – the French word for meat is *viande*, derived from the Latin *vivenda*, meaning "living," but when it is without the "e," the word refers to victuals in general – has also had a lengthy usage in English, meaning all kinds of sustenance. "Flesh," by comparison, which derives from German and Scandinavian sources, is explicit, referring to that which covers the framework of bones and is enclosed by the skin of an animal – whether human or nonhuman. In the context of this book, "flesh" has a double referent: it is the lust of the human flesh for animal flesh and its rejection that we seek to understand. Nonetheless, as a concession to custom, I have sometimes mentioned "meat" where there is no doubt about the meaning.

## THEMES OF THE BOOK

There are several themes in this book. The overarching theme is that, despite the occasional presence of ascetic and cultural vegetarianism, full ethical consideration for animals resulting in the eschewing of flesh did not arise until after the Aristotelian period in Greece. It was then repeated in Rome before disappearing until its revival at the turn of the nineteenth century. There are a number of partial exceptions to this, as with certain early Jewish and Christian vegetarian sects; with Leonardo da Vinci, Thomas Tryon, George Cheyne, and David Hartley; with aspects of Eastern thought; and in a few other minor but engaging instances. A subsidiary theme is that the human species was probably quasi-vegetarian and perhaps even fruitarian in origin. Further, the vast majority of the frequent eighteenth century advocates of vegetarianism preached without practising. It took the general questioning of authority and fundamental change in expectations encouraged by the culture of the French revolutionary era to bring about a vegetarianism usually practised by those who preached it. A further argument, exemplified at points throughout the book, is that historically there has been a paradoxical incongruence between the development of sensibilities to animals and the declination to consume their flesh.

A society may best be understood less by how it answers questions and more by what questions it perennially fails to ask itself. Whether we should consume flesh is rarely pondered. Customarily, we have treated what is done traditionally as a compelling criterion of what we ought to do. For the vast majority of persons, custom and virtue are, from a practical perspective, almost synonymous. There is a propensity to believe that what is normal – or what has become normal – is what is right. It takes an event of the enormity of the French Revolution to persuade inquisitive voices to ask the relevant questions and consider it morally imperative to act upon the answers.

According to Plato, Socrates said that the unexamined life is not worth living.[30] Few humans have examined their omnivorous practices with any degree of rigour. It should not be forgotten, however, that some very honourable and intelligent people have examined their diet and reached very different conclusions from those formulated by the historical figures examined in this book. Often, the ecologically minded will argue a certain amount of flesh eating and predation is necessary to maintain an appropriate species balance and to allow for the use of barren land otherwise unproductive in farming. But the flesh eaters' arguments are customarily derived from the proclaimed superiority of humans over their fellow creatures. Paradoxically, this might be a reason for not eating animals rather than eating them. Would we expect Sir Isaac Newton to feel entitled to eat an intellectually handicapped person? No. We would expect Newton to have sympathy for those so inferior to him in intelligence, following the dictum of theologian and church father Clement of Alexandria about "training men to gentleness by their conduct toward those beneath them."[31] Would we

expect a victorious side in hockey to eat their vanquished foe? Of course
not. Despite the fact that the victors killed the vanquished in the Mayan
ball game (they did not eat them), we are inclined to think of the practice
as a cathartic ritual not to be repeated in more "civilized" climes. And
although the word "cannibalism" derives from the Caribes, who practised
it on those "inferiors" they had defeated, no one today proposes to reintro-
duce the practice – a practice still known in medieval Europe and, even
later, in times of famine.[32] Should we, then, practise such rituals on "inferior" animals? To know the attitudes with which this question was answered
in the negative is what this book is all about.

## Purported Vegetarians

Some avid vegetarians will be disappointed not to find much discussion of
their favourite "vegetarians" in these pages or mention of some of the most
famous "vegetarian" quotations from these and other authors. The unfortunate reality is that the Internet is replete with entirely invented "quotations" from some of those authors who were vegetarian but presumably did
not say what the inventor wanted them to have said. Numerous websites,
even those of a reputed national vegetarian association, also contain lists of
vegetarians that include a number who, quite simply, were not vegetarians
at all. In some cases, the relevant statement was made by one vegetarian
and then applied mistakenly to another historical figure. Perhaps the purported vegetarians are included in the lists because they have impressive
names and their inclusion gives greater prestige to the cause. Perhaps sometimes a person of one surname is confused with another of the same surname. Perhaps easily misread statements in books on vegetarianism have
led to the assumption that some historical figures were vegetarian who were
not. Perhaps the logic of statements made by these actors on the world stage
*ought* to have led to vegetarian practices, but the logic was not followed and
they continued to consume flesh. In reality, the frequent errors serve only
as an embarrassment to vegetarians who care for honesty and accuracy.

There are numerous inaccurate "quotations" to be found – from Albert
Einstein, for example, who became a vegetarian toward the very end of his
life. And numerous lists of vegetarians include both Henry David Thoreau
and Charles Darwin, neither of whom gave up flesh or claimed to do so. To
make the matter worse, these gross errors have crept into print in the writings of quite reputable authors. One such modern list from an author I
respect, as well as a historical conference presentation that made the same

error, included Sir Isaac Newton, who was concerned to eliminate excessive cruelty from the stockyards and the kitchen but not to eliminate their associations with flesh. In fact, Newton ate a very limited amount of food, with little flesh, and he was often claimed by eighteenth-century vegetarians as one of theirs. He certainly appears to have preferred vegetables, and he perhaps went without meat for periods of time. Perhaps Newton's recognition that animals were entitled to earnest ethical consideration was extended further than warranted. But he wasn't a vegetarian. Or, at least, there is no convincing evidence that he was – and, thus, no good grounds for claiming him as one. Another spurious website list produced by a Monterey, California, physician practising holistic medicine included Jeremy Bentham, William Blake, Charlotte Brontë, Charles Darwin, Ralph Waldo Emerson, John Milton, Isaac Newton, Plato, Socrates, Jean-Jacques Rousseau, Henry David Thoreau, H.G. Wells, William Wordsworth, Oliver Goldsmith, Martin Luther, Alexander Pope, Arthur Schopenhauer, and Voltaire – for not one of whom is there any convincing evidence of their vegetarianism and for most of whom there is incontrovertible evidence they were not vegetarian. Some, including H.G. Wells, were decidedly antivegetarian. Another list named Shakespeare, the economic and social theorist Adam Smith (an advocate but not a practitioner), and that avid hunter Prince Charles as "famous vegetarians." There is no evidence to support the vegetarianism of any one of them – and a great deal to indicate otherwise. By comparison, the content of the International Vegetarian Union (IVU) webpages is most impressive. The union is both even-handed and impeccably concerned to report the historical reality. Nonetheless, even here readers are often misled into thinking that omnivorous animal advocates – listed under "history of vegetarianism"! – either also advocated vegetarianism or practised it. Frequently, they did neither. To be sure, the IVU adds a disclaimer acknowledging that some of those listed might not have been vegetarians at all. But an impression of their vegetarianism is left nonetheless. And why would they be listed as vegetarians if there was no convincing evidence that they were vegetarians?

## RELATIONSHIP TO MY PREVIOUS WRITINGS

Having already written extensively on the history of animal ethics and the development of attitudes to animals in general, I was interested in applying my findings to the specific matter of ethical vegetarianism, a topic close to my heart. But that would mean revisiting and reiterating aspects of my previous work to provide the context in which vegetarian thought could be placed, as well as restating some of the details mentioned elsewhere. Consequently, especially, but not solely, in parts of the first half of the book, above all in the first half of Chapter 8, I have recapitulated, and sometimes substantially so, some of what I have previously written elsewhere. Not to have done so would have left gaps in the story and its framework. The narrative would not have read as a continuous whole. Accordingly, where appropriate, I have borrowed occasional ideas, passages, and quotations from my *Animals and Nature: Cultural Myths, Cultural Realities, Awe for the Tiger, Love for the Lamb: A Chronicle of Sensibility to Animals,* and *Brute Souls, Happy Beasts, and Evolution: The Historical Status of Animals.* Where these have been borrowed, they have been reoriented to a different audience and to questions relevant to the development of vegetarian thought. My sincere apologies are due to those who may have read some of my previous work and thus to whom I may be unnecessarily repeating myself on occasion. I trust that the entirely new remainder of the book will make up for the repetition they endure. Vegetarianism is a topic I have touched upon but, despite my abiding interest, have never entered into in any depth before, other than in my edition of George Nicholson's *Primeval Diet of Man.* However, much of what I have written over the past two decades is tangentially relevant to vegetarian history. Thus, I do not feel I come to the matter entirely anew.

## MANNER OF APPROACH

A half-century and more ago the academic norm was to attempt to produce objective and impartial argument, to be "value-free." In recent decades the majority of social scientists, historians, and philosophers have moved away from such an approach. Today, the far greater likelihood is to encounter an emphasis on rights, compassion, and justice rather than on impartiality. There is an intermediate position that may be said to encompass both traditions. Compassion may be said to be an appropriate concept that should guide our ends. Impartiality, or detachment, however, remains of great importance as a vehicle. It is vital that one's compassion and predilections should not influence how one reads the evidence. Nor should compassion control the direction that the analysis should take or the evidence that is investigated. When one discusses events of the past, the task is to write not as an advocate, although an advocate one is, but as a historian of ideas. Put another way, it is vital that our research not be influenced by wishful thinking, as so often happens in the field of animal ethics. It remains as true today as in the heyday of "scientism" that our values should not predetermine the weighing or selection of the material. It is with this precept in mind that this book has been written. In the words of Tacitus in *The Annals* (bk. 1, ch. 1), history should be written *sine ira et studio* – with neither bitterness nor partiality. A further apology is in order. Although gender-neutral language is distinctly preferable, the requirements of historical analysis sometimes enjoin the use of "he" and "man" if one is not to misrepresent the thoughts of those of earlier eras about whom one is writing.

# I

# The Human in Prehistory

## HUMAN ORIGINS

Most paleontological accounts of the earliest humans depict them as flesh eaters. If these paleontologists are right – on the balance of possibilities, there is a reasonable chance they may well be – it is one of the most astonishing facts of human history, one that cries out for explanation, that most societies, including our own, possess or possessed primal memories, or myths, of a time when we were not flesh eaters at all and of the circumstances in which flesh eating began.

Whether it is from the account in Genesis, or from the tales of the Makritare of the Orinoco, or from the legends of the Cheyenne, we learn of a time when no animals were consumed in the societal diet. Do these legends tell us something about human origins? And if so, if humans were originally vegetarian or even vegan, what would, then, have occasioned their introduction to an omnivorous diet? Why do we all share very similar dietary legends? Is it an implicit recognition of our primordial nature? Was it the fact, when humans left the original homeland of East Africa and year-round vegetation was no longer available, almost 2 million years ago, that humans first turned to the eating of flesh? Such an explanation of the change to flesh eating, if change it is, must at the very least be incomplete because the inhabitants of the African homeland were also omnivores, and the fossil evidence indicates a continued period of the human as both predator and prey there as well as in the new habitats. Perhaps a lightning-induced forest fire destroyed all the immediate vegetation, and the corpses

24

of the animals burnt in the fire were the only source of food. The merit of such an explanation is that it would allow us to begin to understand how humans came not only to eat flesh but also to eat cooked flesh. That raw flesh is, on the whole, too tough for our teeth to tear and chew suggests prima facie an original vegetarian or at least quasi-vegetarian lifestyle to be a distinct possibility for the human species. After all, the earliest humans not only lacked fire but also had no sophisticated tools with which to kill or capture animals, nor the speed with which to entrap mammals or flying birds. Nonetheless, it should be noted that we tend to cook vegetable food as well. If the cooking of flesh is a strange artifice, so, presumably, is the cooking of other foodstuffs. Although it would not be as difficult as to chew raw flesh, the chewing of some uncooked vegetables would also prove troublesome. That would suggest that we were perhaps fruit eaters before we used fire and cooked many of our comestibles.

The classical Greek vegetarian Dicaerchus believed the first person sated with the produce of the oak tree took the step to war with the animals and with other humans.[1] Theophrastus, also a vegetarian pupil of Aristotle, and his successor as head of the Lyceum, thought that animal consumption had begun as a consequence of the destruction of crops in war. If so, it is notable that there was no general attempt to return to a vegetarian diet once the crops had recovered. In his "Essay on Flesh-Eating," the Greco-Roman Plutarch (c. AD 46-120) speculated that before there was adequate agriculture, the infertility of savage earth provoked original humans to kill animals for food. Humans of his own era, he added, had no such excuse. "Nature," he tells us in the same essay, "firmly forbids humans to feast on flesh." But he has rather more to say on the abject horror of the first person's handling of flesh as food and eating it than on the causes that invoked it. The seventeenth-century Pythagorean Thomas Tryon declared flesh to have occasioned violence among men and appears to believe the eating of flesh arose from the quarrelsome nature of human beings. George Nicholson, at the turn of the nineteenth century, proclaimed the eating of animal flesh to have begun in ancient times in order to prevent the cannibalism that he believed had become common as a result of famine.[2] In 1811, John Frank Newton cited Pliny on blaming the origin of flesh eating on Hyperbius, son of Mars, who killed the first animal, and on Prometheus, who slew the first ox – and discovered fire, on which presumably to roast the slaughtered ox. Keith Thomas has observed that seventeenth- and eighteenth-century biblical "commentators argued as to whether meat-eating had been permitted [after the flood] because man's physical constitution had degenerated and therefore required new forms of nutriment, or because the cultivation of the soil to which he was condemned required a more robust food, or because the roots and herbs on which he had fed in Eden had lost their former goodness."[3] By contrast, the most common modern paleontological view is that the beginning of flesh eating requires no explanation, for we have always been omnivores.

Perhaps, when adequate vegetation and fruit were scarce, scavenging the marrow of, say, a leopard's prey introduced humans to animal fare. Usually, the leopard, or some other powerful carnivore, would drag its prey, sometimes a hominid, into the fork of a tree to escape competition from other predators, such as lions, and the successful predator would usually consume about two-thirds of the prey. The remnants of the flesh would be devoured by eagerly waiting hyenas, jackals, vultures, and the like, perhaps even by the competing lions. With the flesh now torn away and no easy pickings to be had, the weaker human's manual dexterity would allow for the breaking of the bones and the extraction of the marrow. In fact, Raymond Dart, the South African paleontologist who discovered the early hominid Taung child in 1924, first believed that australopithecines were in essence scavengers of animals, before Dart developed fully the now unconvincing idea of "man the butcher" (my term, his analysis) by the 1950s. Even the scavenger thesis is now doubted. Perhaps instead, on a particular occasion of scarcity and extreme hunger, anything edible would have seemed acceptable, and a habit begun in scarcity was then repeated in abundance. One other possibility, one bearing the ring of truth, is that, as the African climate became more arid several million years ago, the equatorial forests went into a decline, and the transitional zones between forest and savannah became, it would appear from the fossil record, the primary human area of habitation. From a primarily fruit diet, humans would have had to turn to more variegated fare, including leaves, vegetables, tubers, insects, lizards, and small mammals. In other words, environmental change would have brought about a change in diet. Thereafter, as human technology improved through increase in brain size, we would have learned to co-operate effectively with other humans and to entrap larger animals – and the period of "man the hunter" would have begun, with an ever-present conflict in the human unconscious mind between the vegetarian of Eden and the omnivore of Arcadia (see pages 35 to 44 on the Golden Age). Of course, in the Edenic period, humans would not have thought of themselves as vegetarian – a thoroughly modern concept – as though diet were simply a matter of conscious choice, but would have felt more comfortable, more at ease, more human, more "natural" with a fleshless diet. Perhaps there is a smattering of truth in all these hypotheses. Whatever the origins of flesh eating – assuming there were any origins – it is clear that any hypothesis must, at least for the time being, remain largely speculative and unverifiable. And one must remember always that, so far as is known, no other species has undertaken a complete change of diet unless environmental circumstances have prevented the continuation of the original state.

Why does it matter what we were in origin? In one important sense, it does not matter at all. We have been continuously adapting ourselves to new circumstances in our evolutionary development for millions of years. And those adaptations have allowed us to continue to thrive on a new and ever-changing diet. In Aristotelian terms, it is what we are becoming, not what we were in origin, that is the human fulfilment. In another sense, we tend to feel intuitively that our original diet is likely to have been more in tune with the needs of our constitution than anything developed during the oppressions and general vicissitudes of human history – the traditional argument being that "nature" is preferable to "culture."

Perhaps most important, whether a flesh or tuber or fruit diet is more in accord with our dietary origins does not obviate the ethical requirement – a requirement that must stand until countered – not to harm other sentient creatures. It is not the responsibility of the vegetarian to show why other sentient beings should not be harmed – that is prima facie an essential part of all just treatment of others. It is the responsibility of the flesh eater to demonstrate why there should be an entitlement to the breach of the rule in the case of nonhuman animals. This must involve a demonstration of the justifiability of the slaughter of animals to fulfil an unnecessary human purpose, which in turn involves the demonstration of the worthiness of the human to have other animal lives sacrificed for its pleasure. And perhaps an important aspect of any such discussion involves talking always of eating animals rather than of eating meat. To talk of eating meat is to avoid the psychological impact of the ethical question.

Perhaps the discrepancy between the paleontological accounts of human omnivorousness and the societal vegetarian legends arises in part through a different understanding of "animal." Today, we tend to think of an animal as any living organism, whether as complex as a dolphin or as simple as a worm, that is distinguished from plants by feeding on organic matter. Moreover, animals are related to each other by biological descent and distinguished from plants in the same manner. They also usually possess specialized sense organs and nervous systems. Typically, they are self-directed and respond more rapidly to stimuli than do plants. By contrast, in hunter-gatherer societies there are no such "refinements" of understanding. "Animal" is the "higher food," which is caught by the male hunters. Everything else, including small birds, eggs, lizards, and tiny mammals, is that which is gathered by the females and categorized separately as "lower food," as "vegetable."[4] The act of hunting with artificial weapons determines the classification of "animal." In biblical usage, blood is deemed the essence of human and animal life, an identification continued in Western culture for many centuries thereafter and not entirely extinguished now.[5] Perhaps this would account for the apparent exclusion of fish in early Christian culture from the notion of animal, for blood in the fish is not immediately apparent. This view is suggested in the writings of St. Augustine, who, knowing full well of the biblical fishing stories, still said Christ forbade flesh in his disciples' diet. In classical Greece, a prevailing distinction was not between mammals and fish but between land animals and sea animals, a distinction that persisted in later Catholic dietary laws, thus including whales, seals, and squid along with cod, mackerel, and bass. Habitat was the defining characteristic. Other Greeks thought of animals as being recognized by the fact that they breathed – air being taken into or expelled from the lungs – which would suggest that only certain complex beings counted as "animals." Likewise, Hindus, following the *Rig-Veda*, deemed *Atman* (breath or soul) the principle of animal life, which was apparently not shared by plants. The neo-Platonist Plotinus (c. AD 205-270) claimed animals feel pleasure and pain, whereas vegetables do not – a distinction that begged the question of the status of the least sentient members of the animal realm, those that almost two millennia later the pre-Darwin evolutionist Jean-Baptiste Lamarck would call the "apathiques" – the insentient. Begging the same question, at least by our scientific criteria of what constitutes an "animal," Plotinus's student Porphyry (c. AD 233-304) declared animals to be rational, whereas plants were not, a distinction repeated in the seventeenth century by Jean de La Fontaine, querying whether we should not allow animals at least this one distinction from other living matter.[6] The classification of "animal" has thus usually been a matter more of culture than of scientific taxonomy. Hence, the customary critique of those who oppose vegetarianism and animal rights that many small animals are insentient, lack reason, and are thus not worthy of ethical consideration entirely misses the point. It is, in the first instance, with the elimination of pain and suffering, not with the scientific concept of "animal," that the ethical vegetarian is concerned. Occasioning the demise of an animal microbe may be thought no breach of the vegetarian ethic.

Why do the paleontologists think of humans as primordial flesh eaters? Perhaps tendentiousness is present to a degree in the mind of the paleontologist because we have conceived of ourselves for millennia as primordial hunters, because being the head of the food chain and the dominant creature on earth is a part of our self-image, an image that would have arisen as we became hunters. The paleontologist *may* be predisposed to find a flesh-eating ancestor. Yet as the seventeenth-century political philosopher Thomas Hobbes reminded us with his rhetorical question: "When a lion eats a man and a man eats an ox, why is the ox made more for the man than the man for the lion?"[7] In part, paleontologists find humans as omnivores in the distant past because they *expect* to find humans as omnivores – the ox, it would appear, is thought to be made more for the man than the man for the lion. The idea of head of the food chain seems to follow not from evidence but from imagination or assumption. Far from the human's being head of the food chain, in some parts of the world carnivorous animals remain a constant threat to human life, as they once were over the whole planet in great profusion. Sometimes, potential victims, as with the inhabitants of the Sundarban delta in India, wear a face mask on the backs of their heads so predators, in this case tigers, will think they have been spotted and thus abandon the chase. Elsewhere, predation is common; almost everywhere, predation was once common. Indeed, in light of the obvious error about our natural place in the food chain, why would we, whether paleontologists or not, ever *imagine* ourselves head of the food chain and the principal animal? Why should we not recognize, as any understanding of the general human prehistorical role and the contemporary role in parts of the world, especially Asia and Africa, would suggest, that the human lies somewhere in the middle of the food chain? The only possible answer lies in human conceit, prompted by our innermost psychological inheritance.

It should be noted there is no consistency in the paleontological accounts of the diet of the earliest humans. Or perhaps we should say the greatest consistency in such accounts is their variability over time. For example, until very recently the image of the Neanderthal was that of a snarling and grunting failed vegetarian species that died out, while flesh-eating *Homo sapiens* became master of the world. Flesh eating was thus seen to make us the most successful and the dominant animal. Increasingly, the picture today of the Neanderthal is changing to one of an intelligent and emotionally complex melodious creature who interbred with *Homo sapiens*. At one time, humanity's fruitarian origins were taken for granted, later likewise humanity's omnivorousness. In the past couple of centuries each generation has differed from the previous generation in its account of the circumstances of human origins. Very often, the flesh-eating accounts read like rationalizations of those who wish to find some "natural" justification for their diet and their conquering demeanour as hunters. Descriptions of vegetarian origins read sometimes as convenient rationalizations of the accuracy of the sacred scriptures or of the virtue of denial or as a psychologically satisfying confirmation of our intrinsically vegetarian nature. Less ideologically oriented accounts include, on the one hand, Desmond Morris in *The Animal Contract* taking the traditional view that we were originally fruit eaters before we became flesh eaters and, on the other, Jared Diamond in *The Third Chimpanzee* taking the now more customary view that flesh eating has been a perennial human characteristic.[8] Certainly, we should read all accounts (including this account) with a degree of reservation, waiting for a time – if there ever will be one – when there is a great deal more convincing physical evidence than currently exists. What now exists as evidence is subject to a variety of competing but almost equally persuasive interpretations. As the vegetarian molecular biologist Randall Collura says, the "evidence presented ... has never been definitive, and I don't believe it ever will be."[9] We should certainly be very wary of the grandiose image of humankind built on scanty evidence and interpreted to elevate humanity without any great degree of reliability, other than the certainty of human hubris.

But let us not imagine that competing interpretations of human origins are of recent vintage. At the turn of the nineteenth century George Nicholson, originally a Bradford printer, wrote an intriguing book entitled *The Primeval Diet of Man,* based on a conception of the natural human as prey and as naturally vegetarian in contrast with the following century's glorification of the prehistorical human predator.[10] Nicholson quoted many of the purported historical authorities stretching back over two millennia who had maintained over the centuries – as, indeed, the biblical book of Genesis also proclaims – that humans were originally vegetarian, even vegan, in their dietary habits. Slowly, the idea of "man the hunter" came to supersede that of "man the vegetarian." Of course, it had long been proclaimed that "man the hunter" was the path taken over a few thousand years (biblical literalness predominated decidedly until the 1830s and lingered into the twentieth century, when all animal species, even the earth itself, were thought to be a mere few thousand years of age, six thousand being the compilation of Archbishop Ussher of Armagh). And, of course, it is now known that humans have been at least occasional small-animal eaters for a hundred thousand years and more. The question, however, that is constantly raised inquires about the *fons et origo* of humankind: are humans by *nature* and *origin* flesh, fruit, or vegetable eaters? Are we *by nature* and *origin* savannah hunters or tree-top fruit pickers in the same manner that a cat is a carnivore *by nature* and *origin?* The assumption throughout recorded history appears to have been that whatever we were in our origins best expresses our fundamental moral nature. And the answer commonly accepted is in constant flux. Every quarter-century or so, the scientific community offers a very different interpretation of human nature and origins.

In our answers to questions of human origins, much will depend on what we consider "human" in our prehistory and what we count as "proto-human" (usually termed "hominid"). If we restrict the idea of "humanity" to the past hundred thousand years or so, it would appear certain we have always been flesh eaters, at least to a degree. However, if we seek "humanity" shortly after our evolutionary break from the other great apes, we probably ate flesh very rarely, if at all, perhaps the occasional insect or lizard but probably nothing as large as a rabbit. Indeed, answers to these questions of origin depend equally on what is meant by animal, which probably varied greatly from our current ideas based on scientific taxonomic differentiations among animals, vegetables, and fruit, distinctions that would have been completely alien to the mind processes of our early ancestors. Indeed, only in the eighteenth century did the Western mind become imbued with questions of classification in anything approaching a rigorous manner, notably with John Ray and his associates at the beginning of the century and with Carolus Linnaeus three decades later.

Those who consider humans by nature vegetarian often rely largely on the biology of humans for their evidence. Thus, it is said that whereas a natural herbivore has, for example, a long and complex intestine, a carnivore has a very short and simple one in order to excrete the poisonous effect of a flesh diet very quickly from the animal and to not allow the flesh to permeate the whole body. This begs the very question of the biological nature of humanity, for few have ever claimed the human to be a natural carnivore but, like pigs, to be natural omnivores (animals who are opportunistic feeders, capable of consuming a large variety of different foodstuffs, including both flesh and vegetable foods), many of whom have structures very similar to those of the vegetarian animals. Certainly, we do not possess the physical characteristics possessed by, say, carnivorous lions or tigers, but nor do omnivorous pigs share these characteristics. There is a great deal of variety in animal and human dietary behaviour and physical structure. The choice is not restricted to being herbivores (strict vegetarians), carnivores (flesh eaters), or omnivores. There are also frugivores (animals who eat fruit predominantly), gramnivores (animals who eat nuts and seeds primarily), folivores (those who exist mainly on leaves), and insectivores (who consume insects and small vertebrates along with fruit and vegetation). And the comparison of our bodily structure with those of the carnivores involves more than the merely superficial but requires us to notice, for example, that cell types distinguish species from each other according to the diets they consume. In addition, plant eaters generally possess large chambers of food deposits. Horses, rhinoceroses, and colobine monkeys have posterior sacs, whereas cattle and deer ruminants have forward sacs. There are no such sacs, either posterior or anterior, in humans. Dogs (which are natural carnivores, although not so completely as cats) have intestines that resemble those of omnivores more than they resemble those of other carnivores, such as raccoons. The small canine teeth of humans are sometimes thought to indicate that the human lacks adequate teeth for a flesh diet, but the size of the cranium and relative smallness of the human jaw brought about by evolutionary developments of the brain may be more important than diet in determining the size and power of the teeth. Moreover, the predominantly vegetarian gorillas and gelada baboons have very large canines, which function as bark-tearing devices, defence weapons, and visual threats rather than being essential for food consumption. Generally speaking, the human seems prima facie very well equipped structurally as an omnivore rather than there being one sole legitimate interpretation of the human as a creature structurally suited to a wholly vegetarian diet. As Randall Collura expresses it, the "bottom line is that nothing about our anatomy or physiology dictates a vegetarian diet (or precludes one either)."[11]

Very often, those who claim the human to be in origin a fruitarian or a vegetarian compare humans to their closest relatives, the apes. There is, however, considerable variety among apes. The only frugivores appear to be gibbons and siamangs, and they are primarily rather than exclusively so. The orangutans are also fruit eaters, although they consume a large amount of general vegetation as well, but no substantial flesh. Gorillas eat vegetation in general, especially leaves, and again no substantial flesh. It was traditionally thought that our closest genetic and evolutionary relatives, the chimpanzees, were also almost entirely vegetarian, but it is now known that they consume animals occasionally, both mammals and insects, just as others of the great apes eat insects. However, chimpanzees eat mammal meat very infrequently, and flesh is a very small proportion of their diet. Baboons prey occasionally on antelope. What this suggests to us is that there would appear to be a general inclination toward fruit and vegetable food among the apes but that habitat and availability play significant roles in the specific kinds of food eaten. Certainly, the flesh-eating chimpanzees, not unlike the gibbons, would appear to differ from most of their great-ape relatives, and one is led to wonder from the accounts of chimpanzee meat eating whether it is an aspect of bravado and machismo rather than any real dietary preference, whether the choice depends more on psychology than on biology. Thus, young male chimpanzees capture and kill small monkeys in an apparent attempt to impress females, who are offered a morsel of the prey, rather like human teenagers with marijuana, alcohol, or tobacco. The biblical idea of "the fruit of the forbidden tree" is not without merit in the case of the chimpanzees.[12] The human has many close relatives who have restricted fruit or vegetarian diets, but they do not include the very closest cousin.

When we look at the body structure of early humans and recognize that they lacked talons and claws, could not match a cheetah, a tiger, or even a rabbit for speed, and possessed far weaker and smaller teeth than a crocodile or a lion and less agility than a monkey or a squirrel, we soon realize how implausible it is to think of our human ancestors as specialized hunters, as has sometimes been thought. Investigating the fossil evidence – skulls, other bones, footprints – of *Australopithecus afarensis*, who lived between 5 and 2.5 million years ago, we are led to the speculative conclusion that they were bipedal, stood around four feet tall on average, weighed around eighty pounds, and had teeth pretty much like our own. Moreover, they did not have tools to cut flesh (the first tools were constructed about 2 to 2.5 million years ago), and they had no fire on which to cook flesh. The first solid evidence for controlled fire comes from significantly less than 1 million years ago, although some suggest the control of fire began "perhaps as far back as ... 1.8 million years ago."[13] No satisfactory flesh digestion, at least of the tougher portions of flesh, could have occurred before the control of fire. Indeed, we are led to wonder why fire was introduced for cooking if other animals were our natural diet. Would we not have expected to eat them raw? It is very difficult to conceive of humans, as we have already noted, as generally raw-flesh tearers and eaters other than of the very smallest of mammals, birds, and lizards. It is worth recalling that in zoology the Carnivora is an order of mammals – comprising the cats, dogs, bears, hyenas, weasels, civets, raccoons, and mongooses – that have powerful jaws and teeth adapted for tearing and eating flesh. The human does not fit at all as a primary flesh eater. Nor do humans escape the problem of the lack of carnivorous characteristics by conveniently designating them as omnivores instead. They are still expected to be consumers of significant quantities of flesh.

The famous *Australopithecus*, Lucy, discovered in Ethiopia in 1974, had "an exceptionally long big-toe," Donna Hart and Robert Sussman tell us in *Man the Hunted*, "that was divergent like our modern human thumbs and could be used to grasp and climb trees."[14] Customary tree climbing suggests prima facie a fruit-eating lifestyle. Moreover, the evidence for systematic organized hunting of anything other than small mammals suggests hunting began no more than sixty thousand years ago, at most ninety thousand. When we consider further that there were very many times more large predators in the distant prehistoric past than today and that those in existence were far larger than their modern counterparts – sabre tooth tigers, hyenas, crocodiles, lionesses, and the like, which would find a human to be a tasty supper – it is not unreasonable to assume, as the fossil record suggests, that the human was primarily a fruit, tuber, and nut eater who stayed well away whenever possible from the predatory carnivores. Moreover, the human did not possess the weapons necessary to kill any but the very smallest of animals and lacked the speed or stealth to catch all but the very slowest. Further, humans were without the social organization necessary to arrange a hunting expedition, and many early skeletons have been found with carnivore teeth indentations in their skulls, indicating humans' status as prey. It is perhaps likely that a few insects, and maybe small lizards and the like, were consumed along with the fruit and vegetation, but *Australopithecus afarensis* was probably an *almost* complete vegetarian, living certainly no less comfortably in the trees as on the savannah, as indicated by the long arms – hanging by them to pick fruit – and relatively short legs. Thick jaw bones and small incisors and canines compared to the molars, which are large, flat, and blunt, were characteristics of *Australopithecus afarensis*. Strikingly, there were no long shearing crests on the teeth required for the chewing of substantial flesh. The evidence overwhelmingly suggests an animal that ate leaves, fruits, seeds, and tubers predominantly. M. Teaford and P. Ungar conclude that "early hominids were not dentally preadapted to eat meat – they simply did not have the sharp, reciprocally concave shearing blades necessary to retain and cut such foods."[15] Nonetheless, sometimes when we look to modern hunter-gatherers, we often tend, sadly and prejudicially – "*they* are closer to human origins than *we* are," we imagine – to assume that their preferred flesh diet is likely to be similar to the diets of our early ancestors. It is certainly true that no aboriginal societies, or significant groups within such societies, are vegetarian, although it is estimated that the gatherings of the women constitute over two-thirds of the diet. The male hunters would not like it to be so. Yet their preference for flesh eating may be understood, like that of Western culture, as a part of their Arcadian rather than Edenic character, as will be explained in the next section of this chapter.

It has customarily been argued that it was in the organization of the hunt that humans began to learn to develop their skills and their minds, thus becoming the large-brained ape with far more reason and sagacity than other species. Yet it is just as likely that the brain evolved not in hunting but in trying to outwit the predators. Indeed, co-operation and socialization would have developed in like manner not as mutual advantage in the hunt but as necessary steps to provide defence. Predators are often solitary animals, or they may act in pairs. Diurnal primates find it necessary to live in permanent social groups both to provide sufficient voices to sound a predatory alarm and for there to be more individuals to confuse their foes by scattering, or to mob them, if attacked. The most that can be said is that the evidence suggests a human who was originally prey and quasi-vegetarian as a distinct possibility, although this is a supposition without any *absolute* certainty. At the same time, with absolute certainty it can be said the relatively recent human is the only primate ever to have regularly eaten large animals – as large as a rabbit, that is. In fact, mainly through the paucity of large animals there, the European "discoverers" of the Caribbean islands were astonished to find the inhabitants living predominantly on worms, spiders, and other insects. They were insectivores. We can be sure that if early humans ate any flesh, it was not of the large-animal variety that we encounter in our grocery stores.

## The Golden Age

The Golden Age is a period of human prehistory remembered or imagined in the legends of almost all societies. The idea of the Golden Age played a major role in Chinese and Indian thought. In India, the age is thought to have long disappeared, now replaced with the corrupt Iron Age of Kali. Still, today, the Pitjantjatjara aborigines of Australia revere *tjukurpa,* the mystical past and its legendary heroes. A similar conception is present in many contemporary foraging societies. Islam, too, holds to a conception of the highest of all humans as the *insan-I-kamil* – the primordial man of fully realized spiritual qualities. And the one-time doyenne of medieval studies Hélène Guerber acknowledged it also as a Western legend, albeit derivative. "Of all the romances of chivalry," she tells us:

> The most mystical and spiritual is undoubtedly the legend of the Holy Grail. Rooted in the mythology of all primitive races is the belief in a land of peace and happiness, a sort of earthly paradise, once possessed by man, but now lost, and only to be attained again by the virtuous. The legend of the Holy Grail, which some authorities declare was first known in Europe by the Moors and Christianized by the Spaniards, was soon introduced into France, where Robert de Borron and Chrestien de Troyes wrote lengthy poems about

it. Other writers took up the theme, among them Walter Map, Archdeacon of Oxford, who connected with it the Arthurian legends. It soon became known in Germany, where in the hands of Gottfried von Strassburg, and especially of Wolfram von Eschenbach, it assumed its most perfect and popular form.[16]

The Anglo-Saxon word "aergod" means "as good as at the beginning." The thought persists in the writings of Aquinas. The idea of the original as somehow the best is to be found in most cultures.

Was there a Golden Age? Certainly not, if what we mean by that is the utopian ideal outlined by its historical promoters. Nonetheless, the question is answered less easily if what is meant is a time when cultural novelties were not always sought and a time before knowledge was desired as an end in itself. The conception of a prior Golden Age could well have arisen from a perception that not all arts, knowledge, and wisdom had proved beneficial to humankind and that something of inordinate value had been lost in the course of time. After all, the serpent, the symbol of the fall, was always portrayed as wise. And wisdom was associated with cunning and hence with deceit or evasion.

A modern expression of the return of the Golden Age and the victory of the virtuous is to be found in the rapturous chant of the Iranian people awaiting Ayatollah Khomeini's return from exile in 1979:

The day the Imam returns
No one will tell lies anymore
No one will lock the doors of his house
People will become brothers
Sharing the bread of their joys together
In justice and sincerity.[17]

As Francis Ween wrote of the endeavours of the Khomeini sycophants, "Iran goes back to a past that seems a lost paradise."[18] This lost paradise would appear to be an integral part of the human psyche, a desire to overcome what are seen as perennial, but not inevitable, human characteristics associated with our historical experience.

There is a decided possibility of the legend being a part of earlier Western oral myth, even if it first arrived in popular literary form only in the Middle Ages. In religious literary form the legend goes back at least to Genesis within the Judeo-Christian tradition and much earlier in other countries of the Middle East, in India, and in China. And it plays an important role in classical philosophy. It has, as indicated, long been a part of popular literature, again exemplified through Voltaire's Dr. Pangloss in *Candide:* "Men ... must in some things have deviated from their original innocence; for they were not born wolves, and yet they worry one another like those beasts of prey."[19] Likewise, in *Madame Bovary*, Gustave Flaubert refers to "the cradle of human society" as the time of "the savage ages when men lived off acorns in the depths of the forest. Then they cast off their animal skins, garbed themselves in cloth, dug the ground and planted the vine. Was this an advance? Didn't their discovery entail more disadvantages than benefits?"[20] The acorn myth was already present in Pliny the Elder's *Natural History* (first century AD), where we read: "Ceres discovered corn; previously men had lived on acorns."[21]

Our image of the early human or hominid begins to change from that of the essential hunter when we come to recognize that the early human, and for that matter all other great apes, were in origin far more prey than predator species and that their behaviour corresponded to this predominant reality. In light of the distinct possibility that the earliest humans were vegetarian, or at least quasi-vegetarian, the primal memory of the Golden Age becomes readily comprehensible, especially when we understand that the legend consists of two competing elements or stages: the Edenic and the Arcadian – primal memories occasioned by different periods of human prehistory.[22] The first is a primal memory of our period as prey (see the next section of this chapter), whereas the second is a primal memory of the early stage of our predator period, and the two are ever in tension within the human psyche. These periods, or stages, may be understood as the vegetarian (prey) and omnivore (predator) stages, as depicted in the human journey from "man the hunted" to "man the hunter." The conception of the human as in essence hunted or hunter turns out to be a question not really about essence at all but about the human in different periods of prehistory and the impact these stages have left on the human mind. Each stage informs a part of the human psyche and is incompatible with the other part informed by the other stage. Being both hunted and hunter is a part of the human primal memory. In its pure form, as what Max Weber called an "ideal type" (although such types certainly never existed in their entirety in actuality), the Edenic is rural, simple, peaceful, altruistic, symbiotic, innocent, loving (agape), co-operative, compassionate, meek, tender, egalitarian, and vegetarian – in short, the Edenic world is the world of the angelic and saintly.

This is the Eden of Genesis before humans and animals became flesh eaters and before the fruit of the tree of knowledge was eaten, as so many religions depict, the time of an essential difference from our present nature. It is viewed as the earliest stage of human prehistory, a period when, in the words of Elijah Buckner in *The Immortality of Animals* (1903), a view shared by the vegetarian founder of Methodism, John Wesley: "the earth, teeming with every variety of useful productions, was the great storehouse of the Almighty, from which all living things were commanded to help themselves. They were all vegetarians, for they were commanded by God to live on nothing else. There was no necessity to destroy one life to support another ... In this primeval innocence, there was surpassing beauty in every animate and inanimate object, and every living thing in the heavens above and all that moved in the waters below, were at peace."[23] Few would accept today such an account as prehistorical reality. Even more secular writers such as Virgil and Jean-Jacques Rousseau took humankind's originally simple and vegetarian past for granted. The first written expression of the Golden Age in Western literature came from Hesiod (eighth century BC) when he contrasted in *Works and Days* our present "age of iron," a degraded age of "toil and misery," of "constant distress," with the Golden Age, in which "all good things were theirs, and the grain-giving soil bore its fruits of its own accord in unstinted plenty, while they at their leisure harvested their fields in contentment and abundance."[24] "Every reference to a 'golden age' in Western literature and speech," M.L. West tells us, "derives directly or indirectly from ... Hesiod," although there was a previous passing reference to such an age (unnamed) in Homer's *Iliad* (bk. 1, 260-68).[25] The vegetarian emphasis was likewise expressed by Plato (c. 428-347 BC) in the *Statesman* (269-74) and by the Roman poet Ovid (43 BC to AD 17): "content with foods produced without constraint [i.e., compulsion, force, killing], they gathered the fruit of the arbute tree and mountain berries and cornel berries and blackberries clinging to the bramble thickets, and acorns which had fallen from the broad tree of Jupiter."[26] Even earlier, the Pythagorean poet Empedocles (c. 490-430 BC) had told us that in such an age: "the altar did not reek of the unmixed blood of bulls, but this was the greatest abomination among men, to snatch out the life and eat the goodly limbs."[27] Moreover, in that bygone age, Empedocles says, "all [animals] were gentle and amenable to men, both beasts and birds; and kindness glowed."[28] He showed his preference for the sacrifice of costly perfumes rather than flesh. In fact, Empedocles commended the life of ancient humans, who, he believed, were peace-loving vegetarians who eschewed animal sacrifice to the gods until Strife entered the world and the perennial conflict began between Love and Strife that epitomized what he thought of as the modern world, with Strife ever in the ascendant.

The "ideal type" of Arcadia, by contrast with Eden but sharing some of its characteristics (again never fully achieved in actuality), is rural, simple, industrious, adventurous, loving (eros), loyal, courageous, strong, honourable, respectful, hierarchical, hunting-based, and omnivorous – in short, the world of Pan, King Arthur, and the "noble savage." According to the renowned anthropologist of religion Mircea Eliade, this desire for a return to the past, of which, I am postulating, both Eden and Arcadia are reflections, arises in an attempt to overcome the inevitable decay involved in the march of history, which removes us from the perfection of the creation of the gods.[29] If the origins provide security and change produces disharmony, then the creations of the gods are far superior to the civilizations developed by humankind. But they are different securities provided by the "origins." They are similar in that both Eden and Arcadia are in conflict with the cultured soul of the city and its technology, which delights in "progress," books, learning, the arts, and the finesse of civilization, as well as, of course, in science and luxury. But whereas Eden is an object of beauty, serenity, and reverence, Arcadia relates more to the awesome, the sublime, and the majestic. In Arcadia, it is the rugged laws of nature that are respected, whereas in Eden it is the individual lives of animals. It is even thought that in the ideal Eden carnivorous animals would be neither predators against us nor against the other vegetarian animals. Together, the ideas of Eden and Arcadia are in constant historical tension in the human mind and breast – hence the impossibility of connoting the ideal nature of humankind: there are competing ideals in constant tension within our minds. We do not endure moral relativism. We endure conflicting moral absolutes.

In the Mesopotamian *Epic of Gilgamesh,* composed on twelve tablets about three thousand years ago, the path from Eden to Arcadia is exemplified. Here, Enkidu is a primitive human who lives in accord with the animals, sharing in common with them a vegetarian diet. The temple girl, Shamat, and the symbol of early civilization, Gilgamesh, escort Enkidu on an adventure to prove him capable of valour, lust, reason, and the robust virtues. When he returns to the animals temporarily, they no longer acknowledge him as one of their own, and he no longer possesses their speed and strength. Enkidu has arrived in Arcadia. He no longer sees himself as an animal in the way that other animals are animal.

Before Arcadia is reached, most societies have legends of a wholly vegetarian past, now lost in the mist of time. Thereafter, humans and certain other animals become flesh eaters. Thus, the Makritare of the Orinoco believe that, in the conclusion of the vegetarian stage, "Mantuwa, the Jaguar, approached and took a bite of the serpent flesh. That was the first eating of meat. When the others saw the red blood flow, they all pressed in for a mouthful."[30] The elders of the Bassari of West Africa teach that before the time of flesh eating, the deity Unumbotte gave the people "seeds of all kinds" and said, "go plant these" so that "the people might live from their fruit." In remarkable similarity to Genesis, "Snake" tempts "Man and his wife" to eat forbidden fruit – flesh – instead.[31] They become aware of their differences from other animals, develop a separate language from that of the other creatures (that is, their interests diverge), and become flesh eaters. George Nicholson repeats one of the traditional interpretations of the origins of flesh eating, suggesting the practice arose after an animal sacrifice to the gods when a Phoenician priest picked a piece of burnt offering from the ground and licked his lips.[32]

The myth of the Golden Age is treated in modern literature as an ahistorical imagination. But we need to ask: how ahistorical is it, and what function does it perform? According to the *Concise Oxford Dictionary*, "myth" is "1. a traditional story concerning the early history of a people or explaining a natural or social phenomenon, and typically involving supernatural beings or events. 2. a widely held but false belief – a fictional person or thing – an exaggerated or idealized conception of a person or thing." Thus, a myth may be true or false. There are various kinds of myths. Some are myths that explain. Some are myths that instruct. Some are myths that instruct while providing a true or false historical explanation. And as Maynard Mack has it, "most myths are caramelized fragments of common sense."[33] Being accustomed to scientific explanation, we tend to forget how the explanations of science evolve, at least in part, from our own cultural stance. To be sure, the explanations offered by science may be more convincing explanations to us than those offered in the absence of scientific method, but the latter are very persuasive in the cultures in which they are developed. For earlier humans, explanations would have to be of the prescientific variety. To experience something of a mythic awakening, it is worth watching a magnificent, shimmering dawn and then imagining, in the absence of scientific explanation, in what terms the societal elders would have explained the shimmering dawn to the initiates and the difference between it and a dull and cloudy dawn. A bright, beautiful dawn may well be explained as the gods speeding across the heavens and lighting the day. A dull dawn may be explained as the gods being hindered in their progress by the enemies of life-giving light. The night, which the dawn is dispersing, is a time of darkness and danger. (It is difficult to discern when candles were invented, but it was probably not until Roman times. Their use did not become widespread until the later Middle Ages. Until then, the primary diminution of the darkness of the night was the light of the moon. Flaming torches were notoriously unreliable.) The moon may thus have been worshipped as the provider of a measure of respite from the unseen terrors of the dark. And upon the fears of the night, the promise of the day, and the experience of mysterious events, a whole pantheon of gods – some threatening, some at least occasionally benevolent, including the life-giving Sun and the twilight-giving Moon – will have emerged.

The conflict between the Edenic and Arcadian versions of the Golden Age myth will allow us to understand how it is that a myth may retain competing elements: a pride in the original human as being at one with the animals and an equal pride in having become flesh eaters. Thus, for example, in the Cheyenne creation myth, originally "every animal, big and small, every bird, big and small, every fish, and every insect could talk to the people and understand them. The people ... went naked and fed on honey and wild fruits; they were never hungry ... During the days they talked with the other animals, for they were all friends."[34] This was, of course, the Edenic stage in which pride is expressed. These conditions did not last, however, for the "Great Medicine taught" the Amerindians

> to catch and eat fish at a time when none of the other people knew about eating meat ... the Great Medicine blessed [the Amerindians] and gave them some medicine spirit to awaken their dormant minds. From that time on they seemed to possess intelligence and know what to do. The Great Medicine singled out one of the men and told him to teach people to band together, so that they all could work and clothe their naked bodies with skins of panther and bear and deer. The Great Medicine ... gave them corn to plant and buffalo for meat, and from that time on there were no more floods and no more famines.[35]

Human co-operation permitted hunting, and hence flesh eating and pelt acquisition, which, thus, according to the myth, ensured human survival. The utopian ideal of Eden was being replaced by the courageous and adventurous ideal of Arcadia. The pride in the Edenic stage did not disappear but existed alongside that of Arcadia, albeit in a weaker form. In the precarious earlier period, so the Cheyenne legend of the origins of the buffalo hunt tells us, it was initially the buffalo who was the meat eater, but eventually the human vanquished the buffalo in a contest and won the right to consume the buffalo instead. In other words, at first, nonhuman animals were the predators, and human animals were the prey. Later, as we shall see, the period of the human as prey was replaced by that of the human as predator. The Cheyenne legends depict clearly the conflict between the "natural" ("original") and the cultural, the instinctive and the learned, the primitive and the developed – in short, the Edenic and the Arcadian, which have come to confound human ideals ever since. Aboriginals everywhere inhabit the world of Arcadia rather than Eden, which, paradoxically, may come later (or perhaps constitute a return) in human conscious development. For the aboriginal, as for the supposedly "civilized," the Arcadian is seen as the decidedly superior stage, one in which the human has changed from prey to predator, but the lingering pride in Eden is never quite lost.

What if there were no vegetarian stage in human prehistory, as, we must constantly remind ourselves, most paleontologists continue to believe? Even the ethical vegetarian scientist Randall Collura states that we "evolved eating a wide variety of diets containing both plants and animal food" and that "humans don't really have a natural diet."[36] In this circumstance, the Edenic vegetarian ideal must be seen as a deeply held moral value – the absolute, if difficult to attain, ethical ideal. If such is the case, the Golden Age does not in any manner represent historical reality; instead, the pervasiveness of the myth suggests that it was an intuited moral goal of humankind. It is what the human is conceived to be in ideal form – the Form, the Idea, of Plato's justice, if you will. It is human perfection; it is a primal moral memory, to express it in quasi-Wordsworthian and Jungian terms.[37] It is an expression of the sense of justice present in every human, however distorted culture may have rendered it. But it is also seen as an impractical ideal. Its alternative is viewed as the necessity of culture replacing nature in human consciousness. The addition of Arcadia alongside the perennial myth of Eden suggests a permanent contradiction in humanity's primal memories. Neither culture nor contradiction is a recent acquisition. We have to return to Eden to escape the contradictions, if they can ever be escaped at all. But the image of Arcadia is so deeply implanted in the human mind that any retrogression to Eden is a daunting task.

The moral imperative may be weakened given the "would it were so" nature of the myth of the Golden Age in that, according to the myth, natural carnivores become vegetarian when it is clearly incompatible with their biological constitution that they be so, even though it is worth noting that many well-intentioned, but *perhaps* misguided, vegetarians have attempted to render their carnivorous companion animals likewise vegetarian.[38] Of course, it would not have been possible that in the distant past carnivorous animals would have been vegetarian, as the myth requires. Or that herbivorous animals could have been carnivorous at one time, as suggested in the

Cheyenne legend. The use of the buffalo as predator in the myth, rather than the real predators from whom the Amerindians have suffered, provides a convenient justification for the slaying of the buffaloes in revenge. The myth is, in fact, a rejection of the cruel realities of carnivorous "nature" – namely, that there are carnivorous animals, notably carnivorous animals from whose teeth and claws humans traditionally have suffered. Nonetheless, it is equally clear that such a restriction on the myth would not necessarily have applied to omnivorous humans. It may well be that the human part of the moral or history is valid as history, whereas that of the carnivorous animals is merely a wish based on a utopian image of the eradication of competitive and aggressive nature, which humans prehistorically had to endure – a nature frequently deemed deplorable by such prominent historical figures as Leonardo da Vinci, Victor Hugo, Charles Darwin, Thomas Hardy, and George Bernard Shaw.[39] To refer to the words of Darwin alone, writing to J.D. Hooker in 1856: "What a book a Devil's Chaplain might write on the clumsy, wasteful, blundering, low and horridly cruel works of nature."[40] In short, vegetarian impulses constitute an attempt to replace the rancour of a world of natural conflict with the tranquility of the utopian peaceable kingdom, to overcome the morally wasteful and harmful in favour of the morally pristine. The Edenic primary premise may be expressed in the dicta of various traditions, such as the saying of the Christian desert father Abbot Moses that "a man ought to do no harm to any,"[41] the Judaic adage of *Bal Taschit* (do not destroy), and the Jain principle of *ahimsa* (nonharm). Despite the adages, Arcadian harm to others remained the norm. At the very least, the earliest time of the Golden Age presents itself as the essential human moral lesson. In the words of Porphyry expressing the vegetarian mandate: "We should imitate those that lived in the golden age, we should imitate those of that period who were free. For with them modesty, Nemesis and Justice associated, because they were satisfied with the fruits of the earth."[42] Randall Collura says that today, in contrast, the "first thing we need to do ... is to abandon the Garden of Eden mythology."[43] But do we? If one has serious doubts about the historicity of the Golden Age, as many will, the doubt does not eliminate the appeal. As the philosopher Daniel Dombrowski has pointed out, although "'once upon a time' stories of a contract between man and animal are merely stories, so are the 'once upon a time' stories between man and man. In that this condition has not bothered the history of social contract theory from Plato to Kant to Rawls, it should not bother us. That is, these stories of an ancient vegetarian past, even if not true, offer insights into the beliefs of the people who told them."[44]

What if neither the claimed historicity nor a manifestation of the intuited good appears convincing as an explanation for the persistence of the myth of the Golden Age? Then the myth would appear to stand as a symbol for that which humanity has striven throughout its history. For example, in Dostoevsky's *The Devils* (1871-72), Stavrogin has a "Golden Age" vision of a primeval earthly paradise of happiness and innocence, inspired by Claude Lorraine's painting *Acis and Galatea*: "A feeling of happiness, hitherto unknown to me, pierced my heart till it ached ... Here was the cradle of European civilization, here were the first scenes from mythology, man's paradise on earth. Here a beautiful race of men had lived. They rose and went to sleep happy and innocent; the woods were filled with their joyous songs, the great overflow of their untapped energies passed into love and unsophisticated gaiety. The sun shed its rays on these islands and that sea." Yet Dostoevsky is aware of the illusion, although it is an illusion that loses nothing by being an illusion. Stavrogin continues: "A wonderful dream, a sublime illusion! The most incredible dream that has ever been dreamed, but to which all of mankind has devoted all its powers during the whole of its existence, for which it has died on the cross and for which its prophets have been killed, without which nations will not live and cannot even die."[45] Whether history, intuition, or symbol of human goals, the Golden Age stands as a remarkable signpost of the finest ideals of humanity. It is a signpost whose clarion call resonates deeply in the human breast.

### THE HUMAN AS PREY

Myth depicts humans as vegetarian in origin. And myths usually have some historical, moral, or explanatory justification. But on what hard evidence, we must ask, should we believe the human animal to have been originally a predominantly vegetarian and prey creature rather than a natural predator? We have already met some significant hard evidence, but there is more. *Paranthropus boisei*, discovered by the Leakeys in Olduvai Gorge, Tanzania, was said to be "robust" – referring not to overall stature but to the extremely large jaws and molars, suited to grinding hard, fibrous plant material. The teeth of australopithecines were also decidedly not those of a flesh eater. However, because intestines do not fossilize, it is impossible to discern whether the intestines of primitive humans resembled those of vegetarian animals most completely or not.

Few flesh-eating predators are also natural prey, although there are a significant number of exceptions. An adult animal usually belongs to one category or the other. Thus, human flesh eating along with a tradition of being hunted must be seen as something of a rarity, even if the antitheses occur at different periods of human development. But it is a rarity borne out by evidence and argument. Holes in the skulls of some early hominid fossils match perfectly with big-cat fangs. Many human fossil bones bear the marks of being gnawed. Hans Kruuk, an authority on predators, argues that our horror, yet fascination, with man-eater tales is based on a hard-wired fear of our history of having been hunted, a fear developed over millions of years.[46] The horror, together with fascination, reflects that one meets danger with both anxiety and excitement: witness the attraction of horror films, an attraction scarcely explicable in the customary terms of "entertainment" or "pleasure." The strange reality – unfathomable in conventional terms – is that many people are excited by events that arouse fear. Paradoxically, fear may itself be fulfilling on occasion, as exemplified by the synchrony of terror and the sublime.

During the Raj, the British kept statistics on the numbers of humans lost to tiger predation. Between 1800 and 1900, they estimated some three hundred thousand humans had been killed.[47] In the summer of 1996 in Indian Uttar Pradesh, there were thirty-three fatal wolf attacks on children.[48] Ignorant, weak, and inexperienced human children are especially easy prey. Self-confident, aggressive carnivores can afford to live alone; weaker animals must live communally. And the human is a decidedly social animal, out of prehistoric need. As the protoanarchist William Godwin wrote: "There is nothing that the human heart more irresistibly seeks than an object to which to attach itself."[49]

As the number of large predators has declined in general through human population explosion, habitat destruction, effective hunting, urbanization, and "civilization," a few areas of the world have remained rife with predation. Nile crocodiles are still feared as creatures that dine on human flesh and that of other primates. In the already mentioned Sundarbans region of northern India and Bangladesh, tiger predation is a constant threat. In a four-month period of 1988, sixty-five people were killed there by tigers. Even in Canada, bears (grizzly, polar, and very occasionally, black) and mountain lions take a small toll.[50] In Australia, Florida, and California, humans are at risk from sharks. Predation was a constant threat in the past both more frequently than now and far more extensively in the areas affected. In the not so distant past, in his *Descriptive Sketches*, Wordsworth numbers bears, ravenous wolves, and bandits as objects of fear in his Swiss wanderings. At Dmanisi in the Republic of Georgia, paleontologists have discovered fossils from *Homo erectus* some 1.7 to 1.8 million years ago – perhaps the first hominid to venture beyond the confines of Africa. The fossils give a clear indication of having been preyed upon. Indeed, Hart and Sussman report on a "Dmanisi skull [that] bears the signature set of holes into which sabre-toothed fangs fit with perfection."[51] Gnaw marks on one of the hominid lower jaws demonstrate that some of the Dmanisi population were eaten by large cats. And there are good grounds for the belief that the human brain still stores fear and threat memories, albeit unconscious memories, of those early ages. Cornell University's Colin Campbell, a reputed bio-chemist, stated to the *New York Times* that, far from being primordial hunters, "we're basically a vegetarian species and should be eating a wide variety of plant foods and minimizing our intake of animal foods."[52] The history of the human as prey would confirm Campbell's claim. Humans are more likely to have been primordial quasi-vegetarians whose later history has endowed the human psyche with a sense of being an essential omnivore.

## Animal Sacrifice

"In the beginning no animal was sacrificed to the gods, nor was there any positive law to prevent this, for it was forbidden by the law of nature."[53] So said Porphyry. How, then, did animal sacrifice to the gods originate – the product of which was eaten primarily by the human sacrificers? Perhaps it should first be noted that there are many misleading suppositions made with regard to animals and worship. Worship is often thought an adoration of the object worshipped. In fact, adoration in worship arrives late in the history of prayer. In many instances, although by no means all, beings are worshipped because they are feared. Animals that are neither feared nor food are not customarily the object of prayer. Where sharks are a constant threat to human life, as in the South Pacific, they are worshipped (by the Tuamoton, for example) in the hope that the sharks will thereby spare the lives of the kith and kin of the worshippers. The Ainu of Hokkaido, Japan, prayed to the bear but treated the caged (although, of course, "worshipped") bear abominably. The object was to render the potentially harmful bear innocuous. Certainly, it is important to distinguish between reverence and awe derived from fear or terror and reverence and awe based on love, admiration, and wonder. The latter shows a respect for the being as an entity in itself, reflecting an evaluation of its appealing qualities; the former reflects the urgency to escape the consequences of the worshipped being's wrath, the desire of the worshipped animal being to have oneself as food. In some instances, the worship will also reflect that we are in awe of the animal's powers. Animals were often themselves deities precisely because they were feared. Nonetheless, totemism was a common practice – a lingering remnant of Eden. Under totemic belief a tribe considers itself a descendent of a particular animal, to which it bears a special kinship relation. Only occasionally is a totemic animal sacrificed, and then as a special gift to a favoured god. Even under totemism, contrary to common interpretation, there is no "oneness with nature," for animals other than the totem animal are regularly sacrificed and eaten.

Certainly, in many incipient states and among hunter-gatherers, animals were usually worshipped, but we should not imagine that those worshipped benefited from the worship. Nowhere were animals worshipped more assiduously than in ancient Egypt – from crocodiles through snakes to baboons. Yet the "worship" was of no benefit to the animals. So many "worshipped" animals have been found in human graves in Egypt that they must have been acquired in the neighbouring lands specifically for the purpose of sacrifice. Let us avoid the easy error of imagining that treating animals well in myth, drawing pictures of them on cave walls, or making statuary of them meant that they were well treated or well respected, in the positive sense of that term. More often than not, they were killed for their divinity. Animals were useful symbols to help humans develop rules for living, and for saving, their own lives. Only rarely did the animals matter as ends in themselves.

Nor should we confuse positive symbols with benevolent treatment. In India, the cobra is still worshipped in places. Before the religious ceremony involving worship of the cobras, their mouths are sewn shut. In 1994 the Indian government released dozens of such tortured – yet "worshipped" – cobras back into the wild, after the sutures had been removed, of course. In the *Euthyphro,* Plato has Socrates proclaim that "where reverence is, there is fear."[54] Likewise, the Greek poet Stasinus as well as Thomas Hobbes emphasized the connection between fear and reverence. None of this should persuade us to ignore saying no. 17 of the *Pancatantra:* "In blind darkness are we sunk when we offer sacrifices with beasts. A higher religious duty than harmlessness (*ahimsa*) has never been nor shall be." But the *ahimsa* of the *Pancatantra* is followed no more faithfully, other than as rote, than are the New Testament admonitions to pursue peace and turn the other cheek. Bulls, goats, and sheep are slaughtered in ritual sacrifice in India still today. In the Hindu Kaharingan region of the Dayaks of Borneo, the *tiwah* – the funerary ritual – involves the sacrifice of animals to protect human lives from evil spirits. The Toraja of the highlands of Sulawesi in Indonesia sacrifice as many as 250 buffaloes on the death of an important person. These "sacred" animals are bred for the specific purpose of their sacrifice. Being "sacred" and being thus "worshipped" is of absolutely no benefit to the animals.

In the Great War of 1914 to 1919 – to take but one of myriad potential examples – the soldiers of the Allied forces, and equally their enemies, imagined themselves on the side of God and justice. They did not imagine themselves full of rage or hatred toward their foe, at least not in the early years of the war. Instead, they thought of themselves as noble. They had a strong sense of solidarity with their compatriots, an attitude that the war fostered; they were patriots, they belonged, and they revelled in their belongingness. Likewise, hunters see themselves engaged not in enmity with the prey but in solidarity with their fellow hunters. They "cherish the noble art of venerie," as Walter Scott wrote in *The Talisman.* They share the sense of being part of a body, of being subsumed, lost almost, within a greater whole – hence the blood-smearing ritual of the foxhunt, which integrates the novice recipient of the blood into the fraternity. The comradeship of the hunters gives them a sense they are pursuing a just end, even though the object of their enterprise involves the killing of another being – an innocent being, a "respected" being, but one who is on "the other side," just as, at first in the First World War, the Germans and Austrians were "respected" but on "the other side." Despite the "respect," they were killed if the opportunity arose. Certainly, hunters feel without any doubt as they slaughter their prey that the animal is deeply "respected." With undoubted exaggeration, but nonetheless meaningfully from the perspective of the hunter, we are often told that "traditional hunters typically view the animals they hunt as their equals. They exercise no power over them."[55] This is, of course, because the aboriginal has few artificial weapons with which to wield extraordinary power. But there is little equality in that the human predators are rarely successfully hunted by the prey. In fact, the ethical vegetarian deems the claimed respect a malevolent subterfuge if death or harm of the prey is intended, but it would be churlish to deny that hunters *feel,* persuade themselves they possess, a sense of respect toward the object of the chase, however much it is anathema and unconvincing to the ethical vegetarian. War and hunting are useful analogies for understanding some aspects of the human-animal relationship, especially with regard to animal sacrifice to the gods and to flesh eating.

Rituals of societal blood sacrifice – both human and animal – celebrate and reenact the transition from prey to predator, from hunted to hunter, from Eden to Arcadia. Animal sacrifice, with roles reversed, reenacts the predation of animals on humans. Now it is the animal that is prey. Being hunted by predators must have played a supreme role in human evolution. In moving from prey to predator, one lives in constant tension, often ambivalence, retaining sometimes admiration, often respect, and usually fear for nonhuman animals in the prey stage alongside the sacrificial, vivisecting, flesh-eating habits of the predator stage. Violence is not a *necessary* part of the primordial human psyche, but it is expressed in the traditional glorification of the warrior and the hunter that is a consequence of our transition from prey to predator, from Eden to Arcadia.

Only the horrors of war's excesses in the past century have dimmed the glorification of war. As long as war was fought on a restricted battlefield between limited numbers of soldiers, with the vast majority of the population involved no more than peripherally, war and warrior could be readily glorified. And sport – all sport is an imitation of war and the chase – has come to be war and hunting's modern replacement to the extent that real war can be avoided. Hunting today and animal sacrifice to the gods are traditionally substitutes for war; they are blood sacrifices in the tradition of war in which the victim is viewed as "only an animal," on the one hand, but as a worthy fellow creature, on the other. The animal has to be worthy as an admirable object for sacrifice if the gods are to be truly respected.

As Barbara Ehrenreich explains in *Blood Rites,* "blood sacrifice is not just 'a' religious ritual; it is the central ritual of the religions of all ancient and traditional civilizations ... it is probably through ritual killing that humans approached the experience of the transcendent."[56] Today, it is in part through the killing involved in hunting that the animal becomes "sacred" and is thought by hunters to be "respected" – its blood, the symbol of life, is sought. Among the ancient Greeks, no important decisions or important events could occur without sacrifice – without blood – and ancient Greece was merely an "advanced" representative of the norm. It was, oddly, as shown in the rituals of numerous societies from Papua to Hawaii to Australia, less death than blood that was required. Yet often blood is seen as the essence of life. And loss of blood leads to loss of life.

Ancient Greeks, Hebrews, Canaanites, Maya, and more were all obsessed with sacrifice. The gods demanded sacrifice. Sacrificing the animal to the gods was in part to thank the gods for past mercies and in part to persuade them to act benevolently by turning the tide of history in the supplicant's favour, but most of all the purpose of sacrifice was to propitiate the gods, to avert their wrath. Threatening forces must be thwarted, and those forces include, or once included, predatory animals. The threat from the large carnivorous animals must be thwarted through worship. Sacrifice is society's sanction of violence, which the transition from prey to predator seems to demand as a signal of the new-found power of humankind. René Girard in *Violence and the Sacred* argues convincingly that war and sacrifice serve ultimately the same end – the suppression of internecine conflict and the direction of conflict outward instead.[57] The primary function of war and sacrifice is communal – the compact of warriors, the bonding of sacrificers, the camaraderie of hunters. Communal prayer encourages the integration and the sense of oneness. And if this is so, then there are countless millennia of hardwired tendencies in the human psyche, especially the male psyche, because it is from the males that the warrior and hunter caste is mainly drawn, fighting to withstand the logic and the ethics of the vegetarian argument. Thus it is that for most flesh eaters, animal consumption seems an essential part of being human, or at least "civilized," despite the strength of the vegetarian's ethical argument. Indeed, omnivorousness often seems almost impervious to the ethical argument.

War and sacrifice must be seen as vindications of the superiority in some manner of one's tribe or nation or religion if the sacrifices are to be justified to oneself, if acts of aggression and oppression are to be countenanced as acceptable. One must think of one's nation as especially protected by a particular god if one is to justify preferential consideration for one's own compatriots. And, likewise, humans must see themselves as in some manner superior to other species, and not subject to the same ethical criteria, if animals are to be treated as subservient to human ends. If vegetarians are to succeed in their task, they need not mere successful ethical argument but must replace the warriors' and hunters' subliminal need for blood, the promptings of our evolutionary history, with some other fulfilling passion – war with hockey or soccer, even chess; hunting with archery, javelin throwing, or billiards and, ultimately, with the fully satisfying meal, equally acceptable and ritually meaningful to all members of the community and absent of the now customary flesh component. The meal must be communal and integrational, an especially difficult task when the vegetarian is in a decided minority.

Animal sacrifice came to replace human sacrifice, to be directed toward more socially acceptable goals, as the idea of the value of all human life came to predominate. It is now commonly recognized that human sacrifice has been widespread throughout much of human history – in both tribes and urban civilizations. It is mentioned in the Indian sacred Vedas and was practised by the Aztecs and Maya. Britain, Mexico, and Carthaginia are among the lands where human sacrifice appears to have been commonplace. But at some point, almost everywhere, human sacrifice was replaced by animal sacrifice. The sacrifice of animals instead of humans was deemed worthy of pleasing the gods. As Girard has recognized, the sacrificial victim must be seen primarily as a scapegoat – one who is blamed for the sins of others. The victim was sacrificed to excuse some iniquity or to avoid some calamity, such as an alien invasion, an epidemic, or an internecine conflict. Indeed, the very term "scapegoat" is derived from the Yom Kippur practice of transferring the sins of the faithful onto the goat – from the human culprit to the goat substitute, which is to be sacrificed in the human's stead. And the harmless goat stands as the representative of all animal life, including the dangerous predators. If the beasts that once killed humans almost at will, and for whom considerable "respect" was still felt, were to become sustenance, then the ultimate revenge was achieved. What is perhaps an example of the fear of the potential reversal of roles once again is expressed in the Hindu *Kausitaki Brahmana* and *Satapatha Brahmana* when, in the legend of Bhrgu, a visitor to the yonder world sees an animal eating a human in revenge for his having been eaten by a human on earth, just as the human in reality has wreaked revenge on the animal.[58] The famous adage of the military theorist Carl von Clausewitz is appropriate: "War is not an independent phenomenon but is the continuation of politics by other means." Sacrifice is the politics of revenge – a reversal of traditional politics – against the once feared but now dominated enemy. And the domination is practised primarily not on the dangerous predators but on the harmless animals whom it is so much easier to dominate.

In the story of Cain and Abel, God is said to prefer Abel's flesh offerings (deemed valuable and apposite!) over the "fruit of the soil" offerings (deemed insufficiently grateful and unfitting) from Cain. Thus, flesh rather than fruit becomes the diet of the gods. Of course, in reality, humans consume most of the sacrificed animal and not just in the lands of the Bible. Thus the formal meal comes into existence – as a part of one's ceremonial duty to the gods. Flesh could be consumed only if it had been sacrificed according to the prescribed ritual and for the appropriate divine recipients. Animals must thus undergo a ritual death and be consumed in the temple according to the usually observed rites, without which the practice is seen as a serious moral transgression akin to murder. Eden has not quite disappeared, for, in many instances, the value of the animal's life is recognized and the animal is apologized to for its treatment. The same apologetic practice continues today among many Inuit, a practice that suggests an awareness that the killing and eating are wrongs in themselves that require some external justification, usually in the form of a religious or mythical permission.

Girard goes so far as to say that the awe-inspiring nature of the ritual would be lessened significantly if it did not include the element of transgression. What should be clear is that animal sacrifice is recognized as a substitute for human sacrifice. Human sacrifice is an evil in itself, which reverential circumstance once excused. Animal sacrifice remains a transgression, but it is a lesser transgression than the taking of human life. For the vegetarian, it is apparent that now that the then presumed need for animal sacrifice and hence animal eating has disappeared, meat eating is as readily dispensable as sacrifice itself. Nonetheless, the very real difficulty for the vegetarian is to determine in what communal and integrative manner the nonflesh substitute might be made communally and socially satisfying to the omnivore.

Humans differ from natural carnivores and from other omnivores in that our flesh consumption depends on religion and ritual to authorize its practice. After millions of years of evolution, the trauma of being hunted was replaced by the trauma of being the hunter, and religion and ritual served to assuage the trauma. Especially when confronted with danger, when there is an external threat, we move closer together in common cause and solidarity, even in war (hunting and sacrifice) against the predatory enemy. And the vehicle of the solidarity was initially the common belonging expressed in a religion.

It is a human propensity derived from our evolutionary history to side with the weak (ourselves) against the strong (predatory animals) and to rejoice in our legends (animal-related myths and others) of the victory of the naturally weak over the naturally strong. As Ehrenreich expresses it, "The transformation from prey to predator in which the weak rise up against the strong is the central 'story' in the early human narrative."[59] And what greater victory can we have in devouring the erstwhile and now vanquished foe than by eating what once ate us? It is what, like it or not, makes most humans feel "human" as the once dominated but now dominant animal – head of the food chain, as humans imagine themselves to be.

Throughout human prehistory and human history, *Homo sapiens* has been developing a moral conscience, although never sufficient entirely to overcome human evolutionary impulses. Vegetarians usually believe they have adopted a necessary stage in human ethical development, but the human is far more the rationalizing animal than the ethical animal, far more the product of evolutionarily developed genes than of the philosophical imagination. The human as predator plays a greater subliminal role than the human as moralist in the human psyche. If the vegetarian ideal is consistent with Edenic morality, it is not consistent with the morality of Arcadia and later stages of human history. And this fact persuades most people, albeit subliminally. It is a sufficient justification for their dietary habits. The vegetarian has many of the nonrational elements of human psychology to overcome, an almost insuperable task. Thus it is that the ethical task of the vegetarian is an arduous one – to overcome the lust for animal flesh that is a constituent part of the Arcadian human primal memory.

Yet it must not be forgotten that the once pervasive lust of the human for the flesh of fellow humans – cannibalism – has been overcome. Symbolically, partaking of the blood and body of Christ in the Eucharist, a practice of several Christian denominations, is reflective of this aspect of our prehistory. Humans once thought they acquired the virtues of conquered humans by eating them and later thought they acquired the courage and guile of nonhuman animals by eating them. We no longer, in general, possess these beliefs – although most still tend to imagine a flesh diet makes us stronger and healthier, a remnant of our Arcadian history. And thus the task of the vegetarian, although still immensely difficult because of the continuing influence of the evolutionary forces, is eased. Because we no longer fear animals, we no longer look on them as superiors or even equals. In the West, we are often sentimental about some of them and treat them through "love" and sentimentality as decidedly inferior creatures, as our "toys." Where predation is still a reality, no such pampering or sentimental affection can be enjoyed. Where predation is no longer a reality, pampering and sentimental affection still ascribe lower status to the nonhuman animal. Both being prey and treating animals sentimentally reflect that, as a species, we have never come to acknowledge humans as animals in quite the same way we acknowledge other species as animals. Recognition of humans and other species as animals in the same manner is perhaps the *sine qua non* of ultimate vegetarian success. Although at least quasi-vegetarian origins are not a *proven* part of human prehistory, the evidence and argument is undoubtedly persuasive, perhaps compelling.

Despite the apparent vegetarian aspects of human prehistory, it is not until the Indian experiences of around the millennium before the time of Christ, rapidly followed by, or perhaps contemporaneous with, the Middle East and Eastern Europe, that we encounter explicit vegetarian practices.

# 2

# Eastern Religions and Practice

Perhaps more misleading pious prose and wishful thinking have been expressed about the purported pervasive vegetarianism and respect for animals of Indian religious and philosophical traditions than about any other aspect of historical vegetarianism. It is certainly true that India has provided far more of the impetus to vegetarianism than has any other single country, but to listen to some accounts, by Western vegetarians in particular, of the doctrines of Hinduism, Buddhism, and Jainism is often to hear a very distorted story. Indeed, in the words of the renowned doyen of the anthropology of religion Mircea Eliade, in his profound study *Yoga: Immortality and Freedom,* "the analysis of a foreign culture principally reveals what was sought in it or what the seeker was already prepared to discover."[1] The result has been a host of misinformation. Nonetheless, India's vegetarianism had an abiding impact on many travellers to the subcontinent from the late sixteenth to the nineteenth centuries and on administrators of the British Raj. And via the travellers and the administrators, in time naturalists, essayists, poets, and philosophers were awakened to the vegetarian appeal. At the very least, many were impressed that the Indian experience demonstrated that humans did not require flesh to live a healthy life, a fact they could have learned just as easily from the poor of their own countries or from the slaves on the West Indies plantations, who were in most instances served the same fodder as the working animals. It was an important awakening because the more common prior view, even held by many who thought of vegetarianism as an ideal, was that the human constitution had over time come to necessitate the consumption of flesh. And many others – Isaac Newton, for example – were persuaded by the reports from India of the need to treat animals with respect and to eliminate gross cruelties from the kitchen. To be sure, it took the addition of the culture inspired by the French Revolution to encourage a sense of the possibility of all kinds of political and social reform, but the Indian experience was instrumental in helping to develop an awareness of a potential European vegetarian practicality.

Many centuries previously, the early Fathers of Christianity had commended the Brahmins for their abstemious life. Frequently, later stories that emerged from India treated an idealized Brahminism, or occasionally Buddhism or Jainism, as though it were the whole of the Indian reality. That the Indians were reported to live healthy lives to the age of 200 (sometimes even 300) is an indication of the degree of gross inaccuracies born of wanting to have a good story to impart. Many did not come to vegetarianism from the practices of India but came to the practices of India from vegetarianism, finding in them a practical exemplar of their ideals at work and misrepresenting the reality of India in the process. Others embellished the reality of India in the stories they told to impress their audience with wondrous tales. In many other such stories told in Europe, it was Turkey that was treated as the ideal of a country wholly considerate of its animal population. This was especially so from the seventeenth to eighteenth centuries among the literati. And, again, there was more idealization than reality. This was not unlike the idealization of the aboriginal beginning in the late fifteenth century and developed by Peter Martyr, Oviedo, Montaigne, and others.[2]

Several contemporary writers on Indian vegetarianism provide a very one-sided and quite misleading account of its practice. They act the part of rationalizing apologists rather than that of informative scholars. It is necessary, therefore, to attempt to provide some healthy balance in the understanding of modern vegetarianism's most worthy forerunner. Voltaire's eighteenth-century admonitions are as apposite to the current intellectual traveller as to his fellow physical travellers then: "Our European travellers for the most part are satyrical upon their neighbouring Countries, and bestow large Praises upon the Persians and Chinese; it being too natural to revile those who stand in Competition with us, and to extol those who being far remote from us, are out of the reach of Envy."[3] The less we know of a civilization and the further removed it is from us culturally, the easier it is to imagine an improbable utopia and to use that culture as a cudgel with which to flagellate ourselves.

Other than depictions in very broad strokes about Aryans – who were probably tribal peoples from the Caucasus mountain region – and others invading the land now known as India, about their very nomadic pastoral economy, and about incipient agriculture, including cattle sacrifice, little can be offered with confidence about India's early cultural traditions that arrived from the steppes. We can be confident, however, that in a conjunction of the beliefs of the conquered Dravidians and the conquering Aryans, Brahmanism, the early form of Hinduism, was developed. There are unfounded yet firm beliefs among many traditionalist Hindus in the practice of the veneration of the cow in the earliest thus developed Vedic customs and precepts. But there are equally adamant and well-documented denunciations by some Hindu scholars that no such customs or precepts existed.

India is a land of many subcultures, often interrelated but with very considerable divergence. Although it is an oversimplified account, one may say Aryan culture forms the basis of the north, whereas the south has been predominantly Dravidian. Dravidians speak a Tamil-related language and are thought to have occupied the Indian subcontinent before the invasion of the Aryans. But the two were never entirely separate after the invasions. It is impossible to describe *the* culture of the nation with any degree of accuracy and clarity, for the varieties from region to region are legion, the discrepancies between rural and urban lifestyles are notoriously rife, and the cultural diversity of the nation is acknowledged as official in the Indian Constitution's recognition of fifteen regional languages. These are scarcely surprising facts about the most populous country in the world after China. Despite governmental efforts to change the culture of caste – indeed, to outlaw it – the caste system continues to have a major and direct impact on the practices and beliefs of Hindu India today, although it is undoubtedly in a measure of decline. Nonetheless, the caste system – no less oppressive than the former apartheid system of South Africa – continues to be rigorously upheld by many from the upper castes. With such disparaging treatment of the lower castes and, of course, outcasts, it would at first seem surprising if animals were treated with a respect rarely accorded some fellow humans.

It was pointed out in the Introduction that approximately one-third of the population of India is vegetarian – a commendably far higher proportion by a significant amount than any other country. That figure may itself be a little misleading, however, in that some 40 percent of India's population lives in dire poverty, although the prospects for change are now beginning to improve substantially, even dramatically. Thus, some of the poor may be vegetarian not out of cultural practice or ethical principle but because they cannot afford flesh. In the areas outside India where Hinduism is the recognized religion, its beliefs and practices differ greatly from those proclaimed as the Indian Hindu norm, and although Buddhism has practically died out in India, it has flourished elsewhere since leaving its birthplace. Where it is practised abroad, the differences among the varying forms are so great that it is in some respects difficult to see them as having sufficient in common to identify the various strands as Buddhism in common, other than that they are derived ultimately from a single original source.

What we can say of the religious constitution of present-day India – from which country Hinduism, Jainism, and Buddhism have all sprung – is that some 80 percent of the population is Hindu, including so-called "seculars" of Hindu origin; 14 percent is Muslim; fewer than one-half of 1 percent is Jaina; and the remaining 5 plus percent is divided among Christians, Sikhs, Buddhists, and a few Parsees (Zoroastrians), whom I shall discuss in the next chapter. Neither Muslims nor Sikhs nor Christians are customarily vegetarian. The Buddhists in India consist largely of refugees from Tibet, together with a few converts, almost entirely from the lower castes of Hinduism. While the proportion of Jaina is extremely small, the influence of Jainism has far exceeded the numbers of its adherents.

## HINDUISM

Almost everything about Hinduism is paradoxical, confused, and accordingly, unclear – which, of course, could be said with no less truth about a number of other religions as well, Christianity included. The real India is as elusive for modern Westerners as it was for the British characters of E.M. Forster's *A Passage to India*. There are innumerable strands and sects within Hinduism, and it has no well-defined ecclesiastical organization or system of orthodoxy. Its three most common traditional features are world renunciation (now diminishing), adherence to the caste system, and acceptance of the Aryan Vedas – Sanskrit sacred scriptures of the period from c. 1500 to c. 600 BC – as the scriptural basis of the religion. The earliest and most authoritative of these scriptures is the *Rig-Veda*, although, as notoriously with the Bible and the Koran also, there is no agreed upon interpretation of the varying and apparently contradictory decrees contained within the Vedas or even consensus on their meaning.

Vegetarianism and nonvegetarianism, which co-exist peacefully in India, are rather a matter more of caste and tradition than of ethical principle or choice. The tradition of the caste into which one is born – the complexity of caste is reflected in the fact there are over 3,000 castes and subcastes today – predominantly determines the dietary practice that will be followed. Brahmins (the priestly and intellectual caste) in general and those of the farming and mercantile caste (Vaishya), also called Banias (traders), are traditionally vegetarian. Today, it is especially the women who renounce flesh. Among the Brahmins, the Vaishnava are said to be devout in their rejection of flesh, whereas Shaivite and Shakti Brahmins are known to indulge their fleshly appetites on occasion. The warrior, or administrative, caste (Kshatriya), the labourer caste (Shudra), and the untouchables (Pariahs, or Harijans [children of God], as Gandhi renamed them) – formally, "untouchability" has disappeared but not in fact – are predominantly flesh eaters. Nonetheless, a remarkable feature of India is that even the flesh eaters have great respect for vegetarianism and regard its practice as in principle worthier than their own less commendable omnivorous habits. Still, by and large, vegetarianism is promoted and deemed worthy of practice because it is seen as an intrinsic part of the appropriate human condition, as a part of earthly renunciation, not because our moral responsibilities to our fellow animals warrant it. Vegetarians are admired because they are seen to be releasing themselves from the shackles of the mundane sphere.

What, then, can be said with any degree of confidence about the earliest Indian dietary practices? From long before the Aryan invasions (occurring from the middle of the second millennium BC), animal bones and stone tools, deposited in the period from between one hundred thousand and ten thousand years ago, have been found in abundance at excavation sites throughout the Harappa civilizaton area – the remarkably advanced Indus Valley civilization of the second half of the third millennium BC – indicating the prevalence of flesh consumption. The pre-Aryan invasion evidence is relevant because Aryan culture syncretized with – that is, married its own cultural practices with – the prevailing practices of the peoples of the conquered territories, usually said to be Dravidian. There is abundant archeological evidence that flesh eating continued after the Aryan invasions. Beef, pork, mutton, venison, fish, fowl, and river turtles, along with the flesh of carnivorous animals, appear to have been consumed.[4] Large numbers of charred bones with cut marks, indicating the cooking and eating of flesh, have been excavated, covering both the Vedic and post-Vedic periods. Moreover, there is frequent reference in the Vedic texts, according to D.N. Jha, author of *The Myth of the Holy Cow,* to "the cooking of the flesh of the ox for offering to gods, especially Indra, the greatest of the Vedic gods, who was strong-armed, colossal, and a destroyer of enemy strongholds." At one place, it is said: "they cook for me fifteen plus twenty oxen." At other places, Indra is said "to have eaten the flesh of bulls, or of one or of a hundred buffaloes or 300 buffaloes roasted by Agni or a thousand buffaloes."[5]

Agni is a god who acts as an intermediary between heaven and earth and who takes the sacrificial offerings to the higher gods. It would be strange if the dietary preference of the gods was entirely alien to that of the supplicants, at the very least on festive occasions such as the birth of a son or the marriage of a scion. Indeed, there is ample documentary evidence of frequent flesh consumption on such occasions throughout recorded history.[6] Nonetheless, the Vedic texts seem to suggest that a substitute for animal sacrifice might be desirable. And, apparently, sometimes rice and barley effigies were offered in place of flesh, a practice we also hear about among the Pythagoreans. This desire to eradicate animal sacrifice might best be understood in the new cultural context permitted by the change from pastoralism to settled agriculture, animals being no longer central to all human experience. Although there are clear indications of Vedic preference for the purity of behaviour among the Brahmins through the denial of flesh, it would appear largely an aspect of the preferred asceticism of the priestly class (noticeable even today among Eastern Orthodox monks in the Christian tradition as well).[7]

It is difficult to determine when vegetarianism became a common practice in India, both among the Brahmin caste and in certain regions of the country. There is no consistency on the subject of vegetarianism in the religious commentaries and digests between the eighth and nineteenth centuries, Jha tells us, although it is generally agreed that in the earlier centuries it was a customary expectation that even a cow would be killed for a learned *brahmana* (a respected member of the Brahmin caste) or even for a less exalted guest – and even today beef consumption, in preference to the more expensive mutton, is not at all rare, especially among the lower castes.[8] However, it is probable that some of Brahmin caste renounced flesh as early as 1000 BC to be ascetically pure. Thereafter, albeit very slowly, vegetarianism came to be seen as a preferred way of life, entailing some respect for animals, not just by Brahmins but around the seventh or eighth century BC, with varying degrees of success, also by Hindus in general, some areas becoming vegetarian completely. This occurred mainly in the south, where agriculture is more suitable to the practice of vegetarianism, where the influences of Buddhism and Jainism were stronger, and where religious competition was accordingly more keenly felt. When the inhabitants had become vegetarian, however, they tended to retain their vegetarianism for cultural and religious reasons rather than because they considered it a right of the animal not to be eaten. Steven J. Rosen, who regards vegetarianism as generally pervasive on ethical grounds in the Hindu tradition, concedes that "the non-vegetarian diet has become widespread among Hindus in the modern world, just as it had in the early part of the Vedic restoration process."[9] (The Vedic restoration process is the period of Hindu revitalization in response to the increased popularity of Buddhism in India, effectively eradicating Buddhism eventually.) Vegetarianism remains something of an ideal, but not always a consistently practised ideal, and where it is the ideal it is primarily for the saintly interests of the devout. As James Gaffney rightly has observed: "reluctance to kill animals did not necessarily entail an equal reluctance to eat them – so long as they were killed by others less spiritually elevated."[10] That animal wellbeing is not a prominent purpose in vegetarian India is reflected in the fact that many cows are slaughtered in a most inhumane manner solely for their hides. They are killed, despite their holiness, to provide leather for shoes, seats, belts, and the like.

Despite the common contradictions in the scriptures, the precepts of the various religious commentaries contained significant animal-respecting directives in their hortative edicts. In numerous impressive instances, vegetarianism appears prima facie to be based on ethical principles, or at least to relate to them in some manner. Thus we find, for example, the *Mahabharata* announcing: "Dharma [religious duty] exists for the general welfare [*abhyudaya*] of all living beings. Thus, that by which the welfare of the greatest number of living beings is sustained, that for certain is Dharma."[11]

In G. Naganathan's *Animal Welfare and Nature: Hindu Scriptural Passages,* we read that the *Pancatantra* states: "The holy *first* commandment runs: not harsh but kindly be – and therefore lavish mercy on the louse, the bug and the gadfly." Further, "Whether it is the worm in the excrement or the being in Indra's heaven, their love of life is the same, their fear of death is the same."[12]

But our confidence in the substance of the passages is a little shaken when we turn to Chandra Rajan's translation of Vishnu Sarna's edition of the *Pancatantra* and find no equivalent to the passages cited by Naganathan.[13] In fact, there are considerable divergences in the translations of Hindu scriptures in general. Thus, for example, the same passage from the opening words of the *Ishopanishad* is translated in quite different ways by three different scholars. Naganathan renders the relevant opening passage as: "The entire universe and everything within it, animate and inanimate, is His. Let us treat everything around us reverently, as custodians. We have no charter for dominion. All wealth is commonwealth. Let us enjoy, but neither hoard nor kill. The humble frog has as much right to live as we."[14]

By comparision, R.C. Zaehner's version is far simpler and devoid of reference to animal ethics, other than an implicit acknowledgment that all beings are ensouled: "The whole world must be pervaded by a Lord – / Whatever moves in this moving [world] / Abandon it, and then enjoy: / Covet not the goods of anyone at all."[15] And Juan Mascaró translates the same passage as: "Behold the universe in the glory of God; and all that lives and moves on earth. Leaving the transient, find joy in the Eternal: set not your heart on another's possessions."[16]

Whereas Zaehner and Mascaró have treated the passage as being concerned primarily with abandonment of the self, renunciation of the mundane, recognition of soul in other beings (including animal beings), disparagement of greed, and human worship of the godhead, Naganathan seems to have treated the passage quite differently as a profound statement regarding animal ethics; he appears to have imposed his own gloss, values, and preferences on the material and tried tendentiously and unwarrantedly to differentiate it explicitly from the commonly condemned but commonly misunderstood "dominion" language of Genesis – a language that in fact enjoins a measure of ethical consideration for other animate beings.[17] We thus have grounds for being suspicious of some of the more elaborate of the Hindu statements on animal ethics offered to us, which must accordingly always be treated with some caution.

There is, nonetheless, a general, if far from complete, consistency in some of the statements we encounter. Accordingly, always being wary of potential tendentiousness in the translations we meet, whose originals are themselves open to easy misinterpretation, as we shall see from John Mackenzie's statements (below), we should delight in such pronouncements as: "*Ahimsa* [freedom from harm] is the highest dharma, self-control, gift, penance, sacrifice, power, friend, happiness, truth [and] scripture."[18] In the same scripture, we are also told: "Everyone in the [meat] business, the one who cuts, the one who kills, the one who sells, the one who prepares, the one who offers, the one who eats, all are killers."[19]

And again, this time in pantheistic mode, in the *Bhagavad Gita:* "I [the godhead] am the Self established / In the heart of all contingent beings; I am the beginning, the middle and the end / Of all contingent beings too."[20] The pantheistic message is repeated even more emphatically in the *Mahabharata:* "We bow to all beings with great reverence in the thought and knowledge that God enters into them through fractioning himself as living creatures."[21] Nor is the *Mahabharata* alone in such expressions of reverence. The *Hitopadesa* asks: "What is religion? Compassion for all things which have life. To animals in this world, health. What is kindness? A principle in the good. What is philosophy? An entire separation from the world."[22] If this beautiful passage enjoins compassion, it also enjoins the do-nothing of quietism, as we will also see in the Sadhu response to Gandhi (below): feel benevolently but do not act to right the wrong. Finally, from the *Bhagavatam* (there is much more, but the respectful pattern is clear): "The perfect devotee of the Lord is one who sees *Atman* [the soul, breath, the principle of life] in all creatures as an expression of the Supreme Being and all beings as dwelling in the supreme spirit."[23]

It is difficult to interpret these edicts as anything other than an immediate and thorough concern with animals as ends in themselves, but it remains a fact that numerous Hindu sages interpret such scriptures as a part of our duties to the godhead rather than expressing any concern with animals for their intrinsic selves. At the very least, such Hindus are able to point to passages in the scriptures that lead in a different direction. And as we have seen, we find conflicting interpretations of the same passages, some quite at odds with each other. Contradiction is the nature of many religions. Despite the lack of certainty, the evidence appears on the whole to suggest that the Hindu expression of benevolence toward the animal is a part of a sincere, if not extensive, concern for the animal in itself. Nonetheless, both sides of the story should be heard.

In *Holy Cow: The Hare Krishna Contribution to Vegetarianism and Animal Rights*, Steven J. Rosen accosts D.N. Jha, author of *The Myth of the Holy Cow*, claiming that "scholars of Hinduism ... point out that animal sacrifices were a departure from the overall spirit of Vedic dharma [religious duty], even if these sacrifices are mentioned in the Vedas themselves."[24] And, of course, Rosen is right that some always found animal sacrifice illegitimate, just as several writers of the Hebrew Bible also found animal sacrifice unacceptable, whereas others said God demanded it. But it is equally right that some Hindus advocated and practised animal sacrifice, and there is no good ground other than wish fulfilment to imagine the former more legitimate or numerous than the latter. What Rosen conveniently neglects to tell us is that animal sacrifice continues in Hindu temples even today, although it is less prevalent than before. Mahatma Gandhi felt compelled in his autobiography to mourn the continued practices:

> I saw a stream of sheep going to be sacrificed to Kali [the Hindu goddess of destruction] ... I asked him [a religious mendicant]: "Do you regard this sacrifice as religion?"
>
> "Who would regard the killing of animals as religion?"
>
> "Then, why don't you preach against it?"
>
> "That's not my business. Our business is to worship God ... it is no business of us *sadhus*."

We did not prolong the discussion but passed on to the temple. We were greeted by rivers of blood. I could not bear to stand there. I have never forgotten that sight.

That very evening I had an invitation to dinner at a party of Bengali friends. There I spoke to a friend about this cruel form of worship. He said "The sheep don't feel anything. The noise and the drum-beating there deaden all sensation of pain."

I could not swallow this. I told him that, if the sheep had speech, they would tell a different tale. I felt that the cruel custom should be stopped. How is it that Bengal with all its knowledge, intelligence, sacrifice and emotion tolerates this slaughter?[25]

It was *not* stopped and it *was* tolerated. Joseph Campbell said of a slightly later time, in the second half of the twentieth century, on the occasion of a visit to India: "I noticed that the place where a goat is sacrificed every morning (and a buffalo on feast days) is situated about where the *nandi* [sacrifice] is placed in a Siva temple compound ... It is said that earlier the goat sacrifice in this temple was a human sacrifice."[26] The goat is the symbol of lust and the buffalo of anger; thus, these passions are supposedly sacrificed along with the sacrifice of the animals. The sacrifice is undertaken to assuage human ills but, of course, at the expense of the animals.

Nor did Gandhi consider the treatment of the cow to be consistent with her supposed holy status: "How we bleed her to take the last drop of milk from her. How we starve her to emaciation, how we ill-treat the calves, how we deprive them of their last portion of milk, how cruelly we treat the oxen, how we castrate them, how we beat them, how we overload them."[27] In the Hindu religion cows are considered in principle the mother of all life – indeed, the mother of the gods – the symbol of wealth, and the most sacred of animals. But, clearly, Gandhi was of the view that, although they might be "revered," they were in fact treated poorly. The reality of the contradiction between Hindu religious philosophy and Hindu regular practice is best summed up by Joseph Campbell in *Baksheesh and Brahman: Indian Journal, 1954-1955:* "Indian society is not a function of Indian philosophy, but on the contrary Indian philosophy is a function of *one* section of Indian society. Consequently Indian society as a whole does not illustrate ... the ideals of Indian philosophy."[28]

The idea of sacrifice in the Vedic tradition is said by Hindu apologists (Rosen, for example) to have encouraged inveterate and unalterable flesh eaters to continue animal sacrifice as an act of worship prior to the consumption of flesh, if it had to be done at all.[29] Of course, this is equally true of the practice of other religions – and it is no less true to point out that Christianity, say, or pagan monotheism in early Rome, abolished animal sacrifice altogether a couple of millennia ago or thereabouts, whereas it still exists today in Hindu temples in India. Rosen continues, telling us that the *Laws of Manu* (c. 200 BC to AD 200) conclude by firmly discouraging the eating of meat: "The merit of not eating meat, which involves killing, is equal to the merit of performing hundreds of horse sacrifices."[30] What Rosen does not point out is that the *Laws of Manu* thereby declare horse sacrifice to be meritorious in and of itself, even if decidedly less meritorious than abstention from flesh. To equal the abandonment of flesh, one must perform numerous horse sacrifices! Religious devotion seems a principle prior to, and independent of, animal ethics. Moreover, the *Satapatha Brahmana,* one of the Hindu commentaries on the Vedic scriptures, declares unequivocally that "meat is the best kind of food." And cattle hide was used widely in a variety of ways. By the time of the *Upanishads* (sixth century BC or so), we find a parent being encouraged to eat a beef or veal stew if, on the birth of a son, a learned child is desired, although, alternatively, the child may be fed a diet of bird flesh and fish at the age of six months.[31]

In *Hindu Ethics: A Historical and Critical Essay,* John Mackenzie has argued that the vegetarian principle was considerably weakened in practice through the *Laws of Manu,* which he quotes as follows: "One may eat meat when it has been sprinkled with water, while Mantras were recited, when Brahmanas desire (one's doing it), when one is engaged (in the performance of a rite) according to the law, and when one's life is in danger."[32] And again: "He who eats meat, when he honours the gods and manes, commits no sin, whether he has bought it, or himself has killed (the animal), or has received it as a present from others."[33]

One is tempted to conclude that the purpose of (partial) flesh abstention is more the purity of the Brahmin and Vaishya castes than the wellbeing of animals. Indeed, Basant K. Lal, a professor of philosophy at Magadh University, Bodh Gaya, India, has observed that: "The Hindu recommendation to cultivate a particular kind of attitude toward animals is based not on a consideration about the animal as such but on consideration about how the development of this attitude is a part of the purificatory steps that bring men to the path of *moksa* (salvation)."[34] He adds: "Hinduism in all its forms teaches that we have no duties toward animals and thus implicitly denies that they have any rights."[35] The phrase "in all its forms" is relevant in implying that such Hindu doctrine applies as much to the Brahmin caste as to others.

Rosen's apologetic commentary would have been more balanced if he had added that in the Vedic *Laws of Manu* transmigration means that "people of darkness always become animals." The purpose of the transmigration of the soul was to release humans from the baseness of the animal character within. The very reason was to reject the animal aspect of character within the human breast, not at all to respect the animal. According to the *Laws of Manu,* animals are the lowest of "the three-fold level of existence," which is itself divided into three, some animals being distinctly lower than others, and all being far lower than humans. Manu tells us that animals were created by the gods to be sacrificed, that killing, when it is done as religious ritual, is nonkilling, and that injury *(himsa)* permitted by the Vedic scriptures is nonkilling *(ahimsa).* Manu also provides a detailed list of animals whose flesh was edible. The killing of cattle, the bearers of the most frequently proscribed flesh for food, continued until about the twelfth century.[36] Still, although there are undoubtedly limitations to the Hindu concern for animal wellbeing, it would be churlish to deny that such concern exists in some measure, even if countered by other sayings of the scriptures.

John Mackenzie adds insightfully that there are limitations "to the doctrine of ahimsa" – the doctrine of nonharm to other beings – which normally so arouses our admiration, noting that it "does not apply to the taking of lives in battle, or to the infliction of capital punishment. By qualifications such as these the force of the doctrine is considerably weakened. The exception to the general principle that life should not be taken, and that the flesh of animals should not be eaten, were so many and of such diverse kinds, that we can believe it would be exceedingly difficult to determine whether a particular act was a breech of the law or not. We know that hunting and fishing continued in spite of all laws."[37] If Mackenzie's interpretation is in accord with cultural reality, it would be reasonable to conclude that the doctrine of *ahimsa* is not very different in practice from less seemingly altruistic doctrines elsewhere.

The rose-tinted interpretations of Rosen's account pale against the animadversions of Ranchor Prine, who, confronted with the realities of life in modern India, insists that "for nearly two centuries Indians have been estranged from their own [ecology-sympathetic] culture by English education. They have been encouraged to think in Western ways and to value the things which the West values. Their own traditional values have been marginalized. In many cases they no longer know what these values were or why they were held because those things are no longer taught."[38]

To some extent, Prine may well be right about the orientation of modern Indian values – in which case modern Hindu vegetarianism, respect for animals, and care for the environment may be seen to be seriously impaired. But it would be grossly misleading, for example, to blame the fact of animal sacrifice on the British. First, animal sacrifice existed throughout India for millennia before the establishment of the Raj; indeed, as we have seen, it is acknowledged in the Vedas. Second, the British disapproved of animal sacrifice in India and tried to discourage it, although they accepted it as preferable to the continuing practice of human sacrifice. If "English education" had succeeded in its efforts "to value the things which the West values," it would have succeeded in eliminating this particular misuse of animals for human ends. Moreover, the once extensive practice of overt female infanticide among Hindus was a consequence of the dowry system, not some alien British innovation.[39] It is inappropriate to blame the decline in family values on the modernity introduced to India by the British, a charge found in the same book. Indeed, if female infanticide is declining, the introduction of the alien value system is at least in significant part to be thanked. Likewise, the same is true of child marriages. And that the ritual burning alive of widows was made illegal in 1829 is due to the same foreign source. No one should doubt the ills imposed on India by the Raj. But the fictions offered of Hindu purity reflect, understandably, indignant self-righteousness more than a concern with Indian practical or philosophical reality.

Still, none of this should persuade us to discount the fact of a significant vegetarian tradition in India nor to imagine that Hindu vegetarianism was based entirely on considerations other than the wellbeing of animals, although animals – at least other than the cow – clearly never held an exalted status. But it should persuade us to look at these vegetarian origins with a warier eye than is customary in the Western vegetarian practice, which tends toward evaluation in a decidedly unidimensional vein. It is certainly worth bearing in mind the admonition of Gandhi, who was a cultural vegetarian from birth but who learned his ethical vegetarianism from the writings of Percy Bysshe Shelley and Henry Salt after visiting a vegetarian restaurant on Farringdon Street in London while resident in England: "The ideal of humanity in the West is perhaps lower but their practice of it very much more thorough than ours. We rest content with a lofty ideal and are slow or lazy in its practice. We are wrapped in deep darkness, as is evident from our paupers, cattle and other animals."[40] Moreover, to put the conception of "Hindu diet" into perspective, it is worth noting that, in practice, it is not seen as a generally vegetarian diet. For example, Canada's Via Rail offers various "special meals" in its food service. Those meals include "Asian vegetarian," a category to which about one-third of India's population would belong, but under the heading of "Hindu meal," composed with the assistance of Hindu religious authorities, lamb, eggs, fish, dairy products, rice, herbs, and spices are seen as allowable, whereas beef, veal, or pork and its derivatives are excluded.

The island of Bali in Indonesia has had a Hindu population since the seventh century. Currently, Hindus constitute about 2 percent of Indonesia's total population but have little of the animal-oriented attitudes that are said to be found in Indian Hinduism. A reading of the Balinese Hindu legend of *Bhima Swarga* confirms a significant degree of ambivalence. Cruelty for fun is decried but slaughtering animals for food or sacrifice is improper only when the prescribed ritual is not followed.[41] Likewise, Malaysia also has a small Hindu population, but Hindus are vastly outnumbered by Muslims. There is also a smattering of Hindus in omnivorous Pakistan, but they constitute less than 3 percent of the population, whereas Hindus in Bangladesh are a proportionately greater 10 percent. Among the population of Sri Lanka, Tamil Hindus comprise 18 percent. Although the Hindus of these states differ somewhat in belief and culture from the Hindus of the Indian homeland, the differences are rather less than those to be found among the different branches of Buddhism. For, in none of the Hindu groups, abroad or in India, is vegetarianism central to ethical doctrine. It is merely a part of cultural tradition or is not. The one exception may be said to be the Hare Krishnas, although their relationship to traditional Hinduism is obscure. Hare Krishna practice, formalized with the founding of the International Society for Krishna Consciousness, emerged not in India but in New York City in 1966, basing its philosophy on the teaching of the sixteenth-century Bengali sage Chaitanya Mahabraphu, who regarded the Hindu god Krishna as the supreme personal God. Hare Krishnas practise vegetarianism and an ascetic lifestyle, and they strive to attain enlightenment by chanting the mantra Hare Krishna (Lord Krishna). To the extent that the vegetarianism of the Hare Krishnas is an ethical vegetarianism and moves well beyond asceticism, it may be said, as its foundation in New York might suggest, to owe its creed to Western as much as Hindu mores.

The lack of centrality of vegetarianism and animal ethics to Hinduism can be readily gauged. While browsing in the World's Biggest Bookstore in Toronto, for instance, I found five shelves of books devoted to Hinduism. For none of the books was vegetarianism in any way a principal topic. Very few of the books even had "vegetarianism" in the index. And of those that did, Gandhi's autobiography excepted, all treated the subject in a quite superficial way in one or two lines. Moreover, in the lengthy and multiauthored *Movements and Issues in World Religions,* there is no mention of vegetarianism in the several chapters on Hinduism and Buddhism, even where ethics is the stated topic, and there is only one mention of *ahimsa* in the book – and this without reference to animals.[42] According to such books, the vegetarianism of Hindu India does not seem to play a major role in the *ethical* considerations of the practitioners. Nonetheless, vegetarians should rejoice in the considerable degree to which vegetarianism is practised and remains a significant, if declining, matter of cultural significance.

## BUDDHISM

The Buddhist religion and philosophy were founded around 525 BC in India by Siddhartha Gautama. After its birth in India, Buddhism at first attracted a significant following, mainly among lower-caste Hindus, primarily, it would appear, because of its opposition to the caste system. A similar rejection of caste encouraged the success of Islam at a later date. Today, on the subcontinent, Muslims inhabit mainly the former Raj-occupied lands of Pakistan and Bangladesh, although some 14 percent of India's population is also Muslim, together with Afghanistan, which the British ultimately failed to incorporate into the Raj.

Buddhist canonical works written in the Pali language and commentaries in Pali and Sanskrit demonstrate with both clarity and certainty that the early Buddhist diet was nonvegetarian; at the very least, flesh was a fairly frequent delicacy. Although the Buddha (Gautama) was unequivocally opposed to animal sacrifice both for ritual and for food thereby derived, there is solid evidence that early Buddhists, including Buddhist monks, ate flesh.[43] The *Vinaya Pitaka* informs us that Buddha proscribed the flesh of certain animals to monks but, by implication, permitted the consumption of other animals by those monks.[44] And again, the use of animal hides was widespread. The doctrine of the Middle Path – midway between self-indulgence and total asceticism – was inimical to vegetarianism because consistent vegetarianism was seen to represent an extreme. The idea of the Middle Path was in essence a pragmatic doctrine, making religious life not too great a burden either for the laity or for the religious orders, in contrast with what was seen as the essential hardship of Hindu devotion. There is even an unverified but oft-repeated tradition that the Buddha himself died from eating tainted pork. Others say it was from poisonous mushrooms. Yet others say it was from the weakness of his body but do not deny that he consumed flesh. The very fact that there developed a tradition of death from eating tainted flesh reflects that flesh eating was not thought to be proscribed or to be abnormal. The first claim that Buddha himself was a vegetarian came from Sri Lankan Buddhists in a Theravada text written in the third century BC, hundreds of years after the Buddha's death, but there is no evidence of it in his life and circumstantial evidence that he most probably was not a vegetarian. Indeed, Japanese Buddhists acknowledge explicitly that he was not. In reality, we know as little with any certainty of Buddha's life in India in the sixth century BC as we know of Pythagoras in Italian Magna Graecia a few years earlier.

The greatest successes for Buddhism in India occurred during the reign of the Buddhist Emperor Asoka (c. 273 to c. 232 BC) of the Mauryan dynasty. He managed through bloody conquest to unite almost the whole of India, together with some of the neighbouring territories. Tradition has it (bolstered, if not occasioned by, inscriptions on pillars and boulders, as well as by Asoka's direct edicts) that he was so remorseful for the sufferings inflicted by his wars of aggression that he renounced conflict, tolerated all faiths, declared his belief in *ahimsa,* and regulated the slaughter of animals, exempting certain species from it. It is even said of Asoka, and with the ring of truth, although without hard evidence, that he enjoined his subjects to treat animals with kindness and consideration. Indeed, he is said to have provided animals with medical care. Whether true or not, many European travellers to India over a millennium later were astonished to find animal hospitals there, and it is quite probable this was a practice instituted in Asoka's time. More certain is that he prohibited animal sacrifice to the gods. Under his auspices, it is also said, Buddhism was elevated from an Indian sect to a major world religion. Upon his death, the Mauryan Empire rapidly declined, and India returned to its particularist roots.

The traditional association of Asoka and his realm with vegetarianism seems scarcely tenable. Asoka refers to the slaughterhouse and to the state office of the superintendent of cows, although it is possible, if improbable, that the superintendence should not have been of their slaughter. Asoka required butchers to be just toward their customers by charging them a fair price, an unnecessary edict if animals were not slaughtered for food. When we read of the animals exempt from slaughter, it becomes clear that many other animals, including cows, were not exempt. Indeed, as Jha tells us, "in one of his edicts Asoka informed his subjects that two peacocks and a deer continued to form a part of the royal cuisine every day, though he had the noble intention of stopping even this killing in future."[45] But if vegetarianism was not practised, there is at least in Asoka's edict a clear indication that a vegetarian diet would be preferable. Moreover, an animal ethic was vociferously proclaimed. Asoka at least pointed the way to an idyllic vegetarian and cruelty-free future.

A seventh-century Chinese Buddhist visitor to India – author of the regulations to be observed by a Chinese monastic order in which flesh eating is depicted as a minor character flaw akin to losing one's temper, rather than as a major sin – enumerated the flesh foods that were proscribed for Mahayana Buddhists and those that they were allowed to eat. Hinayana Buddhists also ate flesh despite an apparent royal edict not to slaughter any animal for food on pain of death.[46] It is doubtful, Jha believes, there ever was such a proclamation.[47] Nonetheless, the very tradition of there having been such a proclamation indicates something of its deemed desirability. Hunting and butchery were proscribed for Buddhists, although the edict was often ignored, and flesh eating was deemed acceptable provided that the flesh was served by non-Buddhists and that the butchery and hunting, when the proscription was observed, were undertaken by non-Buddhists. Whereas some Mahayana and Hinayana texts preached against the eating of flesh, the evidence strongly suggests little heed was taken of the preachings – any more than, as we have noted, the New Testament persuaded Christians always to love one another, to treat others as they would themselves be treated, to seek the path of peace, or to turn the other cheek. Indeed, in light of these biblical exhortations, which persuade no one that they were commonly practised principles of Christianity, one has to wonder why the exhortations contained in other scriptures are so readily thought to represent the cultural reality of the traditions in which they are expressed. They are there as admonitions to the faithful, not as descriptions of cultural practice.

Buddhism is today very largely absent from India (and has been since the thirteenth century) but continues elsewhere in Asia, albeit in different forms. There are two main schools: Theravada (or Hinayana) Buddhism in Southeast Asia (Sri Lanka, Myanmar, Thailand, Cambodia, and Laos); and Mahayana Buddhism in Korea, Japan, Mongolia, Tibet, Nepal, and China. A third way, the Vajrayana school, has a lengthy tradition in Tibet and Japan but is at least temporarily in recession. Other minor schools include Zen – which concentrates on immediate enlightenment through meditation – Pure Land, Lamaism, Tendai, Nichiren, and Soka Gakkai. Formally, Theravada Buddhism retains essentially the same doctrines it adopted in the third century BC, conforming to the strict and narrow teachings of the early Buddhist writings, and Mahayana Buddhism has, also formally, remained true to the style it developed in northern India in the first century AD, being more liberal than Theravada Buddhism and making concessions to popular piety and to the idea of a personal saviour (*bodhisattva*). In China there has been a subscription to pure vegetarianism among some of the Mahayana Buddhist laity, but it has been far from pervasive. In Paris, for example, where there are in excess of five thousand Chinese Buddhists, after the New Year visit to the temple, and following Buddhist tradition, the celebratory dinner must include wonton soup (wontons are usually filled with minced pork), duck, and fish, a portion of which must be left on the plate as a sacrificial offering. Hong Kong does, however, have a vibrant and inventive tradition of Buddhist vegetarian cuisine, and it is this that has often been imported to the West. Elsewhere, it is sometimes – but far from always – expected that the monks will be vegetarian, except when their alms dish is provided with flesh, when it would be a greater sin to offend the giver than to eat the flesh. And flesh is commonly given. In China, Buddhism arrived in the first century AD, became almost exclusively vegetarian by the sixth century, but was in significant decline by the thirteenth, being replaced by a neo-Confucianism that had come to intellectual and cultural dominance.

Often, the subscription to a particular creed is no more effective in Buddhist than Christian countries. Thus, for example, in Myanmar, where Theravada Buddhism predominates, goats, pigs, cattle, and poultry are raised for food. In Sri Lanka, whose inhabitants likewise profess Theravada Buddhism in the main, beef, fish, venison, and hare constitute a significant part of the regular diet. In Lamaic Tibet beef, mutton, poultry, yak, and pork are consumed as a part of the everyday fare. Japanese Mahayana Buddhism appears to have encouraged the frequent use of fish in cuisine and does not appear to have objected to other flesh foods either – at least after some early vegetarian orientations – although it was instrumental in the denigration of those involved in animal butchery for food. Although theoretical principles of Buddhism seem to commend vegetarianism, there are so many exceptions to the commendation that both Mahayana and Theravada theology acknowledge that flesh consumption does not constitute a breach of fundamental Buddhist laws. Tibetan Buddhists believe that tantric practice makes vegetarianism unnecessary. As Jha explains, "while theoretical debates on meat eating and dietary practices persisted among the Buddhists, the flesh of animals including milch cattle continued to please their palate."[48] He thus denies there is much basis for the view of a broad Buddhist vegetarian past or present in practice.

Self-proclaimed Buddhists in Western countries are of course very largely vegetarian and often imagine Buddhism to have a wholly vegetarian and animal-respectful belief system. They possess a very misleading picture of the tradition as a whole to which they have come to belong, especially where it has syncretized with indigenous practices and beliefs. It is worth noting that entries regarding different types of Buddhism were consulted in several general encyclopaedias during the preparation of this volume, and not one mentioned vegetarianism as an aspect of Buddhism. This does not, of course, deny the relevance of vegetarianism to Buddhism, but it does indicate that where the religion is explained in short compass, vegetarianism is considered low on the list of priorities to be discussed. A part of the misconception of the centrality of vegetarianism to Buddhism lies in the fact that *ahimsa* (nonharm) is said to be the first law of Buddhism. But there is no agreement on what *ahimsa* requires. Nonetheless, there is no doubt that a general subscription to compassion is a hallmark of Buddhism.

Because animals lack the faculty of *prajna* (insight) necessary to understand Buddhist teachings, they cannot obtain nirvana. They are therefore, for Buddhists, intellectually and morally beneath humans, but, like humans, they live a life of adversity and they suffer. Therefore, despite these evaluations of animals by early Buddhists, the adherents of the faith were persuaded to preach, if not always to practise, *ahimsa* toward animals as a principle appropriately practised toward all breathing beings.[49] Perhaps the central aspect of Buddhism in all its forms is its acceptance of the pan-Indian presupposition of *samsara,* a flux in which all living beings pass through a continual cycle of life and death via the transmigration of souls. Karma may eventually lead a human (although not an animal, even though the human may descend into an animal form) to escape the cycle and reach nirvana. Buddhism opposes all killing as one of its primary ethical principles, but as with Hinduism, killing (especially of animals) may be treated as a form of nonkilling – that is, as acceptable killing, a principle not unlike the opposition to killing (ultimately, an opposition to the killing of innocents) in Christianity, which appears in practice not to apply to innocent animals.

There is no doubt that many animal-respectful passages are to be found in Buddhist writings, especially in *The Dhammapada* – probably composed in the third century BC – which has far greater strength in this regard than most other Buddhist literature. Thus, for example, *The Dhammapada* stresses the similarity between human and animal: "All beings tremble before danger, all fear death. When a man considers this, he does not kill or cause to kill."[50]

And it describes *ahimsa* as the measure of superiority among humans: "A man is not a great man because he is a warrior and kills other men, but because he hurts not any living being he in truth is called a great man."[51]

"He who hurts not any living being, whether feeble or strong, who neither kills nor causes to kill, him I call a Brahmin."[52]

The strength, however, is somewhat diminished when we realize that in some circumstances nonharm, noninjury, and nonkilling (or *ahimsa*) allow for harm, injury, and killing (or *himsa*) – acceptable killing is nonkilling – as is likewise true of the Hindu doctrine, although with far less frequency in the Buddhist than the Hindu cases.

The difficulty of making general statements about Buddhist vegetarianism is reflected in the disparity among the practices of Buddhist monks – that is, those most likely to eschew flesh within the Buddhist tradition. In Vietnam, the monasteries are mainly vegetarian; in China, sometimes so. In medieval times the Japanese monks were vegetarian but ceased to be so many generations ago. At one time in Korea, the Buddhist monks were largely vegetarian; today, many eat flesh. Tibetan monks are usually meat eaters. So, too, are those of Sri Lanka, Myanmar, Thailand, and Cambodia. If there is a generalization to be made, it is that many more Buddhist monks are flesh eaters than not, and in the general population most Buddhist laity by far are flesh eaters. In fact, because of its attitude of nonviolence toward nature, vegetarianism has been more common among Taoists than practitioners of any other creed, although, even in Taoism, there is no direct instruction to avoid flesh.

## JAINISM

Jaina were, and are, far less compromising on the ideal of *ahimsa* than Buddhists or Hindus, approaching a strict veganism in their practices, at least among the monks initially and more broadly later. In the tenth century, when Buddhism still retained some of its adherents in India, that Buddhists were frequently nonvegetarian was a common Jaina complaint against them – especially against the *bhikku,* the monks, who regarded as pure everything, including flesh, that was put into their alms bowls. *Ahimsa* was very probably a Jain principle before it was adopted by Buddhists and Hindus, and it has probably remained more central to Jainism than to any other creed. To be sure, the Jaina subscribed to a similar animal hierarchy as did the Hindus, distinguished by their capacities for feeling – the more sentient being of greater value than the less sentient. But all were of value and all were to be considered, if not to the same degree.

Although early Jain references to flesh eating are significantly less frequent than those in the Hindu and Buddhist literature, they are nonetheless present in both the canonical and exegetical writings.[53] But they disappear earlier, indubitably by the eleventh century, and vegetarian practices are the rule, although there are exceptions even to this when we read of royal cock sacrifice and the eating of the proceeds or of the slaughtering of bulls by the wealthy, or when we find exegetical texts proscribing certain flesh items, implying that it was acceptable to consume certain others. Nonetheless, later in the sacred scriptures *ahimsa* is rarely interpreted as acceptable *himsa*, as it is more frequently in both Hindu and Buddhist texts. Still, there are some doubts about Jaina consistency even in the modern era. On a visit to India in the 1930s, George Bernard Shaw commended the equality and humanity of the Jaina tradition in principle but declared Jainism in modern times to have been corrupted by idolatry.[54]

There are certainly inconsistencies in some of the Jain texts, not merely in those of recent vintage. Thus, the twelfth-century guide to Jain yoga, the *Yoga Shastra*, is initially emphatic against *himsa*: "*Ahimsa*, truth, non-stealing, continence and non-possession are the five major vows which are concomitant to charitra [good conduct]."[55]

Perhaps the fifth and least important requirement – that of nonpossession, *ahimsa* being the first duty – should surprise us as a proclaimed principle of a merchant class, a class to which the Jaina belong predominantly, and we may rightly imagine it was not assiduously practised. But the denunciation of hunters and hunting is undeniably and emphatically pronounced: "Are these flesh-eating humans who hunt the innocent deer, dwelling in forests, and living on air, water and grass, any better than curs? Why should the people who feel pain at the slightest prick of a thorn, attack the innocent animals with sharp pointed weapons? These cruel hunters destroy the life of these poor creatures for the sake of some momentary pleasure. If an animal faces danger of death he is terribly pained, then how much will he suffer when attacked with terrible weapons?"[56]

We can be sure that hunting is entirely alien to the Jain tradition. Nothing is ever simple, however, in Eastern thought. In the same book, *The Yoga Shastra of Hemchandracharya*, killing for religious sacrifice is expressly permitted. Religious ritual appears to have outweighed the protection of animal life in the order of principled priorities. Thus, animal protection must be seen, at least in significant part, as a promotion of ascetic purity.

This priority is seen also in the well-known Jain practice of going to extraordinary lengths to protect even the tiniest of animals. The Jaina are known to wear a cloth over their mouths so as not to ingest tiny air-borne insects. As Heinrich Zimmer explains in *Philosophies of India*, "wherever the Jaina ascetic walks, he has to sweep the way before his feet with a little broom, so that no living thing may be crushed by his heel."[57] Sometimes, they employ someone to do the sweeping for them. It should, however, be clear on a moment's reflection that the purpose of this endeavour must be to maintain the purity of the Jain rather than to save the lives of the insects. Indeed, Zimmer refers explicitly to the Jaina as ascetic. Far more insects will be killed by having a path swept for him, or even sweeping it himself, than if the Jain were to take fewer elaborate measures to avoid stepping on the animalcules. The insects will still be killed, but the Jain will have escaped the sin of having caused the death, at least directly. Yet the Jain will also have vicariously created the sin of the sweeper, for the Jain's desire to escape being the direct cause of the insects' death, or some lesser *himsa,* will have required the sin still to be committed but by someone else. When the Jain himself sweeps, more will be killed or harmed than if there were no sweeping. As a result, the animalcules certainly are no better off. Zimmer tells the story of a couple of Bombay beggars "carrying between them a light cot or bed alive with bedbugs. They stop before the door of a Jaina household and cry: 'Who will feed the bugs? Who will feed the bugs?' If some devout lady tosses a coin from a window, one of the criers places himself carefully in the bed and offers himself as a living grazing ground to his fellow beings. Whereby the lady of the house gains the credit, and the hero of the cot the coin."[58] It is the divine credit the woman seeks, not food for the bugs, who would do quite well without the beggarly body. Nonetheless, that Jaina are forbidden by their religious vows from participating in occupations that even indirectly harm animals encourages the idea that nonhuman animals are entitled to freedom from harm for their own sakes.

Looking at the vegetarian tradition in India as a whole, it would appear, as it seems to appear in origin for religious vegetarianism everywhere, that ritual worship and asceticism – self-purity, self-denial, world renunciation, and the elimination of passion – played a greater role than did consideration for the wellbeing of animals, although it would also appear likely that vegetarianism itself encouraged a belief that animals were sufficiently akin to humans that they were entitled to a significant ethical consideration. If Indian vegetarianism did not arise out of a consideration for the wellbeing of animals, and does not always proclaim it a prominent ethical principle, it almost certainly spawned a healthy measure of it.

# 3

# Pythagoreanism

---

At approximately the time the *Upanishads* were being composed in India, Pythagoras was born in Ionia among the first stirrings of Western philosophy. He is usually presented to us as the father of Western philosophical vegetarianism and as an ethical vegetarian who derived his animal ethics from the kinship between humans and animals via the transmigration of souls.[1] To kill an animal would potentially be tantamount to killing a human relative. Yet there are inadequate grounds for such a presentation, although there are persuasive hints of aspects of it. Not only are there marked discrepancies in the early sources – for example, Apollonius said Pythagoras bit a snake to death, whereas others have presented him as treating all animals with respect – but, in fact, we also know almost nothing of the life, practices, and doctrines of Pythagoras, and this despite the tremendous amount of scholarly speculation about these matters.[2] Pythagoras wrote nothing down, so far as we can tell. A manuscript or two would have helped to give us a clearer picture, although some Pythagoreans have claimed lost books to have been written, including *Hieros Logos* (Sacred Word). If so, it is curious that no one in antiquity whose books remain appears to have referred to any of those by Pythagoras before they were lost. We certainly know some of the content of other books that have been lost and can be confident they once existed. One of the reasons so little is known of Pythagoras and Pythagoreanism, apart merely from age, is that, it is said, the adherents of the Pythagorean cult took a vow of secrecy so that nothing potentially damaging to the sect would be divulged. That in itself would reflect the mystical, perhaps even conspiratorial, rather than philosophical nature of Pythagoreanism.

By unverifiable, but persuasive, tradition – and the word of Isocrates – Pythagoras is thought to have visited the priests of Egypt, and also Babylon and Persia, where he learned the basis of much of his religious philosophy.[3] The Indophile theosophist Annie Besant went so far as to say, ingenuously, that "he brought from Ind the wisdom of the Buddha, and translated it into Greek thought."[4] She was not alone. The Irish Unitarian William Drummond, in *The Rights of Animals* (1838), apparently relying on Ovid, as probably did Besant, claimed Pythagoras visited India and studied under the Brahmins.[5] By contrast, Thomas Tryon (1634-1703) thought Pythagoras to have visited India and taught the Brahmins their philosophy. Lucius Apuleius (AD 124-170) claimed that Pythagoras had learned much of his philosophy from Indian wisdom but not that he visited the subcontinent. Such are the confident but unverifiable assertions born of historical imagination! But if it is improbable that Pythagoras reached India, it is nonetheless quite plausible that he was introduced to Indian religious and philosophical ideas when he was in Persia. If Pythagoras possessed a pronounced animal ethic, either he learned respect for other species in the countries he visited or he developed one independently. But there is nothing definitive in the religions or philosophies of those countries now known as comprising the Middle East that would account for his supposed profound animal sensibilities. And there is no convincing evidence that he developed an animal ethic independently. One thing that he almost certainly did learn in his youthful years, and one common to the traditions from which he probably learned, was the necessity of purging oneself of one's animal nature in order to become as purely spiritual as possible, to approach the gods, to separate oneself from the world. It was an orientation reminiscent of Brahmin world renunciation. He is said to have learned this doctrine from his teachers Thales and Anaximander before he visited Egypt and Babylonia, where it would have been reinforced. By contrast, in the fifth century BC, the atomist Democritus took pains to remind his contemporaries that at root we were no more than animals ourselves. It appears to have been a poignant message and one necessary for the times as a reminder to those who would divest us of our essential animal being. The Pythagoreans attempted to escape their animal nature. They were ascetics first and foremost.

Pythagoras is also said to have learned the composition and use of hallucinatory drugs on his visits abroad – hence his reputation as a magician.

The historian of antiquity Martin West regards him as "part philosopher, part priest, part conjuror."[6] The Victorian-era Pythagorean Edouard Schure observed that "Porphyry and Iamblichus have depicted the commence-ment of his life there [i.e., in Croton, Magna Graecia] as being that of a magician rather than a philosopher."[7] The German classicist Walter Burk-ert views him as a shaman. The scholarly image of Pythagoras is certainly not primarily that of a philosopher devoted to ethical vegetarian principles.

The overwhelming belief of the epoch, as with Platonists later, was that the human was divine in nature. Other species, of course, were not. The task was to express human divinity by purifying the human soul as fully as possible – that is, by divesting it of its animality. We can be confident that Pythagoras taught the immortality of the human soul, and as Charles Kahn says, "in the Greek tradition deathlessness is the attribute of the gods."[8] Thus, in pursuing human immortality, the Pythagoreans aspired to be godlike and far removed from other species. If we turn to the Golden Verses, so named by Iamblichus, which were composed probably about 250 BC – and certainly several centuries before the fifth century AD, when the Stoic Hierocles wrote a commentary on them – we find no mention of anything pertaining to an animal ethic. Purporting to replicate the original instructions from Pythagoras to his flock, the Golden Verses tell us: "And when, after having divested thyself of thy mortal body, thou arrivest at the most pure Aether, Thou shalt be a God, immortal, incorruptible, and Death shall have no more dominion over thee."[9] The task was to divorce oneself as completely as possible from one's animal nature in favour of one's spiritual potential, to achieve immortality no less. Biological kinship with the animals, and the transmigration of souls between humans and animals, did not imply a recognition of a common nature, any more than they did for Plato – in *Lysis* (221E-222D), Plato pointed out that to esteem one an-other as kin *(oikeios)* is not the same as to esteem another as a being like oneself – and to the extent that any commonality might be implied, Pythagoreanism was intent on divesting humans of that nature, removing themselves from earthly matters, to reach the gods. Nonetheless, we can recognize that there was something ethical, an inkling at least, implied in the idea of biological kinship in the culture of the epoch, when, according to Plutarch, the early evolutionist Anaximander, "having declared that fish are at once the fathers and mothers of men, urges us not to eat them."[10] Still, biological kinship does not ipso facto imply an affective relationship. Kinship may of course be affective, but there is no compelling reason that it be so.

In his *Pythagoras and the Pythagoreans,* Charles Kahn points out that "we have three lives of Pythagoras from late antiquity, by Diogenes Laertius, Porphyry and Iamblichus, in that order, and each one is more marvelous than its predecessor."[11] The more distant the biographer from Pythagoras's time, the more confident he is of Pythagoras's doctrines and the more wondrous the biographer imagines them. The first was written several centuries after Pythagoras's death, rather like writing about Charles II of England today in the absence of reliable historical documentation. To be sure, each of the biographers had an array of snippets of prior commentary on which to build the life they were writing, but there was little on which they could depend with any great degree of confidence, resorting to selection here and there from a host of not always consistent observations and with no adequate criteria for selection – other than the desire to present a persuasive picture of a historical giant among men. Hagiography did not begin with the lives of the saints! There was an earlier book, *Concerning Nature*, by Philolaus, written close to the time of Pythagoras, but very little of the book remains and nothing on diet or metempsychosis. One would have thought the book more reliable, being closer in time to Pythagoras, but some of the remaining passages utterly fail to convince, smacking more of myth than reality. Being a near contemporary of Pythagoras does not appear to have improved the recollection. But perhaps the most influential book in creating the Pythagorean myth is Book 15 of Ovid's *Metamorphoses* – written well over a half-millennium after the demise of the Ionian sage. There, Ovid provides us with a most engaging picture based primarily on his vivid literary imagination, Pythagoras emerging as a pronounced advocate for the interests of animals. And it is the Ovidian Pythagoras that had the most influence on public conception thereafter.

Colin Spencer states that some say Pythagoras died at the age of 70, others at 104, a discrepancy of a large number of years.[12] For Howard Williams, the age is no less vague, being "variously computed at eighty, ninety, or one hundred years."[13] Today, Pythagoras's lifespan is normally depicted as around 582 to around 507 BC. When there is so little agreement on basic facts, and when no record has been left, how can we feel confident on matters of doctrine or personality? Charles Kahn views the matter aright when he avers: "The historical figure of Pythagoras has almost vanished behind the cloud of legend around his name."[14] We can feel confident, as noted, that Pythagoras taught the doctrine of immortality, and we can be almost certain of his teaching of the transmigration of souls – Eduard Zeller tells us that in the century following his death it was for the teaching of immortality and metempsychosis that he was known.[15] An almost contemporary, Xenophanes, poked fun at Pythagoras, according to Diogenes Laertius, when, on seeing a dog being whipped, Pythagoras ejaculated: "Stop do not beat it, for it is the soul of a dear friend."[16] But we do not know whether the story is true or whether Pythagoras was more concerned about harm to the dog or to the friend. It would not be at all surprising if transmigration were a part of the credo given that the frequency of the doctrine's appearance in early societies is remarkable and quite independent of any ethical notions connected with kinship. It existed in a number of aboriginal societies, including those of Amazonia, Indonesia, and Australia, among the Druids of Celtic France in mythological form, and among the Aztec warriors, whose favourite form was that of the hummingbird, sipping nectar forever.

If we can be reasonably confident of immortal souls and transmigration as aspects of Pythagorean doctrine, what else can we believe beyond a reasonable doubt? He was probably a vegetarian, at least on the whole, but for the sake of the purity of his own soul, not for the sake of the animals. Erich Frank is perhaps a little harsh in his conclusion that all the discoveries attributed to Pythagoras belong to Magna Graecia scholars of a century later and that the Pythagoreans were "a religious sect similar to the Orphics."[17] By contrast, Charles Kahn reported in 2001 that "recent scholarly opinion seems to be inclining to a more positive view of Pythagoras as a mathematician and philosopher."[18] Nonetheless, whereas Pythagorean scholars, such as Moderatus (first century AD), claim that Platonism is a plagiarism of Pythagoreanism – "they have taken for themselves the first fruit of Pythagorean thought" is the common conception – the modern German scholar Walter Burkert has shown convincingly to the contrary that what is taken as Pythagorean philosophy was first brought to us by Plato and his successors.[19] Howard Williams tells the apocryphal story of how Plato spent an enormous sum to purchase a book by Pythagoras, the *Pythagorean System* by purported name, and is said to have incorporated the principal part of it into his *Timeaus*.[20] Certainly, what we know of the supposedly Pythagorean ideas on numbers and music are known to us primarily through the *Phaedo* and the *Timaeus* of Plato, and to a lesser degree from the *Meno, Republic,* and *Phaedrus,* but this of itself does not argue for a Pythagorean source for the ideas, despite Plato's expressed preference in the *Republic* (600 AB) – the only time Plato ever mentions Pythagoras by name – for the philosophy of Pythagoras over the poetry of Homer. The impressive Irish scholar Dominic O'Meara observes that ever "since [the time of] Plato and his Academy[,] Platonists have shown great interest in the figure of Pythagoras and a strong inclination to 'Pythagoreanize.'"[21] And so they have. However, the Pythagoras they have sought is not the unknowable Pythagoras clouded in mist but, in Platonic terms, the Form, the ideal type, of themselves. To "Pythagoreanize" is to Platonize. If the thought of Plato replicates in some manner that of Pythagoras, as it would prima facie appear to do, Pythagoras wished to separate himself as fully as possible from everything animal, as Plato did, not to revel in his relationship to it.[22]

We should not be at all surprised that so much of the earliest Greek philosophy seems obscure to us and often appears strange. We are standing at the beginning of a whole new way of thought. It did not arrive fully clad with Thales — traditionally deemed the first philosopher, following Aristotle's assertion to that effect. And Thales was an older contemporary of Pythagoras. The distinctions among myth, religion, science, and philosophy were not at all clear, and not until Socrates was there anything like a clear conception of ethics. What philosophy there was in the beginning concerned itself with the nature of nature *(physis)*, not with the nature of the good or the just. Nor was philosophy all of apiece, a readily recognizable subject matter or approach. As Martin West has explained: "Early Greek philosophy was not a single vessel which a succession of pilots briefly commanded and tried to steer towards an agreed destination ... it was more like a flotilla of small craft whose navigators did not all start from the same point or at the same time, nor all aim for the same goal; some went in groups, some were influenced by the movements of others, some travelled out of sight of each other."[23] Now called early Greek philosophy, pre-Socratic philosophy was an essentially unclear, uncoordinated, and fumbling — if sometimes brilliant but also sometimes wildly inaccurate — myth-replacing adventure of the speculative minds of Ionia and Magna Graecia. We should not expect, nor do we get, cohesion and clarity or always even meaningfulness. Religion, myth, and the beginnings of philosophy at first intermingled. It is appropriate to imagine Pythagoras as clinging tenuously to all three.

Iamblichus considered Pythagoras "the prince and father of divine philosophy," whereas Heraclitus regarded him as a clever charlatan: "much learning, artful knavery."[24] In the words of Charles Kahn, Heraclitus viewed him as one whose "learning is great" but whose "wisdom is fraudulent."[25] Diogenes Laertius and Iamblichus present Pythagoras as an at least almost consistent vegetarian — he ate flesh only rarely, when the gods demanded it, noted Iamblichus. But we are not told how often the gods demanded it. The renowned classicist Jonathan Barnes, in *The Presocratic Philosophers,* casts doubt on the idea he was a vegetarian at all.[26] The playwrights of the New Comedy (c. fourth century BC) certainly thought the Pythagoreans to be supposedly vegetarian, for they occasionally made the failures to meet the requirements of the Pythagorean diet the butt of their jokes. Aristoxenus (fourth century BC) reports that Pythagoras ate suckling pigs and tender young kids but abstained from ox and sheep.[27] Perhaps Aristoxenus acquired this information (or misinformation) from a Pythagorean sympathizer. Perhaps he or his informant was defending Aristotle's reputation in a cynical and quasi-rationalist age from suspicion of his being too primitive. The facts are unclear. Aristoxenus apparently wrote an early biography of Pythagoras, but it has now been lost. The Byzantine patriarch Photius also claimed that Pythagoras and his followers ate sacrificial flesh on occasion.[28] Athenaeus mocked the Pythagorean Epicharides for eating dog flesh.[29] Plutarch said the Pythagoreans abstained from mullet but implied that they ate other flesh.[30] In the *Ethics of Diet,* Howard Williams concludes: "The obligation to abstain from the flesh of animals was founded on mental and spiritual grounds rather than humanitarian grounds."[31] The Golden Verses of Pythagoras state: "But abstain thou from the meats which we have forbidden in the purifications and in the deliverance of the soul," which, of course, implies that other meats could be consumed.[32] In the "symbols of Pythagoras," contained in the same book of Golden Verses, we are told (symbol 39), contradicting the implications of the above verse, "Abstain from animals," but we are left in doubt as to the reasons for the abstention, be it kinship, or purificatory worship, or an explicit animal ethic. Nowhere in the Golden Verses is there any suggestion it might be a matter of ethics. Porphyry tells us, "fish he ate rarely," but then the cold-blooded fish may not have been recognized as animal in the same manner as other beings were animal.[33] Nonetheless, Plutarch tells us Pythagoras did not eat fish because he thought of them as akin to humans, belonging with us *(oikeia)*.[34] Thus, with such a host of inconsistencies, we cannot be sure whether Pythagoras declined all flesh and, if he did, whether on the grounds of purity of soul alone or whether the supposed doctrine contained at least the elements of a respect for animals in and for themselves.

In *Universal History,* Diodorus presents the transmigration of souls – "metempsychosis" – as a central doctrine of Pythagoras.[35] By contrast, Howard Williams claims that "by it Pythagoras intended merely to convey to the 'uninstructed,' by parable, the sublime idea that the soul is gradually purified by a severe course of discipline until finally it becomes fitted for a fleshless life of immortality."[36] But what can we make of the transmigration of souls? As only the souls of the corrupt, at least according to the Pythagorean Empedocles, enter the bodies of animals, one has to acknowledge that the claimed "kinship" relation is one of the vastly superior to the vastly inferior, not only in reason and ethics but also in overall status. It is, again, a doctrine reminiscent of Indian religious philosophy. Certainly, there is no incontrovertible reason for assuming that kinship – that is, being animals in common – will have led to considerate treatment. Nor is there any good reason to believe, as does Colin Spencer, for example, that "the very concept of metempsychosis implies that all creatures are equal."[37] It certainly did not imply equality, for instance, among the Aztecs. They were decidedly not vegetarian and kept an imperial zoo of the natural, the strange, and the deformed. But they believed in metempsychosis nonetheless. No one in today's society who committed the greatest atrocities against nonhuman animals would deny that he or she and the victim were animals in common. No one who was an omnivore and ate animals would deny being biologically related to nonhuman animals. "Kinship," merely because of the word's emotive persuasion, encourages us to expect it to imply more, but there is no incontrovertible, or even good, reason why it should. After all, even Saint Thomas Aquinas, normally thought to have been one of the prime exemplars of the philosophy of animal denigration, wrote: "The Word [logos] also has an essential kinship not only with the rational nature, but also universally with the whole of creation, since the Word contains the essence of all things created by God."[38] Aquinas acknowledges his kinship with the animals through logos, but this fact does nothing to persuade Aquinas to raise the status of animals – and certainly not to consider them equals.

Diogenes Laertius and most succeeding authors say that Pythagoras and his followers ate no beans. Aristotle tells us that others disagreed, both about flesh and beans, stating that a "false opinion of long standing has gained ground and increased in strength – the opinion that Pythagoras the philosopher did not eat meat and also abstained from beans."[39] Aristoxenus reported beans to have been Pythagoras's favourite vegetable.[40] Apparently, they were a fine laxative – "they soothe and gently relieve the bowels."[41] Whereas almost all the evidence is on one side, and Empedocles himself warns "wretches" not to eat them, we do not know on what grounds beans were eschewed, if they were eschewed. Cicero was confident Plato believed the ban was because of flatulence.[42] Historically, scholars have engaged in the most imaginative, even bizarre, speculations on the potential grounds. Sometimes, they provide entertainment but not much persuasion. It has been suggested, with greater reason than some of the wild speculation, that perhaps the beans bore little relationship to what we know as beans today. Perhaps they were considered unhealthy for some reason, or at least perhaps that was a common medical opinion. Pythagoras probably learned the practice as a piece of mysterious lore from the Egyptian priests, who also abstained from beans, as did the Zoroastrians. But he could have learned it earlier from Thales. Was this a primitive taboo, as has been mooted? Probably. All that we may glean from this abstention is that Pythagoras, it seems not unreasonable to conclude, still stood on the side of superstition in significant respects, not yet fully in tune with the requirements of the philosophic disposition. He was more shaman than philosopher. Was the renunciation of flesh also an aspect of taboo?

Even if there were absolute consistency in the accounts of Pythagoras and his doctrines, this alone would be insufficient to convince us of the nature of his philosophy, although it would give us less anguish. How did Diogenes Laertius find information for his first biography? From sycophantic accounts by contemporary Pythagoreans, themselves centuries removed from Pythagoras? From general impressions in the public mind that may well have been formed in one way and developed quite differently over the intervening centuries? From the scarce and often contradictory documented historical comments? And was the second account based on the first with a few added further speculations, which gave rise to the third? What if by contrast they all concurred, but the first was faulty historiography? Historically, telling a good story, putting one's hero in the light in which one wants him to be seen, was often more important than veracity. Does the biographer want to defend Pythagoras from the potential suspicion of being opposed to whatever the current conventional wisdoms might be at the time the biographer is writing, and does this defence account for the differences in the biographies? As Spencer has rightly expressed the matter, "modern scholarship points out that each new biographer reinterprets the material in the subjective light of his age and beliefs."[43]

Whatever his beliefs, how did Pythagoras come to achieve his undoubtable reputation as a giant among men? A "figure of consequence," Jonathan Barnes deems him in a moment of understatement.[44] Was Pythagoras a philosopher, mathematician, musicologist, priest, magician, shaman, or charlatan, as has been variously thought – or all, some, or none? "A man of great charismatic authority" appears to be the only answer we may give with confidence. If we turn to Homer's works from the eighth century BC, or to Homer and the *Homeridae*, as it is no longer believed that the works attributed to Homer were composed by a single person, we find warriors and hunters as the exclusive heroes – except perhaps for the dog Argos in the *Odyssey*, the battling frogs and mice in the *Batrachomyomachia*, and "goodly-brave steeds" in general. The warrior heroes' passions were wine and flesh. There were lesser heroes in Greece of that time, too – the poets, the storytellers, the musicians – but none were anywhere near on a par with the warriors. What then of the philosophers? Perhaps in Pythagoras's case he was esteemed as much for his commanding presence and mystical priestly function as for his arcane knowledge, but – if not yet alongside the ranks of the warriors – the new breed, nay new species, of philosophers, the mysterious possessors of previously unimagined half-truths, purveyors of uncommon knowledge, were coming to the fore. They were viewed with suspicion but also with awe and dread. They were men to be reckoned with. Whatever else might be said, Pythagoras was viewed as a towering authority, a man beyond normal men. It has been said there were three kinds of men: ordinary men, philosophers, and Pythagoras. That is probably how he was seen in his own time. This perception is given credence by the unverified but persuasive historical claim that only the elevated *mathematikoi* – the initiated of his school – were allowed to see Pythagoras. The inferior *akousmatikoi* – the novices – were forbidden to see him, although they could hear him. They were separated from his august presence by a screen. The mystique of Pythagoras was being created. At least we can be sure that Pythagoras was a highly charismatic figure who dominated his time and space.

## EGYPT, BABYLONIA, PERSIA

Whence did Pythagoras derive his ideas? What were the major influences that encouraged him to adopt an orientation toward the immortal soul, metempsychosis, vegetarianism, and animal ethics, if that is what he did, which were, or seemed to be, novelties to Western culture? If Isocrates, a contemporary of Plato, is to be trusted, Pythagoras studied "sacrifices and temple purifications" with the Egyptians.[45] By repute, he set out on his voyage to Egypt at the age of twenty-two. What he learned there about the secrets of the Egyptian doctrines maintained in the temples he was sworn to secrecy not to reveal. The priests by whom he was instructed in Egypt were vegetarian for the same purificatory reasons that seem to have moved Pythagoras. In this way the priests were raised above the mere mortals. Fortunately, because the Egyptians have had a uniform system of writing for some five thousand years and, in general, adequate records have been kept, information about Egypt is rather more reliable than for most other nations – despite the antiquarian efforts to delete the records of queens who aspired to be pharaohs. We can thus be confident of priestly asceticism but must note that such asceticism, hence vegetarianism, was not enjoyed (or suffered) by the populace at large. Denying themselves the impurities of animal flesh raised the priestly class above the mere laity. The priest-hood, which possessed powers well beyond that of strictly religious author-ity, constituted a relatively small but elite group within Egyptian society. Indeed, prior to Pythagoras's time, for nigh on a half-millennium, Egypt was in effect a priest-run theocracy, but by the time of Pythagoras's pre-sumed sojourn the theocratic power had waned. Still, the priesthood re-mained a formidable force.

A large variety of animals were worshipped in Egypt, but as we saw ear-lier, it was of no benefit whatsoever to the animals.[46] In those societies where animals were deemed divine, they were eaten precisely because they were divine. They were sacrificed and eaten because to do so was to partic-ipate in the divine. The Egyptians' belief in the transmigration of souls must be understood not as a vehicle to respect animals but as a means to provide the populace with an avenue to their secular and religious poten-tialities. If people did their duty, their souls would be elevated toward the godhead. If one failed in one's earthly requirements, the soul would de-scend into that of a lowly animal. It seems very probable that there was at least an element, and probably much more than an element, of this in the Pythagorean adoption of metempsychosis. Indeed, the case for the influ-ence of Egypt in particular, and the Middle East in general, on the doctrines and practices of Pythagoras and Pythagoreanism has considerable merit.

Priestly vegetarianism and a belief in the transmigration of souls were also aspects, slightly later in origin, in the culture of Babylonia, the ancient empire of Mesopotamia. It is mooted whether, along with Egypt and Per-sia, Pythagoras also visited Babylonia to study the mysteries of the priestly practices. It has been further suggested that Babylonia is most likely the place where Pythagoras learned the esoteric secrets of the preparation and use of hallucinatory drugs to consort more effectively with the gods, factors that helped to create his reputation as a shaman.

Persia is the third country he is said most likely to have visited . There, it is thought he met Zoroaster (c. 628 to c. 551 BC), the founder of Zoroastri-anism – at least the likely lifespan dates do not rule out such a meeting. By the time he was thirty, Zoroaster (known by some as Zarathustra) had experienced revelations of a new religion he was to preach and proselytize. The religion was concerned with the protection of the harvest of a seden-tary people. It required kind treatment of the animals that had helped to produce the bounty of the harvest. The reason for the consideration of these animals – and apparently they alone among animals – was primarily because kind treatment would result in more efficient performance. How-ever, with the adoption of such a practice, the consideration for animals in and for themselves would likely have ensued quickly. Thus consideration for animals was foreshadowed, we can reasonably project, in the doctrines of Zoroaster.

Gradually, the use of narcotics in prayer and the sacrifice of bulls to the god Mithra, practices that Zoroaster is thought to have abhorred, crept into the practice of Zoroastrianism, and thus the religion's potential for the benefit of the animals diminished. There appears to be little explicit in the practice of Pythagoreanism that was adapted or adopted from Zoroastrianism, although those convinced of a serious animal ethic among the Pythagoreans are likely to find similar influential expressions by the Persians of the Pythagorean era.

## THE ORPHICS

There is a contender for significant influence on Pythagoras and Pythagoreanism far closer to home than Egypt, Babylonia, or Persia: the Orphics. In Greek mythology Orpheus is a celebrated Thracian musician. Thrace occupies the southern tip of the Balkan peninsula, bordering the Black Sea. Orpheus was said to produce such charming music on his lyre that wild animals were soothed, trees danced, and rivers stood still.

The Orphic cult developed in Greece somewhat earlier than the era of Pythagoras but was prominent during the Samian's lifetime. The Orphics, paying lip service to Orpheus, were ascetics who espoused metempsychosis and the abstention from animal flesh in order to purge the animal – hence, evil – aspects of the human character. No doubt, these characteristics of the Orphics were at least somewhat influential on Pythagoras's thought. But there is another aspect of the Orpheus image that can have played very little role, an image that is often confused in considering the Orphic impact on Pythagoras: that of the animal-respecting Orpheus. The image did not come to fruition until centuries after the time of Pythagoras.

It is in Ovid's *Metamorphoses,* written around the time of Christ and over a half-millennium after Pythagoras's earthly demise, that we get an at least partly new image of Orpheus, just as we got a rather different picture of Pythagoras than had reigned previously. Just as Ovid succeeded in giving posterity a probably distorted, but extremely influential, picture of Pythagoras (along the same lines as those that had been previously developing in contrast to its earliest depictions but far more explicit in its ethics and in far more modern guise), he succeeded likewise in producing an equally novel, and probably misleading, depiction of the traditional image of Orpheus. To be sure, the one is an image of a philosopher, the other a portrait of a mythological figure, but they each serve to deceive – however beautifully they are written. They tell us rather more perhaps about one side of the contradictory aspects of contemporary Roman expectations and mores – symbolized antithetically by vegetarian influences and the Roman games – than about the characters they purport to describe. Moreover, from the perspective of understanding the influence on Pythagoras, whatever effect the Orphic tradition may have had cannot include today's customary conception of Orpheus as the great ally of the animals. To be sure, he charmed the wild beasts, but in the original myth he has not much more relationship to the wild beasts than to the dancing trees or to the static rivers. And his ability to soothe the wild beasts tells us nothing more about the beasts than that they were customarily wild. Indeed, of greater significance in this account is the remarkable feat of Orpheus's control of them, which could be said to represent governance and dominance of the animals rather than respect. The original myth tells us something of the remarkable musical accomplishments associated with Orpheus rather than of an idyllic relationship with the animals.

In Book 10 of the *Metamorphoses,* Ovid regales the wondrous story of Cyparissus and the stag, a considerable embellishment on previous accounts of the legend. Ovid has Cyparissus kill the stag inadvertently and then pine away unto death for his misdeed against the beloved animal. In effect, Ovid creates a new myth from an old myth. The story takes place in the groves of Orpheus, and Ovid concludes the tale: "Such was the grove which Orpheus had drawn around him, and now he sat in the midst of a gathering of wild creatures, and a host of birds."[47] An Edenic image of Orpheus and the attendant animals was created. Such an image could never have reached Pythagoras nor had any influence on his philosophy. Nor was the image consistent with the traditional myth.

## THE PYTHAGOREANS

Jonathan Barnes says, "the school of thought founded by Pythagoras lasted more than a millennium."[48] Indeed. But it was the school of *thought* rather than the school itself that endured. Within a couple of hundred years of the founding, the Pythagorean school proper had been driven out of its home in southern Italy, ostensibly over some religious or political dispute with the new authorities. Many Pythagorean followers are reported to have been murdered. There was the remnant of a school still in existence at Tarentum in the fourth century BC. And a new school was in existence for a while in Rome in the first century AD, of which the extreme ascetic Apollonius of Tyana and perhaps the Pythagorean apologist Moderatus of Gades were adherents, but the cultists, if we may call them that, soon fell foul of the strict authorities and disbanded. Apparently, smaller schools remained scattered about Europe, primarily Greece and Italy, for another few hundred years.

Seventeenth- and eighteenth-century texts demonstrate continued interest in Pythagorean doctrines. There was a significant, almost worshipful, revival in the Victorian era, spawning a number of new books, most tending toward the occult, but no books of assistance to the animal cause. Not once did Edouard Schure, perhaps the most prominent and representative of the authors of such books, mention animal ethics in his book on the Pythagorean tradition. Not once in his forty-page chapter on "The Order and the Doctrine" did he deem abstention from flesh worthy of even a passing comment. So little did he see concern for animals as central to Pythagoreanism. Indeed, he saw Pythagoreanism as essentially concerned with purification of the soul, emphasizing our spirituality and attempting to eliminate our animality. Its purpose was to elevate us toward the heavens and thus to repudiate our presumed kinship with other species as far as possible – although, of course, Schure does not express the renunciation of kinship in precisely these terms. It is implied by the purification and the emphasis. He tells us clearly enough that "humanity evolves between the natural and animal world into which it plunges by reason of its earthly roots, and the divine world of pure spirits, its heavenly source, towards which it aspires to rise."[49] He writes further of the Pythagoreans endeavouring to be "freed from the darkness of animality."[50] It is not the commonality of species, not kinship, in which he revels but human exclusivity from the other species that he seeks. One is struck by the vastly different interpretations in play, dependent upon whether one approaches the understanding of Pythagoreanism from the perspective of an animal advocate or from any other bent, be it academic, religious, or spiritual. One must conclude that the perspective tends to inform the interpretation, sometimes radically.

The Pythagorean school, it is said, was divided into *mathematikoi* (the "esoterics" who inhabited the hallowed halls – according to Schure, "Pythagoras called his disciples mathematicians because his higher teaching began by the doctrine of numbers") and *akousmatikoi* (the "exoterics" who awaited "the test" to see whether they were adequate to join those of the higher calling).[51] The primary discipleship was some three hundred strong, according to Williams. Spencer numbers the converts at some two thousand and the philosophers at six hundred. Again, there is a significant discrepancy in the historical record about basic facts. Only the *mathematikoi*, those trained to pursue the ethereal soul, were required to be vegetarian, although on certain days the same fleshless restriction was imposed on the *akousmatikoi*. Surely, if the protection of animals were uppermost in Pythagoras's mind, or even a vague but firmly held principle, all would have been required to abstain from flesh or, at least, would have been exhorted to do so. No such requirement was imposed nor exhortation reported. Instead, becoming a vegetarian is a privilege, a mark of status, an elite emblem. In the Pythagorean world, to be allowed to become a vegetarian is a way to distinguish oneself from all others. These divisions between *mathematikoi* and *akousmatikoi* are reminiscent of the Manicheans, founded by Mani (AD 216-276), whose followers were divided into the elect and the hearers, the latter ministering to the elect, who again were required to abstain from flesh, unlike the hearers. The division, too, evokes the memory of the *brahmana* in early Hinduism and the origins of the caste system with a not too dissimilar resultant distinction between those who were vegetarian and those who were not. The vegetarian requirement was to aid in the renunciation of the world, not to proclaim oneself an essentially animal part of it. To become a member of the *mathematikoi* was to be advanced in otherworldliness.

Whatever may be the truth of early Pythagoreanism, by the second or third century AD the image was firmly set, as we can see from the skeptic Sextus Empiricus in *Against the Mathematicians* (or *Against the Dogmatists*, as it is also known):

> Pythagoras and Empedocles and the rest of the Italians [so called because they resided in Greek colonies in Italy] say that we have a fellowship not only with one another and the gods but also with the irrational animals. [Sextus Empiricus does not believe the animals are irrational. This is merely a sop to conventional usage.] For there is a single spirit which pervades the whole world as a sort of soul and which unites us with them. That is why, if we kill them and eat their flesh, we commit injustice and impiety, inasmuch as we are killing our kin. Hence these philosophers urged us to abstain from meat.[52]

By the time of Sextus Empiricus, the idea of Pythagoras as an advocate for the animals was firmly entrenched. The idea of kinship had come to possess ethical content. Or at least it has been so traditionally interpreted. Of the biographers from antiquity, Kahn deems Porphyry "the least unreliable."[53] Porphyry expresses the doctrine simply: "What he said to his associates no-one can say with any certainty; for they preserved no ordinary silence. But it became very well known to everyone that he said, first, that the soul is immortal; then, that it changes into other kinds of animals; and, further, that at certain periods whatever has happened happens again, there being nothing that is absolutely new; and that all living things should be considered as belonging to the same kind. Pythagoras seems to have been the first to introduce these doctrines into Greece."[54]

In contrast with Sextus Empiricus centuries later, here with Porphyry we have as yet no explicit acknowledgment of a sophisticated animal ethic connected with kinship in Pythagorean doctrine. Indeed, it would appear to be true of Sextus Empiricus only if the "injustice and impiety" he mentions are viewed to be crimes and sins against the animal realm, not infractions against the achievement of the appropriate human goal. Either interpretation would appear reasonable.

Sacrifice was regarded as an important part of the Greek tradition, and the Pythagoreans also practised sacrifice, but it may well have been, at least on occasion, an effigy of an animal, or a cake, or honey, or sweet-smelling perfumes, such as frankincense and myrrh, that were sacrificed to the gods. Some Pythagorean apologists have even indicated it was mathematical speculations that were sometimes sacrificed! But if Iamblichus is to be believed, it was animals that were sacrificed. Porphyry concurs but adds that certain parts, such as the head, feet, testes, and genitals, were not eaten. Aristotle adds heart, sea urchin, and womb among the Pythagorean inedibles.[55] Pythagoras is said by some, however, to have preferred to sacrifice at the bloodless altar of Delos. Nonetheless, according to Iamblichus, the Pythagorean perspective was that one must not eat flesh unless the animal was appropriate for sacrifice and had been sacrificed by the due ritual. The ritual was thus of greater importance than the life of the animal. At the religious festivals the dissection of the carcase would be undertaken by the priests. It is ironic that the butcher is thus the direct descendent of the clergy! Human souls, it seems to have been believed, do not transmigrate into animals that it is appropriate to sacrifice. In other words, it is only the less esteemed – but better-treated – animals into whom the soul is transmigrated.

In the hands of the later classical Pythagoreans, particularly Iamblichus, we are, Dominic O'Meara tells us convincingly, "led up through successive stages of Pythagorean philosophy, the final stage being reached ... in a Pythagorean theology."[56] Yet it should be understood the later Pythagoreans were either completing the process portended in the origins or completing the circle, returning Pythagoreanism to its theological roots. O'Meara allows that, for Porphyry, the value of vegetarianism lies in the fact that "it demands the minimum of attention from the soul, since it is inexpensive to procure, simple to prepare, and unexciting. Porphyry would prefer that we do away with food altogether."[57] Theological asceticism, not animal protection, is at the root of Pythagorean vegetarianism, to the extent the diet was vegetarian.

If there are grounds to be cautious in our interpretations of the animal sensibilities of the Pythagoreans in general, we can feel rather more confident about the animal sensibilities of one of them: the *mathematikoi* poet Empedocles. We met the Sicilian Empedocles (c. 495 to c. 435 BC) already in our earlier discussion of the Golden Age, but there is more to be said. To be sure, he was often regarded as something of a shaman in his practice, and perhaps as something of an extremist in some of his views, but we can see at the very least an element of an animal ethic in his expressions. Naturally, his reasons reflected his primary asceticism. Not only did he abominate animal sacrifice, as we saw in Chapter 1, but the reason he gives is to avoid "defilement" rather than to achieve justice. He was explicit that we should abstain from eating living beings because "the bodies of the animals we eat are the dwelling places of punished souls."[58] He maintains the distinction between potentially divine humans and animals by noting that animal bodies are only the houses for *punished* souls. Human bodies were the houses for potentially pure souls. But Empedocles praises kindness between human and animals and seems to suggest that justice applies in the same manner to all creatures.[59] At least, that is how Aristotle interprets him:

> As everyone somehow surmises, there is by nature a common justice and injustice, even in the absence of community and compacts [a prescient swipe against the Stoics!]. This is what Empedocles says about not killing animate creatures,
>> but a law for all, through the broad
>> air it endlessly extends and through the boundless light.[60]

There is almost in fact, and very probably by implication, an explicit animal ethic here, at least if Aristotle is right that, for Empedocles, justice (probably here synonymous with law – a clear distinction between the two came many centuries later) is the ground for not killing animals. Moreover, at no point in anything extant from the classical period is it suggested that Empedocles thought of himself as differing from the master, although, to be sure, he was regarded as an extremist in his views. Either, we must conclude, there is more of an animal ethic to Pythagoras than our analysis has suggested, or there is less of one to Empedocles than the quotation from Aristotle would seem to imply. Alternatively, Empedocles sees something more in the renunciation of flesh than does the master.

Whether Pythagoras was a philosopher, mathematician, musicologist – his reputation with regard to music is reflected in Voltaire's claim that "Pythagoras ow'd the invention of Musick to the Nose of the Hammer of a Blacksmith" – priest, or charismatic charlatan, we cannot know with any justified degree of confidence.[61] What we do know is that, whatever the truth of the personality and doctrines may be, Pythagoras's name has been indelibly associated with vegetarianism as an aspect of animal ethics throughout Western cultural history, although his purported precepts have been rarely followed. In fact, until just a few years before the time of the founding of the Vegetarian Society in 1847, a person who declined animal flesh was known to partake of a Pythagorean diet. We find Pythagoras honoured in the verse of the self-described "water poet" John Taylor and in the various writings of John Donne, John Dryden, John Wilmot, John Gay, Henry Fielding, and Soame Jenyns, among others. He is lauded in the pages of *The Tatler*. Whether Pythagoras founded Western ethical vegetarianism or not, and the balance of available evidence suggests the answer is distinctly in the negative, Pythagoreanism (like Zoroastrianism) foreshadowed the announcement of a readily recognized, explicit animal ethic but no more than that, *perhaps* Empedocles to the contrary. It is following Aristotle that, as we shall see, such an ethic comes to the fore. The ethic depended on the recognition that nonhuman animals are animal *in the same way* that human animals are animal, not on the kind of minimal kinship between humans and animals that Pythagoras and the Pythagoreans seem to have wanted to promote.

# 4

## Greek Philosphy and Roman Imperium

Whether or not Pythagoras was the harbinger of philosophical and ethical vegetarianism, undoubtedly the manner in which he was presented played a role in the development of some later Greek philosophy. Whereas the classical Greeks were the pioneers in philosophical thought, and in several respects have scarcely been excelled even today, the Romans were masters of empire who relied in large part on the philosophical innovations they inherited from the Greek members of their empire. And although we can see the beginnings of philosophy in the sixth century BC among the Greeks of Ionia (present-day Turkey – Pythagoras was originally from Ionia before he emigrated to Croton in southern Italy), it is not until Socrates (469-399 BC), given literary form by Plato (c. 428-347 BC), that we encounter explicitly ethical principles of the kind that we understand today – even though, it would appear, Empedocles came close. The classical Greek claim was to have discredited the rule, authority, and doctrines of priests in favour of rational philosophy. Nonetheless, especially in Rome, the Orphic mysteries continued to play a vital role. If philosophy – that is, the love of wisdom – was replacing the power of the priesthood and the shamans, it was a hard-won victory with numerous temporary defeats along the way. Animal sacrifice continued until the fourth century AD, and even many of the philosophers still displayed a reluctance to abandon all of the occult.

Flesh was not generally consumed by the Greek population at large other than at religious, political, and formal family religious ceremonies – and then perhaps only a couple of times a year or so. As Oswyn Murray writes: "meat at all times [was] reserved for festival occasions and the eating of sacrifice."[1] The Greeks were "noted among the Europeans for their abstemiousness," Howard Williams tells us.[2] Of course, some of the very wealthy were occasional exceptions. Those who did not partake of the flesh on the occasion of such public festivals were castigated as nonparticipants in public life. Hence they were regarded as less than full members of the community. They were, indeed, to a significant degree, viewed as betrayers of the community or, at least, as alien to it. They were renegades. Nonetheless, almost all participated in animal sacrifice, even if only infrequently. Tradition, a different tradition from the Phoenician tradition reported earlier from George Nicholson, had it that the first ever animal sacrifice was that of a pig after the priests of Delphi had indicated that sacrifice was permissible if the victim concurred.[3] Having had holy water sprinkled on the head, the pig would nod his assent − to rid itself of the annoying liquid − and thus the sacrifice was performed. A version of the myth was retold by Ovid in the *Metamorphoses* (bk. 15, 111-15), this time with greater consistency with previous accounts. The significance of the myth lies in the fact that even before the triumph of explicit ethical philosophy, the pig's agreement was deemed necessary if the sacrifice was to be considered acceptable. If the sacrifice was a crime against the animal unless it acquiesced in its own death, there was a lingering suspicion that the practice was not fully legitimate, that there was something less than acceptable in the killing and eating of animals. The death was excused only if the appropriate rites had been performed. As we saw in the first chapter, eating the flesh of animals was a reversal of the prehistorical role of the human as prey. It was an auspicious event that required special rites, as the Pythagoreans seem to have required earlier. The necessary acquiescence of the animal intimated that animal ethics were beginning, if as yet in inchoate form: while waiting for the new breed of philosophers to address the relevant questions explicitly, animal ethics first addressed only those questions portended by tradition. Such prephilosophical suppositions were the probable extent of animal, or even self-conscious human, ethics among the earliest pre-Socratic Greeks, including the original Pythagoreans.

Between the time of Empedocles and Socrates, we have no reliable evidence that any of the major philosophers were ethical vegetarians. Nor was Socrates himself a vegetarian, as far as we can tell, although some fourth-century commentators claimed he advocated a fleshless diet on grounds of mental purity. Even if he has little to add to the vegetarian story, his role in the development of Western philosophical thought is far too significant merely to pass him over without a mention, for his introduction of ethics into philosophy was seminal. Like Pythagoras, Socrates left no writings to posterity. Indeed, he did not write any of his philosophy down. And the four accounts of his life and teachings – by Aristophanes, Xenophon, Plato, and Aristotle – contain some annoying discrepancies, although the accounts by Plato and Aristotle are pretty much in accord. There is, however, a tradition of thought associated with Socrates that bears the test of scrutiny. This tradition was perhaps most memorably expressed by the Roman statesman, orator, and essayist Marcus Tullius Cicero (106-43 BC) when he informed us that Socrates was the first to call "philosophy down from the heavens and set her in the cities of men and bring her also into their homes and compel her to ask questions about life and morality and things good and evil,"[4] although it again must be confessed Empedocles appears to have travelled a part of the journey, even if he did not quite complete it. Prior to Socrates, Greek philosophy was concerned with nature *(physis)* rather than with the questions of ethics. Prior to Socrates, so it is commonly and persuasively said, *polis* and family, sometimes sect, were the highest loyalties. Now, as a result of Socrates's arguments, the primary loyalty, in theoretical principle anyway, was to truth and justice (effectively synonymous in Platonic dialogue). The love of wisdom was to be prior to the love of compatriots. In both practice and theory, however, only human interests were taken into consideration. If Socrates made ethics explicit, he did not include animals within the beings to whom the ethical principles were to be applied.

In general, early classical Greeks took it for granted that ethical thought was first and foremost about the relations between humans – although, in later classical Greek thought, ethical theory was, as we shall see, not without a significant other side. Only rarely around the time of Socrates and Plato did animals get more than a passing mention, never mind a significant consideration, although there were a few notable exceptions.[5] Xenophon (c. 435-354 BC), friend and student of Socrates, captures the Greek spirit of the age when he states explicitly in his *Memorabilia* (bk. 4, pt. 2, secs. 9-12): "the beasts are born and bred for man's sake." This is perhaps the first statement of the philosophy that underlies so much later opposition to animal ethics and ethical vegetarianism: might makes right, superiority trumps inferiority, law and custom are the standards of justice.

Although Socrates made explicit the rational standards of ethics, he did not apply, as previously noted, any of his ethical principles, related primarily to the virtues, beyond the realm of the human – however, he did point out, via Xenophon, that animals are subject to the same desires as humans.

He transformed the Greek idea of virtue from attaining *any* desired end into that of attaining the morally good end. Via Plato in the *Laches* (196E) and *Lesser Hippias* (375A) – sometimes doubted as a genuinely Platonic work – he is said to have averred that some animals were capable of some of the same character attributes as humans and that some animals were not restricted to acting from instinct alone. Nonetheless, his question always was: what is the standard of *human* happiness, what is *human* virtue? Like Aristotle, as we shall see, Socrates regarded animals, so it was said, as legitimate human food. Xenophon, in his biography, claimed that Socrates found animals appropriate for human consumption, for no better reason apparently than that they were customarily eaten, even if not in the proportions found in later European society. Moreover, in his *Memorabilia*, Xenophon has Socrates maintain that, corporeally, humankind is unique in possessing erect posture, hands, speech, and sexual appetite "unbroken to old age"; we are mentally unparalleled in our awareness of the deities, in our ability to anticipate and thus to provide against the elements and the want of food, and in our capacity for learning.[6] The human being is the distinctly superior being. Of course, we do not know how accurately this represents Socrates, although it certainly fits the mood of the times. But given that what we take as Socrates's thought is derived primarily from Plato's depiction of him and that it is very difficult in Plato's dialogues, where Socrates is almost always a primary character, to discern who is the real Socrates and when Plato is talking through him, we should perhaps move directly on to Plato, who does have something to say both about metempsychosis and about vegetarianism, albeit not in the clearest of voices. In a manner similar to Pythagoras, Socrates, and Aristotle – indeed, to most of the Greek philosophical tradition – Plato believed that humans, at least when they are rational, are divine in their natures. Not so other species. The discovery of objective truth "is a manifestation of the divine in a race which is of supernatural lineage."[7] There is thus every reason to expect Plato to imagine humans to be of a different order from other animals.

I have dealt at some length with the competing versions of metempsychosis and the potential vegetarianism of Plato elsewhere, but the gist of my observations, with some clarifications and amendments for the purpose of this book, bear repetition.[8] Despite his elevation of the human to a quasi-godlike status, Plato has humans share their souls with other animals. Indeed, on death, most take on the souls of other creatures – which, it was sometimes said, is difficult to comprehend if only the human shares fully in the divine, if only the human is of a supernatural lineage. In the *Phaedrus*, Plato describes the cavalcade of gods and purified souls who have escaped the transmigratory cycle of life and death, which is achieved, he remarks in the *Thaetetus*, by imitating the gods as far as possible, a view that in turn he examines more closely in the *Phaedo*. And of course, only the humans can imitate the gods because they alone possess *sophia*, philosophic reason; only they can join the parade – the function of *sophia* is rather similar to *prajna* in Buddhist thought.[9] Indeed, this apparent contradiction persuaded Iamblichus, writing against the transmigration conclusions of Porphyry and Origen, who were followers of Pythagoras and Plato on metempsychosis, to decide that only human souls were of an exclusively rational nature and that, because a rational soul cannot become a nonrational soul, transmigration between nonhuman and human souls was not possible.[10]

Despite all this, Plato has no difficulty accepting the flight of the human soul to the animal soul and vice versa. If deathlessness is the distinctive attribute of the gods through the transmigration of souls, both humans and animals would appear prima facie to be similarly deathless, and hence both partake in a measure of divinity. Yet this is not the message one receives from Plato's dialogues any more than from the Indian philosophies. Thus in the *Meno*, Plato uses the apparently Pythagorean doctrine of transmigration of souls to pursue "an epistemology of innate ideas and a priori knowledge," which he elaborates in the *Phaedo*, insisting that the basis of "recollection is a prenatal acquaintance with eternal Forms" – apparently, for Plato, well beyond the capacities of nonhuman animals to have acquired in their transmigrations.[11] Plato tells us further in the *Phaedo* that "thought is best when the mind is gathered into herself and none of these things trouble her – neither sights nor sounds nor pain nor any pleasure – when she has as little as possible to do with the body, and has no bodily sense or feeling, but is aspiring after *being*." The philosopher is to pursue "absolute justice ... absolute beauty and absolute good," and "he attains to the knowledge of them in their highest purity who goes to each of them with the mind alone, not allowing when in the act of thought the intrusion or introduction of sight or any other sense in the company of reason, but when the very light of the mind in her clearness penetrates into the very light of truth in each."[12] No one imagines a rhinoceros contemplating the absolute good. No one imagines a hippopotamus attempting to divest itself of its senses. For Plato, the body is animal, and the mind is that in which humans can lose their animal nature. The otherworldly similarities with Pythagoras are apparent. Clearly, Plato sees a vast difference between the human capable of such abstruse philosophy and the nonhuman incapable of such intellectual or spiritual elevation.

Metempsychosis is so central a part of Plato's thinking that he discusses it in the *Phaedo, Republic, Phaedrus,* and *Meno.* It is even implied in the judgment myth toward the end of the *Gorgias.*[13] The version of metempsychosis in the *Republic* is rather more respectful of animals than that of the *Phaedo,* the two dialogues in which he treats the transmigration of souls most fully.[14] Having praised Pythagoras and philosophy over Homer and poetry, Plato tells us in the *Republic* of both animals and humans getting to choose the bodies that will next house their souls, the animals sometimes choosing human form, humans sometimes, especially when ill-treated in their present lives, choosing animal form. Here, there is no explicit hierarchy of humans over other animals. Was the idea of the transmigration of souls, for Plato, more a literary and theological device to explain the demands of justice than a serious theory that related to the natures of humans and animals? That there are other ideological myths in Plato makes the suggestion plausible. For example, there is the renowned "myth of the metals," a political device, in which humans are told they belong to different classes of gold, silver, and bronze, each mixed with earth, in order to persuade them to accept their differing lots in life. We can have little doubt Plato hopes to persuade the bronze class above all of their inferior status. Nor should we imagine that he considers the myth a mere metaphor without practical consequences.

Whatever the truth may be about metempsychosis – the transmigration of souls – it is quite clear that Plato did not use it to enhance the idea of kinship, at least not in any ethical sense, between human and nonhuman animals. He used it probably as a similar metaphorical device to that of the "myth of the metals" to explain what otherwise might be inexplicable, the purification of the soul, and the repercussions of sin, none of which had to do with the elevation of the status of animals. Whether the idea of metempsychosis in the Greek past, or in other lands and climes, demonstrated the affinity between humans and animals, as is frequently claimed, is very much to be doubted. That it certainly does not *necessarily* imply any such affinity, requiring us not to harm animals or eat them, must be clear from Plato's treatment of the subject, for Plato was decidedly an omnivore, if an omnivore who believed in moderation. However, Plato does have Clinias remark in the *Laws* that vegetarianism is currently practised and is a worthy tradition. Indeed, it was commonly said that the Spartans practised a vegetarian diet. Nonetheless, metempsychosis and vegetarianism are independent phenomena, and the adoption of the doctrine of metempsychosis does not entail, nor does it necessarily promote, a vegetarian lifestyle, as some have thought. It need not even encourage considerate treatment of other species.

In light of Plato's rejection of Homer in favour of the wisdom of Pythagoras, would one not expect Plato also to have espoused the purported Pythagorean vegetarianism? Apparently, he did not in fact. However, Plato accepts in *Epinomis* (also known as *Nocturnal Council*) that there was a Golden Age in which vegetarianism was practised and that such an age was preferable to the present, but he has little to say there with regard to vegetarianism itself. A case can however be made, and has been made persuasively by Daniel Dombrowski, that Plato wished his republic to be a vegetarian city. Plato's society of the *Republic,* according to Dombrowski, is conceived as a return to the principles of the Golden Age in which vegetarianism will once again be the accepted practice.[15] Likewise, Howard Williams, writing well over a century hence, numbered Plato among the antiflesh dietary reformers.[16] And certainly Socrates's statement in the *Republic* about the division of labour leads readily to this conclusion: "To feed them they will make meal from barley and flour and wheat; some they will cook, some they will knead into fine cakes and loaves." And when Glaucon questions whether they should not also have relishes at their feasts, Socrates replies: "I forgot that; they will have something more, salt, of course, and olives and cheese, onions and greens to boil, such as they have in the country [rural life was far less attuned to flesh than the city]. And I suppose we shall give them dessert, figs and chickpeas and beans, and they will toast myrtle berries and acorns before the fire, with a drop to drink, not too much."[17] These are all wholesome, nonflesh foods, of course, even if a dairy product (cheese) is included. And when Glaucon asks how Socrates would feed the citizens if he were founding a city of pigs (metaphorical pigs, of course) rather than the republic he describes, he replies with disdain that they could continue to consume the luxurious foods they now consume. Yet it seems clear that Plato, through the character of Socrates, is concerned with the mental and perhaps physical health of the citizenry, not at all with the protection of animals, especially as the term "the city of pigs" is used with such disdain for pigs. His opposition is to "fine food ... and ointments and incense and pretty girls and cakes, all sorts of each." His intent is for the city not to exceed "the bare necessities," which epitomized the Golden Age. One can be further confident of this simplicity from what the Socrates character says when discussing the appropriate size of the city: "Yet it still would not be so very large, even if we were to add oxherds and shepherds and the other herdsmen, that the farmers might have oxen for the plow, and the builders draught-animals to use along with the farmers for carriage, and that the weavers might have fleeces for skins."[18] There is no objection to the use of animals for human ends and no objection to the use of the skins of the slaughtered, or at least dead, animals. Moreover, what could be the purpose of keeping sheep if not for their flesh? For milk and wool alone? It is unlikely, although certainly not impossible, that goat, sheep, and pig skin were used for raiment and protection from the elements and that the flesh of the domesticated animal was not consumed. If Plato does intend a vegetarian city, as Dombrowski has valiantly and intelligently argued, it is not out of respect for animals but to maintain an ascetic citizenry. If Plato's recommendations for the republic are truly consistent with Pythagoras's presumed vegetarianism, Williams's nineteenth-century interpretation is well worthy of consideration: "The obligation to abstain from the flesh of animals was founded by Pythagoras on mental and spiritual rather than on humanitarian grounds."[19] Perhaps the same is true of Plato. Perhaps the *apparent* inconsistency of the domestication of sheep and a vegetarian diet was merely an oversight of detail – an offence of which Plato was occasionally guilty.[20]

Aristotle (384-322 BC) expressed a not dissimilar conception to that of Xenophon on human superior attributes, with the moral implications for the human-animal relationship spelled out more explicitly, when he averred at the beginning of the *Politics:* "Plants exist to give subsistence to animals, and animals to give it to men. Animals, when they are domesticated serve for use as well as for food; wild animals too, in most cases if not all, serve to furnish man not only with food, but also with other comforts, such as the provision of clothing and similar aids to life. Accordingly, as nature makes nothing purposeless or in vain, all animals must have been made by nature for the sake of men."[21] Yet a respect for animals was also creeping, inconsistently, into his thoughts. If Aristotle completely ignored the topic of vegetarianism, he nonetheless laid out the factors that would have an effect on his immediate posterity: his student Dicaerchus and his successor Theophrastus, both of whom chose to become vegetarians. Certainly, that two of the most prominent vegetarians in antiquity, and the foremost of their own era, were immediate products of the Aristotelian stable requires an investigation. It was not a feature of the age that students would react against the teachings of their instructors as they are often said to do today. Even Aristotle, renowned for opposing some of Plato's tenets, accepted the tenor of the master's thought by and large. He seems to have been more concerned to ensure his reputation as an original thinker by exaggerating his differences from Plato. We will find that this Aristotelian inheritance of Dicaerchus and Theophrastus should not surprise us too greatly, for although Aristotle was far from becoming a vegetarian himself, his approach to ethics was one that could readily be borrowed and used toward more animal-considerate if not immediately vegetarian conclusions.

Aristotle's reputation is, of course, as one who was diametrically opposed to the interests of animals, as his statement on animals for human use would suggest. Perhaps we should first recognize that the aspects of "use" mentioned by Aristotle, the provision of food and clothing, apply not just to Western societies in general but also to every Oriental, African, and Amerindian society, which are by reputation supposed to be so much more animal-sympathetic than Western society. Moreover, as we are customarily inclined to ignore, far more than 90 percent of the world's human population "uses" animals in precisely the way that Aristotle indicates. Aristotle was doing no more than stating what is, for many animal advocates, a regrettable fact about humanity, although Aristotle may be read to find it a very convenient fact in line with the dictates of nature, as he saw them. It should be added that as a teleologist, he thought this use the very purpose of nature. No one bothers to make a similar accusation against Plato, even though he refers directly to the use of fleeces for raiment and to the domestication of animals for various ends, notably oxen for the plough and draught animals for carriage, presumably because he is not so direct as to talk about the legitimacy of animal use explicitly. Although there is undeniably the animal-hostile aspect of Aristotle, which his explicitness on animal use has exacerbated, the other side, on which a profound animal ethic may be built, is usually ignored. We may surmise that both Dicaearchus and Theophrastus were steeped in Aristotelian thought, even if Dicaearchus deviated from it the more. Still, they both benefited from it. It is worth giving the other side some attention.

Undoubtedly, Aristotle believes that our capacity for reason and the concomitant capacity for speech – which he saw as our godlike qualities – set humans apart from, and above, all other species.[22] It is reason that entitles humans to ethical consideration before all other species. On the other side, in *On the Parts of Animals*, Aristotle remarks: "For all living beings with which we are acquainted man alone partakes of the divine, or at least partakes of it in fuller measure than the rest."[23] Thus if other animals have less capacity for reason than humans, who accordingly possess greater divinity through reason, nonetheless animals possess reason, and hence divinity, in some degree. Accordingly, one might infer, animals are, for Aristotle, entitled to less ethical consideration than humans but to some consideration nonetheless. Aristotle has numerous remarks to make about animal character that would support such a conclusion. He announces that "in all natural things there is something wonderful ... we should approach the inquiry about each animal without aversion, knowing that in all of them there is something natural and beautiful" and that "each animal body must some-how be made for the soul."[24] To be sure, the animal does not possess the human soul with the capacity for speculative reason, but it has a soul capa-ble of sense perception and calculative reason nonetheless. Porphyry went further and said Aristotle allowed animals to participate in *logou* (full rea-son).[25] Perhaps he was relying, as Dombrowki postulates, on Aristotle's passage from the *Historia Animalium* (588: A8): "just as in man we find know-ledge, wisdom and sagacity, so in certain animals there exists some other natural property akin to these ... one is quite justified in saying that, as regards man and animals, certain psychical qualities are identical with one another, whilst others resemble, and others are analogous to, each other." Animals perceive "pleasure and pain."[26] Some animals are suited "for the development of courage and wisdom" and "some are of a more intelligent nature."[27] Some are accordingly, in Aristotle's view, prudent. In the *Poetics* (ch. 7) Aristotle recognizes the potential for beauty in animals. The point about the identity of certain human and animal qualities is persuasive to Theophrastus in particular. Thus, for Aristotle, there is in general a con-tinuum of the mental states between animals and humans. Yet this does not mean that, for Aristotle, animals and humans are almost identical. As he wrote in the *Nicomachean Ethics,* "We do not call animals temperate or intemperate."[28] There is, in other words, something about the human *moral* character that keeps a clear distance between humans and the other ani-mals. We cannot use words appropriate to the description of human char-acter to describe the motives, emotions, or character of nonhuman animals. Nonetheless, if humans are divorced from law and justice, they are the low-est of the animals – "a most unholy and savage being." Animals possess memory and are able to learn, but they do not understand universals. They do not possess intellectual reason, but they are endowed with practical rea-son. In the *Nicomachean Ethics* (701B 1-15) Aristotle describes this wisdom as a low-level practical wisdom. For Aristotle, ethics is a branch of practical rather than theoretical knowledge, and thus it can be argued that animals, who possess practical rather than theoretical knowledge, are the subject of some ethical concern. If anything is consistent, it is that Aristotle is ambivalent about animals. It is difficult to escape the conclusion that when Aristotle's attention was attuned to the interests of the human community – as it was in the writing of the *Politics* and the *Nicomachean Ethics,* for example – he thought almost exclusively in the human interest, but when he turned his attention to animal questions, his conclusions were far more favourable to those to whom his attention was then directed. Undoubtedly, he equivocated about animals throughout his life but was more favourable to them, on the whole, in his maturity than in his youth. Thus, while Dicaerchus and Theophrastus could not have reached their vegetarian conclusions by following directly in the path of the master, there was much in his teachings that could lead them away from the human exclusivity that Aristotle's doctrines are normally thought to imply. Indeed, some of these teachings could be said to have provided an impetus toward a serious animal ethic with vegetarian consequences.

Dichaerchus the Peripatetic, as he was known, appears to have derived his vegetarianism most immediately from his admiration of the men of the Golden Age. Like Aristotle, he believed ethical truths are best understood through the historical approach, and he followed Aristotle's idea of the Golden Mean, although we cannot be sure what he meant by it, for his vegetarian conclusions are certainly at odds with the common practices of the day. Perhaps he thought, as he appears to, that his contemporaries had long abandoned moderation, and he was intent on returning to it. According to Porphyry in *De Abstinentia* (On Abstinence from Flesh), Dichaerchus believed the men of the Golden Age "were akin to the gods and were by nature the best men and lived the best life ... they are regarded as a Golden Race in comparison with the men of the present time made of a base inferior metal."[29] Dichaerchus, it would appear, wished to emulate them. Unfortunately, little remains, other than his work on plants. But if we can rely on Porphyry with confidence, and in this instance we probably can, for he had access to at least some of Dichaercus's other writings, something of his attitudes to vegetarianism may be gleaned. Dicaerchus is said to explain how the first person who had eaten "enough of the oak-tree" (i.e., enough of acorns and other primitive fruits) led the world to suffering through the departure from the simple way of life. Eventually, he mooted, pastoralism, domestication, and then agriculture forged the path to competition over others' possessions, and wars began. It was abstinence from animal flesh that contributed significantly to the satisfaction of those of the Golden Age with primitive life. Cicero, too, in *De officiis* (On Duty), advises us how Dicaerchus thought that, following attacks on "great multitudes of animals," among other factors, tribes had been destroyed by their own aggressiveness, and hence the "wars and seditions" of men had arisen.[30] Thus for Dicaerchus, the primary lessons of history (he took the Golden Age as fact, not parable) teach us the wisdom and justice of the simple life, of which vegetarianism was seen to be an integral aspect.

Theophrastus (c. 372-286 BC) followed his friend Aristotle not only as his successor as head of the Lyceum but also in that the focus of much of his work was on the biology of the natural realm. Their friendship is reflected in the fact that Aristotle bequeathed his library to Theophrastus. As the passage quoted from the *Historia Animalium* indicates, Aristotle accepted the principle of psychological continuity from humans to animals, a principle that Theophrastus adopted and took further than the master. While Aristotle's primary biological work was on marine life, Theophrastus's extant work was on plants, although we are told by Diogenes Laertius he also wrote several books on animals that have not survived. While Theophrastus is enamoured with the men of the Golden Age, he has more convincing grounds for his own vegetarianism than the superiority of the primitive life or, for that matter, the transmigration of souls, which he appears to have discarded as philosophically unworthy. His primary known work, as noted, was on plants, and he stated clearly that plants differ from animals in that the former do not feel pain. He bases his vegetarian conclusions on the fact that humans and animals have similar biological structure and feel alike. They suffer in common. Porphyry tells us in *De abstinentia* (bk. 2, 11-12) that the fleshless diet was no religious matter alone for Theophrastus but that he held the killing of animals to be unjust. In addition, loss of life matters as well as the elimination of suffering. Theophrastus adds that if the gods are thought to require animal sacrifice – which was first caused by famine via cannibalism, he indicates – then, if you must, sacrifice the animals, but do not eat their flesh. He knew, of course, that one of the purposes of the sacrifice was the consequent entitlement to eat the flesh. Thus to follow his advice was likely to lead to a diminution of animal sacrifice. It is also likely, however, that he understood the centrality of sacrifice to the extant social order and feared the consequences of disturbing it too deeply. For Theophrastus, as for Aristotle, doing what was ethically right in the abstract was sometimes politically wrong in the concrete. Ethics was a practical discipline.

Following a different path from Aristotle, Theophrastus argues that respect for animal life is required by our community *(oikeiôsis)* with them. It is the principle of community, or belongingness, that associates all animals, including human animals, he claims, thus beginning the longstanding argument about the appropriate recipients of justice, principally between the Stoics and their adversaries. At least some of the Stoics – Zeno, for example, the founder of the school – denied that humans belonged to the same community as other animals, arguing that humans, therefore, could not owe animals just treatment. Zeno of Citium (c. 336 to c. 265 BC) was in fact one of those ascetic vegetarians whose refusal to eat flesh related in no manner to consideration for animals. The Epicureans, too, were ascetic vegetarians, even though today we tend to use the word Epicurean to refer to a propensity for sybaritic luxury rather than extreme simplicity – the very reverse of its historic manifestation. Epicureans, in fact, believed that pleasure could be most readily achieved through self-denial and the avoidance of desire. Despite Epicurus's vegetarianism, he believed animals existed for human use and that because animals could not enter into contracts, they were beyond the bounds of justice. In this era the practice of a vegetarian diet did not at all imply, or even suggest, a commitment to avoiding harm to animals for the sake of the animals. Theophrastus was the exception to the norm but not a complete rarity. As Plato recognized, there was a vibrant vegetarian tradition in contemporary Greek culture. And some of that had something, if only a smattering, of an ethical impulse.

In Theophrastus's view, we have a right to kill dangerous animals for self-protection but only in the same manner that we have a right to protect ourselves against criminals. Otherwise, animals have a right to their lives for their own sakes. Thus his vegetarian premise is based not on purification of souls, nor on the lessons of primitive history, but on the similarity of humans and other animals in their potential to suffer and on the value of their own lives to them. He draws conclusions from the principle of psychological and biological continuity that seem never to have been entertained by Aristotle. From the vegetarian standpoint, Theophrastus is truly the first of the moderns and the present-day ethical vegetarian's earliest role model, although, yet again, Empedocles comes close and Dicaerchus is a legitimate contender.

## HELLENISTIC GREECE AND ROME

For Aristotle, the Greek *polis* (city-state) represented the perfection of social and political society. He had no conception of how fragile and temporary was the Greek political order that was soon to be overturned forever by Alexander of Macedonia, whom, ironically, Aristotle had earlier tutored for some six years. Greece became but one element within the new Macedonian imperial order, which included Egypt, Persia, Phoenicia, Babylon, Lydia (in the western part of Asia Minor), and parts of the Indian Punjab. The period from Alexander's death in 323 BC to the conquest of Egypt by the Romans in 30 BC is commonly known as the Hellenistic age. Immediately following Alexander's death, the unity of the empire was loosened, and it eventually began to crumble. From the early second century BC, the Macedonian Empire, including Greece, was subject to increasing pressures from Rome, finally submitting with the defeat of the Macedonians in Egypt. Rome now established its own imperial order with a Latin administration in the Mediterranean regions. Eventually, the empire stretched from most of Britain to the Middle East. But if Rome gave Greece a new imperial overlord, it borrowed its philosophy very largely from those Greeks it now administered. When Rome first conquered Greece, what Dombrowski via Brumbaugh calls "teleological anthropocentrism" – the view that everything in the world was created for humankind – was already dominant, if far from universal, in Rome and Greece.[31] There was in effect a united culture of the two originally separate cultures. Stoicism, alongside Epicureanism – which shared much of Stoic thought – and Skepticism, flourished for a half-millennium in the Hellenistic Roman period from around 300 BC to AD 200. Stoicism and Epicureanism maintained the teleological anthropocentrist view on the whole and most steadfastly.

The prevalent Stoics, named after the "Painted Stoa" (colonnade) where they met, followed Aristotle in that they held, by and large – in addition to the view that plants were made for animals and animals for men – that animals, lacking reason, shared no common values with humans and thus that there was no possibility to include animals within the framework of justice. In other words, despite Dicaearchus and Theophrastus, it was the arguments of Xenophon and Aristotle that held sway with the Stoics. Beyond this, the Stoics believed in a rational, materialistic, and deterministic universe in which virtue involved understanding the world as it was and cheerfully accepting it – indeed, withdrawing from it – a view not too dissimilar from Oriental quietism. A few stalwart figures, however, stood out against this prevailing sentiment, and two of them are among the most significant contributors to vegetarian thought in all of human history: Plutarch (c. AD 46 to c. 120) and Porphyry (c. AD 233-304), the latter of whom shall be treated below under the heading of neo-Platonists. The first was born in Greece and the second probably in Tyre, Phoenicia. Both were educated in Athens. Both spent much of their maturity in Rome, reflecting the cosmopolitan nature of the new political order. Plutarch's most famous work was his *Parallel Lives,* consisting of forty-six portraits of Greek and Roman historical figures who shared some semblance with each other and thus showing the purported unity of the Roman and Greek traditions. *Parallel Lives* reflects that this was a period of dislocation, during which Greeks tried to rediscover themselves within the new Roman order and tried to demonstrate the similarity of the Greek and Roman traditions. Despite Stoic dominance in Rome, Nero outlawed the selling of meat in public while permitting its consumption in private at home, a reflection of the belief that there was something less than wholesome in flesh consumption. Moreover, vegetarianism was no new radical fad. It was avidly furthered and supported by the empress Julia Domna (c. AD 267-317) herself during the time of Porphyry. Nonetheless, it should not be imagined that vegetarianism was widespread among the elites or readily tolerated. In fact, wealthy Romans indulged in frequent haute cuisine. Even the more modest dinner table contained game birds, seafood, goat, pork, and chicken.

Immediately prior to Plutarch, we find, surprisingly enough, a wayward Stoic as a prime proponent of vegetarianism. Seneca (4 BC to AD 65), a Roman statesman, philosophical essayist, and playwright, reflected the newly revived interest in Pythagoras and his image as the exponent of transmigration and our consequent kinship with animals as the basis for the refusal of animal flesh. Sextius, by contrast, is presented to us by Seneca more as an ethical vegetarian, although we have to wonder whether the cruelty he condemns is the practice of cruelty to humans learned via butchery of animals, in the manner of Saint Thomas Aquinas and Immanuel Kant, or whether Sextius is condemning cruelty to animals directly. Perhaps there is no clear distinction in Sextius's mind between the two. This passage from Seneca's *Ad Lucilium Epistolae Morales* (Letters on Morals to Lucillus) also reflects both that some of the Stoics were less inimical to animal interests than they are commonly portrayed and that Romans were imbued with Greek thought:

> Inasmuch as I have begun to explain to you how much greater was my impulse to approach philosophy in my youth than to continue it in my old age, I shall not be ashamed to tell you what ardent zeal Pythagoras inspired in me. Sotion [a Pythagorean contemporary of the young Seneca] used to tell me why Pythagoras abstained from animal food, and why, in later times, Sextius [i.e., Quintus Sextius the Elder, renowned for declining an honour from Julius Caesar] did also. In each case the reason was different, but it was in each case a noble reason. Sextius believed that man had enough sustenance without resorting to blood, and that a habit of cruelty is formed whenever butchery is practised for pleasure. Moreover, he thought we should curtail the sources of our luxury; he argued that a varied diet was contrary to the laws of health, and was unsuited to our constitutions. Pythagoras, on the other hand, held that all beings were interrelated and there was a system of exchange between souls which transmigrated from one bodily shape to another ... he made men fearful of guilt and parricide, since they might be, without knowing it, attacking the soul of a parent and injuring it with knife or with teeth ... If the theory is true, it is a mark of purity to abstain from eating flesh: if it be false it is economy ...

I was imbued with this teaching, and began to abstain from animal food; at the end of a year the habit was as pleasant as it was easy. I was beginning to feel that my mind was more active.[32]

Seneca, it is sometimes claimed, continued to practice vegetarianism in his private life – although one might be inclined to doubt it from the tone of his comments to Lucillus below – but returned to meat eating in public to avoid societal and imperial condemnation. His own explanation of his resumption of flesh eating is contained in the same letter to Lucillus: "the days of my youth coincided with the early part of the reign of Tiberius Caesar. Some foreign rites were at that time being inaugurated and abstinence from certain kinds of animal food was set down as a proof of interest in the strange cult. So at the request of my father, who did not fear gossip, but who detested philosophy, I returned to my previous habits, and it was no very hard matter to induce me to dine more comfortably."[33]

He never mentioned having resumed his vegetarian diet at any time. His vegetarianism may thus have been a temporary interlude in early adulthood. Indeed, he seems to imply that the greater comfort of the flesh diet (comfort for whom? certainly not the comfort of the tortured animals) sat better with him. While vegetarianism was certainly practised in Rome, it was not a practice that sat comfortably with those in authority when practised on grounds of ethical principle.

Colin Spencer has described eloquently the conditions of restraint in Rome during this period as contrasted with those of earlier Greece:

In the city states of Greece enquiring minds with unfashionable views were tolerated if not fostered, the city states being small and flexible enough to allow a collection of disparate views to flourish without feeling overly threatened. Rome was another matter; the vast empire always in a state of growth, yet at its heart always insecure, its power vulnerable to criticism, enforced conventional piety towards its gods on all its citizens. The Romans felt hostile to Greek thought which explored anti-social tendencies so the Pythagoreans were denounced or banished. Stoicism was approved of as it emphasized the conventional duties of life and virtue.[34]

Perhaps the Romans were more jealous of Greek philosophical superiority than hostile to it, for they borrowed it willingly enough, even if sometimes less than wholeheartedly. And not merely the Pythagoreans were denounced or banished. Even the Stoics were not fully exempt, for at the age of sixty Seneca was condemned to death by the paranoid Emperor

Nero on suspicion of conspiracy, following which, his execution being bungled, he committed suicide. The commanding authority of the empire was extended to all who met with political or social disfavour.

In the ensuing years, we find significant expressions of animal sensibilities in the writings of Pliny the Elder, Ovid, Marcus Aurelius, Aelian, and Sextus Empiricus. Ovid had a few years earlier written a fine poem extolling Pythagoras's vegetarianism. But none of them, so far as I can tell, ever renounced the eating of flesh. Or at least, I am suspicious that such is the case. However, Williams, Dombrowski, and Spencer are among the advocates of Ovid as a vegetarian. They should not be too readily discounted. To me, he seems to have a greater interest in literary form than in ethical principle. The most the evidence seems to suggest of Ovid (43 BC to AD 17), one might say, is that if he could write such heartrending condemnations of animal cruelty through the supposed mouth of Pythagoras, he *ought* to have been a vegetarian. Yet later, neither Mandeville nor Rousseau was any less effusive. They still continued their omnivorous practices. If they converted others to the bloodless regimen, they did not convert themselves. This period is the first decisive indication of the paradox that suffused Western culture hereafter – the general sensibility to animals ran well ahead of the recognition that respect for animals required the refusal to eat them. Oddly, the thought was born that respect for the animals did not include respect for their lives.

Plutarch was a Greek historian, biographer, and essayist but made several extended visits to Rome, where he was a popular lecturer. In his essay "On the Use of Reason by 'Irrational' Animals," Plutarch argued that animals were not irrational and were in several respects superior to humans.[35] Others – Chrysippus and Sextus Empiricus, for example – concurred on animal rationality but apparently failed to draw vegetarian conclusions from their deliberations. In "Life of Marcus Crato," an eminent Roman statesman, Plutarch discussed our responsibilities toward domesticated species and some of the more salutary aspects of the Greek tradition.[36] But it was in his early and incomplete essay "On the Eating of Flesh" that Plutarch was a plaintiff against the inconsiderate treatment of food animals. And he advocated a vegetarian diet on the explicit grounds of sparing the animals the cruelties inflicted on them and also of saving humanity from its flesh-eating self-degradation. Again, he evokes the memory of Pythagoras in the vegetarian cause:

> Can you really ask what reason Pythagoras had for abstaining from flesh? For my part I rather wonder by what accident and what state of soul or mind the

first man who did so, touched his mouth to gore and brought his lips to the flesh of a dead creature, he who set forth the tables of dead, stale bodies and ventured to call food and nourishment the parts that had a little before bellowed and cried, moved and lived. How could his eyes endure the slaughter when the throats were slit and hides flayed and limbs torn from limb? How could his nose endure the stench? How was it that the pollution did not turn away his taste, which made contact with the sores of others and sucked juices and serums from mortal wounds? ...

You call serpents and lions savage, but you yourselves by your own foul slaughter, leave them no room to outdo you in cruelty, for their slaughter is their living, yours is a mere appetizer.

It is certainly not lions and wolves that we eat out of self-defence; on the contrary, we ignore these and slaughter harmless, tame creatures without stings or teeth to harm us, creatures that, I swear, Nature appears to have produced for the sake of their nature and grace.[37]

Even if flesh eating were morally acceptable, Plutarch adds, the wasteful practices of profligate humans cause unnecessary suffering and death:

But nothing abashes us, not the flower-tinting of the flesh, not the cleanliness of their habits, or the unusual intelligence that may be found in the poor wretches. No, for the sake of a little flesh we deprive them of sun, of light, of the duration of life to which they are entitled by birth and being..Then we go on to assume that when they utter cries and squeaks their speech is inarticulate, they do not, begging for mercy, entreating, seeking justice, each one of them say, "I do not ask to be spared in case of necessity; only spare me your arrogance! Kill me to eat, but not to please your palate." Oh, the cruelty of it! What a terrible thing it is to look on when the tables of the rich are spread, men who employ cooks and spicers to groom the dead! And it is even more terrible to look on when they are taken away, for more is left than has been eaten. So the beasts died for nothing! There are others who refuse when the dishes are set before them, and will not have them cut or sliced. Though they did spare the dead, they did not spare the living.[38]

The sole reason for this profligacy, Plutarch seems to suggest, is the complete indifference of the human being to any pain and suffering meted out to those beyond the human species boundary. Despite the eloquence and persuasiveness of Plutarch's essay – the very first of its kind or, at least, the only one still extant – the sybaritic dining luxuries of the wealthy continued, and so did the barbarities of the Roman games. Even the Stoic Cicero complained about the purposes of the games.[39] He went so far as to write of the "impulse of compassion" for the ill-treated animals, but neither he nor others who claimed to feel compassion felt compassionate enough to forgo the unnecessary titillations of their palate. It is logically odd – but apparently not psychologically incompatible – to express compassion for an entity and then to consign the entity to oblivion. Plutarch certainly thought so.

In fact, Plutarch was the classical vegetarian advocate most commonly cited from the seventeenth century on, but paradoxically, in many instances he was mentioned in defence of flesh eating. Those who were tempted, but not tempted enough, to abandon flesh would recall Plutarch's sentiments as a justification of their carnivorous behaviour. Provided the animals were killed without undue suffering, so it was said, eating them was acceptable – and this in ages when it was even more difficult than today to spare the animal the anguish and cruelties of slaughtering practices.

## THE NEO-PLATONISTS

Initially associated with Plotinus (AD 205-270), neo-Platonism is so called because of its attention to the existence of the One and to the attendant theory of ideas that were aspects of the later writings of Plato, especially in the *Timaeus*. Plotinus was born in Egypt, probably of Roman descent, and studied in Alexandra and Persia before moving to Rome, where he set up his influential school, all of which reflects once more the cosmopolitan nature of philosophical life in the Roman Empire. He advocated a moderate asceticism to allow one to dispense with the senses and achieve a union with the godhead. In Plotinus's work, collected together as the *Enneads* by Plotinus's student Porphyry, he was concerned with understanding the mysteries of the infinite and invisible, but, in fact, his system was a natural extension of the thoroughly rational method of traditional logic and the humanitarian lore of Greece. While there is no conclusive evidence, Plotinus's strict personal asceticism most probably included vegetarianism, although his biographer, Porphyry, could find no writing by Plotinus on the topic. Still, in his *Life of Plotinus* he tells us that Plotinus refused medicine with animal ingredients.[40] It is certain that a number of Plotinus's followers were not just vegetarians but also ethical vegetarians.

The primary neo-Platonist of interest to vegetarians is the polymath and prolific scholar Porphyry, who continued the Pythagoras-Plato tradition that the primary human endeavour was to free one's life from the calamities of the body. Together with Plutarch, he is the only scholar in antiquity to have written a polemic in favour of the abstention from flesh. Along with a biography of his teacher Plotinus, he also wrote a biography of Pythagoras, to which previous reference has been made, as well as a book attempting to harmonize Aristotle's writings on logic with Platonism, in addition to many other writings. His book *On Abstinence from Flesh* is now commonly recognized as the primary classical work related to vegetarianism and animal ethics. It is more than just a polemic. It is a finely reasoned argument of the significant human moral obligation toward nonhuman animal species. In it he makes the anti-Stoic case for extending justice to animals, denouncing the entailed view of the Stoics that animals lack reason. Further, he discusses the distinction between animals and plants. Unlike plants, he says, animals are sentient and rational, and he demonstrates the poverty of the argument that animals are intended for human use. Most important, Porphyry introduces the argument from marginal cases (e.g., the error of rationality being allowed to depraved men but not to members of other species, thereby denying "rationality" to the latter in principle but not the former) that is today considered a mainstay of the argument for animal rights. Animals possess reason, he believes, although not in the same degree as humans, and humans and animals share their senses in common. He makes the customary due obeisance to Pythagoras on a couple of occasions, but he is very well worth quoting at considerable length in his own right, for no one is better qualified than the author himself to state his profoundly logical and compassionate argument. Nor is there a better way to understand the philosophical culture of the day:

> We shall pass on ... to the discussion of justice; and since our opponents [the Stoics] say that this ought only to be extended to those of similar species, and on that account deny that irrational animals can be injured by men, let us exhibit the true, and at the same time Pythagorean opinion, and demonstrate that every soul which participates of sense and memory is rational. For this being demonstrated, we may extend, as our opponents will also admit, justice to every animal ...
>
> Since, however, with respect to reason, one kind, according to the doctrine of the Stoics, is internal, but the other external, and again, one kind being right and the other erroneous, it is requisite to explain of which of these two, animals, according to them, are deprived. Are they therefore deprived of right reason alone? Or are they entirely destitute both of internal and externally proceeding reason?
>
> They [the Stoics] appear, indeed, to ascribe to brutes an entire privation of reason, and not a privation of right reason alone. For if they merely denied

that brutes possess right reason, animals would not be irrational, but rational beings, in the same manner as nearly all men are according to them. For, according to their opinion, one or two wise men may be found in whom alone right reason prevails, but all the rest of mankind are depraved; though some of these make a certain proficiency, but others are profoundly depraved, and yet at the same time, all of them are similarly rational ... If, however, it be requisite to speak the truth, not only reason may plainly be perceived in all animals, but in many of them it is so great as to approximate perfection ...

Since ... that which is vocally expressed by the tongue is reason, in whatever manner it may be expressed, whether in a barbarous or a Grecian, a canine or a bovine mode, other animals also participate of it that are vocal; men, indeed, speaking conformably to the human laws, but other animals conformably to the laws which they received from the Gods and nature. But if we do not understand what they say what is this to the purpose? For the Greeks do not understand what is said by the Indians, nor those who are educated in Attica the language of the Scythians, or Thracians, or Syrians; but the sound of the one falls on the ear of the other like the clangour of cranes, though by others their vocal sounds can be written and articulated, in the same manner as ours can by us ... The like also takes place in the vocal sounds of the other animals. For the several species of these understand the language which is adapted to them ...

The difference, indeed, between our reason and theirs, appears to consist, as Aristotle says somewhere,[41] not in essence, but in the more and the less, just as many are of the opinion, that the difference between the Gods and us is not essential but consists in this, in them there is a greater, and in us a less accuracy, of the reasoning power. And, indeed, so far as pertains to sense and the remaining organization, according to the sensoria and the flesh, every one will grant that these are similarly disposed in us, as they are in brutes. For they not only similarly participate with us of natural passions, and the motions produced through these, but we may also survey in them such affections as are preternatural and morbid. No one, however, of a sound mind, will say that brutes are unreceptive of the reasoning power, on account of the difference between their habit of body and ours, when he sees that there is a great variety of habit in man, according to their race [i.e., species], and to the nations [i.e., breeds] to which they belong, and yet, at the same time, it is granted that all of them are rational.

It does not follow, if we have more intelligence than other animals, that on this account they are to be deprived of intelligence; as neither must it be said, that partridges do not fly, because hawks fly higher ...

Brutes are rational animals, reason in most of them being indeed imperfect, of which nevertheless they are entirely deprived [by the Stoics]. Since, however, justice pertains to rational beings, as our opponents say, how is it possible not to admit, that we should also act justly toward brutes? For we do not extend justice toward plants, because there appears to be much in them which is unconnected with reason ...

To compare plants ... with animals, is doing violence to the order of things. For the latter are naturally sensitive, and adapted to feel pain, on which account also they may be injured. But the former are naturally destitute of sensation and in consequence of this, nothing foreign, or evil, or hurtful, or injurious [in terms of pain] can befall them ... And is it not absurd, since we see that many of our own species live from sense alone, but do not possess intellect and [right] reason, and since we also see, that many of them surpass the most terrible of wild beasts in cruelty, anger and rapine ... to fancy that we ought to act justly toward these, but that no justice is due from us to the ox that ploughs, the dog that is fed with us, and the animals that nourish us with their milk, and adorn our bodies with their wool? Is not such an opinion both irrational and absurd? ...

If God fashioned animals for the use of men, in what [manner] do we use flies, lice, bats, beetles, scorpions and vipers? ... And if our opponents [the Stoics] should admit that all things are not generated for us, and with a view to our advantage, in addition to the distinction which they make being very confused and obscure, we shall not avoid acting unjustly, if attacking and noxiously using those animals that were not produced for our sake ... I ought to mention that, if we define, by utility, things which pertain to us, we shall not be prevented from admitting, that we were generated for the sake of the most destructive animals, such as crocodiles ... For we are not in the least benefited by them; but they seize and destroy men that fall in their way, and use them for food; in so doing acting not at all more cruelly than we do, excepting that they commit this injustice through want and hunger, but we through insolent wantonness, and for the sake of luxury, frequently sporting in theatres, and in hunting slaughter the greater part of the animals. And by thus acting, indeed, a murderous disposition and a brutal nature become strengthened in us, and render us insensible to pity, to which we may add, that those who first dared to do this, blunted the greatest part of lenity, and rendered it inefficacious ...

Since animals are allied to us, if it should appear, according to Pythagoras, that they are allotted the same soul that we are, he may justly be considered impious who does not abstain from acting unjustly toward his kindred. Nor because some animals are savage, is their alliance to us to be on this account abscinded. For some men may be found who are no less, and even more malefic than savage animals to their neighbours, and who are impelled to injure any one they may meet with, as if they were driven by a certain blast of their own nature and depravity. Hence also, we destroy such men; yet we do not cut them off from alliance to animals of a mild nature. Thus, therefore, if likewise some animals are savage, these, as such, are to be destroyed, in the same manner as men that are savage;[42] but habitude or alliance to other and wilder animals is not on this account to be abandoned. *But neither tame nor savage animals are to be eaten; as neither are unjust men.*

He ... who admits he is allied to animals, *will not injure any animal ... since justice consists in not injuring anything, it must be extended as far as to every animated creature ...* when reason governs ... man will be innoxius towards everything. For the passions being restrained, and desire and anger wasting away, but reason possessing its proper empire, a similitude to a more excellent nature immediately follows.[43]

Since we do not eat inferior humans, Porphyry has argued, we should not eat animals either, even if we consider them inferior. The argument for not eating the former applies with equal force to the latter. The passage here quoted from Porphyry at extraordinary length is the most important statement in the history of vegetarianism before Percy Bysshe Shelley a millennium and a half later, and arguably not equalled even then. Most significantly, for Porphyry, justice to animals requires that we do not eat them.

# 5

# Judaism and the
# Earlier Christian Heritage

## The Jewish Tradition

Many are aware of the modest successes of vegetarianism in the classical world, but a great deal less is heard about the modest successes in the early Judeo-Christian tradition. There are, however, significant vegetarian instances to be found. But they are found less frequently than are hints that vegetarianism would have been practised widely if God had not made the concession that flesh could be eaten. Thus, at the close of the eighteenth century, we find Thomas Young, an Anglican priest and Fellow of Trinity College, Cambridge, allowing that there could be no good ground for eating flesh if God had not granted the privilege. Thus Young remarks: "After the flood, God by a particular grant gave permission to Noah and his descendants, to take away the lives of animals for the purposes of food. Now I think it evidently appears from the grant itself, independent of any other arguments, that without it mankind would not have had a right to kill animals for food. For if the right could have been derived from any other source, that grant would have been unnecessary, in which case we cannot conceive that God would in so express and particular a manner have conferred it."[1] Nor did Young stand alone, offering some novel biblical exegesis. A few years earlier, the political philosopher and preeminent Anglican theologian William Paley had observed: "It seems to me that it would be difficult to defend this right [to eat flesh] by any arguments which the light and order of nature afford; and that we are beholden to it for the permission recorded in scripture, Gen IX, 1, 2, 3."[2] Without God's

grant to the contrary, so we are being told, vegetarianism is the diet appropriate to the dictates of nature. God's grant was imperative to the maintenance of the traditional regimen. In his pursuit of ecclesiastical preferment,
Paley also proved himself incapable of accepting the moral conclusions of
his rational insights when they interfered with his rationalizations. So at
odds with nature did God's permission to eat flesh seem to be that in the
third century AD Tertullian went so far as to say the passage permitting flesh
consumption is "intending to enjoin abstinence by the very indulgence
granted."[3] Tertullian, like several others, found the grant so distasteful that
some interpretation was necessary that would imply the reverse of what
was ostensibly being said.

These sentences from Young and Paley contain interesting implications.
They appear to concede that God allowed humans to contravene the then
universally acknowledged natural law, of which God is the source in the
Judeo-Christian tradition. If God were the source, was he not, then, breaking his own moral laws? Or was Tertullian right that in some mysterious
manner the passage furthered abstinence? The original biblical requirement
– arguably written by Ezra some 400 years BC, although it is now usually
conceded that Genesis was written by at least two different authors many
decades and mindsets apart – reads: "Behold, I have given you every herb
bearing seed, which is upon the face of the earth, and every tree in the
which is the fruit of a tree yielding seed; to you it shall be meat" (Gen. 1:29).
We are compelled to ponder whether this was an example of the common
reference to a Golden Age (very probably) or whether there were significant
Jewish vegetarian groups who were the occasion for the writing of the
verse. Although this is a far less likely ground for the inclusion of the verse,
it is not at all implausible that there were numerous vegetarian groups
around at the time, and flesh eating would have been further curtailed by
the practices of those who were wary of animal sacrifice, those who practised animal sacrifice and did not eat the flesh (a common and praisewor-
thy Jewish practice according to Porphyry [*On Abstinence from Animal
Food*, bk. 2, 26]), and those who lived too distant from the Holy Temple at
Jerusalem, the only legitimate place of sacrifice. And sacrifice was the prerequisite of entitlement to eat animal flesh. To be sure, some rural Jews are
reported to have sliced pieces from living animals to maintain a continuous
supply of fresh meat – living larders – but that has been an unfortunate
practice of many cultures. And some more, no doubt, ate flesh without
attending the Holy Temple. It is quite improbable that the vegetarian practices of at least a few of the priesthood in the neighbouring lands of Egypt,
Babylonia, and Persia, and probably others close to home besides, did not

influence at least in some degree the culture of the Jews, especially given that, by biblical tradition in the book of Exodus, they had spent some time in captivity in Egypt, where some had come to practise Egyptian rites.

Was there a specific reason the god they worshipped had decided to abrogate the original injunction not to eat flesh out of temporary necessity? The granting of the permission to eat flesh was of course made after the flood. Roberta Kalechofsky has argued that when Noah disembarked from the ark, he was met with a world denuded of plant food, a view held previously in 1655 by the Leveller mystic Roger Crab.[4] The environmental catastrophe that had occasioned the flood story – a version of the story being repeated in many cultures – had radically altered the ecology, Kalechofsky argues. Humans must either eat flesh temporarily or starve to death. They chose not to starve. Nowhere, however, does God once again reimpose his original vegetarian, and perhaps vegan, restrictions on humankind, a fact usually explained as a concession to human weakness – by Tertullian, for example.[5] Instead, immediately following the concession to eat flesh – "every thing that liveth shall be meat for you" (Gen. 9:3) – we are told: "But flesh with the life thereof, which is the blood thereof, ye shall not eat" (Gen. 9:4). Our immediate response is that the command is of no value to the animals, for with the blood removed, they are just as dead as if they are eaten with the blood intact. However, the appropriate interpretation is rather more beneficial to the animals: one must not take the life of the animal without considerable thought, blood being the principle of life and life being of inherent value. It is a not uncommon rabbinical argument that the stricture in Jewish law allowed the killing of the animal if the needs were strong, and then only very rarely. Whether that became the later Jewish practice is a different matter. What the stricture indicates is that Jewish principles several centuries before the birth of Christ, if not vegetarian, came closer to it as a general rule than those societies that restricted their vegetarianism to one class or one or two castes alone. Indeed, as Clement of Alexandria said, "the Jews had frugality thrust upon them by the [Mosaic] Law in the most systematic manner."[6] And we can read in the Book of Enoch, a Judaic text composed in parts from around 170 to 64 BC – Enoch was connected with and revered by the Essenes – that it was only after the flood that humans "began to sin against birds and beasts and reptiles and fish, and to devour one another's flesh and to drink the blood."[7] The idea mooted is that flesh eating was still a sin despite the concession. In fact, the Jewish prescription regarding blood continued for several centuries among early Christians according to Eusebius in *Ecclesiastical History*.[8]

It is now fairly well known but bears repeating, especially in light of the fact that one hears the contrary view still frequently reiterated, that "dominion" in Genesis – "let them have dominion over the fish of the sea, and over the fowl of the air, and over the cattle, and over all the earth, and over every living thing that creepeth upon the earth" (Gen. 1:26) – does not mean, as pointed out both cogently and memorably by Richard Schwartz, "the rule of a haughty despot."[9] Traditionally, such commentators as Edward Payson Evans, Lynn White Jr., Peter Singer, and Roderick Frazier Nash have interpreted Genesis 1:26 as the legitimizing onset to a Judeo-Christian oppression of the animal and other natural realms.[10] White, for example, interprets the passage to imply that, according to Judeo-Christian scripture, God had created all of the nonhuman realm "explicitly for man's benefit and rule: no item in the physical creation had any purpose but to serve man's purpose." Singer's interpretation has a decidedly political impulse: "To end tyranny we must first understand it." Such interpretations of the text, if not necessarily of the practice, are seriously in error. In fact, *rādā* (the Hebrew word translated as dominion) does refer to a significant power that *may* be used despotically. Nonetheless, an implication of the term is that humans were intended to share not only some of God's prerogative but also, as the theologian Andrew Linzey has explained, "his moral nature," acting toward animated nature as God did toward humans, bringing order to chaos and bringing blessings and goodness rather than tyrannical mastery to the world.[11] Certainly, in Genesis animals are subordinated to humankind, and humans are entitled to their use. But as the detailed research of Elijah Judah Schochet has demonstrated, animals were to be regarded as "the delicate tool," as instruments for human use, to be sure, but to be used with feelings of respect for, and kinship with, animals.[12] Moreover, what we might call limited dominion has been the customary historical interpretation of the grant. To take but two of a host of potential examples, Lord Erskine remarked in a debate in 1809 on the second reading of an unsuccessful animal welfare bill that "the dominion granted to us over the world is not conceded to us absolutely. It is a dominion in trust; and we should never forget that the animal over which we exercise our power has all the organs which render it susceptible of pleasure and pain."[13] In the *Rights of Animals* (1838), the Unitarian Irish preacher William Drummond argued that "man's dominion over [the animals] is a delegated trust, which he is required to use with discretion and lenity ... The [animals] were formed for their own enjoyment of life ... it is a dominion of justice and mercy."[14] Such commentary was common from the sixteenth century onward.

Startlingly, in light of the abuse heaped traditionally on the Judeo-Christian ethic with regard to animals, we find specific practical pronouncements of consideration for animals earlier, more fully, and more consistently expressed in pre-Christian Judaism, taking a culture as a whole, than in any other culture, even though vegetarian conclusions are not usually drawn from these pronouncements, at least not by the orthodox. Thus, for example: "It is forbidden according to the law of Torah to inflict pain on any living creature. On the contrary, it is our duty to relieve the pain of any creature, even if it is ownerless or belongs to a non-Jew."[15]

Although similar proscriptions are to be found in Indian thought, there are others that contradict them. There are no competing instances in Judaic thought other than occasional mention of animal sacrifice, practised less than in most religious traditions. By referring to ownerless animals being entitled to freedom from the infliction of pain, the proscription makes it clear that the duty is to the animal directly, not indirectly to the animal and directly to the owner, as later for both Aquinas and Kant. And the reference to being owned by a non-Jew implies that one must have concern for the animal in and for itself, not because it may be owned by someone to whom one has a natural obligation by being a member of one's own religious community. Several other classical Judaic edicts have similar references to responsibilities to animals owned by non-Jews. Thus, for example, we are told: "When horses, drawing a cart, come to a rough road or steep hill, and it is hard for them to draw the cart without help, it is our duty to help them, even when they belong to a non-Jew, because of the precept not to be cruel to animals, lest the owner smite them to force them to draw more than their strength permits."[16]

As an indication, again, that it is the responsibility to the animal directly that is being promoted, we may read in the Talmud that heaven rewards those who show concern and compassion for nonhumans and that one should not own an animal unless one can feed and care for the animal.[17] Another Hebrew doctrine reads: "a good man does not sell his beast to a cruel person."[18] And again from a classical Hebrew doctrine: "As the Holy One, blessed be He, has compassion upon man, so has He compassion upon the beasts of the field ... And for the birds of the air."[19] There are many precepts of a more precise nature, including:

Jews must avoid plucking feathers from live geese, because it is cruel to do so.[20]
Rejoicing cannot occur at an animal's expense.[21]
Animals are not to be penned up in stables on the Sabbath.[22]
One who prevents an animal from eating when at work is punishable by flagellation.[23]

The Jewish proscriptions against animal cruelty are a signal example of the most advanced expressions of sensibility to animals not being enjoined by the requirement not to eat them.

The renowned Jewish historian Flavius Josephus (AD 37-100), when writing of the fundamental laws of the Mosaic code, observed: "it is not lawful to pass by any beast that is in distress, when it is fallen down under its burden, but to endeavour to preserve it, as having a sympathy with it in its pain."[24] Thus not only is the duty direct to the animal, but the moral also imposes a responsibility both to refrain from cruelty and to act in a manner supportive of the animal's interests. Nor is there any quasi-Aristotelian sense of animals intended for human use, although there is certainly a reality that they were so used: "Thou thinkest that flies, fleas, mosquitoes are superfluous, but they have their purpose in creation as a means of a final outcome ... Of all that the Holy One, blessed be He, created in His world, He did not create a single thing without purpose."[25] Of course, such assertions were made precisely because the implied ethical imperatives were not followed. Even Samson, according to Judges 15:4, caught three hundred foxes and had torches placed between their tails and lit. They were then driven through the fields of the Philistines.[26] Indeed, ethical imperatives were advanced for similar reasons of noncompliance in other traditions.

There is more in the Hebrew Bible besides, alongside the recommendations to perform sacrificial rites – although some passages do deem such sacrifice to be evil and displeasing to God (e.g., Psalms 66:4 and Hosea 6:6). Thus, to mention but three of the relevant animal-considerate verses:

A righteous man regardeth the life of his beast: but the tender mercies of the wicked are cruel (Proverbs 12:10). [In other words, upright persons have compassion for their animals, whereas the heart of the wicked is ruthless.]

You shalt not plough with an ox and an ass together (Deuteronomy 22:10). [That is, yoked animals must share an equal burden and thus not be harmed by an unequal burden imposed by the yoke.]

Thou shalt not muzzle the ox when he is treading out the corn (Deuteronomy 25:4). [The farmer is being instructed that the ox must not be deprived of a due portion of the fruits of the animal's labour.]

Unlike the Homeric Greek tradition, Jewish mores did not, and do not, celebrate hunters as heroes. Nimrod and Esau, who enjoyed the chase, are not well regarded in Jewish tradition. As Roberta Kalechofsky has explained, "there is no record of blood sports ... or any use of animals for any purpose of entertainment, nor gladiatorial combats, bullfighting, cockfighting, dogfighting etc. There is no tradition of the hunter as hero, romantic figure, or macho exemplar."[27] Her view is well confirmed with regard to blood sports in W.E.H. Lecky's nineteenth-century *History of European Morals,* where he remarks that "the rabbinical writers have been remarkable for the great emphasis on the duty of kindness to animals." He adds there is "no record of any wild beast combats existing among Jews."[28]

Other societies have animal-friendly pronouncements of perhaps a rather earlier period, but they are balanced by statements that treat animals a great deal less than respectfully. Among the Jews, the pronouncements consistently treat animals with respect and consideration, exemplifying and extending Zoroastrian protection of working animals. Such pronouncements are both significant in number and quite specific. Even the methods of slaughter were intended to be considerate of food-animal interests, although whether they were and are remains, in fact, a matter of significant dispute. However, although these statements indicate a clear duty to the animal, the stronger duty by far was to God – "the earth is the Lord's," everything that exists belongs to Him, and *correspondingly,* we have no right to harm anything.[29] The later Jews, as similarly the Christians, took the permission to eat animals more or less as an injunction to do so. For the Jews, this was especially so on festive occasions or at Friday family dinners to celebrate the commencement of the Sabbath, although gluttony was expressly forbidden. Whereas vegetarianism made little headway among mainstream Judaism, it appears to have played a role among nonconformist sects. The consistency of the ethical statements gives one cause to wonder whether vegetarianism was more common than the available evidence indicates. Or was this simply one more instance, as in so many cultures, where sensibility toward animals permits, paradoxically, the right to bring their lives to an inordinately early end and consume their carcases?

None of these positive pronouncements appears to have led to any *widespread* vegetarianism among the nonconformists – although, again, we cannot be sure. The historical record is not at all clear. Even if we take the Essenes as a strictly Christian example of a vegetarian community in the early Christian era, as some have been inclined to do – and it is quite inappropriate to do so given the community's existence for over a century before the birth of Christ – it would be probable that any early Christian quasi-vegetarian group would find its roots in the immediately preceding Jewish traditions.[30] Moreover, for the first eighty-five years or so of the Christian tradition, there is no clear distinction between Christianity and Judaism, Christianity being in effect an expression of a tendency within

Judaism, just as later Protestantism became an aspect of Christianity with the initial intention not to cause a schism within the Catholic Church but to reform the church. In fact, early Christians were not called by that name but as Nazarenes (Nazoreans), referring to themselves as "the way," "the poor ones," or "keepers of the light." They thought of themselves as Jewish and followers of Christ. At least until the time of John Chrysostom (fourth to early fifth century), many Christians continued to engage in Jewish worship rituals.

The Essenes were a fairly small, but perhaps widely dispersed, Jewish, but nonconformist, male, mainly celibate, religious order originating in the second century BC and lasting until the second century AD. What we know about them comes mainly from the Dead Sea Scrolls, discovered at Qumran in 1949. The Essenes regarded themselves as strict followers of the law of Moses, believed in the immortality of the soul, and probably at least at first practised ritual sacrifice, as evidenced by archeological remains, even though Philo Judaeus (Philo of Alexandria) said they did not. But perhaps he was referring to Essenes after the birth of Christ. They may well have fused with early Jewish Christianity, and some even say that they were led in the first century by James, brother of Jesus. Perhaps not surprisingly, there is evidence of Persian, but also of Hellenistic, influences in their doctrines. Certainly, they were deemed to be of a type from which primitive Christianity descended. Indeed, early church fathers claim that John the Baptist was an Essene who restricted his diet to locusts and honey, as a consequence of which locust beans (carob) are known as Saint John's bread. The Essenes were mentioned frequently in antiquity. According to Porphyry (*De abstinentia* 4.3) and Jerome (*Against Jovinianus* 2.14), they were vegetarian. The Jewish historiographer and military leader Flavius Josephus (*Antiquities* 15, 10.4) stated unequivocally, if not fully convincingly, at least if the traditional view of Pythagoras is the correct view, that the Essene and Pythagorean principles were identical. In fact, in general, the Essenes permitted themselves grasshoppers and fish, which, again, may not have been seen as fully animal. Likewise, the Nazoreans of Mount Carmel were a vegetarian or quasi-vegetarian Judeo-Christian brotherhood, closely related to the Essenes. According to the *Panarion* of Epiphanius, another Jewish sect, the Theraputae of Egypt, restricted its members' diet to bread, hyssop (a wild bush whose twigs were used in Jewish purificatory rites), salt, and water.[31] Like the Essenes, although of later origin, the Ebionites (literally, poor men) were a Judeo-Christian vegetarian sect that followed the Mosaic law. They also regarded Jesus as a virtuous man anointed by the spirit and, although the Messiah, not in fact divine.

Clearly, for the Jews, as later for the Christians, humankind is made in the image of God, and as a consequence, the interests of humankind trump those of the animal creation – but only where there is a conflict between human and nonhuman interests. Otherwise, the interests of the animal creation are entirely worthy as the interests of an inherently valuable part of God's creation. Nonetheless, there always was a clear conflict between the interests of animals as ends in themselves and the use of animals as creatures subservient to the overriding interests of humankind. Neither mainstream Jews nor later orthodox Christians were ever able to resolve the contradiction. The potential for ethical vegetarianism, inherently possible in light of the high regard for animals as entities with their own ends and purposes, was always subordinated to the dominant human interest in continuing to exploit the power of animals, to domesticate, and, we presume, to slaughter and eat animate beings, whose intrinsic value as a consequence of the many Judaic pronouncements was in principle inconsistent with their being employed as a part of the human diet. Thereafter, much of the history of the Western relationship to animals, beginning in the classical era, hangs on the same contradiction, with significant numbers lauding animals as inherently worthy creatures, ends in themselves no less, but continuing at the same time to enjoy them as a part of their supper or, at the very least, on festive occasions.

## EARLY CHRISTIAN PRACTICE

The *Panarion* by the Christian-despising Epiphanius and the pseudo-Clementine *Recognitions* and *Homilies* point to rigorous ethical vegetarian sects in early Christianity.[32] The apocryphal second-century *Acts of Andrew*, widely employed by Gnostic and heretical groups, claimed a connection between demons and flesh. As Stephen H. Webb has argued, apocryphal or not, "it demonstrates that the Christian revulsion against animal sacrifices" – the customary occasions of flesh consumption – "was widespread."[33] Clement of Alexandria called Christian communal meals *agapes* – literally love feasts – for being in essence "heavenly food," claiming that such meals "should not include the smell of roasting meat."[34] He recommended and adopted a strict regimen, but his idea of a nonflesh diet is instructive. He tells us "the Apostle Matthew lived upon seeds and nuts, and vegetables without the use of flesh." Yet he continues: "And John, who carried temperance to the extreme, 'ate locusts and wild honey.'" Locusts, then, did not appear to count as flesh. Neither, it would appear, did fish: "And the fish which, at the command of the Lord, Peter caught, points to digestible and God-given moderate [i.e., nonanimal flesh] food."[35] Clearly, the early Christian conception of a fleshless diet does not conform to modern conceptions of such a diet. "Animal" was not yet a scientific concept. Nor, evidently, was it for the Jews. The idea of a fleshless diet was one restricted to not eating mammals or birds.

Undoubtedly, there were a significant number of vegetarian or quasi-vegetarian groups within early Christianity. We have already seen the habits of the Essenes, who became Christian after their origin as Jews and, quite likely, without renouncing their Judaism. And we have also noticed the Ebionites. The relevant question is whether these groups practised vegetarianism or quasi-vegetarianism entirely as an ascetic matter of ritual purification or whether they were also ethical vegetarians who maintained their practice in part out of consideration for animals. So excellent an authority as Benedicta Ward, the finest of the commentators on the desert fathers, observed that "the aim of the monks' lives was not asceticism, but God, and the way to God was charity. The gentle charity of the desert was the pivot in all their work and the test of their way of life. Charity was to be total and complete."[36] By contrast, the widely read and eminently well-researched Colin Spencer takes the now customary view that early Christian vegetarianism was entirely ascetic, referring to the Essenes as beginning "the long tradition of asceticism that was to influence the early church fathers."[37] Not once does he mention an animal-ethical aspect of their vegetarianism. On what side does the preponderance of evidence fall?

Only rarely is the matter made explicit in the historical record. Thus interesting accounts could be read with either explanation. The following account, reflective of distinctions between the church hierarchy and the groundlings, is instructive as an example of a tale that could be interpreted either as ascetic or as ethical vegetarianism. Theophilus, who was Archbishop of Alexandria at the time Augustine was Archbishop of Hippo, relates the following story, Ward tells us: "As the monks were eating with [the archbishop], they were brought some veal for food and they ate it without realising what it was. The bishop, taking a piece of meat, offered it to the old man beside him, saying, 'Here is a nice piece of meat, abba, eat it.' But he replied, 'Till this moment we believed we were eating vegetables, but, if it is meat, we do not eat it.' None of them tasted any more of the meat which was brought."[38] In the long run, the flesh of the bishops outweighed the vegetables of the abbas in the development of Christian attitudes and practices.

Clearly, the grounds for the rejection of flesh could have been the sake of the slaughtered animals, or the purity of the monks, or both together. The following reflects the reality far more clearly. Saint Athanasius wrote of the desert-dwelling Saint Anthony that his food was "bread and salt, his drink only water. Of meat and wine it is needless to speak, for nothing of this sort was to be found among the other monks either" – hence the generality of the fleshless diet among the monks. And the grounds for the diet were not solely purity of spirit, for "the wild beasts kept peace with him," as enjoined by Job 5:23: "the beasts of the field shall be at peace with thee." When there was a drought Saint Anthony released his camel that it might seek for itself and survive. The inherent value of the camel outweighed Anthony's right of possession. "My book is nature," he is reported to have said, "and wherever I will, I can read the word of God."[39] There is surely at the very least an element of ethical vegetarianism in Anthony's denial of flesh and communion with the beasts. Even clearer is the story of Saint Jerome about Theon, one of the vegetarian monks of Egypt, whose "food was cooked on no fire. They said of him that at night he would go out to the desert, and for company a great troop of the beasts of the desert would go with him. And he would draw water from his well and offer them cups of it in return for their kindness in attending him. One evidence of this was plain to see, for the tracks of gazelle and goat and the wild ass were thick about his cell."[40] It was no mean feat of generosity to offer water from one's well in the desert! The stories were probably apocryphal, almost certainly exaggerated. No matter. Such stories of whatever tradition are prone to reflect more of the desirable than the real. The tale imparts what was thought an epitomizing attribute – the appropriate ethic – of the saintly person, and this included a respect for animals and an intimation of a closely felt ethical kinship.

The early Christian abbot Moses listed seven ethical principles, the fifth of which was: "A man ought to do no harm to any," as derived from Isaiah 11:9: "they shall not hurt nor destroy in all my holy mountain" – a doctrine very similar to the Jaina *ahimsa* (the principle of nonharm) and the Judaic *Bal Taschit* (do not destroy).[41] The patristic scholar and translator Helen Waddell wrote of the early seventh-century monk John Moschus, author of the *Pratum Spirituale*, that "he was a lover alike of man and beasts, and never weary of stories about the goodness and guilelessness of lions, and the wisdom of the little dog of the abbot Subena Syrorum."[42] Moschus told tales of Abba John the Eunuch, who "had more compassion than anybody we ever saw, not only for men but also for animals." An entirely ascetic portrait of early Christian vegetarianism misses a great deal of the wondrous affection that was evidently displayed. Nonetheless, asceticism was certainly present and in a manner that is scarcely conceivable to modern minds. Thus, for example, Saint Simon Stylites was a fourth-century monk to whose shrine near Antioch (the third city of the empire) many medieval, and some later, pilgrims made the journey of homage. The early-twentieth-century journalist and travel writer H.V. Morton remarked that Simeon "believed that only by the complete humiliation of his body could his soul set itself free and fit itself to contemplate God." To this end, he devised "all kinds of self-torture ... It was a world in revolt against materialism."[43] We should wonder not only at the infliction of self-flagellation but also at the surprising fact that for many centuries so many found the behaviour – which was not all that unusual for the time, we might add – as worthy of pilgrimage and hence veneration. But not even Stylites was entirely ascetic, at least if there is any truth to tradition. By legend, he is supposed to have cured a blind dragon, "dragon" being symbolic of a large and dangerous animal. Even if the story is untrue or, at the very least, an exaggeration, as surely it must be, it is important. That the story was worthy of being invented reflects that it was deemed admirable to respect and care for other species. Similarly, Saint Macarius was renowned for being gentler with a blind hyena kitten than with his own kind. In the instances of both Simeon Stylites and Macarius, it is not at all unreasonable to infer that their belief in kindness to animals lay behind the development of the vegetarian traditions.

There were numerous philosophers and theologians – as though there was much of a difference in those days! – as well as common or garden commentators in the early Christian era who subscribed, usually literally and sometimes figuratively, to the idea of the Golden Age as the requisite standard to be achieved or a past paradise no longer recoverable because of man's original sin. In such images the primitive state was always superior to the fallen state, and the vegetarian practices always superior to the present age of flesh consumption. Many idealized the vegetarian lifestyle, but we do not know whether many of them, other than some monks, practised it. Probably precious few. Among the glorifiers of primitivism, we find the heretics Tertullian and Novation, as well as Philo Judaeus (or Philo of Alexandria) – a Jewish thinker, the most significant before Moses Maimonides – who developed a sophisticated form of the doctrine and who had a significant influence on Christian theology in general through his development of the idea of the scriptures as allegory.[44] Saint Jerome (c. 347-420) practised regular fleshless fasting, which he believed was a temporary return to paradise. He was not otherwise a vegetarian, although he remarked that at Christ's resurrection we would all cease to be flesh eaters. The reason that the prospects for vegetarianism within orthodox Christianity were slim is perhaps explained by Saint Paul's edict to Timothy (1 Timothy 4), where Paul refers to the "doctrines of the devil" (verse 1), which included "commanding to abstain from meats" (verse 3) not because such abstention is a wrong in itself but because such rigid requirements would detract from the primary Christian duty – the quest for salvation. A general vegetarian requirement would diminish the likelihood of Christian conversion.

Helen Waddell translated forty charming stories from Latin in a delightful little book entitled *Beasts and Saints* (1934) about what she called "the mutual charities" between man and beast in the early Middle Ages. Waddell depicted a world alive with interspecies respect among the desert fathers, the saints of the West, and the saints of Ireland. The task is to relate these "mutual charities" to vegetarian practices beyond those of the desert fathers. An inviting candidate is the Scottish and Irish Culdeans (or Kildeans), as they were popularly called, a monastic order founded in the fifth century AD. They were ascetic monks with vegetarian practices. In a report on the monastics, we read that they ate "cooked vegetables, seasoned only with salt. Never did they eat flesh or fish, nor did they permit cheese or butter, except on Sundays and feast days."[45] One assumes it is the cheese and butter allowed on the special days. "They were true monks," we are told further, "imitating the monks of Egypt [the desert fathers] and leading a life like theirs." George Boas claims their practice to have been "in reality more like that of the Essenes."[46] His report continues: "They had not a single ox or other animal for cultivating their fields, or for doing any work whatever, for each was ox or horse for working."[47] To be sure, "the little old abbot had a pony for travelling and a few cows for milk." They also kept a few sheep for wool. In part, the dispensation of the animals and their labour was in practice an early acclamation of the dignity of labour, almost unknown in this period of the early Middle Ages. But in part it was to save the animals from having to labour on behalf of humans. Although the evidence of their ethical vegetarianism is not incontrovertible – as usual for this early medieval period, the records are inadequate for absolute confidence – it is nonetheless quite persuasive. If purity of soul was the primary purpose of vegetarianism, the evidence suggests a significant concern for the animals as well.

It is significant both that many, if decreasingly fewer, of the monasteries were vegetarian, although not generally for ethical reasons, and that most of the saints, if not ultimately the most influential of them, were known for their protection of animals. Rev. Andrew Linzey has estimated that more than two-thirds of the medieval saints demonstrated "a practical concern for, and befriending of, animals."[48] Another theologian, Stephen H. Webb, has confirmed that "one of the criteria for sainthood seems to be the compassionate treatment of animals."[49] Again, many stories of the saints may be apocryphal or exaggerated. But they demonstrate both how saintly persons were perceived and the ethic they were expected to pursue.

Not all the stories were undocumented myths, however. Thus, for example, the Abbot of Spoleto, Saint Isaac the Syrian, who died around 700 AD, said:

> What is a charitable heart? It is a heart which is burning with love for the whole creation, for men, for the birds, for beasts ... for all creatures. He who has such a heart cannot see or call to mind a creature without his eyes being filled to tears by reason of the immense compassion which seizes his heart; a heart which is softened and can no longer bear to see or learn from others of any suffering, even the smallest pain being inflicted upon a creature. That is why such a man never ceases to pray for the animals ... [He is] moved by the infinite pity which reigns in the hearts of those who are becoming united with God.[50]

If this is in any degree an exemplification of the feelings of the vegetarian monks, we can feel confident theirs was an ethical, not merely an ascetic, vegetarianism.

There were certainly in these years examples of a broader Christian respect for animals. Thus, for instance, Saint Basil (c. 329-379), Bishop of Caesarea, reminded his audience of Psalm 36:6 in saying God "has promised to save both man and beast." Moreover, the animals "live not for us alone, but for themselves and for God."[51] Basil writes of "a sense of fellowship with all living things, with our brothers the animals ... to whom [God] hast given the earth as their home in common with us."[52] The prolific Saint John Chrysostom (c. 347-407) – Howard Williams tells us he wrote 700 homilies, orations, doctrinal treatises, and epistles – was Archbishop of Constantinople until he was deposed and exiled.[53] He observed: "Surely, we ought to show [other species] great kindness and gentleness for many reasons, but above all because they are of the same origin as ourselves."[54] He was himself for a while a vegetarian, at least for his four years spent in a monastery, but probably returned to flesh to pursue his career in the ecclesiastical hierarchy. Still, he praised the abstinent monks their diet: "no streams of blood are among them; no butchering and cutting up of flesh; no dainty cookery; no heaviness of head. Nor are there horrible smells of flesh meats among them or disagreeable fumes from the kitchen."[55] The idea of a *purely* ascetic Christian tradition that did not care for animals is without merit.

## GNOSTICS

There was not always a clear distinction between the orthodox and the Gnostics, many of the latter continuing to worship in the churches of the former, and many of the former coming perilously close in their thinking to the heresies of the latter, as well as some, such as Tertullian, who became a Montanist, being respectably orthodox for much of their lives but discovering something in late maturity they had come to regard as absent from the customary worship and practice. Tertullian tells us: "So great is the privilege of a circumscribed diet that it makes God a dweller with men, and, indeed, to live on equal terms with them."[56] The purpose of the diet is thus to achieve union with the deity. Valentinus (c. 125 to c. 160), often considered the first and greatest of the Gnostics, approaches the esoteric essence when he teaches that ultimate reality is a procession of aeons! God was knowable only gnostically as the being beyond all concepts of God. Knowledge of God, in other words, came from an essentially mysterious, spiritually motivated intuition. And the state in which this intuition could be achieved was thought to come in significant part from a fleshless diet.

Having the source of their ideas in Jewish mysticism, Hellenistic mystery cults, and Egyptian, Babylonian, and Persian mythology, the Christian Gnostics – and there were many other Gnostic cults in many of the religions of the region – came to the fore in the second century AD, promising salvation through occult knowledge that they, the privileged, alone possessed. In general, the cults held to a dualistic conflict between good and evil, spirit and flesh. Humanity's salvation was to be achieved through the divine spark of spirit and the abomination of all matter and flesh. The adherent's life was to be spent in the glorification of the one and the utter rejection of the other. The later development of the high-medieval Jewish Kaballah, which so influenced Robert Fludd and John Milton in the seventeenth century, found its spiritual impetus in Christian Gnosticism and Catharism.[57]

Although these Gnostic sects were vegetarian in the main, this vegetarianism had very little, if anything at all, to do with a concern for the lives of the animals from whom the Gnostic sects abstained. The Gnostics were not, at least in this respect, legitimate descendants of the desert fathers.

Three examples should suffice. Novation was a third-century schismatic who, on the grounds of the failure of the traditional church to maintain appropriately rigorous religious standards – that is, with respect to human worship – opposed the election of Saint Cornelius as pope and declared himself pope in his stead. He claimed the original diet of humankind was restricted not merely to nonflesh food but also to the fruit of the trees. It was the commission of sin that cast the eyes down to the ground for sustenance. Humans were creatures who had an upright posture and, accordingly, were not meant by nature to find their sustenance on the ground.

They were thus unlike other animals. Accordingly, as with some later fruitarians, Novation thought even the eating of grains did not belong to the natural human diet. It was with the introduction of toil after the Fall that the concession to eat flesh was granted so that the strength necessary for husbandry would be acquired.[58] Now it was time to return to the vegetarian past. There was no indication in his writings that the interests of animals were to be considered.

Marcion (c. 85 to c. 160) was an early Christian bishop who founded the Marcionites, one of the first major professions of heresy to rival the Catholic Church. He claimed there to be two gods in conflict: the stern Hebrew deity and the compassionate, merciful God of the New Testament. "Nature" – as the physical world, including the animal realm – far from being an indicator of the just, was the work of the evil god and the enemy of the Christian God. Thus, for the Marcionites, even sex was an abomination as that which would further the existence of the material world. The animals, even more "natural" than humans, were, George Boas tells us, "objects of contempt to the Marcionites."[59]

The Montanists were founded by Montanus of Phrygia (fl. AD 170) and were strict ascetics, encouraging ecstatic prophesying and believing the day of judgment was at hand. The Montanists and Marcionites shared the belief that their Eucharist should consist of milk and honey to recreate the Edenic vision of Exodus 3:8, in which God came "to bring them ... to a country rich and broad, to a country flowing with milk and honey." Milk was symbolically opposed to blood, and honey was seen as a foretaste of heaven.[60] The Montanists' most famous convert was Tertullian, but even though the movement died as a viable sect in the third century, the vegetarian Cathars and Emanuel Swedenborg were influenced at a much later date by their anti-intellectualism. Tertullian (c. 160 to c. 230) left the Catholic Church in 213 to join the Montanists because of their more rigorous theology and practical ethics, although animals were not included in the ethics. His saving grace was that he believed animals possessed immortal souls. And unlike many Gnostics, he did not despise Nature in principle but avowed that "the innocence and purity of nature being restored, animals shall live in harmony with each other, and infants will play without harm with animals once ferocious"[61] – presumably a reference to Isaiah 11:6-8 and the peaceable kingdom to be introduced after the redemption. However, he shows no concern for animals as they are here and now before the new Eden has been created. It is, indeed, difficult to find even a remnant of an animal ethic among the Gnostics, even though they were almost all vegetarian. The asceticism of the Gnostics seems to have differed substantially from the animal respect displayed by the earliest Christian fathers and can be viewed as an instance of Christianity turning away from its early respect for the animal creation.

## MANICHEANS

Early in the third century AD, Mani, or Manes (c. 216-276), the founder of Manicheism – "a belief in the inherent evil of all matter"[62] – broke away from the Gnostic sect, the Elchasaites, to which his father, Patik, had been converted and which had been instrumental in developing Mani's early religious and philosophical thoughts. The Elchasaites were an anti-Pauline, Jewish-Christian, vegetarian sect whose members thought of themselves as strict followers of the Mosaic law. The sect inhabited Persia, where the semiofficial religion was Zoroastrianism. By the time he was twenty, Mani was developing a strictly dualist system of thought in which, in common with the now customary Gnostic division, everything emanating from the body was evil in nature, whereas that emanating from the spirit was heavenly. He derived much of this doctrine from the earlier Gnostics, especially the Marcionites, even if the debt was never acknowledged. Although the division between mind and body was strict and although sex was cast out along with flesh, Mani's rejection of the body was not as rigid as that of other Gnostics.

In Mani's view, the world was divided into the people of darkness and the people of light. It was humankind's heavenly task to promote the Spirit of Light and abominate the Spirit of Darkness. In line with Marcionite doctrine, animals belonged to the kingdom of darkness, a view also expressed in the Hindu *Laws of Manu*. One might have expected the proximity to the Zoroastrians and their incipient concern for animals in their own selves to have influenced the Manicheans, but this would appear not at all to have been the case. After considerable, even violent, opposition to what the Elchasaites saw as arrogance and sloth – Mani thought fruit and vegetables should be received as alms, not collected, a practice reminiscent of Buddhism – a few, including Patik, came to regard Mani as the true prophet of God, and thus the Manichean religion was born.

Blasphemous speech, the consumption of all flesh, the practice of sex, and the drinking of wine were forbidden, but the sole reason for each appears to have been the purity of the spirit. Reminiscent of the Pythagoreans, the Manicheans were divided into the elect and the hearers. For the latter, the rules were less strict – without some laxity the propagation of the species, or at least sect, would have been in peril. The hearers were allowed to marry, eat flesh, and possess property, all forbidden to the elect. The Manicheans also adopted the doctrine of the transmigration of souls, perhaps from contact with neighbouring India. Simply from proximity, Indian ideas are likely to have had greater influence in Persia than elsewhere in the region. To the contrary, however, it is possible that the doctrine began in the Middle East and spread from there to India. Or of course, the idea could have developed in more than one place at the same time, not at all a rare occurrence in cultural history. With animals belonging to the kingdom of darkness for the Manicheans, once and for all the idea that transmigration of souls implies human-animal kinship and that kinship necessarily implies a respect for animals should be forever dismissed.

After Mani died from torture by the Zoroastrian Sassanians in 276 while on a mission of conversion, the Manicheans did not wither away but appear to have prospered, if the continued opposition to their effective proselytizing is a measure. In Rome at the beginning of the fourth century the emperor Diocletian warned of the threat from the Manicheans. He followed this by persecuting the Manicheans as well as more orthodox Christians. Later in the century Timothy, the patriarch of Alexandria, felt orthodox Christianity sufficiently threatened by Manicheanism that he required the meals of his clergy and monks be inspected regularly to check whether the supposedly devout were eating their customary flesh diet or a Manichean fleshless diet. The emperor Theodosius banned the Manicheans in 381. Later, Manicheism spread as far as China, where it appears to have flourished, although always in a minority, until the fourteenth century, and a few groups appear to have survived until the beginning of the sixteenth century, after which they were heard from no more.

Eventually, within Christendom, the name "Manichean" became in effect a synonym for almost every kind of heresy and, for centuries, was a term of abuse within mainstream Christianity. Both the Manicheans and the desert fathers were competing symbols in Rome of the simple and abstemious life, vying with each other to persuade many to adopt a vegetarian lifestyle. For a time, each had some successes. In rather longer time, neither prevailed. Catholic orthodoxy remained a fleshy orthodoxy.

## THE AUGUSTINIAN REACTION

In *Of the Morals of the Catholic Church*, Saint Augustine, Bishop of Hippo, indicated that, among Christians, vegetarians were "without number."[63] The fact appalled him, and he helped to establish the orientation of the

Catholic Church thereafter with regard to flesh. He clearly recognized there were ethical aspects to vegetarianism, claiming in *The City of God*: "We do not apply 'Thou shalt not kill' to plants, because they have no sensation; or to irrational animals that fly, swim, walk, or creep because they are linked to us by no association or common bond. By the Creator's wise ordinance" – it was of course no ordinance at all but a permission granted, as we have seen, in special circumstances – "they are meant for our use, dead or alive. It only remains for us to apply the commandment 'thou shalt not kill' to man alone, to oneself and others."[64] There was an ethical responsibility to fellow humans but none to fellow creatures of other species, which, he implied, some of his vegetarian opponents affirmed.

Augustine's defence of flesh eating has both Aristotelian and Stoic philosophical elements. It also appears to be born of his formerly having been a Manichean hearer. Desiring to demonstrate his own rejection of his former Gnostic adherence and to assert at the same time his refound Catholic purity, his reasoning involves an element of rationalization. If the ground on which we are entitled to kill plants is that "they have no sensation," one is entitled to wonder why the sensation criterion does not apply to animals as well as to plants but, of course, with the opposite consequences. Moreover, since animals "die in pain," as Augustine acknowledges, even if animals "are meant for our use, dead or alive," one is led to wonder why "man disregards this in a beast." The only possible answer, for Augustine, is that a being must have *both* sentience *and* the kind of reason possessed by humans – which of course, for Augustine, meant, tautologically, that the kind of reason possessed by humans only humans have! – if it is entitled not to be harmed, killed, and eaten. Humans win and animals lose – a predetermined victory and defeat occasioned by the arbitrary selection of a category only humans are deemed a priori to possess! Augustine had set the stage for the flesh-eating victory within Christendom for centuries to come against both the Gnostic and ethical considerations that had been advanced and remained effective, although in decline and never dominant, up until this time. But as we shall see, it was not quite a total victory, even if the apparently fairly wide practice of vegetarianism prior to the Council of Gangra in the fourth century was never to return. That there were reservations is expressed in the Easter 2007 view of Pope Benedict XVI that the Passover was probably celebrated without a sacrificial lamb.

# 6

# Bogomils, Cathars, and the
# Later Medieval Mind

## Bogomils

If laic vegetarianism was moribund in the Catholic Church from the very early medieval period, it raised its head elsewhere within Christianity. From the sixth century through the remainder of the medieval period, Howard Williams tells us in *The Ethics of Diet:* "The merits of monastic asceticism were more or less preached during all these ages, although consistent abstinence from flesh was by no means the general practice even with the inmates of the stricter monastic or conventional establishments – at all events in the Latin Church. But we look in vain for anything like the humanitarian feeling of Plutarch or Porphyry."[1] Indeed, we find an ascetic vegetarianism from at the very least the eighth to fifteenth centuries, one beyond the confines of the monasteries, but as Williams indicates, there was no return to the respect for animals found in these Greco-Roman vegetarians or, for that matter, found in the Christian ethical vegetarianism of the desert fathers.

The Roman Empire in the West was formally ended by the defeat at the palace of Soissons in 627. This was the titular collapse of civilization that led in the West if not to the Dark Ages, as they were once commonly called, at least to the temporary but long-lived decline in the yearning for learning and effective administration, an overwhelming concern to eradicate heresy – perhaps more as a matter of power and control than of doctrine – and continuous conflicts between church and state, except when their interests coincided. Among those who had been declared heretical were the Paulicians

– so called, it would appear, from their perhaps single-minded devotion concentrated on the Pauline Epistles. In the eighth century they were exiled from Armenia to Thrace. A Syrian branch was deported in the tenth century to the Balkans by the Byzantine emperor Basil I, where they are said to have combined with the Bogomils.

In line with the Marcionites, the Paulicians were dualist, believing that the Old Testament God created matter, which was evil, and that the God of Christ was the author of spirit, which was good and was the nature of life to come. Thus, like the Marcionites and other Gnostics, they castigated animal life as the life of the flesh. They were sometimes deemed Manichean – by now the customary term of heretical abuse – as were the Bogomils and Cathars. Nonetheless, the record is silent on their abstention from flesh, although their joining with the Bogomils is a likely enough indication of at least a measure of it. The influence of the Paulicians on the Bogomils seems fairly certain. The medieval historian and expert on medieval heresy Malcolm Lambert states that: "At some stage ... the Bogomils underwent some Paulician influence: this affected their understanding of their history and gave them a tradition which linked them to the early Christian centuries. Paulicians as individual converts to Bogomilism carried over something of their history, traditions and texts; they may also have influenced their hosts in the direction of radical dualist beliefs."[2]

Whereas the author of *The Yellow Cross: The Story of the Last Cathars' Rebellion against the Inquisition*, René Weis, deems the Cathars and their ilk Manichee – "the pedigree of this dualist, Manichean heresy reaches back at least to the eleventh century" – Lambert, who authored *The Cathars*, describes, to the contrary, the doctrine "so often labelled Manichee" as having "nothing to do with Mani and his movement, which had long died out in Western Europe. The [Bogomils and Cathars] were not the endpoint of a line of ancient heresy: their roots lie in the religious and social history of their own age. They were individualistic, *sui generis*, sporadic, the fruit of particular circumstances, coteries, isolated leaders."[3] Perhaps the discrepancy between Weis's and Lambert's accounts is to be explained by the fact one is thinking of sharing certain aspects of a doctrine and of the labelling of the sects by the orthodox, whereas the other is thinking of the causes and immediate antecedents of the professors of the heresy. Justified or not – and, strictly speaking, probably not – the term Manichean continued to be employed as a description of the Bogomils and Cathars.

Peter, tsar of Bulgaria, wrote to Theophylact, the Patriarch of Constantinople, some time in the middle of the tenth century, describing "an ancient and newly appeared heresy ... Manicheanism with Paulicianism."[4]

He was referring to the Messalians (or Massalians), who were not in fact new but had been around in Bulgaria for a century or so. They were sometimes called "enthusiasts" or "corentes" because of the agitations they received from the holy spirit – rather like the Quakers of a later period. Epiphanius thought these heretics first arose in the time of Emperor Constans (earlier fourth century), whereas Theodoret, friend of Nestorius, dated the origins to the time of Emperor Valentian (later fourth century). Whatever the origins, the adherents prayed frequently, almost incessantly, and were successful in their proselytizing, having spread throughout Asia Minor by the fifth century. The orthodox also claimed "they taught Manichean impieties," and these ideas, they said, were then the source of some of the doctrines of the Bogomil sect.

It is rumoured of the Messalians that they practised sexual libertinism and also that they enjoyed the worldly pleasures of wine and flesh after completing the requisite three-year abstention. If so, and it is to be doubted given that slander of the practices of one's adversaries was commonplace, it was not this libertinism the Bogomils inherited. At least not at first. Toward the very end of the Bogomil era, they too were tarnished with the libertine brush by their persecutors.

As with much of the history we have encountered to date, the record of the Bogomils is a great deal less than complete. It is said they were founded by an uneducated Bulgarian village priest, named Theophilus or Bogomil – meaning beloved of God – about the beginning of the tenth century on the basis of Paulician and *perhaps* some Messalian influences. What we know beyond these bare likelihoods is that, around the turn of the first millennium, a certain monk, Basil by name, came from Macedonia to Constantinople to preach the Bogomil heresy. He was arrested, imprisoned, and burned at the stake, along with other Bogomil leaders. However, the Bogomils not only survived but, at least for some considerable time, appear to have also flourished in Bulgaria. Perhaps because they prayed eight times a day! As previously noted, the Bogomils were strictly dualist. They adopted the Marcionite-Paulician doctrine that the bad God of the Old Testament had created matter, the good God of the New Testament having created spirit. Even to touch flesh was to obey the command of Satan. Animals lacked the divine spark that infused humans and were thus an entirely diabolical product. Likewise, wine was condemned. However, the success of the sect was predicated perhaps more on its political than on its doctrinal appeals. The movement was intensely nationalistic, reflecting and profiting from resentment of Byzantine power and culture as well as the suffering of Slavic serfdom.

In the West the Bogomils extended their influence into Serbia, where they managed to convince the king to adopt Bogomilism as the state religion. The king brought some ten thousand of his subjects, it is said, into the religion with him. The papacy and neighbouring monarchies eventually combined to convince the king, Ban Kulin, by show of arms to return to the Catholic fold. Still, against all odds, the heresy persisted, and still it was fought from Rome. Eventually, by the second half of the fifteenth century, the forces of Islam invaded. Shortly thereafter, the victorious Turkish sultan allowed the nobility its land and privileges, provided they adopt the Islamic faith. In a matter of months Bogomilism perished forever in the Balkans, but a different form of a similar heresy, the Cathar heresy, had by then flourished in, and perhaps departed to, parts of southern France and Italy, reaching both Britain and Germany.

## Cathars

Although it is unknown whether there was any causal connection between the Bogomil and Cathar faiths, there seems to be no probability of such a connection. We are not even entirely sure which came first, even though, on balance, the evidence seems to point to the Bogomils – we first hear of the Cathars at the beginning of the eleventh century. Whatever the causal relationship, Lambert describes "striking likenesses between Eastern Bogomolism and Western Catharism, especially in their ritual practices and their attitudes towards the beliefs, order and ritual of the great churches against which they struggled and protested."[5] He adds that "powerful as it is, all our evidence of a link between Bogomilism and Catharism before 1143 is inferential, based on likenesses between ritual, diet, religious practices and doctrines."[6] The movement rejected traditional baptism, the cross as an appropriate symbol, marriage, and the eating of flesh. In general, the Cathars, at least the perfect, or elect, eschewed all flesh and even milk, for they were born of coition, and every form of food associated with animal fat. Eggs were also forbidden. They permitted themselves fish because the creation of fish in water was deemed somehow to escape the pollution of animal coition. They opposed the killing of all forms of animal life, fish excluded, because, again, that would involve them in the world of the flesh. The acceptability of fish as a nonflesh item is reminiscent of the earliest Christian "vegetarian" practices and perhaps derives in some measure from Cathar understanding of those original practices. Unlike the Bogomils, they did not reject wine, except during their frequent fasting periods.

The sect was divided into the perfect and the *credentes,* a division not unlike in the Pythagorean and Manichean practices. Whereas the prohibitions against the perfect were fairly strict, those against the *credentes* were far more lax. The *credentes* were permitted all forms of flesh. The perfect sullied flesh dishes, gravy and stew in particular, with the derogatory term *feresa* – in effect, meaning deadly, namely to one's heavenly ambitions.

The complexities of the diet, the desire for absolute purity, the menial relationship of the *credentes* to the perfect, and the effect of constant persecution are expressed in informative detail by the *credens* Pierre Maury in his account of a supper on the night of 17 June 1307 at an inn in Laroque d'Olmes in the modern-day *département* of Ariège in the South Pyrenees region:

> And since at the inn conger was already being cooked in another pot, when we wanted to cook ours separately in the newly purchased one, the hostess of the inn told us not to run up such an expense, but rather cook up all the conger together in one. Bernard replied that she should not worry about the expense, because she would be well paid for the fire. Because there were many pots with meat on the hearth, Bernard and I were anxious to ensure that no *feresa*, that is meat or gravy from the meat, should enter our pot; even though our pot was covered, we still stayed close to it until the fish were cooked.
>
> During the time the Perfect slept Bernard and I were about to sit down at the table when the Perfect advised us to buy eggs for two pennies and put them in front of us on the table, to ensure that our diet would not betray us as a heretical party. We bought the eggs. Then after Bernard had prepared a dish of fish and fish broth for the Perfect, he lifted the [remaining] fish out of the pot, and he and I broke the eggs into it. Then Bernard and I ate the eggs as well as the fish, but the Perfect did not eat eggs, but only fish and broth ... Our bill was paid by myself and Bernard Bélibaste, and between us we spent that day about four shillings.[7]

The ritual was pure, but there is absolutely no evidence that the well-being of animals was given any consideration. Indeed, Cathar vegetarianism seems, like Gnostic vegetarianism, to have been totally ascetic.

By the time of the meal at Laroque d'Olmes, the Cathar heresy had long been under strenuous proscription – hence the considerable care at the inn that the creed be neither suspected nor discovered. The Albigensian Crusade against the Cathars had begun in 1209 but had been reinforced by the institution of the Inquisition in 1232. In 1243 a force of some 10,000 French troops besieged the primary Cathar stronghold of Montségur, which finally surrendered in March 1244, although some of the Cathar faithful escaped and continued to practise their religion in the Languedoc area of France. At least two hundred were burned to death following the surrender. By the fifteenth century Catharism was finally destroyed by the efforts of the Catholic Church with the aid of monarchs willing to stamp out heresy.

## THE LATER MEDIEVAL MIND: FROM THE BESTIARIES TO DIVES ET PAUPER

Although the European Middle Ages witnessed little vegetarianism outside the "enthusiasm" of heretical sects and the more modest asceticism of the occasional monasteries and nunneries, we can recognize in these times hints of the resurrection of the animal sensibilities that are a prerequisite of ethical vegetarianism. Among the most striking of new mediaeval appearances were the bestiaries. It has become customary to regard the bestiaries as a mere means of socialization, in which the animals are no more than characters on the stage playing their moralizing roles for the edification of the audience. But as Ron Baxter has shown in *Bestiaries and Their Uses in the Middle Ages,* if that is how bestiaries began, editions produced in the later part of the medieval era showed a decided interest in animals for their own sake: "they made it more of a reference book and less of a lecture script."[8] Europeans were beginning to think *about* animals rather than merely *through* them. And although the religious hermit Richard Rolle of Hampole's fourteenth-century "The Nature of the Bee" is still dependent on ethological inaccuracies derived from Aristotle and is still largely concerned with demonstrating the animals' role as no more than a lesson for our moral behaviour, it is difficult to read the essay without recognizing an authentic respect for the birds and bees of the story.[9]

In fact, a respect for animals appears to have been emerging among some of the more notable figures of the time. For example, John of Salisbury (1110-1180), biographer of Thomas à Beckett and writer on government, criticized the aristocratic practices of his day, pointing out in his *De nugis curialium* (Trifles of the Court) how hunting demeaned humanity but also expressing some sympathy for the victims as well.[10] Walter Map (c. 1140-1209), archdeacon of Oxford, states in a book of the same name as that written by Salisbury how courtly life has degenerated humanity's nature, whereas the animals have maintained the grace first given them.[11] But this pales against the statement of Richard de Wyche (c. 1197 to c. 1253), Bishop of Chichester, who said of the farm animals: "Poor, innocent little creatures: if you were reasoning beings and could speak you would curse us. For we are the cause of your death, and what have you done to deserve it?"[12] We have already mentioned the numerous saints who received their sainthood through consideration for the wellbeing of animals. In addition, there is Brigit of Sweden, who urged compassion on animals, and the Franciscan Bernardine of Siena, who preached the moral superiority of animals.[13] Together, they served to raise the status of animals in general. In fact, animal respect was growing in the established church, at least among the less orthodox laity, whereas ascetic vegetarianism was the province of the heretical sects. Ironically, respect for animals and vegetarianism in these Middle Age centuries developed in entirely antithetical ways. Those who learned a serious measure of respect and affection for the animals continued to eat them, whereas those who forbore to eat them failed to respect them at all. Indeed, the vegetarians deemed animals to be of the world of Satan!

Almost all the medieval legends have animals as heroes, from the horse Bayard in the *Legends of Charlemagne* to the horse Bucephalus in the *Legends of Alexander the Great,* from King Arthur's animal helpers in the *Mabinogian* to the birds of *Parzival* – and many more besides. In the fifteenth-century poem *Piers the Ploughman,* by William Langland, we can read: "Yet the thing that moved me most, and changed my way of thinking, was that Reason ruled and cared for all the beasts, except only for man and his mate, for many a time they wandered ungoverned by Reason."[14] It is the portent of a new era of respect to which Langland is pointing the way.

What should perhaps puzzle us most about the lack of consequent ethical vegetarianism upon the frequent recognition of animal worth in the Middle Ages is the enigmatic case of Saint Francis of Assisi. Francis admonished his flock, informing them that "all the creatures under heaven, each according to his nature, serve, know and obey their Creator better than you."[15] Both Thomas of Celano and Saint Bonaventure, the earliest of the Franciscan biographers, described Francis as a benevolent friend to the animals. Francis's first biographer, Celano, described him as a man of "very great fervor and great tenderness towards lower and irrational creatures ... he called all creatures *brother,* and in a most extraordinary manner, a manner never experienced by others, he discerned the hidden things of nature with his sensitive heart."[16] Francis's disciple Saint Bonaventure tells us that "when he considered the primordial source of all beings, he was filled with even more piety, calling creatures, no matter how small, by the name of brother or sister, because he knew they had the same source as himself."[17] Wondrous tales are told of Francis's relations with, and experience with, all manner of animal life. Yet neither biographer suggests Francis to have been a vegetarian, either of the ascetic or ethical strain. If he had been an ethical

vegetarian, it would have been a matter of astonishment, would surely have
been mentioned by Bonaventure and Celano, and would have been looked
at askance by the ecclesiastical authorities. If he had been an ascetic vegetarian, such vegetarianism would have surely been a requirement of Francis's order. But as Michael Allen Fox says in referring to the medieval saints,
"whose kindness to animals is legendary": "Saint Francis of Assisi (1181-
1226) is merely the most celebrated of these ... Yet Saint Francis did not
compel his followers to adhere to a vegetarian diet, nor is such a rule part
of the Franciscan order today."[18] To be sure, it is worthy of note that the
Poor Clares, the female equivalent to the Franciscan Order, founded by
Saint Clare of Assisi (1193?-1253), have been vegetarian for centuries: "meat
may not be used, even on Christmas." Yet even here the reasoning is almost
entirely ascetic. Perhaps it is also worth mentioning that the Franciscans
abjure flesh on feast days – as many as two hundred in a year at one time.
But that leaves well over a hundred days of feasting on flesh! Perhaps we
might also note that Amerindians also call animals "brother" and that all
Native tribes have traditionally been omnivorous. If we find Saint Francis
enigmatic, the enigma belongs no less to those of other cultures. Calling
animals "brother" as an expression of kinship does little to save the animals
from unnatural and early deaths.

The essay of the Middle Ages that by far most clearly announces the evil
of cruelty to animals is a moral treatise of the late fourteenth century, certainly no later than 1410, entitled *Dives et Pauper*. Keith Thomas has said of
it that "it is a notable passage and a very embarrassing one to anybody trying to trace some development in English thinking about animal cruelty.
For here at the very beginning of the fifteenth century we have a clear statement of a position which differs in no respect whatsoever from that of most
eighteenth-century writers on the subject."[19] The title means "the wealthy
and the ordinary" because, as Henry Chadwick points out, "*pauper* means a
person of modest means rather than someone without food, roof, or clothing; Ovid defined him as 'a man who knows how many sheep he owns.'"[20]
The passage from *Dives et Pauper* on the Ten Commandments reads:

When God forbade man to eat flesh, he forbade him to slay the beasts in any
cruel way, or out of any liking for shrewness. Therefore, He said, "Eat ye no
flesh with blood (Gen IX), that is to say with cruelty for I shall seek the blood
of your souls at the hands of all beasts." "That is to say, I shall take vengeance
for all the beasts that are slain out of cruelty of soul and a liking for shrewness." For God that make all hath care of all, and He will take vengeance
upon all that misuse his creatures. Therefore, Solomon saith, "that he will

arm creatures in vengeance on their enemies" (Sap. V); and so men should have thought for birds and beasts and not harm them without cause, in taking regard they are God's creatures. Therefore, they that out of cruelty and vanity behead beasts, and torment beasts or fowl, more than is proper for men's living, they sin in case full grievously.[21]

This may not be good biblical exegesis. But the moral message is impressive, even if it does not lead toward vegetarianism. Killing animals for requisite food is acceptable — it is not "without cause" — but no gratuitous harm is to be tolerated. Certainly, it is a tremendous ethical step in advance on the vegetarian Cathars, but the food animals did not prosper therefrom.

If, as the evidence suggests, there was a professed general sentiment in favour of the interests of the animals present in the minds and, by repute, in the actions of many individuals in the medieval era, why did this sentiment and these actions have almost no influence in persuading the populace to adopt a vegetarian diet on ethical grounds? After all, it would seem incongruous to profess respect, admiration, and affection for animals and then to consume their bodies, although it must be stressed that many were deprived of the opportunity to eat flesh more than very occasionally by their poverty or were prevented from obtaining flesh foods by the power of the nobility, who kept the flesh produce for themselves. Still, this deprivation must not be exaggerated, as we saw in the apparent abundance expressed in the flesh pots of the hostelry at Laroque d'Olmes.

Why, then, were animals eaten? In the first instance, through acculturation. If all of one's family, friends, and acquaintances apparently consider animals an appropriate nature- or God-given and necessary food product, and if, as they do, people desire a connection to and acceptance by their families, associates, and communities, they will find it hard to conceive that the general opinions of the group are unethical. Initially, the group is, for most people, the very *source* of moral and acceptable opinions, and these are later buttressed by the wider authority of church and state, which both help to establish and then to reinforce the customary opinions of the community. Moreover, at that time it would have been very difficult in Europe to maintain health on a year-round vegetarian diet without significantly greater nutritional knowledge than was available.

In the second instance, it is the oppressive force of power that is effective. As Lord Acton said wisely, all power tends to corrupt and absolute power corrupts absolutely. Thus, if there is no legitimate authority or devoutly believed doctrine that interferes with the exercise of power, then the power possessed by humans to treat many animals as appropriate foodstuff will have its way. If people are not constrained to act otherwise, our pre-dilections will not permit our sensibilities to interfere with our selfish power. For the vast majority in the Middle Ages, the legitimate authority in social matters, and hence power in those matters, was the church. Most accepted as a matter beyond question that the authority of the church was granted by God and was thus unassailable. And God had "ordained" the eating of flesh. To maintain its authority, and hence power, the church felt constrained to oppose all forms of organization and doctrine that threatened its omnipotence. Whatever did not conform with its interests was heresy. The most significant form of heresy seemed always to include a doctrine that rejected the eating of flesh foods. Thus, more than ever, the church was not only coerced by force of circumstance to regard the eating of flesh as proper and normal, and the rejection of the eating of flesh as intrinsically heretical, but also came frequently to regard flesh eating itself as a mark of normality and hence acceptability. Thus a commonly professed respect and consideration for animals persisted incongruently, if not outright contradictorily, alongside a continuation to consume animals. This strange ambivalence was to continue into posterity. No one did more to state the medieval church's attitude to these matters more effectively and influentially than Saint Thomas Aquinas, the prime representative of Catholic orthodoxy in the late Middle Ages. Notoriously, Aquinas followed Aristotle in the belief animals were entirely appropriate as a means to the fulfilment of human purposes, including dietary purposes.

# 7

# The Humanism of the Renaissance

## THE CARNIVOROUS CONSENSUS AND THE REBIRTH OF THE PROFANE

In their instructive book *Ethical Vegetarianism: From Pythagoras to Peter Singer*, editors Kerry S. Walters and Lisa Portmess divide the included essays into four historical parts, culminating in Part 4, on the twentieth century. Part 1 consists of six contributions from antiquity. The book then jumps from Porphyry to Part 2, on the eighteenth century. With a considerable measure of justification, there is nothing deemed worthy of inclusion between Porphyry and the eighteenth century. To be sure, the editors could have found short and valuable snippets from a variety of authors over the one and a half intervening millennia, but nothing of both length and substance was found for inclusion. And of the "eighteenth-century" contributors, only two of the five authors who are selected practised vegetarianism, one (Shelley) not becoming a vegetarian until the nineteenth century (at the start of which he was only seven years of age). He is more properly included in Part 3, among the nineteenth-century contributors. Such is the general dearth of the practice of ethical vegetarianism between Porphyry and the turn of the nineteenth century. Nonetheless, in those intervening centuries several brave figures braced themselves against the carnivorous consensus, and a few more contributed to the development of animal ethics.

Whereas the thought of the Middle Ages was first and foremost religious, with at least one eye cast continuously toward eternity, Renaissance thought fixed the other eye firmly on the mundane. Life on earth became an acknowledged, although not the sole, end in itself, as Thomas Aquinas had tentatively already affirmed in the latter part of the thirteenth century, not merely a preparation for heaven, as Augustine had insisted. But if this was the age of Reason, and it was, it was no less the age of Superstition. If the one augured well for the animals, the other did not. Nor did all of Reason. And seemingly like never before, it was in Europe an age of severe cold that limited the growing season, bringing famine to an already undernourished people. Naturally, the lack of vegetable produce encouraged an increase in stock production, but vegetable food was also lacking with which to feed the livestock. Again, if this was an age of Reason, it was not an age that rejected Christianity. It was, however, an age that questioned seriously the practices of the church and its clergy, a query that resulted in the outbreak of the Reformation immediately prior to Leonardo da Vinci's death.

The Renaissance introduced the idea that became the governing conception of the Enlightenment: all nature was continuous, simple, and uniform. Most important, nature was knowable entirely through reason and empirical investigation. No heavenly or mythical intermediary was necessary or appropriate to the acquisition of knowledge. The Accademia Nazionale dei Lincei (National Academy of the Lynx) was instituted in Rome, the forerunner of all national scientific societies, to promote objective and scientific thought. The tyranny of the priesthood was on notice. Yet if Renaissance scientism was a spur to the most heinous vivisection, its humanity was also a spur to its vehement denunciation.

What humanism appeared intent to overcome was the truly ecclesiastical medieval attitude of what the Thomist scholar Jacques Maritain described as "keeping men from thinking about themselves." In the second half of the fourteenth century, Francis Petrarch, poet laureate at Rome and no less one of the early great Renaissance humanists, announced: "I am an individual and would like to be wholly and completely an individual; I wish to remain true to myself as far as I can."[1] This is indeed the Italian reveille of the Renaissance, although, to be accurate, as Michael Seidlmayer has demonstrated convincingly, the clarion was heard a century earlier at the time of the Hohenstaufen – "the most creative and intellectually the most important of the Middle Ages ... one of the summits in the development of European culture. It was *then* and not at the time of the Renaissance that what Burkhardt called 'the discovery of the world and man within it' really began."[2] Or as Percy Bysshe Shelley saw: "Dante was the first awakener of entranced Europe ... He was the congregator of those great spirits who presided over the resurrection of learning."[3] Certainly, ever since the mid-thirteenth century, minds had been slowly turning toward nature and the secular.

Petrarch's statement is the announcement of an awakening from the slumber of seeing everything about the individual in terms of relationships – to family, for example. The Renaissance version of the story of Romeo and Juliet – it is in origin of much earlier vintage – is a striking instance of the conflict arising from the awareness of the new importance of the self rather than that of one's family. Knowing one's place, especially as to class, had long been the hallmark of one's identity – through traditional kinship associations rather than through choice, emotion, and reason. Church and state, for example, were primary but frequently conflicting obligations to which the self must be inescapably subordinated.

Petrarch's words are a prerequisite of being able to recognize individuals as ends in themselves. If we had to await Kant and the closing decades of the eighteenth century before ethics were formulated in these terms, that was how the Renaissance was beginning to think. It culminated at the time of the French Revolution in the notion that the purpose of the state was to serve the individual, not the individual to serve the state, but the first rumblings were already underway. To recognize individual humans as ends in themselves is a prerequisite of recognizing individual animals as ends in themselves. It is only when we can look to ourselves and say "I" that we can look to animals and acknowledge their right to be perceived, if not necessarily conceive of themselves, as an "I" too. If the Renaissance and its aftermath witnessed among some a deplorable conception of the human as the only truly worthy animal – as with the Cartesians, for example, who treated animals as automata – it also experienced a conflicting and growing compassion and respect among the large body of people who thought in non-Cartesian terms, who treated animals as intelligent and sentient creatures. But only very few of these were persuaded that these attributes entitled the animals to their unfettered lives.

## Luigi Cornaro

Luigi Cornaro (1465-1566), an upper-echelon Venetian by birth and breeding, was not an ethical vegetarian but a quasi-ascetic vegetarian, if he was one at all. And he probably was a vegetarian. To be sure, he was known to eat an occasional egg. But this was no hindrance to his apparent principles. In his time he was celebrated in all Europe through his writings for the

Spartan regimen he pursued, persuading many he ought to be imitated, although we have no evidence of the number who did so. He published several short treatises during the last few years of his life, celebrating his healthy longevity, which were translated, Howard Williams tells us: "into all the civilized languages of Europe [and one of which] was once a most popular book. There are several English translations of it, the best being one that bears the date 1779."[4] Joseph Addison commented favourably on the "temperance" of Cornaro's diet in the pages of *The Spectator* in October 1711, noting that "Nature delights in the most plain and simple diet. Every animal, but man, keeps to one dish. Herbs are the food of this species, fish of that, and flesh of a third."[5] The term "simple diet," or "natural food," a phrase employed by Cornaro, was a common way to refer to a human regimen of fleshless fare. However, Addison concluded his article in *The Spectator*, "I have not here considered temperance as a moral virtue, but only as it is the means of health."[6] His promise to return to the ethical aspects of the issue, so far as I can discern from the articles attributed to Addison in *The Spectator*, was not kept. Nor is there any evidence Addison pursued the recommended course with any degree of rigour himself. The only time Addison appears to have broached anywhere near the topic again was in October 1712, when he discussed the chain of being in an article on "Meditations on Animal Life" and acknowledged even the worms as "my mother and my sister."[7] But there is no discussion of the ethical appropriateness of a fleshless diet. Still, that Addison indicated clearly in the October 1711 issue of *The Spectator* that temperance was an appropriate topic for discussion suggests it was not alien to the public mind. Temperance, one of the four cardinal virtues, meant self-restraint and, as with the temperance movement later, would commonly imply abstinence.

And he considered the matter a question of "moral virtue." Certainly, Addison's comments and the continued English publication of his writings are a reflection of the influence that Cornaro continued to wield centuries after his demise. Addison's comments are also a reflection of the fact that ethical vegetarianism was not *entirely* alien to public consciousness.

Cornaro tells us, writing in the then common third person, switching to the self-referenced vocative, and then to the first person: "he has now a better relish for his dry bread than he had formerly for the most exquisite dainties. And all this thou hast effected by acting rationally, knowing that bread is, above all things, man's proper food when seasoned by a good appetite ... It is for this reason that dry bread has so much relish for me, and I know from experience, and can with truth affirm, that I find such sweetness in it that I should be afraid of sinning against temperance were it not for my being convinced of the absolute necessity of eating of it, and that we cannot make use of a more natural food."[8] "Natural food," it would appear, included neither the produce of the chase nor that of animal domestication and butchery. Nor, we can imagine, did a diet of dry bread appeal to many who enjoyed their food!

Of particular interest about Cornaro is his apparently vegetarian diet based on grounds other than the intended holiness of the practitioner. To be sure, it is still the purification of the body he seeks, but the difference between Cornaro and his ascetic predecessors is that he is an apparent vegetarian on primarily secular grounds, seemingly the first since the early Christian centuries to be so. And this reflects the fundamental change of tenor of thought of the Renaissance from that of the Middle Ages. If it is appropriate to think of Machiavelli (1469-1527) as the first exemplar of modernity in political thought, on the grounds of his rational and empirical methods, and it is common to do so, then Cornaro is the first of the modern rational and secular vegetarians, although not a vegetarian on ethical grounds. Still, as we can see from the intention of Addison, Cornaro's temperance led toward ethical considerations.

Influenced by Cornaro and determined to imitate him was the learned Belgian Leonard Lessius (1554-1623). Lessius extolled the virtues of a temperate, apparently fleshless, diet in *Hygiasticon* (1614), again entirely for reasons of health. Joseph Ritson, an early-nineteenth-century writer on, and practitioner of, vegetarianism, unearthed another "hygienist," a certain Dr. W. Moffat (d. 1604), the title of whose book on the topic of *Health's Improvement* also places him in the Cornaro camp. Nonetheless, Moffat's writing indicates it was not health alone that moved him. He asks *inter alia* whether "civil and human eyes [can] yet abide the slaughter of an innocent 'beast,' the cutting of his throat, the smashing him on the head, the flaying of his skin, the quartering and dismembering of his limbs, the sprinkling of his blood, the ripping up his veins, the enduring of ill-savours, the heaving of heavy sighs, sobs, and groans, the passionate struggling and panting for life, which only hard-hearted butchers can endure to see."[9] There was clearly an ethical dimension à la Plutarch to Moffat's regimen. Indeed, there was a significant distaste, revulsion even, at the injuries inflicted through butchery. As an aside, it is worthy of note that Moffat frequently employed the word "meat" to mean a great deal more than flesh alone, and the word "beast" placed in quotation marks indicates both that the term was becoming primarily one of abuse and that some were less than satisfied by the prejudicial usage. Linguistic forms as well as animal ethics were changing. It was becoming less acceptable to malign the animals by seemingly pejorative expressions.

## LEONARDO DA VINCI

If Cornaro was the first of the modern vegetarians, having wholly secular reasons for his vegetarianism, and if Moffat was a man of at least aesthetic disapprobation, Leonardo da Vinci (1452-1519) was the first since Porphyry to fuse animal ethics with principled vegetarianism, although a good dimension of it existed in Moffat. Da Vinci was thus the first of the modern ethical vegetarians, basing his thoughts solely in the ethical realm. This is not to deny his apparent religious devotion but to realize that the grounds for his vegetarianism were entirely humanitarian. It is morality, not the desire to placate perceived authority or the deity directly or to respect health considerations, that impels his conclusions. From the perspective of his enlightened outlook on the arts and sciences, da Vinci is the very epitome of the Renaissance "man." From the perspective of his ethical vegetarianism, he would have been quite at home in the early nineteenth century.

We have no *incontrovertible* evidence that da Vinci was a vegetarian. He did not state that he was, and we even find evidence of the purchase of flesh in his accounts, although that very probably was for staff, guests, and art students. He also designed meat-roasting jacks and stoves, a reflection of his inventive interests. Moreover, according to Giorgio Vasari in 1550, da Vinci created stores of dead small animals as models for his art, but it is possible that, rather than killing them, he collected them shortly after their natural deaths. It would appear that da Vinci, stating very little of his own life and worldview, was regarded by others as vegetarian. Thus, for example, Andrea Corsali wrote to his patron (also patron of da Vinci and brother of Pope Leo X), Giuliano de' Medici, stating: "certain infidels called Guzzarati [Hindus of North West India] do not feed upon anything that contains blood, nor do they permit among them any injury be done to any living thing, like our Leonardo da Vinci"[10] – an exemplary use of "blood" as the apparent defining characteristic of an animal for both contemporary Europeans and Indians. A biographer of da Vinci, Serge Bramly, states that he "dined off salad, vegetables, cereals, mushroom and pasta; he seems to have been particularly fond of minestrone."[11] Da Vinci himself asked of humanity: "Does not nature produce enough simple food for thee to satisfy thyself?"[12] As with Luigi Cornaro, the simple food means nonanimal food. This could be read, as with Cornaro, as no more than vegetarianism on health grounds, but his comments on cruelty to animals would emphatically suggest otherwise. The closest he came to announcing his ethical vegetarianism was when he implied that he would not let his body become a "tomb for other animals, an inn of the dead ... a container of corruption," and he expressed great despair of humanity for doing so.[13]

Writing in 1550 of the lives of several Renaissance artists, Giorgio Vasari commented very favourably on da Vinci's concern for animals and clearly expected his readers to rejoice in this respect and consideration along with the writer. Da Vinci, he remarks,

> was so pleasing in conversation that he attracted to himself the hearts of men. And although he possessed, one might say, nothing and worked little, he always kept servants and horses, in which latter he took much delight, and particularly in all the other animals which he managed with the greatest love and patience; and this he showed when often passing by the places where birds were sold, for, taking them with his own hand out of their cages, and having paid for them what was asked, he let them fly away into the air, restoring them to their lost liberty. For which reason nature was so pleased to favour him, that, wherever, he turned his thought, brain, and mind, he displayed such divine power in his works, that, in giving [the animals] their perfection, no one was ever his peer in readiness, vivacity, excellence, beauty, and grace.[14]

Da Vinci's notebooks are replete with condemnations of humanity for its lack of wisdom in general and cruelty to animals in particular. A few representative examples will suffice to express the tenor of his objections to human cruelty. For example, on bees, he wrote: "And many will be robbed of their stores and their food, and will be cruelly submerged and drowned by folks devoid of reason O justice of God! Why dost thou not awake to behold thy creatures thus abused?"[15] Writing of "sheep, cows, goats and the like," he bemoaned that "from countless numbers will be taken away their little children and the throats of these shall be cut, and they shall be quartered most barbarously."[16] In discussing "asses that are beaten," he exclaimed to Nature: "I see thy children given up to slavery to others, without any sort of advantage, and instead of remuneration for the good they do, they are paid with the severest suffering, and spend their whole life in benefiting their oppressor."[17] Christian opinion, as expressed by the church and heavily influenced by Saint Thomas, and occasional laic Christian opinion, as expressed by the compassion of a da Vinci, have little in common.

Da Vinci observed the foolishness and depravity of humans seen in their environmental degradation through shipbuilding and mining, in their cruelty to animals (containing even a hint of awareness of the gross immorality of habitat destruction), and in their often unwarranted belief in their own heavenly immortality:

Animals will be seen upon the earth who will always be fighting with one another, with very great losses and frequent deaths on each side. And there will be no end to their malice; by their strong limbs we shall see a great portion of the trees in the vast forest laid low throughout the universe; and when they are filled with their food, the satisfaction of their desires will be to deal death, and grief and labour and fear and fright to every living thing; and from their immoderate pride they will desire to rise towards heaven, but the excessive weight of their limbs will keep them down. Nothing will remain on earth or under the earth or in the waters that will not be persecuted, disturbed and spoiled, and those of one country moved to another. And their bodies will become the tomb and the means of transit of all the living bodies they have killed. O Earth! what delays thee to open and hurl them headlong into the deep fissures of thy huge abyss and caverns, and no longer to display in the sight of heaven so savage and ruthless a monster?[18]

The animal that da Vinci condemns is of course the human animal.

Cornaro, Lessius, Moffat, and da Vinci were not the sole vegetarians of the era. Although records are scanty, we know also of Saint Philip Romolo Neri (1519-1595), known as the "Apostle of Rome," who ate but one meal a day consisting of "bread and water to which a few herbs were added."[19] His was undoubtedly an ascetic vegetarianism. And some monasteries were full of at least part-time ascetic vegetarians. But we can find a literary hint of an ethical touch in Miguel de Cervantes's *The Ingenious Gentleman: Don Quixote de la Mancha* (1605-1615). The book exhibits sensibilities to animals beyond those to the horse Rocinante, not least to Squire Sancho Panza's ass. What is perhaps less commonly noticed is that in Chapter 11 he pays due regard to the Golden Age and its vegetarian lifestyle, although it is probably little more than a rhetorical flourish, and it is most unlikely Cervantes was ever persuaded to forgo flesh. Still, it is a signal portent of the role that the idea of the Golden Age was to play, as it had played centuries previously, in the development of vegetarian thought.

## RENAISSANCE SENSIBILITY TO ANIMALS

If the Renaissance produced few vegetarians, it produced an abundance of ideas that set animals on a higher plane than that to which they had sometimes been accustomed, even higher than they had been placed in 1567 by the denunciation and prohibition of bullfighting by Pope Pius V, although the Spaniards at whom the proscription was directed contrived to ignore it.

In line with John of Salisbury, the great Catholic humanist Erasmus condemned hunting and asked what pleasure there could be in the slaughter of animals. The one-time chancellor to King Henry VIII and martyred Catholic saint Sir Thomas More (1478-1535) likewise castigated the habit of hunting, telling us that "hunting is the lowest thing even butchers can do" and deploring the hunter's pleasure derived "from killing and mutilating some poor little creature."[20] The inhabitants of his *Utopia* "kill no living animal in sacrifice, nor do they think that God has delight in blood and sacrifice, Who has given life to the animals to the intent they should live."[21] Nor does he approve of the transference of arable land to grazing land. However, paradoxically, the Utopians continue to slaughter animals for food. Such thinking takes us little further than the finer sensibilities expressed in the late Middle Ages. With Montaigne, however, animal sensibilities are raised well beyond those conceived in the medieval mind, even though he does not ultimately opt for vegetarianism in practice.

Michel Eyquem, seigneur de Montaigne (1533-1592), held that there is "a kind of respect and a general duty of humanity which tieth us ... unto brute beasts that have life and sense, but even to trees and plants ... unto men we owe justice, and to all other creatures ... grace and benignity ... there is a certain commerce and mutual obligation between them and us."[22] Prima facie, this is little more than an expression of Stoic philosophy, rejecting our owing justice to the animals. But if it is Stoicism, it is Stoicism with some novel twists and one that recognizes our obligations toward the animals. With the customary obeisance of the animal advocate to Pythagoras, but also to Plutarch, Porphyry, Pliny, Democritus, even Plato, and others of the classical period, Montaigne showed a particular concern to limit pain to animals. In his essay "Apology for Raymond Sebond," Montaigne denounced human hubris and the manner in which humans distinguish themselves from all other animals. He described the qualities and remarkable capacities he believed animals to possess in considerable superiority to humans. He even quoted Lucretius approvingly to ascribe a general equality between humans and animals. And he then concluded that "the very share of the favours of nature that we concede to the animals, by our own confessions, is very much to their advantage."[23] If he does not himself turn away from flesh foods – at least we have no evidence that he did – he understands the case from original nature for doing so:

> As for use in eating, it is with us as with them, natural and without instruction. Who doubts that a child arrived at the necessary strength for feeding himself, could find his own nourishment? The earth produces and offers to

him enough for his needs without artificial labour, and if not for all seasons, neither does she for the other races [i.e., species] – witness the provisions which we observe the ants and others collecting for the sterile seasons of the year. Those nations whom we have lately discovered, so abundantly furnished with natural meat [i.e., nonflesh meats] and drink without labour [i.e., without domestication and hunting], have just instructed us that bread is not our sole food [i.e., there are other nonflesh foods than bread] and that without toil our mother Nature has furnished us with every plant we need, to shew us, as it seems, how superior she is to all our *artificiality;* while the extravagance of our appetite outruns all the inventions by which we seek to satisfy it.[24]

Clearly, he is promoting a vegetarian diet, although he acknowledges the great difficulties the varying seasons afford the vegetarian diet. Montaigne's unspecified era of the Golden Age is not the Golden Age of Eden in the Genesis account nor the age of primordial Arcadian man in the forests; perhaps it is something more like what would have been familiar to the inhabitants of classical Greece. The characteristics he ascribes to the age would fit more comfortably with this option. Still, Montaigne appears to be the first of the postclassical literary luminaries to have described a vegetarian state of nature *in principle* preferable to that of carnivorous culture. He is followed later, as we shall see, by many other nonpractising preachers. It is the first clear indication that somewhere lurking in the mind of many vegetarian advocates is the supposition that a fleshless diet was once an achievable moral goal – indeed, a reflection of the human ideal – but that, because of the path pursued by human vice over the centuries, the human – or at least Western – constitution can no longer endure such privation.

The increased awe toward the animal realm expressed in the later editions of the bestiaries was increased many fold by the science of the Renaissance, to which da Vinci himself contributed. It was an awe based on precise description of the animals, their movements, and the causes. But there was also the mysticism of those like Giordano Bruno (1548-1600) and Jakob Boehme (1575-1624), which complicated the culture of the later part of the high Renaissance. Bruno developed a pantheistic conception of the world in which the animals had a respected place, all parts of the world soul being animated by God. In *Cause, Principle and Unity,* he described "the universal intellect," of which animals are a part, as "the innermost, most real, and essential faculty, and the most efficacious part of the world soul. It is the one and the same thing, which fills the whole, and directs nature in producing her species in the right way."[25] If, for Bruno, animals do not participate in the rational life, they are nonetheless themselves the product of universal reason and are thus kin with all species. Jakob Boehme proclaimed: "And Adam knew that he was within every creature, and he gave to each its appropriate name."[26] Not only is there a kinship with other species, but a certain common identity among all species is also being expressed. And the personal naming of the animals is seen to give them a greater respect than the merely cultural or scientific means of identification. This kinship implied for Boehme – or so it would appear, everything in Boehme being opaque – a unity of the animals with the deity, a unity that should not be broken for human use. In fact, via Pythagoras and Plutarch, Boehme developed a system of influential ideas, known as Behmenism, that resembled nineteenth-century theosophy, preaching radical nonviolence.

In *Measure for Measure*, William Shakespeare (1564-1616) acknowledges the significant sentience of animals. In *As You Like It*, he describes "melancholy Jacques" approvingly as a man of considerable animal sensibility. In the poem *Venus and Adonis*, he expresses great sympathy for the hunted hare and acknowledges sentience even in the snail. Nonetheless, in *Macbeth*, the witches' cauldron contains parts of snake, frog, bat, dog, blind-worm, lizard, owlet, dragon, wolf, and shark – all creatures maligned by general superstition. And the issue of saving animals from slaughter as food is never raised by Shakespeare. In *Metempsycosis*, John Donne (1572-1631) shows sympathy for the life of the unfortunate fish, the prey of the angler. Francis Quarles (1592-1644) shows sympathy for food animals – "How full of death is the life of momentary man."[27] But he can go no further than recommending: "Take no pleasure in the death of a creature; if it be harmless or useless destroy it not; if useful, or harmful, destroy it mercifully."[28] Use as food is sufficient to ensure the animal's death, but at least the importance of a merciful death is recognized. Still, it was by and large the nobility and their aides who had the opportunity to decimate the wild and the domesticated, which they took in great quantities. The severity of the antipoaching laws, in Britain in particular, sufficed to hinder most illegal hunting, with all flesh of any size reserved for the peers of the realm. A typical lunch for a relatively prosperous peasant might consist of bread, cheese, and ale, with salted herring perhaps being added to the same menu for supper. Colin Spencer has observed that, with remnants of previous flesh meals still in the cauldron, the pot being emptied perhaps once a year, "all the cooking of Christendom, from whatever region, was designed around the consumption of animals."[29] In fact, only the wealthiest peasantry enjoyed more than the scantiest portion of flesh, and then infrequently. If, for some, the cooking was designed around flesh, for most, the flesh portion was decidedly meagre. And for more than a few, it was no more than a whiff of lingering memory.

If, in general, the Renaissance seemed to augur well for the increased regard for animals, the publications of Descartes seemed very much to dim the prospects. Indeed, the general opinion has been that Descartes had an enormously negative impact on the treatment of animals. In the next chapter we will investigate the influence of Cartesianism and the question of whether Cartesianism and the inauguration of the era of unregulated vivisection occurred independently.

# 8

# The Cartesians and Their Adversaries in the Seventeenth and Eighteenth Centuries

## CARTESIAN AUTOMATA

The prevalent but quite erroneous view that prior to modern times there was no consideration for animals in the West is still repeated in some of the most recent relevant literature. Thus, for example, Gary Francione, writing in 2004, states: "Before the nineteenth century ... Western culture did not recognize that humans had any moral obligations to animals because animals did not matter morally at all. We could have moral obligations that concerned animals, but these obligations were really owed to other humans and not to animals. Animals were regarded as things, as having a moral status no different from that of inanimate beings."[1] As we have seen, and will see again in this chapter, this view is without merit, but it is based on an episode in European history that has commonly, if unwarrantedly, led to such a conclusion.

Infamously, in the seventeenth century the French rationalist philosopher René Descartes determined in *The Discourse on Method* that it is not merely that "brutes have less reason than men, but that they have none at all." Moreover, "it is nature which acts in them according to the disposition of their organs, just as a clock which is only composed of wheels and weights, is able to tell the hours and measure the time more correctly than we can do with all our wisdom."[2] Animals lack reason because they lack sentience. They lack sentience because they are machines like watches. So Descartes was interpreted to have said. Speech and flexible response are, in Descartes's view, exclusive to humanity and are prime indicators of rationality.

Thus we arrive at the idea of the insensible machine and at the animal-watch analogy: animals are not thinking, sentient beings but complex machines like clocks and watches. Descartes reinforced this view in the groundbreaking *Meditations on the Foundations of Philosophy* (1641) when he observed: "looking from a window and saying I see men who pass in the street, I really do not see them but infer that what I see is men ... yet what do I see from the window but hats and coats which may cover automatic machines? Yet I judge these to be men ... solely by the faculty of judgment which rests in my mind, I comprehend that which I believed I saw with my eyes." Whatever I perceive, he added: "I can ... not perceive ... without a human mind."[3] For Descartes, possession of a *human* mind is a prerequisite of inference, perception, and judgment. Moreover, it is a prerequisite of ethical consideration.

There has developed a consensus among animal advocates that René Descartes and his conception of animals as automata had an extraordinary influence on the European mind, one very much to the lasting detriment of animals. However, a close inspection of the European culture of the seventeenth and eighteenth centuries reveals a more nuanced picture.

In recent decades, there has been a resurgence in the traditional dispute over whether Descartes allowed for any animal sensation, John Cottingham and A. Denny, for example, arguing the affirmative, whereas Gary Steiner, for his part, holds to the negative.[4] But if we cannot be entirely confident of Descartes's view of animal sentience, or at least cannot be confident of its consistency in Descartes's writings, we can be confident of his denigration of the animals and his objection to what he calls "the superstitions of Pythagoras," although he was not above practising vegetarianism himself at times on health grounds. We cannot be confident the views ascribed to him were entirely his, but we can be confident his self-proclaimed followers held the belief of animals as unfeeling automata completely – "possessing eyes in order not to see, ears in order not to hear, and so on."[5]

In France, Descartes was followed by Pierre Chanet, M. Des Fournelles (nom de plume of Géraud de Corderoy), Antoine le Grand, and above all, Nicolas Malebranche, who proved very much more of a mechanist than the master. His animal automata, he thought: "eat without pleasure, they cry without pain, they grow without knowing it, they desire nothing, they know nothing, and if they behave in a seemingly intelligent manner, it is because God, having made them thus to preserve them, has so formed their bodies that they avoid mechanically and fearlessly everything capable of destroying them."[6]

Although Cartesian rationalist philosophy, even in Malebranchian guise, was in general greatly admired and highly influential, it is remarkable how many expressed their conviction in the validity of its arguments *except* with regard to what they saw as the preposterous notion of animals as *bêtes machines*. For example, Marin Cureau de la Chambre, physician in ordinary to the king – and one who knew both human and animal anatomies from practical experience – argued in adamant opposition in *Traité des Connoissance des Animaux* (1646) that animals could reason and were ingenious. On the grounds of animal capacities, he even questioned the right of human dominion over them.

The Catholic abbot Pierre Gassendi (1592-1655), who, as we shall see, argued the case in favour of vegetarianism, was appalled at what he saw as Descartes's blindness where animals were concerned. In fact, long before Descartes had published his *Meditations,* which denied definitively that animals possessed the capacity for reason, Gassendi had announced his position in the preface to *Exercises in the Form of Paradoxes in Refutation of the Aristotelians* (1624): "I restore reason to the animals; I find no distinction between the understanding and the imagination," which was a distinction the Peripatetics (Aristotelians) employed, one affirmed by Descartes, to indicate what they saw as a significant distinction between human and animal thinking. He went on to argue that it is simply a prejudice to deny animals the faculty of reason, that animals reason in the same manner as humans, and that "all knowledge" – whether human or animal – "is in the senses or is derived from them."[7] Thus, when the *Meditations* appeared Gassendi was prepared to do battle.

In the second meditation, Descartes observed, as we have seen, a grand distinction between the human and the animal in the faculty of judgment. Only humans possessed the capacity to draw rational but unverified inferences from their experience. Thus, Descartes opined, as we have noted, if looking on a street from a window we saw only moving hats and clothes, we would correctly judge that they were worn by persons. A dog, it was thought, would be quite incapable of performing such a feat. Gassendi wrote privately to Descartes, expressing what he called his "Doubts." Descartes responded publicly, dismissing Gassendi's reservations. In return, Gassendi went into print with what he now termed his "Rebuttals":

> You deny that any dog has a mind and leave him wholly with an imagination [as the Peripatetics had done]; but the dog also perceives that a man or his master, is hidden under the clothes, and even under a variety of different forms ... Is it not true that if you think the existence of a mentality is evidenced by your realization that there is a man underneath when you see

nothing but his hat and clothes, and if likewise a dog realizes that there is a man underneath when he sees nothing but his hat and his clothes, is it not true, I say, that you should also think that the existence of a mentality like yours is evidenced by the dog?[8]

Gassendi not only granted rationality to the animals but determined on the basis of humanity's natural constitution that we had no right to eat them. He drew at least quasi-ethical theories about vegetarianism from his rejection of the Cartesian notions of what it is to be human. Gassendi wrote to his friend the renowned Belgian physician and natural philosopher Jan Baptista van Helmont, rejecting his conclusions on the carnivorous nature of humankind, claiming:

I was contending that from the conformation of our teeth, we do not appear to be adapted by Nature in the use of a flesh diet, since all animals ... which Nature has formed to feed on flesh have their teeth long, conical, sharp, uneven, and intervals between them – of which kind lions, tigers, wolves, dogs, cats, and others. But those who are made to subsist only on herbs and fruits have their teeth short, blunt, close to one another, and distributed in even rows. Of this sort are horses, cows, deer, sheep, goats, and some others. And further, that men have received from Nature teeth which are unlike those of the first class, and resemble those of the second. It is therefore probable ... that Nature intended them to follow, in the selection of their food, not the carnivorous tribes, but those races of animals which are contented with the simple productions of the earth ... As for flesh, true, indeed, it is that man is sustained on flesh. But how many things, let me ask, does man do every day which are contrary to, or beside, his nature? Can use so noxious be called natural? Faculty is given by Nature, but it is our own fault that we make a perverse use of it.[9]

Gassendi added, "there is no pretense for saying that any right has been granted to us by [natural] law to kill any of those animals which are not destructive to the human race."[10] Gassendi's argument is the teleological one that we ought to act in the way that Nature has intended for us. That ethical implications are to be drawn from the "scientific" findings is clear from his use of such words as "noxious," "fault," "right," and "perverse." Nonetheless, strangely, Gassendi failed to follow the ethical implications of his own argument. He is one of those – we will meet several more in the next chapter, and we already encountered Montaigne in the last – who were persuaded by facts and arguments conducive to vegetarian conclusions but found it far more convenient to continue to dine on flesh. Stranger still is that, in a manner, Descartes was on Gassendi's side. He concurred with his rationalist ally Sir Kenelm Digby that a vegetable diet would prolong human life and began to practise that diet, albeit not without an occasional reversion to flesh. Of course, this did not change his views on the mechanical nature of the animal creation.

Among those distraught at Descartes's argument was the Cambridge Platonist Henry More (1614-1687), Fellow of Christ's College, Cambridge. Writing to Descartes in 1648 to praise his work in general but to abominate his views on animals as automata, More complained bitterly of the "internecine and cutthroat idea you advance, which snatches life and sensibility away from the animals":

> But I beg you, most penetrating man, since it is necessary by this argument of yours, either to deprive animals of their senses, or to give them their immortality, why should you rather set up inanimate machinery than bodies motivated by immortal souls, even though that may have been the less consonant with natural phenomena so far discovered? In this, indeed, most ancients judged and approved: take Pythagoras, Plato, and others. Certainly, the persistent idea is presented in all the works of Plato, and has given courage to all the Platonists. Nevertheless, such a remarkable genius [as yourself] has been reduced to these straits, that, if one does not concede immortality to the souls of brutes, then all animals are of necessity inanimate machines.[11]

Although both Gassendi and More took the side of the animals against Descartes, Gassendi declared in favour of a fleshless diet and against animal immortal souls, whereas Henry More took the opposite view – in favour of immortal animal souls but against flesh denial. Such is the nature of the human paradox! Both took the view that animals were sentient and rational creatures.

Other than probably Descartes, certainly Malebranche, the few Cartesians previously mentioned, the Jesuit François Garasse, Jacques-Benigne Bossuet, the seminarians of Port Royal, and perhaps a handful of Englishmen, Kenelm Digby being the most prominent, very few were fully persuaded of the thesis that animals were truly insentient. A few managed to make Descartes a laughing stock on the issue. Thus in 1672 the famous author of letters addressed to her daughter, Mme de Sévigné, wrote incredulously of Descartes's infamous "beast machines": "Machines which love, machines which choose one fellow over another, machines which are jealous, machines which are afraid! Surely, surely, you are making fun of us;

not even Descartes could have aspired to get us to believe that."[12] In England, Lord Bolingbroke, noting Descartes's analogy between an animal and a watch, declared that the plain man would persist in believing that there was a difference between the town bull and the parish clock.[13] Bernard Fontenelle delivered the deepest cut of all: "You say that animals are both machines and watches, don't you? But if you put one male dog machine in close proximity with a female dog machine, a third little machine may be the consequence. In their place you may put two watches in close proximity with each other for the whole of their lifetime without their ever producing a third watch. Now, according to our philosophy, all those things that have a capacity to render three out of two possess a greater nobility which elevates them above the machine."[14] Despite this ribald opposition to Descartes, reflecting a raising of the animals in their stature, few took the view we should cease to eat the animals. Fontenelle declared the animals to "possess a greater nobility," but this nobility did not save them from his dining table.

It is perhaps the Cartesian clergyman John Norris of Pemberton (1657-1711) who illuminates the issue of Cartesian influence best, indicating that however persuasive Cartesian arguments might have been to the contemporary mind, there is something in human conscience and experience that makes the whole scheme with regard to animals dubious and dangerous. Writing in 1701, Norris avers:

> To conclude now with a word concerning the *Treatment* of Beasts. Tho' it is my Opinion, or if you will, my Fancy, that Reason does most favour that side which denies all thought and perception to brutes, and resolves those Movements of theirs which seem to carry an appearance of it (because *like* those we exert by Thought) into Mechanical Principles, yea after all, lest in Resolution of so abstract a Question our Reason should happen to deceive us, as 'tis easy to err in the Dark, I am so far from incouraging any practices of Cruelty, upon the Bodies of these Creatures, which the Lord of the Creation has (as to the moderate and necessary use of them) subjected our Power, that on the contrary I would have them used and treated with as much tenderness and pitiful regard, as if they had all that Sense and Perception, which is commonly (tho' I think without sufficient Reason) attributed to them. Which equitable Measure, that they [who] think they really have that Perception, ought in pursuance of their own Principle, so much the more Conscientiously to observe.[15]

Norris's statement is significant for several reasons. First, it makes clear what we customarily doubt: that despite well over a half-century of

Cartesianism, "Sense and Perception ... is commonly ... attributed to" ani-mals. That is, the Cartesians had, on the whole, failed to convince. Second, it indicates that the primary problem with the idea of animals as automata was not merely a metaphysical one but was understood to lie in the fact that it provides an ethical justification for cruelty to animals, including invasive animal experimentation. Third, it suggests that intellectual specu-lations need to be tested against our ethical intuitions and, if counter to those intuitions, need to be thought through again. And Norris is trying to think them through again, for if they appear to convince his reason, they utterly fail to persuade his conscience. Finally, Norris's statement affirms that even those who might have been persuaded of the general validity of Cartesianism and who might have accepted the proposition that animals were for human use should deem it appropriate that animals should be treated with tenderness and compassion. The *logically* surprising conse-quence is that despite the "tenderness and pitiful regard," few drew the conclusion that we should cease to eat the animals. If this was little more than a part of the beginning of a general compassion toward animals, it was no more than an elementary beginning. Norris and almost all his fellows continued to think that eating animals was a part of "moderate and neces-sary" use. "Necessary" is important here, for it reflects that most continued to believe, whatever our origins, that we had become carnivores by ac-quired nature. Any other dietary regimen, it was thought, would be delete-rious to human health and longevity. If Digby and Descartes recognized the long-term benefits of a vegetarian diet, the vast majority, including most of Descartes's own supporters, did not.

The evidence seems incontrovertible that whereas Descartes, and to a far lesser degree Malebranche, may have influenced the European mind on the status of animals to some degree, the majority concurred that animals were sentient and at least somewhat rational creatures who met the standard for ethical consideration of their interests. However, custom and societal com-munitarian reasons ensured that those ethical considerations did not ex-tend to a *profound* respect for animals and certainly did not customarily lead to vegetarian conclusions.

## ANIMALS AS TOOLS

It ought to be a matter of some surprise that the vast amount of animal experimentation that arose in the Renaissance brought about considerable opposition – indeed, although equally invasive and counter to animal interests, far more than was directed against the eating of animals. This reflects that carnivorism was far more an ingrained element of the human constitution than were the experiments, which were designed as much to increase human knowledge as to effect improvements to human medicine. It was not until the twentieth century that animal experimentation resulted in significant improvements to human medicine, and even then there were many who argued that the increased benefits could have been achieved just as readily, perhaps more readily, than those derived via the detriment of animals.

Long before the Cartesians, the Greek scientist Galen (c. 131-200), who resided chiefly in Rome from about the age of thirty and was imperial court physician to Marcus Aurelius, correlated extant medical knowledge with his own theories derived from dissections of animals, chiefly apes and pigs. He did not require a metaphysical distinction between irrational soul and immortal soul to justify his research to himself or to others. Power over the animals and lust for knowledge were quite sufficient. His frequently inaccurate – and sometimes *quite* erroneous – conclusions remained received authority until the publication of *De humani corporis fabrica* (The Structure of the Human Body) in 1543 by the Flemish anatomist Andreas Vesalius working at the University of Padua in Italy. Vesalius's research was based on dissections of human corpses rather than of animals, the latter having sometimes led Galen widely astray.

Not surprisingly, scientists were interested more in function than in structure, for which experimentation on living bodies was thought to be necessary. And it was naturally deemed impermissible to conduct such experiments on humans. No such strictures applied to animals. As a consequence, invasive research on animals became commonplace from the sixteenth century on. Through his research on animals, William Harvey demonstrated the function of the heart and complete circulation of the blood in his 1628 *Exercitatio anatomica de motu cordis et sanguinis in animalibus* (The Movement of the Heart and Blood in Animals). This was received as a great advance in knowledge and served to legitimate live-animal experimentation. Harvey's work was published fully thirteen years before Descartes published his *Meditationes de prima philosophia* (Mediatations on the Foundations of Philosophy, popularly known as the Meditations). The willingness to count animals as beneath earnest ethical consideration was expressed most directly not by Descartes, and not using his metaphysical principles, but by the Oxford chemist Robert Boyle, who bemoaned in his 1686 *A Free Inquiry into the Vulgarly Receiv'd Notion of Nature:* "The veneration wherewith men are imbued for what they call nature has been a discouraging impediment to the empire of men over the inferior creatures of God: for many have not only looked upon it, as an impossible thing to compass, but as something impious to attempt."[16]

Seeing the stars through a telescope, Boyle was compelled to reject the idea that everything was created for human benefit, a truth accepted equally by Descartes.[17] Still, Boyle – Descartes, too – continued to experiment on animals. For example, Boyle invented an air pump that he gratuitously tried out on animals to show that they could not live without air. He chose, as later did Charles Darwin, with myriad scientists in between, to place the importance of knowledge over the pain and suffering of animals. There are two relevant factors about the statement from Robert Boyle. First, he acknowledges that there was significant opposition to the dominance over nature, which included invasive research on animals. Second, he indicates that empire over the animals was to be welcomed not because of some fine metaphysical distinctions in the Cartesian manner but because animals were inferior, and the use of animals without consideration for their interests would increase human knowledge. To be sure, Descartes had been conducting experiments on animals long before this, but it did not take the notion of animals as mechanical beings to allow for the continuation of animal experimentation, although no doubt Cartesian metaphysics gave some added rationalized justification of the practices that would have been undertaken anyway. By the time of Robert Boyle and René Descartes animal experimentation had become a veritable parlour game – to prove, for example, that parrots would die if deprived of oxygen!

Fortunately, there were loud and shrill voices raised in opposition to these practices, although, unfortunately, far more vociferously and broadly than ethical arguments against the torturing and killing of animals for food. Surely, the cruelty to food animals was no less than that perpetrated on those animals under the scientific knife, and those people who lived, worked, and walked within earshot of the abattoirs could not fail to be fully aware of it. The diarist Samuel Pepys (1633-1704) complained against the "petty experiments" of the new amateur "physiologists," who tortured animals for the amusement of their guests. The essayist and editor Joseph Addison (1662-1719) wrote in *The Spectator* of a "barbarous experiment" involving a bitch and her pup.[18] The poet Alexander Pope (1680-1744) protested against the experiments of surgeon Dr. Stephen Hale, commenting: "He commits most of these barbarities with the thought of being of use to man, but how do we know we have a right to kill creatures that we are so little above as dogs for our curiosity, or for some use to us."[19] The printer and compiler George Nicholson reported on a mid-eighteenth-century case of experiments by a Dr. Browne Langrish (d. 1759). Having described the revolting experiments in gruesome detail, Nicholson tells us how "these privileged tyrants sport away the lives and revel in the agonies and tortures of these creatures, whose sensations are as delicate, and whose natural right to an unpainful enjoyment of life is as great as that of man."[20] The *Monthly Review* for September 1770 referred to "numerous and cruel experiments" and to the "*most deliberate and unrelenting* cruelty" before concluding "surely there are moral relations between man and the fellow-creatures of the brute creation."[21] The *Monthly Review* never made mention of the "unrelenting cruelty" to farm animals at the slaughterhouse or of the moral relations that ought to pertain to animal husbandry. It was not that food animals were of a lower order than other animals, merely that it was seen as a *necessity* that we live from their bodies.

It was the master critic Dr. Samuel Johnson who administered the *coup de grâce*. He referred to vivisectors as "a race of men who have practised tortures without pity, and related them without shame, and are yet suffered to erect their heads among human beings."[22] Writing in *The Idler* for 5 August 1758, he complained:

> Among the inferiour professors of medical knowledge, is a race of wretches, whose lives are only varied by varieties of cruelty; whose favourite amusement is to nail dogs to tables and open them alive; to try how long life may be continued in various degrees of mutilation, or with the excision or laceration of the vital parts; to examine whether burning irons are felt more acutely by the bone or tendon, and whether the more lasting agonies are produced by poison forced into the mouth or injected into the veins ... It is high time that universal resentment should arise against these horrid operations, which harden the heart, extinguish those sensations which give man confidence in man, and make the physician more deadly than the gout or stone.[23]

Despite these stirring words, Johnson was a renowned frequenter of the London clubs, where he dined on succulent flesh. Indeed, he was famous for his large fleshly appetite. Was this a double standard? Was it a failure to conceive of the food animal's plight? Was carnivorism a matter so ingrained that the alternative seemed unthinkable? Or was there really an essential difference between abattoir butchery and surgical incision? The extant accounts of life at the eighteenth-century slaughterhouse would suggest that the difference, if any, was quite minor. There was something about the human constitution, it was thought, that made flesh eating an essentially human activity.

The Frenchman Jean Antoine Gleizès (1773-1841) was intended for the medical profession, but in the 1790s his "intense horror of the vivisectional experiments in the physiological torture dens," Howard Williams tells us, "soon compelled him to abandon his intended career."[24] By the end of the decade he had adopted a vegetarian diet, although, like fellow vegetarian Thomas Tryon, he failed to persuade his wife to join him in the abstinence from flesh. He wrote enthusiastically to call others to the path of his conviction, observing the lack of compassion, born of habit, among humans toward fellow creatures:

> Thus men continue to accuse themselves of being unjust, violent, cruel and treacherous to one another, but they do not accuse themselves of cutting the throats of other animals and of feeding upon their mangled limbs, which nevertheless, is the single cause of that injustice, of that violence, of that cruelty, and of that treachery ... Men believe themselves to be just, provided they fulfil, in regard to their fellows, the duties which have been prescribed to them. But it is goodness which is the justice of man; and it is impossible, I repeat it, to be good towards one's fellow without being so towards other existences.[25]

Of those we have mentioned, other than Nicholson and Gleizès, none of these abominators of the cruelties of animal experimentation extended their compassion to refraining from having animals killed for their food. This is surely a clear indication of the customary human conviction in the appropriateness of the flesh diet and the difficulty in overcoming the practice with ethical argument alone. It would be fair to say that almost all those who refused to dine on flesh for ethical reasons also opposed animal experimentation, whereas among those who opposed animal experimentation, only a relatively small proportion were also committed vegetarians.

As we have seen, Cartesianism was not the original inspiration for animal experimentation, and the experimenters enjoyed not an unassailed victory but a victory that was contested by numerous opponents. The primary reason for animal experimentation was that there were no laws to restrict or control it – there were few laws to prevent or restrict anything not of a threat to the state, directly or indirectly – and there were more influential persons with greater interest in medical and scientific knowledge than there were persons willing to pursue the moral course and deem the pain and suffering of animals a necessary factor in ethical discourse. Ethical vegetarianism faced an even greater uphill battle because a mere intellectual victory over the Cartesians would have been even less effective. The experimenters acted not from metaphysical and moral principles that ran counter to those of their adversaries – other than a belief in human superiority – but rather from a lack of them. In the absence of medical successes, they were prompted by sheer self-glorification, professional ambition, and parlour boredom – and the physicians had their professional status on their side. By contrast, the flesh eaters had an even easier task. They acted from the "lust of the belly," as Saint Basil termed it, from primordial habit, convention, and societal togetherness, even more difficult opponents to conquer. And they had religion on their side in an era when religious pronouncements were treated with the utmost reverence by the majority. And religion looked askance at any dietary practice that might smack of heresy or unorthodoxy. The vegetarian argument was far less legitimate than that of abolition or control of animal experimentation in the culture of the times.

If the new scientific age succeeded in providing a preliminary understanding of the orbits of the planets, of the general laws of mechanics, and of scientific method, it did not always proceed very far in our knowledge of the animal realm. If we were beginning to ask the right questions, the very essence of a successful scientific strategy, we were still mired in myth where animals were concerned. To be sure, the later bestiaries were written with an increasing interest in animals for their own sakes, and this was furthered in the Renaissance. But the first "scientific" treatises on animals left almost as much to be desired as the bestiaries themselves. In Konrad Gesner's *Historia Animalium* (in five volumes between 1551 and 1587) we still encounter the satyr (a woodland spirit man-beast), and several of the animal imaginings from Physiologus's second-century exemplar of the bestiary are repeated. Representations of these animals invented in the mythic mind had not changed in fourteen hundred years. In Ulisse Aldrovandi's fourteen-volume *Natural History*, beginning in 1599, a harpy – part bird, part woman – is duly described in detail. Edward Topsell's *History of Four-Footed Beasts* (1607) contains a sphinx, dragons, and basilisks (reptiles that can kill a man with a look but are harmless to women), and in a 1655 volume of his we find portraits of an Indian zebra and four kinds of unicorn. At the end of the seventeenth century the University of Leiden's "Indian Cabinet Hall" of scientific curiosities proudly housed a winged cat, the hand of a mermaid, and a cockatrice (a synonym for the basilisk, a monster hatched from a hen's egg). This was indeed the age of science but far from fully so. Science can provide understanding only when its data correspond with reality, and much available material, even from the most reputable of sources, did not correspond with reality. And to the extent that justifiable sympathies are dependent on appropriate factual knowledge, and respect emphatically so, misinformation is likely to distort that sympathy and respect. The impetus to animal respect, and ultimately to vegetarianism, had poor prospects when the object requiring respect was so misrepresented.

To be sure, Francis Bacon (1561-1626) – who commended but appears not to have always practised vegetarianism – had made great strides in putting the acquisition of knowledge on a scientific foundation, but it was John Ray (1627-1705) and Carolus Linnaeus (1707-1778) who did most to systematize our understanding and provide a context in which sensibilities toward animals could be confidently expressed. By the very close of the seventeenth century, John Ray had developed a systematic classification of the animal and vegetable realms, assisted by his student Francis Willughby and many clerical and lay associates. And Ray's observations persuaded him of the justice of a vegetable diet, even though the persuasion was apparently insufficient to alter his dietary habits. If the age of science spawned many amateur parlour physiologists, it stimulated an even greater number to undertake investigations into natural history, which is not of itself any guarantee of animal sensibilities but often a happy precursor nonetheless. By 1737, Carolus Linnaeus had published his groundbreaking *Systema naturae fundamenta botanica* and *Genera plantarum,* creating a scientific taxonomy applicable in the first instance to plants but also to animals. Such taxonomy provided a sounder footing from which to view the animal realm, and some of the benefits of more rigorous science were now of benefit to the vegetarian cause. Thus, as Keith Thomas has stated, "Later seventeenth-century scientists like Walter Charleton, John Ray and John Wallis were much impressed by the suggestion that human anatomy, particularly the teeth and intestines, showed [as it had shown Pierre Gassendi earlier in the century, as we have seen] that man had not originally been intended to be carnivorous."[26] Even the diarist John Evelyn wrote a short book, *Acetaria: A Discourse of Sallets,* to show that humankind could live quite agreeably on a vegetable diet and dispense with animal flesh, again without changing its cuisine. "Science" was, albeit haphazardly, providing a knowledge of the reality of animals – their organs, their sentience, their structure – that would allow us to understand how analogous, perhaps even homologous, they were to us.

The reality was that Bacon's age of scientific understanding proved a difficult age for many – although, of course, not all – to arrive at self-convincing moral conclusions. To be sure, common sense held that animals feel pain and suffer and that they have a modicum of reason, but the Renaisssance brought such new and surprising speculative knowledge in almost every sphere that confidence waned in the customary certainties. As John Locke saw, among others, Cartesianism seemed to contradict common sense. But who could trust common sense any more? The Renaissance and its aftermath should not be understood as a time of increasing certainty but as a time of troublesome quest. It was a time that invoked a questioning among a stalwart few of the time-honoured flesh-eating traditions. Whereas those who did raise questions did so predominantly from an ascetic perspective, we increasingly find ethical considerations underlying the justifications offered. And ethical deliberations were aided by appropriate scientific – physiological, psychological, taxonomic – knowledge. Nonetheless, most retained the conviction that a fleshless diet was possible only in an ideal world.

## VEGETARIAN VARIETIES

Although vegetarians were scarce in the seventeenth and first half of the eighteenth centuries, they were not unknown, and they were increasingly common. First and foremost, they were ascetics who eschewed animal flesh in order to punish their own flesh. And they achieved some notoriety. For example, in the 1620s Thomas Bushell, an English Civil War royalist and Baconian disciple, was determined to follow the master's vegetarian advocacy. He restricted himself for three years to a regimen of herbs, oil, mustard, honey, and water and ended his days on a meager fleshless regimen. The Ranter John Robins, a self-styled resurrected Adam – despiser of the authoritarian Stuarts and Cromwell alike – enjoined his numerous mid-seventeenth-century London disciples to abstain from flesh and alcohol. Judith Traske, wife of the Judaist leader John Traske, refused flesh for at least seven years while imprisoned during the reign of Charles I.[27] "In the eighteenth and early nineteenth centuries," Keith Thomas informs us, "there were sectarians, influenced by the German mystic Boehme and by William Law's *Serious Call* (1738) who, along with some Southcottians and Swedenborgians, followed a similar austere regimen of abstinence from animal food."[28] At the same time, a few religious fundamentalists adhered rigorously to the injunction of Genesis 9:4, refusing to eat any flesh with blood in it. And the pantheistic Gerard Winstanley, leader of the Diggers, the most radical wing of the parliamentarians during the English Civil War, showed a decided antipathy to all forms of violence, ostensibly including violence to our animal brethren. So did a number of those who had been sickened by the bloodshed they had witnessed and inflicted in the conflict. There was undoubtedly an animal ethic among the more radical of these parliamentarians. The radical Presbyterian Richard Overton's views on animal immortality and the significant human similarities with animals, via the French army surgeon Ambroise Paré, exemplify that perspective. And as later became a commonplace among radical (and even some moderate) animal advocates, both Diggers and Levellers were said to believe that the Golden Rule of doing unto others as you would be done by applied to animals. It was even engraved on the vegetarian Leveller Roger Crab's tombstone.

Apart from the ascetics – and whether many of the others were at least partly ascetics in different guise is open to question – there were those who opposed the killing of animals on almost any ground. In *Man and the Natural World,* Thomas mentions the opponent of animal ethics Thomas Edwards, who in 1646 discussed with disgust what he saw as the unfortunately prevalent doctrine that one must not kill any lawful creatures ("lawful" meaning, presumably, those not injurious to humankind); a certain Mr. Marshall of Hackney, preacher and former soldier, disciple of Giles Randall of the Family of Love, who believed it wrong to kill any of God's creatures; and Roger Crab, the Leveller mystic, who opposed all flesh consumption, primarily on the ground that it encouraged human lust – the "sinful lusts of the flesh," as the *Book of Common Prayer* had warned about in a different context.[29] As a sign of solidarity with the poor, Crab renounced flesh as an aspect of sybaritic luxury. He went further. Eating meat, he believed, was the cause of almost all human illness. Thomas Edwards added more than a touch of animal sensibility in *Gangraena,* although expressing not his own views but those of members of the Family of Love whom he was condemning, in stating their apparent view that: "God loves the creatures that creep on the ground as well as the best saints; and there is no difference between the flesh of a man and the flesh of a toad."[30] The radical Ranter Jacob Bauthumley added a pantheistic flourish, averring: "I see God in all creatures, man and beast, fish and fowl and every green thing from the highest cedar to the ivy on the wall; and that God is the life and being of them all."[31] Thomas Parr, of whom legend has it that he died at 152 in 1635, was "of old Pythagoras's opinion," according to John Taylor, the self-described "water poet," although on what grounds we are not sure. His diet was "old cheese, milk, coarse bread, small beer and whey."[32] The diarist John Evelyn said of him: "As soon as old Parr came to change his simple homely diet to that of the Court of Arundel House [to which he had been invited as a celebrated guest] he quickly sank and drooped away."[33]

Of the seventeenth-century English vegetarians, by far the most significant in terms of the combination of animal ethics and the refusal to eat flesh was Thomas Tryon (1634-1703), who was a convert from Anabaptism – which he had adopted at the age of nineteen – to the so-called Pythagorean diet at the age of twenty-three in 1657, inspired by the mystical writings of Jakob Boehme, although he failed to convince his wife to forgo flesh. Sometimes, probably for political reasons in the unfriendly culture of the Restoration, he advised his readers merely to limit their flesh eating. At other times, he was far more forthright: "Refrain at all times from such Foods as cannot be procured without violence and oppression. For know that all the inferior Creatures when hurt do cry and send forth their complaints to their Maker or grand Fountain whence they proceeded. Be not insensible that every Creature doth bear the Image of the great Creator according to the Nature of each, and that He is the Vital Power in all things. Therefore let none take pleasure to offer violence to that life, lest he awaken the fierce wrath and bring danger to his own soul."[34]

Nor did he resist condemning his fellow citizens their cruelties: "The inferior creatures groan under your cruelties. You hunt them for your pleasure and overwork them for your covetousness, and kill them for your gluttony, and set them to fight one another until they die, and count it a sport and a pleasure to behold them worry one another."[35] Humankind's duty, he added, was: "as it bests tends to the helping, aiding and abetting beasts to the obtaining of all the advantages their natures are by the great, beautiful and always beneficent creator made capable of."[36]

Tryon blames flesh consumption on custom and culture rather than on human nature, noting how a visitor from a non-flesh-eating nation would be horrified at our markets and our practices on seeing: "the communication we have with dead bodies, and how blythe and merry we are at their funerals, and what honorable sepulchres we bury the dead carcasses of beasts in – nay, their very guts and entrails – would he not be filled with astonishment and horror? Would he not count us cruel monsters, and say we were *brutified*, and performed the parts of beasts of prey, to live thus on the spoils of our fellow creatures?"[37]

Tryon was profoundly impressed by what he had read about Indian practices, largely inaccurate although they sometimes were, and ruminated on the kind of world that could be created if an Indian vegetarian and animal ethic could be imported into Europe.

He seems to have had an especial concern for the birds. Speaking for them, he asks: "But tell us, O men! We pray you to tell us what injuries have we committed to forfeit? What laws have we broken, or what cause given you, whereby you can pretend a right to invade and violate our part, and natural rights, and to assault and destroy us, as if we were the aggressors, and no better than thieves, robbers and murderers, fit to be extirpated out of creation. From whence did thou derive thy authority for killing thy inferiors merely because they are such, or for destroying their natural rights and privileges."[38]

This was probably the first time the newly coined concept of natural rights had been applied to animals rather than to humans alone. In fact, Tryon would have been loath to apply the concept to many humans. He elevated the animals while denigrating humankind, "this proud and troublesome Thing, called *Man*" – proud and troublesome because it had the unmitigated gall to inflict its unnecessary greed on their innocent bodies. The vegetarian diet that should be the consequence was "Wisdom's Bill of Fare."

Like many animal advocates, he did not restrict his ethical concerns to animals. He entered the lists on greater gender fairness, the atrocious treatment of slaves, the ill-treatment of the insane, the barbarities of criminal punishment, the need for religious toleration, and the horrors of war. He influenced the feminist, playwright, and purported spy Aphra Behn (1640-1689) with what she saw as his rustic eloquence. She acknowledged her indebtedness to Tryon and said she was persuaded to try his vegetable regimen for a period. When Benjamin Franklin (1706-1790) became a vegetarian for a time in his youth, he attributed the decision to reading Thomas Tryon. Even after returning to flesh eating, Franklin said "he never went a fishing or Shooting," and he continued to speak favourably about an abstemious diet.[39] Tryon was one of those rare figures: a man for whom the elimination of injustice seemed to infuse his whole being, even if in his last years he affected the role of wealthy landed gentleman.

Tryon is probably the first in the anglophone world to provide a predominantly ethical justification for vegetarianism, although he understood it had health benefits as well. He was probably vegan, to boot. And if political circumstance after the Restoration (1660) convinced him to temper his message, it was circumspection, not philosophy, that persuaded him to do so.

On the continent of Europe there was a man who had a similar vegetarian influence as did Tryon in the English-speaking world: Antonio Celestina Cocchi (1695-1758), Professor of Medicine at the University of Pisa and later Professor of Anatomy at the University of Florence. He was the celebrated author of *Del vitto pitagorico per uso della medicina* (1743). The book was translated into English as *On the Pythagorean Diet*. The sympathies of both Voltaire and Rousseau for a vegetarian regimen were based in significant part on the writings of Cocchi. However, the influence on these Franco-Swiss *philosophes,* if less than orthodox *philosophes,* comes as something of a surprise given that, in contrast with Tryon's, Cocchi's argument is based in large part on the health benefits of a vegetable diet rather than on the protection of animals. He was, for example, the first to argue that scurvy was occasioned by a lack of vegetables. He regarded "the Pythagorean diet ... as useful in medicine and, at the same time, as full of innocence, of temperance, and of health."[40] When Cocchi is writing to vindicate Pythagoras, the Samian is regarded as a great physician whose vegetable regimen arose "from the desire to improve health and the manners of men."[41] But although Cocchi clearly approves of the "innocence" and the attempt to improve "the manners of men," they receive relatively short shrift in his discussion. Almost all the attention is on health. It would appear that the portrait of Pythagoras and Pythagoreanism, although still based largely on the imagination of Ovid, was subject to change according to the whim and convenience of the advocate. In Cocchi's case it was Pythagoras the healer.

Vegetarian advocacy was also a province of the highly influential Swedish scientist, prophet, and mystic Emanuel Swedenborg (1688-1772). His mystical theology was both intricate and confusing but sufficiently inspiring to many that a few years after his death a new church (most commonly called New Jerusalem Church or simply New Church) was established with a number of branches, all devoted to the preaching of his doctrines. His theology, including the advocacy of a vegetarian diet, thereby acquired a limited but significant public expression. And this vegetarian creed contained the rudiments of an animal ethic, albeit an obscure one. Certainly, it was a great deal less explicit and direct than that of Tryon. Thus, for example, Swedenborg stated that "the Divine is in each and every thing of the created universe,"[42] which appears simple enough in itself. It may also be said to possess ethical implications, even though the predominant reason for the eschewing of flesh was ascetic. The obscurity is exemplified not only in Swedenborg's own words elsewhere on occasion but also in the discussion of his biographer, Martin Lamm: "even at the time when he was professing a philosophy ... distinctly mechanistic ... we detect in Swedenborg's mind a leaven of mysticism ... his *Animal Kingdom* attempts an empirical penetration, not merely of the essence of the soul and its intercourse with the body, but even the state of the soul after physical death."[43] Although "the Divine," as we might expect, applied in the first instance to humans, Swedenborg observed that animals have their organs, limbs, and viscera in common with humankind and that they all have a spiritual nature. In fact, he remarked: "living creatures of the [animal] kingdom" are like humans "except in the matter of speech," a facility on which he placed significant weight.[44] Martin Lamm advises us "that the thoughts of the nonreasoning animals are no more than tremulations produced by external sensations," although perhaps not much different from what Swedenborg imagined much human thought to be.[45] The soul is a machine but not insensible, for it is a *machina animata* – a living machine.[46] It is an idea perhaps no more enlightening than Malebranche's insentient machines. Nonetheless, the emphasis on the similarities between man and beast encouraged an acknowledgment among the believers that, although there were differences and these to the benefit of humankind, there were sufficient similarities that we owed a responsibility to all of God's creatures.

Despite his recognition of a good measure of human continuities and similarities, Swedenborg's primary reason for advocating abstention from animal flesh is rather more scriptural and prehistorical than ethical, referring back to man's original condition as worthy of recapture, although the suggestion is clear that such a state was morally as well as historically pristine. Cruelty was not a perennial human characteristic but had arrived along with the change of diet. Animal cruelty was thereby condemned:

> Eating the flesh of animals, considered in itself, is somewhat profane; for in the most ancient times they never ate the flesh of any beast or bird, but only grain ... especially bread made of wheat ... the fruits of trees, vegetables, milk and such things as are made from them, as butter, etc. To kill animals and eat their flesh was unlawful [i.e., contrary to the law of God or natural law and hence unjust], being regarded as something bestial. They only took from them uses and services, as is evident from Genesis 1, 29-30. But in the course of time, when man became cruel like wild beasts, yea more cruel, first they began to kill animals and eat their flesh. And because man had acquired such a nature, the killing and eating of animals was permitted and is permitted at the present day.[47]

Like most of his contemporaries, he took the idea of the Golden Age in the scriptures literally, telling us "the earth was formerly like heaven, and the age like a celestial amusement" and mentioning explicitly "the Golden Age of [humankind's] primitive state."[48] It was a paradise to be recaptured.

Often associated with Boehme and the theosophists in manner of spiritual thought, although with less relevance to modernity, Swedenborg would be relegated to a mere footnote in vegetarian history were it not for the impact of two of his followers, William Cowherd and Joseph Brotherton: the one for his major influence on Christian and secular vegetarian developments in both Britain and via some of his disciples the United States, the other for his organizational skills and his important voice in the founding of the Vegetarian Society in England.

Like Swedenborg, the French physician Philippe Hecquet (1661-1737) argued the warrant of Genesis 1 and "the Garden of Eden" for a vegetarian regimen. Rather like Luigi Cornaro and unlike Swedenborg, he was concerned with diet largely from a health perspective alone. Mechanist in the Cartesian manner, and an ascetic to boot, Hecquet lauded the health provided by a monastic diet compared with the sybaritic luxury of the urban gentry, and he ended his days housed among the Carmelites. Reviving, he believed, the temperance doctrines of ancient Hippocratic medicine, he claimed that flesh interfered with the digestion and circulation of the blood. He compiled a list of peoples from Brahmins to Tartars via numerous Spanish and Italians who, he claimed, lived on no or little flesh yet maintained their health and vigour. And he claimed that the fleshless diet was gaining substantial ground among the traditional flesh eaters. Even Hecquet's opponents conceded the growing strength of the antiflesh movement. Fruits, grains, seeds, and nuts should replace meat, Hecquet opined. It was so intended by God and nature. Williams informs us that Hecquet contrasted man with those "animals whom Nature manifestly intended for carnage" and concluded that "since men have neither fangs nor talons to tear flesh ... it is far from being the food most natural to them."[49]

George Cheyne (1671-1743), a British physician who was a contemporary of Hecquet and greatly admired by him, advocated a fleshless diet initially on the grounds of health benefits, as Hecquet had done, but soon saw that it was very much an ethical issue as well. The grossly corpulent Dr. Cheyne had become so after debauching himself on a wide array of culinary novelties he had discovered on his arrival in London from Scotland. In fact, he had been no abstainer during his days as a young man in Scotland either. His only recourse from a threatened early demise, he found, was a milk, bread, fruit, and vegetable diet. He lost some half of his total weight in short order and soon began to proselytize for the vegetable regimen. Like many advocates of the time of the ills of flesh, he also denounced alcohol as a primary contributor to the same maladies brought on by meat. Not surprisingly, he became a thorn in the flesh of the medical establishment, stimulating the formidable physician Dr. John Arbuthnot, friend of Alexander Pope and John Gay and himself no foe to the beneficial effects of a vegetable diet, to organize sentiment against the excesses of Cheyne's sparse regimen. Indeed, a number in the period claimed the effect of Cheyne's regimen was to cause the steady practitioner to waste away unto death.

Cheyne addressed the ethical issues directly in his *Essay on Regimen* of 1740, where he stated:

The question I design to treat of here is, whether animal or vegetable food was, in the original design of the Creator, intended for the food of animals, and particularly of the human race. And I am almost convinced it never was intended, but only permitted as a curse or punishment ... At what time animal food first came to man is not certainly known. He was a bold man who made the first experiment ... To see the convulsions, agonies and torture of a poor fellow-creature, whom they cannot restore nor recompense, dying to gratify luxury, and tickle callous and rank organs, must require a rocky heart, and a great deal of cruelty and ferocity. I cannot find any great difference, on the foot of natural reason and equity alone, between feasting on human flesh and feasting on brute animal flesh, except custom and example.

I believe some rational creatures [i.e., humans] would suffer less in being butchered than a strong Ox or red Deer; and in natural morality and justice, the degree of pain here makes the essential difference.[50]

Cheyne's animal sensibilities are here clearly profound and to the fore. But there are other things to notice about the passage, too. His claim that God had permitted human carnivorousness as a punishment – one, he added, intended to shorten human lives – was treated with derision by his peers. In an otherwise favourable summary of Cheyne's life and accomplishments, the *Dictionary of National Biography* took him earnestly to task on this point. Cheyne's reference to the absence of compensation reflects the common contemporary assumption that, unlike humans, animals do not have the prospect of an immortal life and thus, again unlike humans, cannot be recompensed in the next life for the ills they suffer in this. It was not uncommon to hear the argument – by Alexander Pope and Humphry Primatt, for example – that animals accordingly have an even better claim than humans to be treated well in this life. Cheyne's concentration on the elimination of pain and suffering as the primary moral reason for the avoidance of flesh and on the eradication of cruelty to animals comes long before such was popular – after Moses Maimonides, Montaigne, and William Hinde, to be sure, but well before Richard Dean, Humphry Primatt, Jean-Jacques Rousseau, and then Jeremy Bentham deemed pain and suffering the cornerstone of animal ethics.

In *The Case of the Author,* written just over a decade before the end of his life, Cheyne describes the regimen he follows at present, which consists of "milk, with tea, coffee, bread and butter, mild cheese, salads, fruits and seeds of all kinds, with tender roots (as potatoes, turnips, carrots)." In short, he adds: "everything that has not life."[51] Given the limits of general eighteenth-century conceptions of "life," Cheyne believed we had a responsibility to all the sentient animal realm. Moreover, he had considerable success in persuading others of the necessity of pursuing his recommended regimen. Among his notable converts, we find the Anglican priest and prophet of Methodism John Wesley (1703-1791), who told the Bishop of London in 1747 that since following Cheyne's dietary advice, he had been free from all bodily disorders, and the novelist Samuel Richardson (1689-1761), author of the sentimental *Pamela, or Virtue Rewarded* (1740) and *Clarissa Harlowe* (1747-1748). In the pages of the novels, aspects of the diet are mentioned and treated as a wholesome ingredient of simplicity. Although he was a strict follower of the regimen during Cheyne's lifetime, it seems likely that Richardson returned to a more varied diet after Cheyne's death.

Not all the conversions of the age, however, were ultimate successes. A number of the once-convinced soon managed to unconvince themselves. For example, when he was a student at Trinity Hall, Cambridge, Philip Dormer Stanhope, Earl of Chesterfield (1694-1791), was persuaded on moral grounds to eschew the eating of flesh. In the pages of *The World*, Joseph Ritson reports Chesterfield as stating: "I remember when I was a young man at the university, being so much affected with that very pathetic [i.e., full of feeling] speech which Ovid puts into the mouth of Pythagoras against the eating of the flesh of animals, that it was some time before I could bring myself to our college mutton again, with some inward doubt whether I was not making myself an accomplice to murder."[52]

"An accomplice to murder" again he soon was, rationalizing his new-found flesh-eating convictions based on the natural rights of the strong over the weak, somewhat reminiscent of Hugo Grotius's seventeenth-century views on war, the rights of conquest having gained legitimacy over time by their very success.

The views were reminiscent, too, of what T.H. Huxley, referring to such "rights" of the strong over the weak, would later call "tiger rights." Indeed, having renounced his renunciation of flesh, Lord Chesterfield renounced also any adherence to principles of sensibility toward animals. Although the rights of the strong over the weak were rarely advanced as an argument in favour of flesh eating, perhaps Chesterfield was merely more honest than most. It is quite probable that the idea underlay most thinking of the time: we eat the flesh of animals because we have the power to do so. Eating flesh is the prime symbol of our dominance over other species. In fact, it was very difficult in those days of well-stocked college larders to be an undergraduate vegetarian. Beef and pigeon pies, beef and mutton joints, and roasted duck were regular college fare. The customary tarts, apple pies, cakes, and plum puddings would not alone satisfy the students' appetites. Chesterfield was no exception.

Strangely, William Wordsworth, a student at Saint John's College from 1787, wrote reminiscently of his Cambridge days in *The Prelude:*

> I chaced not steadily the manly deer,
> But laid me down to any casual
> Of wild wood-honey; or, with truant eyes
> Unruly, peeped about for vagrant fruit.[53]

At least it is strange – for a moment we dare to believe we have found a clandestine Pythagorean! – when we know of his common flesh consumption, yet he is not alluding to his diet but to his preferred books of sensibility and to the sexual adventures of which he dreamed and which he sought.

Numbered, like Chesterfield, among the former vegetarians reverting to the consumption of flesh are Benjamin Franklin (1706-1790) and James Boswell (1740-1795). Having been converted to a vegetable diet by the words of Tryon at the age of sixteen, Franklin came to realize that fish ate fish and determined carnivorousness to be the eternal law of nature. Inclination won out over principle. James Boswell turned to the vegetable regimen in his early manhood with protestations of conviction that the diet would last. But he later confessed he had long fallen by the wayside. Nonetheless, both he and Dr. Samuel Johnson read Dr. Cheyne and found his recommended fare a necessary diversion for extended periods on medical grounds from their customary bourgeois feasts. Despite these occasional reversals, vegetarianism made significant strides, especially in medical circles, throughout the later eighteenth century.

## Increasing Animal Sensibility

It was in the main not an awakening to the lessons of Pythagoras, or India, or Turkey, or aboriginal myths and practices that aroused animal sensibilities, however often an idealized version of them was used to paint the scene and explore the possibilities – as did, for example, Tryon of the first version, Goldsmith of the second, Bacon of the third, and Montaigne of the fourth. They were imaginative tropes to show us how the practices of our own culture were lacking and could be transformed within our own changing values. Animal sensibilities were, as we have seen, encouraged by the Renaissance itself, the rebirth of classical inquiry and knowledge, the sensibilities commencing not as often thought in the early sixteenth century but having their first inklings around the midst of the fourteenth. This is exemplified in the fourteenth century by the aforementioned William Langland's *Piers the Ploughman,* an allegorical, alliterative, unrhymed poem that acknowledges a certain animal superiority and that was written long before the renowned "voyages of discovery" had begun. Being asked by Nature to gather wisdom from all the wonders of the world, including the animal creation, Langland investigates the birds, beasts, reptiles, and humanity, perceiving "how surely Reason followed all the beasts, in their eating and drinking, and engendering of their kinds ... And I beheld the birds in the bushes building their nests, which no man with all their wits could ever make." He wonders at the breeding and secreting capacities of the birds, concluding, as we saw previously, "Reason ruled and cared for the beasts, except only for man and his mate; for many a time they wandered ungoverned by Reason."[54] In Chapter 6 we met the fourteenth- or fifteenth-century animal sensibilities expressed in *Dives et Pauper* in some detail. It was an extension of these sensibilities that was rife in the ensuing ages. Langland stands as a symbol of the new era, even though he lived and wrote at its very inception.

Central to the rebirth witnessed in the Renaissance, and seen in profusion in the following centuries, was the discovery of persons and animals as objects rather than subjects, which resulted in their being seen not in relation to ourselves but as independent beings with their own attributes, their own character, their own rights – as ends in themselves no less, although this formulation would come a couple of centuries later. Shakespeare's *Romeo and Juliet* is a telling tale of the changing mores as exemplified in similar Renaissance tales of the loving pair. The Montagues and Capulets represent the dying past, where everything exists in relation to the communal whole. By contrast, Romeo and Juliet are individuals with loyalty to their selves. Their loyalty to each other comes only after their discovery of their individuality. They represent the Renaissance and the new mores of the succeeding eras. As Polonius says to Laertes in *Hamlet,* "This above all: to thine own self be true, / And it must follow, as the night the day, / Thou canst not then be false to any man" (Act 1, scene 3, lines 78-80). Respect for the other as a self, whether human or animal, was predicated on one's own self-recognition. Of course, Langland and *Dives et Pauper* are only isolated expressions among the beginnings – animal sensibilities in embryo, if you will – but they arose precisely from regarding other beings as objective entities, as independent beings who do not exist merely as a part of our community and an extension of ourselves. As D.H. Lawrence saw so well of a later period, but one suffused with the same ideals, the achievement of Paul Cézanne was one in which his "apples are a real attempt to let the apple exist in its own separate entity, without transfusing it with personal emotion. Cézanne's great effort was, as it were, to shove the apple away from him, and to let it live of itself."[55] Novelists and poets, artists and scientists, all frequently acknowledge their need to distance themselves from the object of their attention both to depict it accurately and to appreciate it as it deserves. Unfortunately, along with the incipient sensibility toward animals, the new concern for knowledge for its own sake encouraged the greatest misuse of animals. As always in Western culture, at least from the time of the Renaissance, the two sides were in constant tension: cruelty and sensibility inseparably.

In the century before the French Revolution there was a veritable cultural revolution in "sentiments, manners and moral opinions" – Edmund Burke's words but a popular phrase of the period and one with application beyond Burke's intent. This was the century of Sensibility. The idea was of a revolution in attitudes pertaining to fellow humans, but it applied in lesser degree to the animal realm, too, culminating in the considerable increase in popular advocacy of the vegetarian diet entirely on humanitarian grounds in the years following the Revolution. This advocacy was predicated on the general expansion in animal sensibilities – countered by the experimenting scientists and numerous clerics and their faithful flocks concerned lest the distinction between humans and animals be obscured. From the middle of the seventeenth century most learned voices were heard on the side of the animals, although, as we have noted, this was contemporaneous with the rapid increase in uncontrolled animal experimentation, a consequence of the increased desire to know things for their own sakes; an interest that Thomas Hobbes described in *Leviathan* (1651) as "a lust of the mind that by a perseverance of delight in the continual and indefatigable generation of knowledge, exceeds the short vehemence of any carnal pleasure."[56] It was a lust and delight that countered the tenor of most expressions of animal sensibility. But it was in line with another compatible view, one expressed by François Fénelon, the theologian Archbishop of Cambrai, that because of the faculty of speech, humans were "more perfect" than other animals, with the implication that other animals were not worthy of serious ethical consideration. Paradoxically, Fénelon added, "it happens equally often that I am more perfect when I remain silent than when I talk" – a view that the animal advocates of the time would readily have endorsed.[57] In each nation the Fénelon view existed alongside the growing sensibility.

We find this general tenor favourable to the animals expressed primarily by the literary luminaries of the era but also by the Puritans during the

Cromwellian Protectorate in England, who succeeded in prohibiting the public display of animal fighting until the Restoration. This sectarian sensibility might best be exemplified in the words of William Hinde (1569-1629), curate of Bunbury in Cheshire: "I think it utterly unlawful [i.e., unjust] for any man to take pleasure in the pain and torture of any creature, or delight himself in the tyranny which the creatures exercise, one over another [as in their carnivorousness], or to make a recreation of their brutish cruelty which they practise upon one another [as in cockfighting, dog fighting, bearbaiting, etc.]."[58] It was a common enough kind of utterance. And "fellow-creatures" was a common phrase of the Puritans that helped raise the status of animals. On the other side of the Atlantic, we find the recently immigrated fellow Puritan the Reverend William Ward writing the *Body of Liberties* of the Massachusetts Bay Colony in 1641, which was intended to protect domesticated animals from abuse on the farm and during transportation.[59] Again, the irony is apparent: It is important to provide a measure of justice to those creatures you are soon to treat with the grossest injustice!

Among the literary figures, we find Andrew Marvell (1622-1678) lamenting the death of a fawn; John Wilmot, Earl of Rochester (1647-1680), and Jonathan Swift (1677-1745) comparing animals favourably to humans; the diarists John Evelyn (1620-1706) and Samuel Pepys (1633-1703) denigrating animal "sports"; and Margaret Cavendish, the Duchess of Newcastle (1624-1674), speculating on potentially greater knowledge in animals than humans and deriding human hubris in imagining humans superior. She even questioned whether we had a right to animal flesh. Alexander Pope (1688-1744) stressed the interdependence of all beings, Henry Fielding (1707-1754) abominated cruelty to animals and called for stronger measures against the perpetrators of animal cruelty, and Anne Finch, Countess of Winchilsea (1661-1720), John Gay (1685-1732), and John Dyer (1700-1758) all regretted in their poetry human failure to consider the interests of animals appropriately. Christopher Smart (1722-1771) wrote with grace and charm in praise of his cat, asking that "God be merciful to all creatures in respect of pain."[60] But it is the Scot James Thomson (1700-1748), William Cowper (1731-1800), and Oliver Goldsmith (1728-1774) who perhaps did most to raise sensibilities toward animals, although the Englishman Daniel Defoe (1660-1724), the Scot Tobias Smollett (1712-1771), and the Irishman Henry Brooke (1703-1783) also had passing but significant comments against cruelty to animals in their pages. We encounter, too, Richard Steele (1672-1724) writing in the pages of *The Tatler* in praise of kindness toward animals. In contrast with an exemplar of lack of consideration to animals, he states: "I am extremely pleased to see his younger brother carry an universal benevolence toward every thing that has life."[61] A few of these authors also praised vegetarian practice but did not partake of it.

This was not an age of merely literary consideration for animals. The Cromwellian intriguer Richard Overton (fl. 1642-1649), the French philosopher Pierre Bayle (1647-1706), and the German philosopher Gottfried Wilhelm Leibniz (1644-1716), along with Henry More (1614-1687) and the Cambridge Platonists as well as the parliamentarian Soame Jenyns (1704-1787), concurred in granting immortal souls to animals. The Anglican priests Bishop Joseph Butler (1692-1752), Rev. Dr. John Hildrop (fl. 1742), Rev. Richard Dean (1727-1778), Rev. John Wesley (1703-1791), Rev. Capel Berrow (1715-1782), and the Swiss Protestant naturalist Charles Bonnet (1720-1793) were of like mind. The Reverends James Granger (1723-1776) and Humphry Primatt (c. 1735 to c. 1778) were adamantly in favour of promoting human duties toward animals. In 1683 the Anglican dean of Winchester Richard Meggott preached on the similarity of humans with animals. Even on the questions of reasoning, learning, and knowledge, which humans thought their prerogative, the animals were not without their share, he opined. In America, the devout John Woolman (1720-1772) was not only an advocate against slavery but also wrote with passion against cruelty to animals, and the deist recluse William Wollaston asserted in *The Religion of Nature Delineated* (1724) that animals were better off under the control of man but that they should be taken into account in proportion to their various degrees of understanding.

Among the philosophers, John Locke (1632-1704) used the great chain of being model to narrow the distinctions between humans and other animals, who from species to species "differ in almost insensible degrees."[62] And Locke argued that "children should from the beginning be bred up in an abhorrence of killing or tormenting any living creature."[63] Anthony Ashley Cooper, third Earl of Shaftesbury (1671-1713), condemned those who showed "unnatural and inhuman delight in beholding torments, and in viewing distress calamity, blood, massacre and destruction with a peculiar joy and pleasure." For Shaftesbury, viewed my many as the inaugurator of the cult of Sensibility, this principle applied to the gore "both of our own or another species."[64] The Scottish utilitarian David Hume (1711-1776) argued that humans and animals differed only in degree, not in kind – a formulation that was soon to become commonplace. His *Treatise of Human Nature* (1729-1740) contained chapters on "Of the Reason of Animals," "Of the Pride of Animals," and "Of the Love and Hatred of Animals." "No truth appears to be more evident," he observed, "than that beasts are endow'd with thought as well as men."[65] His countryman Adam Smith (1723-1790), philosopher and economist, had little to say to elevate the animals. But he understood how unnecessary was flesh to the human diet, although he was no vegetarian himself, a recognition held equally by the great historian of the *Decline and Fall of the Roman Empire,* Edward Gibbon (1737-1794). Smith held that "the trade of a butcher is a brutal and odious business," a view shared by many of his contemporaries, butchers being generally disparaged for the vicious work they do. There was even a contemporary pervasive myth that butchers were debarred from jury work on account of the brutality of their trade. Further, because flesh was unnecessary to health, Smith argued, for tax purposes meat should be treated as a luxury item.

The Anglo-Irish parliamentarian and political philosopher Edmund Burke (1729-1797) remarked approvingly that certain "animals inspire us with sentiments of tenderness and affection toward their persons, we like to have them near us, and we enter willingly into a kind of relation with them."[66]

And Frances Hutcheson (1694-1746) tells us that "brutes have a right that no useless pain or misery should be inflicted upon them."[67] He added his voice to those of Thomas Young and William Paley in stating that the right to slaughter animals for food was "so opposed to our natural compassion that one cannot think an express grant of it by revelation was superfluous."[68] Yet later he observed that killing animals for food was necessary and an appropriate human right. He seems to have decided this was *useful* "pain or misery" that was "inflicted upon them."

Commissioner of the Board of Trade Soame Jenyns noted that "God has given many advantages to Brutes, which man cannot attain to with all his superiority ... we are not so high in the scale of existence as our ignorant ambition may desire ... Is not the justice of God as much concerned to preserve the happiness of the meanest insect which he has called into being as the greatest man that ever lives."[69] If a picture is worth a thousand words, perhaps the engravings of Hogarth were more effective than all the writings of the philosophers, essayists, parliamentarians, and poets. In the mid-eighteenth century, William Hogarth (1697-1764) published a series of didactic engravings entitled *The Four Stages of Cruelty,* in which cruelty to animals was depicted as the precursor to cruelty to humans, and although cruelty to humans was clearly in Hogarth's mind far the more serious offence, the lessons on causality and animal cruelty were not lost on the educated public.

Then as now the vast majority of persons gave no thought to the ethics of flesh eating. This was so among many even of the most adamant animal advocates. This is exemplified by Henry Fielding, one of the first English novelists. He was not only profoundly sympathetic to ill-treated animals – horses and asses in particular – but was also probably the first since the Protectorate days of the 1650s to recognize, as early as the 1740s, the need to legislate against cruelty to animals. He thought of himself as "having been sent into this world as a general blessing" with the intent "to redress all grievances whatsoever, and to defend and protect the brute creation" – food animals excepted apparently.[70] Through his son Tom, he was aware of at least one "who professed the Pythagorean principles" and saw some merit in his views on transmigration, but the idea of ceasing to eat animals never seems to have entered his mind.

Clearly, the time was ripe for a general respect for animals to grow into something more – a respect that would extend far enough that the millennia of custom would be questioned and overcome. It is astonishing that all these expressions of animal sensibility had not already resulted in a broad acceptance of the view that we had no right to slaughter for food. It did not. But times were changing. At first, the recommendations to abandon flesh were made but not followed even by many of those who were making the recommendations. It was easier intellectually to reach the conclusion that eating flesh was unnatural or unjust than to overcome the ingrained and convenient practice to which they had become inured. Those who advocated a vegetarian diet for health reasons stood on far firmer ground. Their recommendations were of immediate self-interested benefit to those who obtained the advice, and thus they were relatively easy to follow. The ethical vegetarian had to do the very opposite – persuade the listeners to look out for the interests of others, often at the expense of abandoning their culinary delights.

There is, as previously noted, something incongruous in the claim that one should respect and care for the animals and then eat the objects of this respect and care. Yet that is precisely what happened – by those whose words we have met and probably admired over the last few pages, for example, and even by those who pointed out the incongruence. We must conclude there is something at work deep in the human psyche – not of itself at all a surprising proposition – that limits the capacity to act on the determinations of the inquiring mind. But the incongruity existed not merely among those who advocated concern for animals and were silent on the issue of eating them but also among most in the eighteenth century who wrote eloquently against the eating of flesh while, apparently, downing their mutton chops simultaneously. The prevailing belief among the animal advocates seems to have been that we should and could live from an exclusively vegetable diet in a different world but that humans, as they had become over the millennia since Eden, inhabited a fallen world where they *required* a flesh diet in order to survive. Pythagoras and the vegetarians of the classical era, they readily imagined, lived close to the time of the prelapsarian paradise and shared something of the prelapsarian human constitution. Those attracted to vegetarianism on ethical grounds had to believe the health vegetarians cheated occasionally; they could do so without any fundamental harm to their principles.

# 9

# Preaching without Practising: From Mandeville and Pope to Goldsmith and Wagner

It is a remarkable phenomenon of the history of vegetarianism that a number of prominent persons have concluded – in print no less – that "nature" or "justice" requires the elimination of a flesh diet, have appeared to recommend that diet, but have not themselves behaved "naturally" or "justly" in following the prescribed regimen – Montaigne, Mandeville, Thomson, Gay, Pope, Goldsmith, Voltaire, Rousseau, for example. Or at least, so it would appear. And it would appear that at least some of them have not made much or even anything of an attempt. There are others who have determined that a vegetable diet is the appropriate ethical path, have taken that path, and then at a later date have convinced themselves to the contrary – Seneca, James Boswell, Philip Dormer Stanhope (Earl of Chesterfield), and Benjamin Franklin are instances. Seneca was persuaded by the political considerations of his father to return to flesh. Boswell was converted to vegetarianism as a young man by fellow Scot John Williamson of Moffatt. In a short period, he was to be counted again among the flesh eaters. As we have seen, Chesterfield was a student at Trinity Hall, Cambridge University, when he renounced flesh on reading Ovid's *Metamorphoses*. Later, he observed: "Upon serious reflection I became convinced of its legality, from the general order of nature, who has instituted the universal preying upon the weaker as one of her first principles."[1] Franklin found general carnivorousness in nature sufficient ground to persuade him to return to flesh. So easily are we dissuaded from our ethical considerations and imagine ourselves wiser for being so. Still, despite his reversion, Franklin was known to promote vegetarian practice even afterward and lived in a generally frugal manner himself.

Yet others have simply found themselves too easily tempted away from what they view as the virtuous path. They have not stayed the course – Alfred Lord Tennyson, Lord Byron, and at least on a previous attempt, the current Dalai Lama, for example. The latter had been a vegetarian for a year and a half in the 1960s before returning to flesh. He has now returned to a vegetarian diet, although his consistency as of 2008 is questioned on the International Vegetarian Union website. He appears to be one of those who preaches the virtues of vegetarianism without wholly practising it. Some, such as Alphonse de Lamartine, have found an incompatible tension between the public interests of the private individual and the personal convictions of that individual. The case of Georges Louis Leclerc, comte de Buffon, is seemingly unique in print, if common enough in conversation. He provided a convincingly sound case for vegetarianism but refused to draw what some would think the logical conclusions from it on what they would also consider the flimsiest of rationalizations.

It is not always easy to determine readily who falls into which categories, and either calumny or credulity is a constant danger for the too careless analyst. Sometimes, the data is not readily available, but when not, and when vegetarianism seems to be espoused, one should be suspicious of the espousal if none of the contemporaries have commented on the vegetarian proclivities of a friend or colleague when such practices would have been a rarity. One should be equally suspicious if a biographer fails to mention the vegetarian practices of the subject of the biography, for that would constitute a failure to portray a significant fact of a habit in contrast with prevailing norms. Yet some earlier, and even current, biographers – of Leonardo da Vinci, for example – have failed to comment on an unusual diet. Nonetheless, from the second half of the nineteenth century on, as witnessed by numerous biographies in the *Dictionary of National Biography* as well as by William St. Clair's comments in the twentieth century on the Godwin circle, the eschewing of flesh is considered a matter worthy of mention; and who could imagine a biography of Shelley or Shaw or Gandhi without considerable attention to the diet and the grounds for it? One would also have expected, unless there were good grounds to the contrary, that people would have been sufficiently proud of their vegetarianism that they would have announced the fact publicly. Unfortunately, there may have been times when vegetarians thought it wiser not to announce their ethical or ascetic conviction because of potential official or public reaction. In light of such uncertainties, I shall, in this chapter, be concerned more with the balance of probabilities than with compelling evidence, and I hope that I am able to avoid maligning any historical personages and his or her regimen in the process. The reality is that we are more able to collect reliable evidence about events from the seventeenth century on than about earlier periods, evidence that gives us more confidence in our perceptions of historical reality than before, but it is not until well into the events of the Victorian era that we can enjoy a sufficiency of detail to arrive at conclusions that will not likely one day prove an embarrassment to the speculative historian.

I shall be here, and to some degree in the next chapter, concerned both with those who espoused the fleshless diet but did not practise it and with those whose language suggested the greatest respect for other species, including in some instances a filial relationship, but who continued to eat those they claimed to respect, and be related to, without apparent awareness of any inconsistency. They are each intriguing and enigmatic instances of the expression of the finest animal sensibilities on which ethical vegetarianism is ultimately based. And they are also instances that must cause us to doubt the sincerity or the self-understanding of the advocates. Moreover, it is important to investigate some of them with special care, for they are often promoted in the animal advocacy literature as legitimate vegetarians. It is also of value occasionally to note the justifications offered by some omnivores who were otherwise avid animal advocates for their continuation of their customary habits.

## PIERRE GASSENDI AND MARGARET CAVENDISH

We saw in the last chapter how Pierre Gassendi elevated the status of animals against the *bête machine* conception of his archfoe René Descartes, causing a rift between them that would not be healed until their amicable reconciliation in 1647. Gassendi went further and argued the case that humans were natural herbivores against the carnivorous contentions of his friend Jan Baptista van Helmont. The competing letters they wrote to each other were later published in book form, proclaiming Gassendi's advocacy to the reading public. We wonder immediately how a Catholic abbot (he was a professor of mathematics as well) would have escaped censure by his church on eating a fleshless diet on moral grounds. We can imagine his philosophical opponents tarring him with the brush of "Pythagorean superstition" (Descartes's term) or "empty superstition" (the term of Baruch

Spinoza). But there was nothing to alarm the ecclesiastical authorities or the *savants*. On reading the biographies of Gassendi's life or his own writings, we find no principled evasion of the traditional meals, not even periods of practising the fleshless diet. In fact, Gassendi was far less of a vegetarian than his opponent Descartes (who often practised abstinence on health grounds but did return to flesh occasionally). Moreover, we learn of this failure to practise what he preached from Gassendi himself. He had been bred a carnivore and it would, he thinks, have been detrimental to his health to change his habit of a lifetime fundamentally. Gassendi is in fact ruthlessly honest with his public, conceding his maintenance of the customary regimen and acknowledging he would have been wise gradually to wean himself away from flesh to the natural food from which he would have benefited. It was a step he never took. But he set a standard of honesty in confessing his failure to abide by a principle. It was a standard a number of his fellow advocates would fail to meet. It was not an uncommon view, and one Gassendi may well have shared, that although living on a fleshless diet was our original condition, through millennia of habit and through the deterioration of the earth's produce we had become natural carnivores. Indeed, most who raised the matter to the level of consciousness concluded that whatever our original condition we could not now survive without flesh.

Margaret Cavendish, the Duchess of Newcastle, we also encountered in the last chapter. She indicated, rather less clearly than Gassendi, that humankind was not intended to be carnivorous (to express the matter in the teleological language of the day). She wrote: "As if that God made creatures for man's meat, / To give them life and sense for man to eat."[2] She suggested that the consumers of flesh would suffer for their sin in the afterlife. If her God had intended abstinence from flesh, she does not appear to have followed the intention. Surely, if her practice had matched her language, her diet at ceremonial duchy (or, especially, royal) dinners would have been a matter of public gossip, instigated by others in attendance. It was not. Was it simply that her lifelong love of Ovid, learnt in youth, persuaded her to repeat him in maturity, enraptured as she was? We know she dined with the diarist John Evelyn, her son-in-law, who found nothing out of the ordinary. He would have loved to have reported it in the diary if he had. Certainly, the matter would have intrigued him because he would make similar claims for a fleshless diet himself later, without his ever practising it.

Margaret Cavendish described Shrovetide (Carnival) in Antwerp as "the most pleasant and merry time in all the year in this city for feasting, sporting and masquerading," without suggesting she declined to participate in the regular feasting.[3] Exiled in Paris at the estranged court of Henrietta Maria, and later in Antwerp, during the Protectorate and the Interregnum, Margaret the First, as she has frequently been dubbed, there met her future husband, the much older poetic warrior the Marquis (later Duke) of Newcastle. They were married in Paris in 1645. A friend of Hobbes, Descartes, and Gassendi, a tribute to the marquis's diplomacy, Newcastle himself dabbled in chemistry. He was later a respected author of two books on horsemanship and was a rather less respected dramatist. It was, no doubt, the tyro-poetic endeavours of the noble lord that served as an impetus to the greater literary and scientific accomplishments of Margaret.

The marquis was said to keep "an open table for all comers," especially "such as were excellent soldiers and natural commanders of war,"[4] but also some philosophical figures, frequently including Hobbes – who had earlier been tutor to William Cavendish before he became the Earl of Devonshire. He was scarcely one who would appreciate a vegetarian table! On two occasions the Cavendishes entertained Descartes, who would have been happier with it. After the Restoration, Newcastle opined: "feasting daily will be in merry England, for England is so plentiful of all provisions, that if we do not eat them, they will eat us, so we feast in our defence."[5] If milady had convinced herself, she thus seems to have failed utterly to convince her husband. When, then, does Margaret's vegetarian advocacy come about? It is in her *Poems, and Fancies* (1653) that she expresses her greatest respect for the animals and the reluctance to eat them, condemning the hunt in passing. It was an animal sensibility that was followed by her claim in *Philosophical Letters* (1664) that other species may have a special way of knowing, appropriate to their species experience and beyond the ken of humans. Certainly, in the *Letters* she displays a considerable sensitivity to animals, a sensitivity she sets against what she regards as the inadequacies of Hobbes, Descartes, and van Helmont. Even the neo-Platonism of Henry More does not suffice. Yet her proclaimed sensibilities do not seem to have found a match in her practice. To be sure, the marchioness had a reputation for eccentricity, but this seems to have applied primarily, if not solely, to her quaint wardrobe. Perhaps the secret lies in what she wrote in *Natures Pictures* (1656): "fancy is not an imitation of nature but a natural creation which I take to be the true poetry."[6] Her correspondent the naturalist Walter Charleton, himself of vegetarian inclination, wrote: "Your fancy is too generous to be restrained, your invention too nimble to be fettered."[7] Did her poetry inhabit the realm of fancy and invention, whereas her body rested in the province of nature? The dream has been described as a central element of the English literary imagination from Spenser to Browne, Bunyan,

Blake, and Keats. Were Cavendish"s *Fancies* no more than dreams of what might be? Was the *Faerie Queene* mode of much of her verse a reflection of the illusory nature of her ideals? The illusory nature is exemplified in her *Orations* (1662) when she asks: "Can there be ... more wholesome food than ... new laid eggs, seasoned bacon?"[8] She would not have deemed bacon wholesome if she herself did not eat it. Nor if she had not approved of it.

She praised the animals for their egalitarian lifestyle: "No *Stately Palaces* for *Pride* to dwell / Their *House* is *Common*."[9] But surely this was utopian panacea. She revelled in, rather than renounced, her own privileges. If she did not relish rank, she certainly maintained it. She added: "'Oh, man!' the [birds] all cry, 'how can you treat us so?' Is not love 'Nature's chiefest law?'"[10] Hobbes would have offered a resounding "no" in reply. By contrast, for Hobbes, life is "a war of all against all." In her natural philosopher's breast, for she was an adept naturalist, Margaret Cavendish would have known Hobbes was at least partly right, although grossly exaggerated. In her poet's breast, she would have known him absolutely wrong. If she said she did not like to read romances, undoubtedly she wrote them. *Fancies,* we should recall, was a part of the title of one of her own works. She probably lived on a frugal diet much of the time, seemingly common in her household at Welbeck, but there was enough travel, company, and occasional affairs of state to divert her from the frugal path. Still, we are left to wonder whether the frugality at Welbeck meant she dined frequently on vegetables at home but ate everyday fare elsewhere.

## JAMES THOMSON AND JOHN EVELYN

A friend of George Cheyne, the poet James Thomson wrote *Seasons* (1728), where he extolled Pythagoras, "the Samian sage" (*Spring*, lines 336-73), repeating the message in *Liberty* (1736). In each he gave heartfelt reasons for a fleshless diet. So did the diarist John Evelyn in *Acetaria: A Discourse of Sallets* (1699), where he maintained the possibility "to live on wholesome vegetables, both long and happily." But there are no indications they themselves ever left off eating meat. *Seasons* was primarily a careful study of the workings of nature and an idealized version of the life of the husbandman, based on Virgil's *Georgics*. The primitivism of *Spring* stands in some contrast to the remainder of the romantic nature-descriptive poem, much of it being in the province of the new science and much being "progressive" in the sense of welcoming the commercial revolution in which England was involved. Perhaps the primitivism reflected no more than that the *Georgics* model employed by Thomson also includes a fleshless back-to-nature vision. We know few relevant dietary details directly of Thomson's life between being born near Kelso in Scotland in 1700 and dying early at Richmond, near London, in 1748, although we know enough indirectly. In fact, we know significantly more about his alcohol drinking at the Castle tavern or at the Orange-Tree in Kew Lane, for example, than about his eating – and those who refused flesh commonly denied themselves alcohol as well. We also know that after *Seasons* was published he was a frequent guest of the owners of various country estates from the Earl and Countess of Hertford to Baron Lyttleton, where one would have expected his diet to have been commented on if out of the ordinary. We know he stayed on several occasions at the Dorset home of George Doddington (Lord Melcombe), of whom Richard Cumberland said: he "was excelled by no man in doing the honours of his house and table."[11] It is probably on account of the sybaritic life at Doddington's that the celebrated Dr. Samuel Johnson accused Thomson of "gross sensuality and licentious manner."[12] And we hear that when Thomson caught his death of a cold on the Thames between Kew and Richmond, he was boating and walking from London and stopped at a public house where "he took rest and refreshment," as was apparently his wont.[13] Given the length of the journey, we must assume him to have eaten as well as imbibed, and it is unlikely the public house would have offered a vegetarian meal.

Much is conjecture. Thus, the foremost authority on Thomson, James Sambrook, tells us that after the poet's arrival in London in 1725: "Presumably Thomson's social life, like that of many of his contemporaries, was centred upon the coffee-houses," establishments that served as reading rooms, club offices, and eating and drinking parlours.[14] Some coffeehouses in the theatre district – such as the Rose and the Shakespeare's Head – even functioned more or less as brothels. And the drink was not restricted to coffee, at least as some changed to clubs in the eighteenth century, nor was the food likely to be vegetarian. We find him ensconced at the Old Man's Coffee-House at Charing Cross in March of 1727, when he had probably begun to write *Spring*, and by early 1728 he gave the Smyrna Coffee-House – where Pope and Prior discussed matters of state – on the corner of St. James Street as his address. We certainly know he was a later habitué of a number of coffeehouses. In the fall of 1730 Thomson made a short excursion to Bath, where he met the physician Dr. Cheyne, a fellow Scot, whose "notions on vegetarianism," Sambrook says, "had found their way into Thomson's *Spring*, but not into his diet."[15] On another occasion, Sambrook reports: "Thomson gormandized and drank heavily."[16] In November

1730 Thomson set off on the Grand Tour as paid companion to Charles Talbot. It was notoriously difficult, travelling from inn to inn, to acquire a fleshless meal, as Shelley seems to have found almost a century later. In 1736 we find Thomson telling a Frenchman that salmon is very fatty, a fact he would probably not have known if he did not eat salmon. Andrew Mitchell is reported to have told James Boswell in 1742 that notwithstanding Thomson's "fine imitation of Ovid on the Pythagorean system, he was an egregious gormandiser of Beefsteaks."[17] In James Boswell's *Journal* for 1 January 1763, he reports a conversation about the long-dead Thomson overheard at Child's Coffee-House in which two persons each comment, in passing, that they had eaten beefsteaks with Thomson.[18] If the evidence is not completely conclusive, it is certainly extremely persuasive. Still, it could be said Thomson provides himself an excuse, or an exit at least, in the lines in *Spring* following the proclamation of the vegetarian Pythagorean dream: the "wisest will has fixed us in a state / That must not yet to pure perfection rise" (lines 375-76). Vegetarianism is "pure perfection," but its day is not yet. God and current codes debar it. The Golden Age lies in a dim and distant past. It will come again but not in the present.

John Evelyn (1620-1706) was of affluent gentry stock and lived the life of a country gentleman at Sayes Court, Deptford, a timbered manor house with eighteen rooms, and the last few years as squire of the grand family estate (approximately 7,500 acres) at Wooton. Helen M. Fox, writing in the foreword to the 1937 Brooklyn Botanic Garden reprint edition of *Acetaria,* states: "Evelyn grew to be an ardent believer in vegetarianism and is probably the first advocate in England of a meatless diet," a view that corresponds with that of Howard Williams.[19] But was he a vegetarian? The text of *Acetaria* is certainly a promotion of the products of the garden, and mention is made admiringly of those ancients who, it was thought, had lived from a fleshless diet. And certainly a vegetable diet is primarily what the book is about, although there are also many other avenues explored. Salad, he opined, was both innocent and natural, whereas the product of the shambles was bloody and cruel. Yet Evelyn's biography tells another story.

In wise absence in the Netherlands prior to the English Civil War, Evelyn declared the "Brownists" (i.e., the Presbyterians) "kept the best table."[20] It is an unlikely comment without further explanation from a flesh denier. In exile on the Continent from 1644, when the Civil War was raging, Evelyn praised an inn at St. Cloud for "the excellent manner of dressing the meate and the service."[21] It is scarcely possible that the "meate" could be anything other than flesh. In the same year he finds no distaste in personally serving a "joynt of mutton" to the lion in the zoo of the Grand Duke at Florence.[22] In Naples he stayed at the inn of the Three Kings, where he dined on the "most exquisite meate and fruits."[23] In Bologna he thought the wine better than the sausage.[24] On a Venetian boat he "ate a good dinner of English poudered beefe, and other good meate."[25] In Padua it was potted venison.[26] Back in England in 1647 between the two stages of the Civil War, we find him killing a buck in the chase; in 1654, the war over, we find him coursing a hare; and in December 1661 we find him hunting and killing an otter – scarcely likely practices of a vegetarian on ethical grounds. On a tour of England in 1654 Evelyn and his wife dined to their satisfaction at Great Durnford, finding "pigeons, rabbits and fowl in plenty."[27] The rump parliament being dissolved in 1660, "for joy thereof," Evelyn reported, "were many thousands of rumps [of mutton], roasted publiquely ... this was the first good omen" – not a good omen for anyone who thought animals should not be killed for their flesh (nor a good omen for the sheep, for that matter).[28] He seems to have tolerated the Royal Society's air pump experiments on animals and the transferring of blood from a sheep to a man with far greater equanimity than one would expect of an even mildly ethical vegetarian, although he described cock, bear, and dog fighting on one occasion as "butcherly sports, or other barbarous cruelties" and on another as a "rude and dirty passetime."[29] When fellow diarist Samuel Pepys was unjustly, but temporarily, consigned to the Tower in 1679 – he was consigned again unjustly, and again temporarily, in 1690 – Evelyn sent him venison and dined with him there.

But we must note that *Acetaria* was not published until Evelyn was seventy-nine years of age, although he had been collecting material for the previous twenty years, being very interested in the propagation of plants. Indeed, he had developed extensive vegetable and fruit gardens from his thirties, and from 1664 on he was widely known as "Sylva" Evelyn for his work on forestry – Kneller painted him for Pepys in 1689 with a copy of his book *Sylva* in his right hand.[30] Above all, architecture, art, naval navigation, medals – and who deserved to be commemorated by them, including the "Sappho, Mrs Behn" – and the design of gardens enthralled him.[31] Before writing *Acetaria,* he was constantly in company after the Restoration, from his membership on the Council of the Royal Society to his attendance at the royal court and in senior government circles. There were formal dinners as commissioner for the Navy and commissioner of the Privy Seal: "dined at Guildhall, the feast said to cost a £1000."[32] Another time it was a "magnificent feast."[33] And there were rather less formal occasions when he dined, for example, with fellow commissioner Lord Arlington, or with the Lord Chancellor, Lord Clarendon, or with the later Lord

Chancellor, the notorious Judge Jeffreys, or with various bishops. On receiving an honorary doctorate from Oxford in 1669, the graduands were sumptuously entertained by the president of St. John's College. The failure of his colleagues and other celebrities to note an unusual diet is suggestive. Perhaps Evelyn became a vegetarian advocate and practitioner in old age, reminiscent of Tolstoy in his seventies, after a life of debauchery, advocating abstention from sex. But what evidence we have does not support a vegetarian conclusion even then. As his biographer, John Bowle, has remarked, in *Acetaria:* "Evelyn carefully disowns being a vegetarian, 'preaching down hogs puddings,' even if Adam and Eve did feed on 'hortulan productions' before the 'fatal lapse'; and he prudently ends the subject 'with whatever is advanced in countenance of an ante-diluvian diet we leave to be ventilated by the learned.'"[34]

The late-seventeenth-century diet of the well-to-do in England consisted of large amounts of flesh washed down with copious glasses of ale, although it was not as strong as its modern counterpart. Water was considered dangerous and unfit for human consumption – even bathing was not commonly practised until Evelyn ventured an annual dip. What Evelyn was hoping to achieve was to introduce the French appreciation for vegetables – even the gargantuan feasts of *le Roi soleil* included "salad" – into the meal preparations of his countrymen. If he approved of a solely vegetarian diet, it was not one to be enjoyed in this life.

## JOHN HAWKESWORTH AND ALEXANDER POPE

John Hawkesworth (1715-1775), editor of *The Adventurer,* condemned the infliction of pain on animals, damning the perpetrator with the words: "thou hast offended against thy brother of the dust."[35] In his edition of *The Works of Jonathan Swift,* he was emphatic in his condemnation of the flesh eater, sufficiently so to receive the accolade of Howard Williams, telling us that "the expressions of abhorrence [of] ... Dr. Hawkesworth ... are conceived quite in the spirit of Plutarch."[36] Hawkesworth further opined:

Among other dreadful and disgusting images which custom has rendered familiar, are those which arise from eating animal food; he who has ever turned with abhorrence from the skeleton of a beast which has been picked whole by birds or vermin, must confess that habit alone would have enabled him to endure the sight of the mangled bones and flesh of a dead carcase which every day cover his table: and he who reflects on the number of lives that have been sacrificed to sustain his own, should enquire by what the account has been balanced, and whether his life is become proportionately of more value by the exercise of virtue and by the superior happiness which he has communicated to reasonable beings.[37]

Did Hawkesworth overcome the "habit"? Did he "cover his table" differently? We have no evidence that he did. Hawkesworth was an intimate of Samuel Johnson, who praised the work on Swift but who made no reference to the apparent vegetarian appeal. Indeed, he does not seem to have taken the literary advocacy as more than rhetoric. Hawkesworth dined frequently with Johnson as a member of the Ivy Lane Club, the first of Johnson's many clubs and the one from which *The Adventurer* emanated, which according to John Abbott, Hawkesworth's biographer, "met on Tuesdays at the King's Head, a famous beefsteak house."[38] If Hawkesworth had declined the regular fare, surely Johnson would have had yet another anecdote to tell. Dining on a celebrated occasion with Johnson and others at the Devil Tavern, Hawkesworth tells us: "Our supper was elegant."[39] An elegant Johnsonian supper without flesh would be difficult to imagine! Apparently, Johnson was a frequent diner at Hawkesworth's home in Bromley, where the latter lived with his wife – a butcher's daughter! An unlikely venue for Johnson if the menu was fleshless, and an unlikely wife for Hawkesworth if he were a committed vegetarian. There were no apparent family squabbles about the father-in-law's occupation. Without imagining there to be a dietary issue, Abbott thinks it likely that Hawkesworth and Johnson dined together on occasion at the nearby Bell Hotel, where there would not likely have been vegetarian options in those days.[40] One might imagine a Hawkesworthian conversion to vegetarianism at a later date than the dinners with Johnson, but the Swift work was complete by 1755 and the dinners continued. After Johnsonian dinners came repasts with the thespian David Garrick and then with the music historian Charles Burney, with both of whom it is difficult to imagine a restricted diet. Moreover, if we read the statement on the iniquities of "eating animal food" in Hawkesworth's work on Swift in its context, we will realize these are comments in reference to the Brobdingnagian queen's eating habits and are of only superficial relevance, in Hawkesworth's mind, to the reform of Western mores. They were no more relevant, in fact, than the Gulliver story was to Swift's own eating habits. Swift's antipathies did not create a vegetarian Swift. To be sure, the stories of Lilliputians, Brobdingnagians, Laputians, and Houyhnhnms were relevant to the extent that they showed the undue pride, frailty, and folly of humanity, but no one at the time expected Swift,

Hawkesworth, or others to act on their implied or explicit vegetarian messages.

Samuel Johnson was one who believed "the account has been balanced," to use Hawkesworth's words, reflecting what had become a popular opinion, and he suggests it was a common topic of conversation. Dining at The Mitre in London with Boswell in 1776, and referring primarily to food animals, it would appear, he stated: "There is much talk of the misery we cause to the brute creation, but they are recompensed by existence. If they were not useful to man, and therefore protected by him, they would not be nearly so numerous."[41] The former vegetarian Boswell responded appropriately: "This argument is to be found in the able and benignant Hutchinson's 'Moral Philosophy' [he means 'Hutcheson']. But the question is, whether the animals who endure such sufferings of various kinds for the service and entertainment of man, would accept of existence upon the terms on which they have it."[42] The horse specialist John Lawrence added in 1798 that if beasts were not killed for food, they would overpopulate the earth. Thus "in numberless cases" it was "an act of mercy to take their lives" – a sentiment Johnson would have applauded.[43] We should recall that Johnson was the man, writing in quite different vein, who vilified the vivisectors with such aplomb. It would appear that paradox is the nature of humankind. It is witnessed further when, in 1750, Johnson praised the altruism of the Golden Age but took a quite different approach both earlier and later. When he criticized the back-to-nature ideal, he saw that its espousal was not restricted to a few unclubable vegetarians who saw humans as vegetable, nut, and fruit eaters in origin but, to Johnson's dismay, that it was espoused by many dissenting Christians and especially by deists who held the same "Golden Age" views. Despite his dismay, he did not assume them to be disreputable vegetarians, as he would have viewed them. Nor did he expect the primitivist espousal to turn them into vegetarians. Although contemporary primitivism usually implied a fleshless diet in principle, those who espoused primitivism were not known to eschew flesh in practice – and this despite the fact that the language they employed seemed to suggest they would have.

In *Essay on Man* (1733-34), for example, Alexander Pope praised the men of the Golden Age and appeared to suggest they should be imitated. In those ancient days, Pope tells us, "no murder cloth'd, no murder fed." Pope's biographer, Maynard Mack, says that Pope's Golden Age echoes Boethius's sixth-century lament: "O that our times could go back to the old ways."[44] In his 1713 contribution to the *Guardian*, Pope seems already to have laid out the vegetarian principle in prose: "I know nothing more shocking or horrid than the prospect of one of [the] kitchens [of the contemporary human savages] covered with blood, and filled with the cries of Beings expiring in tortures. It gives one an image of a giant's den in a romance, bestrewed with the scattered heads and mangled limbs of those who were slain by his cruelty."[45] Pope's position appears clear enough. Nonetheless, in the same period in *Windsor-Forest* he describes field sports as "pleasing Toils" (line 120). Further, he wrote to Thomas Dancastle in 1717: "May your gun never fail, and your aim never miss. May your Pouch come swagging home, laden with woodcocks."[46] Mack captures Pope's ambivalence in such matters when he tells us his intent "was to carve out for himself a defensive position between contemporary reality and ancient dream."[47] As an occasional client of Dr. Cheyne, he knew that a vegetable diet would suit his health. But it would not suit his personality.

Discussing imitative writing, Peter Ackroyd has intimated wisely that when Pope wrote in the manner of another, he no longer wrote as himself.[48] Here, he affects to be Plutarch and, accordingly, claims for himself Plutarch's values. As soon as he became himself again, the Plutarchian values dissipated.

Pope continues the *Guardian* essay in rather less abstinent voice than that with which he begins: "The excellent Plutarch (who has more strokes of good nature in his writings than I remember in any author) cites a saying of Cato to this effect: – That 'tis no easy task to preach to the Belly that has no ears. Yet if (says he) we are ashamed to be so out of fashion as not to offend, let us at least offend with *some* discretion and measure. If we kill an animal for our provision, let us do it with the meltings of compassion, and without tormenting it. Let us consider that it is, in its own nature, cruelty to put a living being to death – we, at least, destroy a soul that has sense and perception."[49] Was Pope one who would kill for "provision" with "the meltings of compassion"? – it was even more difficult, nay, impossible, to kill a food animal painlessly then than now. As an unknown author, probably Wordsworth, wrote in 1795: "They read of the afflictions of their fellow creatures, as they would amuse themselves with a romance."[50] To be sure, the "fellow creatures" are here fellow humans. But the point remains. The fellow-suffering is felt momentarily, but the context in which it is felt is unreal. Compassion is felt fleetingly for an abstraction, not for real animate beings. Was it, for Pope, mere literary abstractions that were mourned? If Pope seems on occasion to condone painless killing of food animals, he must surely have known there was no such easy death in the shambles. Was he engaged in literary flights of fancy, or did he place himself on the side of the vegetarian Plutarch? Or did Pope resemble Montaigne? On account of the Périgordian's latitudinarianism – Pope was a somewhat persecuted Catholic – he once deemed Montaigne his "Alter Ego." And Montaigne expressed great sympathy for the animal realm without counting himself a practising vegetarian. The mind is torn on which side Pope might lie but perhaps not for long. Montaigne is a far more likely role model than Plutarch.

To be sure, Pope delighted in growing melons, broccoli, and even pineapples in his extensive garden at Twickenham. But we cannot imagine he lived from them alone. Did Pope really mean, "it is cruelty to put a living being to death"? Was he one who was willing to "offend," to be cruel, provided it was with "*some* discretion and measure"? In Maynard Mack's meticulous thousand-page biography of Pope, no hint of any vegetarianism, however temporary, is adduced. Certainly, Pope was a good friend of the vegetarian advocate under certain health conditions Dr. John Arbuthnot (1667-1735), Physician Extraordinary to the Queen – a portrait of Arbuthnot hung in Pope's home – and he wrote the *Epistle to Arbuthnot* on the physician's death, but he did not consider Arbuthnot's occasional vegetarian advocacy worthy of a mention there.[51] Arbuthnot was founder of the Tory Scriblerus Club, of which the triumvirate of Pope, Swift, and Gay were members, and inventor of the legend of Martin Scriblerus, an Augustan bumbling Colonel Blimp whom the members loved to parody. Any political influence the club might have had disappeared on the death of Queen Anne and the ascendancy of the Whigs under George I – which at least relieved the members from the most extreme political cant. A half-hearted and part-time Tory, Pope was the epitome of the philosophical quietist: "Whatever is, is right."[52] And such a poet can never fully hope to change the world fundamentally or even to see the need to do so – whatever the rhetorical flights of fancy might suggest.

In *Essay on Man*, Pope used the chain of being model to show human-animal-plant continuity. Perhaps, in the end, humans were higher in the scale than the words of *Essay on Man* seemed prima facie to suggest. In another time and another place Pope would probably have been a vegetarian. As it was, he certainly was not. In fact, he frequently gave dinner parties at his Twickenham residence, at which it is inconceivable that no flesh was served. Swift makes a tangential reference to eating beef with mustard and turnips at Pope's residence.[53] If Pope had failed to partake of the flesh, it would surely have been commented upon. From the son of Lord Oxford, he is said to have been "plagued ... with presents of collars of brawn." Moreover, when dining with Lord Bolingbroke, Pope is explicitly said to have supped on "beans and bacon."[54] Nor was this "bacon" seen as a breach of the norm for Pope. No one thought the meal that day worthy of any comment other than to mention its content in passing. From a youthful age, Pope was a frequenter of the taverns, perhaps more to imbibe than to eat – his reputation has him as much pubable as clubable. Yet he maintained a reputation as a heavy flesh eater, too. Thus in 1734, the year of *Essay on Man*, Lord Bathurst wrote to Lady Suffolk (Henrietta Howard): "You do well to reprove him for his intemperance for he makes himself sick every meal [here]. Yesterday I had a little piece of salmon just caught out of the Severn, and a fresh pike that was brought me ... He ate as much as he could of both, and insisted upon his moderation because he had made his dinner on one dish" – the "wicked wasp of Twickenham," as Lady Mary Wortley Montagu said![55] In the same year, on a visit to Bevis Mount, Pope exulted in his meals of "the best Sea fish and River fish in the world."[56] In 1738 William Kent called Pope "the greatest Glutton I know."[57] Pope wrote to Hugh Bethel in the same year: "Take care of your Health, follow not the Feasts (as I have done) of Lords."[58] We find him dining on flesh with Gay. Mack said of Pope that "he never quite learned to curb his impulse to overeat when warmed by the company of friends, and sometimes to overdrink, even with the knowledge that much wine was lethal to him."[59] A vegetarian Pope is as unlikely as a vegetarian pope.

## JOHN GAY

The poet and playwright John Gay (1685-1732), the eloquent Barnstaple-bred rhymer of the Augustan age, praised Pythagoras, condemned humanity its cruelty ("All animals before him ran, / To shun the hateful sight of man") and protested the eating of flesh – "carnivorous sinner," he said. Gay condemned the butcher in his *Fables*, in both "The Philosopher and the Pheasants" and "The Wild Boar and the Ram," but he still bought from him. Two years before his death he was writing to Jonathan Swift how he hated to be in debt to the tailor or the butcher, as though dealing with each was a common occurrence in his life.[60] In *Rural Sports* he bemoaned the angling fate of both fish and worm. In fact, he was always sympathetic to the downtrodden, especially downtrodden women, but to the downtrodden animals only in verse. We have no hint of any practical vegetarian activity that followed from his poetry. Indeed, as the respected author of *Fables,* it would amuse the good-natured Gay that his purported vegetarianism has become a modern fable.

We find Pope writing to him on Gay's return from his secretaryship in Hanover: "Come and make merry with me in much feasting," and we have already seen that, for Pope, "feasting" was not dining on vegetarian fare.[61] In *The Journey to Exeter* (1715) Gay writes explicitly: "O'er our parched tongue the rich metheglin glides / And the red dainty trout our knife divides" ("metheglin" is mead). At Marcombe, still on the journey to Exeter, the coach passengers, Gay among them, "strip the lobster of his scarlet mail." In 1716 he wrote to fellow Scriblerian Parnell "from a chop-house near the Exchange."[62] One doesn't frequent a chophouse without occasionally eating chops. During the South Sea Bubble episode, Swift wrote to Gay in 1721 suggesting he put the money from *Poems on Several Occasions* safely into an annuity that, as Swift said, would guarantee Gay a clean shirt and a shoulder of mutton a day – not the kind of advice one offers a friend who is a confirmed abstainer.[63] In 1726 the celebrated royal mistress, Mrs Howard, received a letter from Gay, or was it Pope? The question is still disputed. No matter. The "Our" refers to Pope *and* Gay. Commenting on a celebratory lunch they had enjoyed the day the letter was written, the author says: "Our entertainment consisted of flesh and fish and lettuce of a Greek island called Cos."[64] In the same year, Gay sent a rhymed recipe for stewed veal in casserole in a letter to Swift.[65]

Gay often lived his life as a guest in the homes of others – including Pope's home at Twickenham. He had, his most recent biographer David Nokes tells us, "the instinctive habit of casting himself in the role of household dependent" – the "gentle parasite," he had earlier been called by another – and never seemed to request vegetarian fare from his hosts.[66] He lived his life, in fact, at the behest of others, whether in the home of the Duchess of Monmouth or as diplomatic secretary to the Earl of Clarendon. Gay and Pope dined together often at the homes of Lord and Lady Burlington in Piccadilly or Chiswick, probably together with Handel, who was a protegé in residence of Lady Burlington, and frequently with the Prince and Princess of Wales at Hampton Court or Leicester Fields, all without appearing to make a fuss about what they ate, as long as there was plenty of it. Gay could be found at the homes of Lords Peterborough, Bathurst, Harcourt, Queensberry, and Pulteney, even at St. James's Palace with the king's court. It would appear he ate what they ate.

In fact, Gay was becoming dangerously overweight – a common condition of the age from unwise eating of the wrong foodstuffs. William Congreve blamed Gay's weight on his hearty appetite. He was "the fat clown," according to Robert Walpole. Gay's reputation was of being as much a glutton as Pope. In fact, Gay was quite unwell from the age of forty and often sought relief in Bath and the spa towns of Europe for his chronic colonic disorder, but there is no evidence he sought the relief in fleshless fare.

Indeed, the spa towns were known for their hedonism, not their abstemiousness. He began to suffer from colitis already in 1721 (aged thirty-six) and was attended at Hampstead by Dr. Arbuthnot, who advised him to abstain from wine, to little avail, but not, apparently, from flesh – abstention from wine was an antidote to his common abode in London, where, as has been said by one of his biographers, "the coffee-house became Gay's spiritual home."[67] Still, perhaps the illness had some effect on his diet, for we find him writing to Swift in 1727: "I refused supping at Burlington House to-night in regard to my health."[68] However, his friends did not hold high hopes of "the cure" at "the Bath," as the city was known, nor of the likelihood of Gay taking it seriously. As Swift penned to Pope in 1728: "I suppose Mr Gay will return from Bath with twenty Pounds more Flesh and two hundred less in Money."[69] Nonetheless, when Arbuthnot repeated the wine abstention warning in 1728, he seems to have met with rather more success, even if Gay did stray on a trip to Scotland. Certainly, Pope believed Gay was still an abstainer in 1730 but only from wine, not from flesh. In fact, staying with the Queensberries at Almesbury in that year, Gay took to the country pastime of shooting and wrote to Pope boasting of his exploits in getting a bag of nineteen partridges that season.[70] A likely boast neither from nor to a vegetarian. Surely, no ethical vegetarian would be a partridge shooter! Gay's health somewhat temporarily improved, Arbuthnot allowed him a partial return to wine drinking. In October of 1732 as a guest of Sir William Wyndham in Somerset, he wrote to Swift that he was eating a lot of fish there. That was his last known mention of food. Just over a month later he was dead at the age of forty-seven from "an inflammatory fever."

The Pythagorean theme was far more popular than practised in the eighteenth century. Yet, in fact, Gay casts some small doubt on his own even theoretical Pythagoreanism in *Trivia, or The Art of Walking the Streets of London* (1716) when, with reference to the issue of transmigration, he questions whether what "the *Samian* taught" is true.[71] Was the apparent vegetarian espousal anything more than the discovery of a convenient metaphor for the innocence of slaughtered animal life? It seems to have been so for William Cowper (1731-1800). In *The Task* (1785) Cowper bemoans that human convenience, health, and safety permit us to dine on flesh and override the rights of animals. Nonetheless, he overrode them himself in his culinary habits. His sensibility to animals, especially the Olney hares, was remarkable but persuaded him only in print, not in practice, that the objects of his compassion were not appropriate items for the dinner plate. Writing of Pope, Gay, and Thomson, Voltaire observed that their interest in form and composition exceeded any concern with substance. Performance over substance was the priority of university education at this time and seems to have pervaded the literary culture generally. It would appear, judging from the silence on the matter, no one expected the literary pronouncements to have any practical dietary consequences; no contemporary thought the literary form was anything other than sanctimonious sentimentalizing.

A number of those who have been viewed as historical representatives of ethical vegetarianism quite simply were not. Vegetarian advocacy was merely a rhetorical flight of fancy.

## BERNARD MANDEVILLE AND DAVID HARTLEY

Dutch by birth and education, Bernard Mandeville (1670-1733) moved to England in 1692, where he earned his living as a physician for the remainder of his life. *The Fable of the Bees: Private Vices, Publick Benefits* (1714, 1723, 1728), based on his 1705 poem *The Grumbling Hive, or Knaves Turn'd Honest,* was his most renowned work and one in which he castigated humankind for its cruelty to animals and its unnatural diet. The 1714 edition contained an extensive prose commentary consisting of *An Enquiry into the Origin of Moral Virtue* and some twenty "Remarks" elaborating the ideas of the poem. The "Remarks" were expanded in the 1723 edition. The following excerpts are from these interpretative "Remarks." In the first excerpt, a lion is speaking:

> 'Tis only Man, mischievous Man that can make Death a Sport. Nature taught your Stomach to crave nothing but Vegetables; but your violent Fondness to change, and greater eagerness after Novelties, have prompted you to the Destruction of Animals without Justice or Necessity, perverted your Nature and warp'd your Appetites which way soever your Pride or Luxury have call'd them ... Man feeds on the Sheep that clothes him, and spares not her innocent young ones whom he has taken into his care and custody. If you tell me the Gods made Man Master over all the other Creatures what Tyranny was it then to destroy them out of Wantonness?[72]

Mandeville now speaks with his own voice rather than through the lion:

> When to soften the Flesh of Male Animals, we have by Castration prevented the Firmness their Tendons and every Fibre would have come to without it, I confess, I think it ought to move a human Creature when he reflects upon

the cruel Care with which they are fatned for Destruction. When a large and gentle Bullock, after having resisted a ten times greater force of Blows than would have killed his Murderer, falls stunned at last, and his arm'd Head is fastn'd to the ground with Cords; as soon as the wide Wound is made, and the jugulars are cut asunder, what Mortal can without Compassion hear the Bellowings intercepted by his Blood, the bitter Sighs that speak the Sharpness of his Anguish, and the deep sounding Grones with loud Anxiety fetch'd from the bottom of his strong and palpitating Heart?

What price now the advocated compassion of Pope with "*some* discretion and measure"? Pope had surely read Mandeville. What methods of slaughter were available to overcome the cruelty? In the eighteenth-century state of abattoir affairs, there would be either the most abject cruelty or abstinence. Mandeville continued:

Look at the trembling and violent Convulsions of his Limbs; see while his reeking Gore steams from him, his Eyes become dim and languid, and behold his Strugglings, Gasps and last Efforts for Life, the certain Signs of his approaching Fate. When a Creature has given such convincing and undeniable Proofs of the Terrors upon him, and the Pains and Agonies he feels, is there a follower of Descartes so inur'd to Blood, as not to refute, by his Commiseration, the Philosophy of that vain Reasoner?[73]

To be sure, Descartes was confounded – but then almost all took Descartes to task on this issue. And sensibility and vegetarianism were vindicated. But what evidence is there of Mandeville's compliance with his own precepts? Unfortunately, there is very little reliable evidence on Mandeville's life other than his work. But there are a few things we know. In the 1690s, he travelled through France and Italy, and travellers would always have difficulty obtaining fleshless fare at the hostelries en route. Perhaps he became a vegetarian afterward. Yet, later in England, he was a frequent guest of the Earl of Macclesfield, the Lord Chancellor, which indicates the exalted circles in which Mandeville moved. What do we imagine Mandeville ate on these frequent visits to the stately home if nothing of a vegetarian nature was reported at large? It is almost as though what we are being told by those who condemned man his cruelty and his diet is that this is how the world could be if humankind were a different animal from what it has become, but it has become what it is, and a fleshless diet is an impractical ideal given the fallen nature of humanity. Would these poets and essayists not have declared their vegetarianism vociferously and with pride, if indeed vegetarians they had become, as did most of the advocates we will meet in the next chapter? The most telling information we have about Mandeville comes from Benjamin Franklin's *Autobiography,* where he tells us of being taken to meet Mandeville at the *Horns,* "a pale Ale-House in ... Cheapside," where Mandeville "had a Club ... of which he was the Soul, being a most facetious [agreeable] Companion."[74] The fare of such a club – clubs usually met over dinner and alcohol – was most unlikely to have been fleshless. To be sure, the vegetarian Dr. Cheyne frequented taverns but was satirized for his declaiming there against flesh. If Mandeville had dined on carrots and cabbage, he would surely have met the same fate. As Basil Willey explained in the classic *The Eighteenth Century Background,* for Mandeville, "virtue is impracticable ... it is to vice that we owe our benefits."[75] Was the denial of flesh, then, an impractical ideal? "Virtue," for Mandeville, Willey continues, "is self conquest ... but ... men never do, in actuality, conquer themselves."[76] Did Mandeville simply fail to conquer the lust for the flesh that he so clearly recognized as a moral necessity? Did he even try? And did his recognition of the vicious nature of humankind, of which he was a member, provide him with ample justification? Did Mandeville "use the loftiest moral ideals purely as a standard of satirical reference, without implicating himself with them," as Willey believed?[77] But if Mandeville himself almost certainly did not practise what he preached, his writings had significant influence later in persuading others, including Joseph Ritson and Sir Richard Philips, to pursue the vegetarian course and cause. It was words, not example, that were effective.

Philosopher and physician – although without a degree in medicine – David Hartley (1705-1757) conceived of all mental phenomena as sensations arising from the vibrations of the white medullary substance of the brain and spinal cord – a doctrine known as "associationism" – a conception that inspired the popular and influential chemist and Unitarian minister Joseph Priestley and was influential in the thought of the philosopher John Stuart Mill.[78] So impressed was Samuel Taylor Coleridge that he had his portrait painted with a copy of Hartley's *Observations* in his hand. This doctrine rendered humans and other animals as essentially, but not entirely, alike and highlighted implications for the moral acceptability of our consumption of animals. In fact, Hartley mentioned five categories of distinction between humans and animals, which amount, as with David Hume, to superior but not exclusive human rationality. Animals, in Hartley's view, are like children, acted upon rather than acting.[79] There is, however, a further distinction, which is the "annihilation" of the human self in a mystical union with the deity as the ultimate goal of humankind. Thus, as with the Gnostics, for example, the task was to separate the human from nature, not to emphasize our oneness with the animals. Nonetheless, unlike the Gnostics, Hartley had an authentic respect for the animals. We differ from them in that we possess what Hartley described as "theopathy" – perhaps best expressed as a religious sense – while the other animals do not, it would appear, although some claimed, strangely, the elephant to possess that sense. Otherwise, we share much, almost everything, in common, by category if not by degree.

In *Observations on Man, His Frame, His Duty and His Expectations* (1749) Hartley announced:

> With respect to animal Diet, let it be considered, that taking away the Lives of Animals in order to convert them into Food does great Violence to the Principles of Benevolence and Compassion. This appears from the frequent Hardheartedness and Cruelty found among those Persons whose Occupations engage them in destroying animal Life, as well as from the Uneasiness which others feel in beholding the Butchery of Animals. It is most evident, in respect of the larger Animals, and those with whom Mankind have a familiar intercourse – such as Oxen, Sheep, and domestic Fowls. These Creatures resemble us greatly in the Make of the Body in general, and in that of the particular Organs of Circulation, Respiration, Digestion, & c; also in the Formation of their Intellects, Memories and Passions, and in the Signs of Distress, Fear, Pain, and Death. They often likewise win our Affections by the Marks of peculiar Sagacity, by their Instincts, Helplessness, Innocence, nascent Benevolence, & c. And if there be any glimmering of the Hope of an Hereafter for them, if they should prove to be our Brethren and Sisters in this higher Sense, in Immortality as well as Mortality, in the permanent Principle of our Minds as well as in the frail Dust of our Bodies, if they should be partakers of the same Redemption as well as our Fall, and be members of the same mystical Body, this would have a particular Tendency to increase our Tenderness for them.[80]

However, Hartley refuses to take the implied next step. Instead, he advises his readers that: "Abstinence from Flesh meats seems left to each Person's Choice, and not necessary unless in peculiar Circumstances."[81] He differs from other figures in this chapter in that he practised the vegetable regimen himself but did not consider it appropriate to recommend to others what he had determined as morally imperative for himself – following the dictates of "Benevolence and Compassion." In contrast with the other figures we encounter in this chapter, Hartley practised without preaching, a worthwhile pointer that there is no uniformity in human affairs. His life shows us that not all of the intelligentsia and educated were of like mind. Not all avoided the potential to act on their professed principles. It is perhaps unfortunate that he was less concerned to advocate his vegetarian beliefs, for there were numerous acolytes, Wordsworth and Coleridge among them, who followed his teachings with care. Coleridge even named his first-born Hartley after the philosopher. But neither Wordsworth nor Coleridge followed his preferred regimen.

John Byrom, member of the Royal Society, as was Hartley, and originator of a system of shorthand, was delighted on encountering Hartley to find a fellow flesh denier. They became firm friends. Early in 1736, we find them, together with a clergyman, Dr. Battely, and Elizabeth, Hartley's wife, enjoying an apparently typical dinner at the Hartley home of "pancake and toasted cheese" – no flesh was ever served. On another occasion, it was apple dumplings, and on yet another, it was messes of spinach. At around the same time, we find Hartley and Byrom attending a lecture "on the globes" at Abington's coffeehouse by Isaac Newton's successor at Cambridge University, William Whiston.[82] Hartley stressed he did not eat supper there. Indeed, he seems to have remained on the fleshless regimen for the rest of his life, after having turned to the vegetable diet probably around the time he left Cambridge University. He was confirmed in his abstemious diet both on health and on moral grounds. It is surprising, then, that he felt no compunction to believe morality required the practice in others. If Hartley was a benevolent and compassionate man, and by all accounts he was, he also thought that "every Man intuitively regards his own welfare."[83] Thus it was that, paradoxically, morality did not absolutely *require* adherence to a universal law. But since Hartley believed also that private happiness was dependent on the promotion of the public good, there is an apparent contradiction – unless, of course, the public good does not include the wellbeing of the animals. Even if not, it must presumably include the health of humans. In fact, Hartley appears to believe that compassion, mercy, and sociability are generated early in life, gradually eliminating the selfish aspects of these impulses and increasingly so as humankind progresses. Perhaps, in Hartley's view, humankind had not yet reached the point in its progress where there was sufficient compassion to do what was right by the animals. Hartley was almost as much a perfectibilist as Shelley – but perhaps refusing to eat flesh was, for Hartley, one of the last steps on the progressive path. If so, it was still a step he took for himself.

## Oliver Goldsmith

Charles Dickens treated the Anglo-Irish author Oliver Goldsmith (1730-1774) as an exemplar of sensibility to animals.[84] And rightly so, judging by Goldsmith's *The Hermit: A Ballad* (1766), where we read:

> No flocks that range the valley free
> To slaughter I condemn
> Taught by the Power that pities me,
> I learn to pity them.[85]

Born in rural Ireland and educated at Trinity College, Dublin, as a sizar (i.e., poor scholar) and at Edinburgh in medicine, Goldsmith prepared himself for a life in the professions rather than as the literary prince he became. Indeed, he practised medicine of a kind in England for a while. But then, from about 1757, he turned to literature, at first as no more than a Grub Street "literary drudge."[86] His *Polite Learning* (1759) is his first serious literary composition, pilloried as it was by some of the Ishmaelites of the press. In time, his work blossomed. *The Traveller* (1764) brought him instant fame. And he became immediately clubbable. In *Citizen of the World* (1762), Goldsmith had previously described the experiences of Lien Chi Altangi, a purported visitor to Europe from China:

> The better sort here pretend to the utmost compassion of every kind; to hear them speak, a stranger would be apt to imagine they could hardly hurt the gnat that stung them. They seem so tender, and so full of pity, that one would take them for the harmless friends of the whole creation, the protectors of the meanest insect or reptile that was privileged with existence. And yet would you believe it, I have seen the very men who have thus boasted of their tenderness at the same time devouring the flesh of six different animals tossed up in a fricassee. Strange contrariety of conduct. They pity and they eat the objects of their compassion ...
>
> Man was born to live with innocence and simplicity, but he has deviated from nature; he was born to share the bounties of heaven, but he has monopolised them; he was born to govern the 'brute creation'; but he has become their tyrant. If an epicure now shall happen to surfeit on his last night's feast, twenty animals the next day are to undergo the most exquisite tortures in order to provoke his appetite to another guilty meal.[87]

Goldsmith extols the virtues of the "bramins of the east," who did not fill themselves with "the miseries of other creatures." But was this mere rhetoric, mere literary licence? We find Goldsmith eating an abundance of flesh as a young man – from chop to steak to partridge – and at no point does he seem to leave off. He bemoaned the fact the French have not good meat.[88] Surely, crusty and pious Samuel Johnson, intimate friend of Goldsmith, would have mentioned, not to say chided him for, his vegetarianism if it had been there, and if perchance not, James Boswell, who was smitten above all with *She Stoops to Conquer,* having been a vegetarian himself for a while, would have been bound to comment. Indeed, it is reported reliably that Johnson and Goldsmith frequently dined together at the tavern of the Wine Office Court on the historic dish of the tavern: beefsteak pudding with larks and oysters.[89] Moreover, when he was a resident of the authors' retreat at Canonbury House in Islington, Goldsmith joined a writers' club at the Crown Tavern and is reported there to have dined at different times on mutton in various styles, rumpsteak, chicken, ham, and Irish stew.[90] In 1769, when Goldsmith published the first volume of his eight-volume *History of Animated Nature,* in good part a synopsis of Georges Louis Leclerc, comte de Buffon, Richard Cumberland observed of the author: "Poor fellow, he hardly knows an ass from a mule, nor a turkey from a goose, but when he sits it on the table" – clearly a reference to eating roast fowl.[91] From the estate of Gosfield Park, a gift of a haunch of venison is said to have been delivered to Goldsmith at his lodgings in The Temple Exchange Coffee House.[92] Surely, the reports are too frequent – and they multiply – not to have had at least a measure of accuracy. And almost all of them arise after he had written *Citizen of the World.*

What did Goldsmith eat when he dined with his associates at The Club – founded in 1763 (i.e., also after *Citizen of the World* ) – for there would surely have been no well-varied menu from which to choose and certainly no vegetarian options? The Club, restricted to nine members, met weekly at The Turk's Head Tavern in Soho. With Edmund Burke, Joshua Reynolds, David Garrick, the Oxford don Topham Beuclerk, and Dr. Johnson as fellow members, there was surely more than a libation to be had. Claret for the boys, port for the men, and brandy for heroes were, according to Johnson, the appropriate drinks. Veal pie with plums and sugar was an item of the standard Turk's Head fare served to The Club. Although we know Johnson ate it, we cannot be absolutely certain Goldsmith did. We know Goldsmith was fond of Madeira – and "Calvert's butt and Parson's black champagne" at the Red Lion – but of his favourite foodstuffs in later maturity we are ignorant.[93] Nonetheless, we know he counted a pig butcher as one with whom he enjoyed at least a degree of convivial fellowship – rather improbable if he were a convinced naysayer to flesh. What did Goldsmith eat at the numerous other clubs, societies, and coffeehouses he was known to frequent (indeed, he once lodged in one: The Temple Exchange Coffee House near Temple Bar) Surely, if it had been anything other than the standard fare, we would have been told about it. Howard Williams says of Goldsmith that his "principles ... were better than his practice, his sensibility stronger than his self-control."[94] We have no evidence that it was ever a principle he espoused for himself, nor that he ever tried to exert any self-control. The fleshless diet appears to have been no more than a convenient intellectual abstraction, a means of arousing the audience through eloquence without imposing obligations on himself or them.

He dined privately with Edmund Burke on more than one occasion. If Goldsmith had declined what was offered, we would assuredly have heard of it. Was Goldsmith one of those who pitied and ate the objects of his compassion? If he ever declined flesh, it was surely only in desperation when he lacked the price during those frequent bouts of poverty he experienced. In fact, as Oscar Sherwin wrote in *Goldy*, rather unkindly but probably justly, Goldsmith "has no desire to become a great writer. He only becomes a great writer to save himself from starvation."[95] It seems likely that his literary espousals arose more from the dictates of the pocket book than from philosophical principle, more from popular expectation of affected cant than from refined metaphysics. If, like Johnson, he intended to be the moralist of the age, unlike Johnson, the particular morals were of no especial importance. Still, we must allow with Sir Joshua Reynolds that "wherever Goldy is, there is no yawning." Perhaps the most frequently quoted sentence in reference to a purported historical vegetarian principle is Goldsmith's: "They pity and they eat the objects of their compassion." It is profoundly ironic that the words were uttered by a consistent omnivore.


## VOLTAIRE

When we turn to France, the experience is little different. Both Voltaire (1694-1778) and Rousseau (1712-1778) were very impressed by the vegetarian arguments of Antonio Celestina Cocchi. In his voluminous writings, the Indophile Voltaire, the proponent of enlightened absolutism, tolerance, and individual freedom, frequently demonstrated considerable animal sensibility.[96] Yet nowhere does he appear ever to have raised the issue of his own vegetarianism directly, although, at the very least by strong implication, he recommended it to others. Not once, it would appear, in his many thousand letters did he mention any principled abstention from flesh on his own part. Nonetheless, his orientations are not difficult to discern, although they must be sought. For example, in *The Treatise on Toleration* he tells us in approving tone: "the compassion we owe all animals ... endures in the peninsula of India; all the Pythagoreans in Italy and Greece abstained constantly from eating flesh. In his book *On Abstinence*, Porphyry reproached his disciple [Firmus Castricius] for having left his group solely to satisfy his barbarous appetite."[97] In reviewing the Hindu culture, Voltaire made a number of significant passing remarks:

> The Christian religion which these *primitives* [Quakers] alone follow to the letter, is as great an enemy to bloodshed as the Pythagorean. But the Christian peoples have never practised *their* religion and the ancient Hindu castes have always practised theirs. It is because Pythagoreanism is the only religion in the world which has been able to educe a religious feeling from the horror of murder and slaughter ... Our Houses of Carnage, which they call Butcher Shops, where they sell so many carcases to feed our own, would import the plague into the climate of India ... Their climate disposes them to abstain from strong liquors and from the flesh of animals – foods which excite the blood and often provoke ferocity ... all travellers agree that the character of these peoples has nothing of that irritability, of that caprice, and of that harshness which it has cost much trouble to keep within bounds in the countries of the North.[98]

Voltaire's view of India was indeed common currency among the learned – Coleridge, for example, referring to the "*Brahman* love & awe of life."[99] Did Voltaire himself practise the vegetarian "compassion we owe all animals"? Was it appropriate to reject flesh only in hot climates? Together with the Conseiller de Cideville, Voltaire translated Mandeville's *Fable of the Bees* into French. There is no suggestion in the fable of a geographical limitation to the fleshless diet. Were the animals just one of Voltaire's "periodic crusades," to be forgotten when the next cause came along?[100]

In the *Philosophical Dictionary*, Voltaire tells us "men fed upon carnage, and drinking strong drinks, have all an imprisoned and acrid blood which drives them mad in a hundred different ways."[101] Along with Rousseau, as we shall see, Voltaire shared the common misconception that diet determined character. And if Voltaire had really believed what he said, he would have known that he himself must be driven mad, for all the evidence is that he regularly consumed flesh and alcohol. Again, despite the implied moral necessity of vegetarianism, no one thought fit to comment on any vegetarian practices of François-Marie Arouet (Voltaire was his assumed name), whether on his extended visit to Britain from 1726, during the three years spent in Berlin from 1750, in residence in his native France, or at his permanent residences from the age of sixty in Geneva and beyond the city gates at Ferney and Tournay. At most, any abstinence was in his youth and thought to be due to ill-health, not will, for, as Norman Torrey wrote of his early years in the classic, *Spirit of Voltaire:* "His physical constitution would not allow physical indulgence, but when after the Duc de Vendôme returned from exile in 1715, the dinners – and orgies – at the Society of the Temple were again in full swing, Voltaire enjoyed them in the body vicariously, but with the spirit in full participation."[102] Voltaire described the dinners as "handsome feasts," although he resisted the shooting sports, having "no desire to assassinate partridges."[103]

In time, Voltaire is said by Archibald Ballantyne to have indulged while in France in "gay suppers," to have been "a welcome frequenter of the best circles of wit and society," to have lived "a pleasant life of writing, feasting and love-making." He "sparkled ... at Parisian suppers of the gods" – and the gods were not abstemious.[104] He dined with the Duc de Sully, enjoying the frivolities of château life, and ate with the governor of the Bastille without occasioning a subsequent comment on his diet. Later still, he gave large house parties at each of his three Swiss homes where flesh was undoubtedly consumed. His secretary, Wagnière, said that "young people came every Sunday to dance at his château. They found there every variety of refreshment."[105] Are we to imagine Voltaire himself did not consume the provisions he supplied? Perhaps conclusive are the words he wrote in 1748 to his Benedictine friend Dom Calmet requesting a cell at the Abbey of Senomes, which he visited for some ten weeks several years later: "If I could have a thick soup, a little mutton, and some eggs I should prefer that happy, healthy frugality to royal fare."[106] Frugality? Voltaire never claimed to practise the vegetarian diet, it should be recalled. It would appear he himself was a consumer of the "carnage," and we know he did consume wine in considerable measure, despite his condemnation of "strong drinks." Was his condemnation of flesh no more effective? The publisher/bookseller and parasitic gourmand, Nicolas-Claude Theriot, travelled from home to home scrounging whatever meals he could. He was frequently a guest of Voltaire. Do we imagine he would have been such a frequent visitor if the fare had not been to his luxurious taste? Voltaire's practical advice on diet seems to have been restricted to what he wrote to Mme. Du Deffand: "Don't eat too much."[107] On his composition of *La Pucelle*, Voltaire wrote: "I wanted to see what my imagination would produce when I gave it free rein."[108] Did "the horror of murder and slaughter" of animals spring from the same temporary and imaginative source?

On his three-year visit to England, Voltaire dined at the residences of Kings George I and II; of Lords Bolingbroke, Lyttleton, Chesterfield, Peterborough, and Melcombe; and of Ladies Walpole and Marlborough. In Germany, he was entertained by Frederick the Great, the Margrave of Bayreuth, and the Duchess of Saxe-Gotha, among others – important to have "a few crowned heads up one's sleeve," he wrote.[109] What do we imagine he ate there if his diet produced no ensuing gossip? He frequently dined in London coffeehouses and bars, including The Rainbow and The Bedford Head Tavern. Surely, there were no vegetarian options. Indeed, Alexander Pope celebrated Voltaire's dietary preferences in verse: "When sharp with hunger, scorn you to be fed / Except on pea-chicks at the Bedford Head." "Pea-chicks" are the young of peafowl. Pope is suggesting Voltaire's taste is refined and tends toward the more exotic flesh foods. Surely, Pope – who knew Voltaire – could not have been hopelessly wrong.

Voltaire says of the English: "No manner of living appears strange. We have men who walk six miles a day for their health, feed upon roots, never taste flesh ... but taxed with folly by nobody."[110] He does not count himself among the "strange," nor does he consider himself subject to the complaint of "folly" elsewhere. The purpose of the passage was to extol English tolerance. On another occasion, he favours the French. Voltaire tells us that "more poultry and game are consumed in Paris in a single evening than in London in a week."[111] And this he counts as a mark in favour of Paris. Moreover, he maintained poultry yards and kept cattle on his Swiss property.[112] Were they merely for eggs, milk, and cheese? He operated a tannery on his property. Did they use merely the hides of the naturally deceased? It is an unlikely possibility if the operation was not to be a serious drain on resources.

In *Le Mondain,* Voltaire wrote of the delights of food and wine taken in the pagan spirit or in the pleasure-loving spirit of his Epicurean contemporary Saint-Evremond.[113] He wrote in a letter penned in old age: "I will not quarrel with my neighbour if he likes beef and I prefer mutton."[114] Of course, he was only indulging in metaphor. But it was not a metaphor likely to be chosen by someone opposed to the eating of flesh. Moreover, a Dr. Samuel Sharpe visited him in 1765 at Les Délices, his home in Geneva, declaring Voltaire as "keeping an open table, to which strangers of every nation find an easy introduction" – a table to which Voltaire had imported his French chef.[115] Indeed, Voltaire declared himself "the innkeeper of Europe."[116] His hospitality – which was frequent and generous, as we have seen – would very much diminish the likelihood of his own rejection of flesh, at least if his diet occasioned no comment from the guests – or himself. One sentence in a letter from Voltaire to Rousseau in 1755 – when they remained, temporarily, on cordial terms, even though Voltaire was in fact in the midst of condemning Rousseau's latest work – gives one cause to reconsider momentarily however.[117] Neither was in good health. Thus, Voltaire wrote from Geneva: "You must come here and restore your health in your native air ... enjoy freedom, join me in drinking the milk of our cows and nibbling our vegetables."[118] But the reconsideration is only momentary. If vegetables were a staple item, so was much else. It was a protestation of the life of rustic simplicity they each extolled and each ignored. One is tempted by Mary Shelley's somewhat exaggerated view of Voltaire as a cynic and of Rousseau as a hypocrite.

Voltaire became famous for the philosophy of tolerance. Was his practice one of tolerant self-indulgence for his own habits that did not meet his rigorous philosophical standards? "French levity dances on the tombs of the unfortunate," he wrote about the cruelties of the *parlement* of Paris.[119] But he seems to have danced himself on the tombs of the permanently unfortunate animals. Surely, it is inconceivable that Voltaire practised a fleshless regimen. If he had a passion for justice, and he did, in practice this justice did not extend beyond human affairs. As we can deduce from Voltaire's superficially primitivist *L'Ingénu*, he is not a primitivist at all – few have ever seriously thought he was. Rather, in all his works we can see him as something of a meliorist who possessed, in the words of R.S. Ridgway in *Voltaire and Sensibility*, "that impulse towards altruism which is the true mark of the man of feeling."[120] But it was not an altruism he was willing to extend to the animals when the price of that extension was a hindrance to his reputation as the grand man of letters welcomed and welcoming everywhere in society – whether in eighteenth-century France, Switzerland, Germany, or England. In the final analysis, we are left with no other conclusion than that on the issue of the fleshless diet, Voltaire, in the manner of Candide, chose to step aside and cultivate his own garden.

## George Louis Leclerc, Comte de Buffon

The author of the famed forty-four-volume *Histoire naturelle* (1749-1804), Georges Louis Leclerc, comte de Buffon (1707-1788) – Rousseau admired him above all other living French writers – discussed the grounds for vegetarianism with remarkable insight for the time but was too tied to tradition to advocate the practice:

Man knows how to use, as a master, his power over animals. He has selected those whose flesh flatters his taste. He has made domestic slaves of them. He has multiplied them more than Nature could have done. He has formed innumerable flocks, and by the cares which he takes in propagating them he seems to have acquired the right of sacrificing them for himself. But he extends that right *much* beyond his needs. For, independently of those species which he has subjected, and of which he disposes at will, he makes war upon wild animals, upon birds and fishes. He does not even limit himself to those of the climate he inhabits. He seeks at a distance, even in the remotest seas, new meats, and entire Nature seems scarcely to suffice for his intemperance and the inconsistent variety of his appetite.

Man alone consumes more flesh than all other animals put together. He is, then, the great destroyer, and he is so more by abuse than necessity. Instead of enjoying with moderation the resources offered him, in place of dispensing them with equity, in place of repairing in proportion as he destroys, of renewing in proportion as he annihilates, the rich man makes his boast and glory in consuming all his splendour in destroying in one day, at his table, more material than would be necessary for the support of several families. He abuses equally other animals and his own species, the rest of whom live in famine, languish in misery, and work only to satisfy the immoderate appetite and the still more insatiable vanity of this human being who, destroying others by want, destroys himself by excess.

And yet Man might, like other animals, live upon vegetables. Flesh is not a better nourishment than grains or bread ... it is proved by facts that [one] could well live upon bread, vegetables, and the grains of plants, since we know entire nations and classes of men to whom religion forbids to feed upon anything that has life.[121]

Yet, *mirabile dictu*, Buffon is not convinced by the invincible strength of the conclusion of his own argument, snidely telling us the denial of flesh is "recommended by some physicians too friendly to a reformed diet" and thus conceding the diet's increased scientific popularity. He tells us that the middle class lives longer than the poor and rustic – as though, even if true, there were not myriad other reasons than the increased consumption of flesh to account for this eighteenth-century "fact"! And accordingly, he does not recommend the diet he has maintained so well in argument, at least if humankind is to avoid the infliction of abuse that Buffon acknowledges is no necessity. It is difficult to imagine a more blatant case of rationalization. Indeed, incensed by Rousseau's claims, he assured his readers that human beings are not naturally herbivorous but need the nourishment of flesh. Upon reading Buffon, Howard Williams bemoaned that "unhappily, Buffon seems to have considered himself as holding a brief to defend his clients, the flesh eaters."[122]


## ROUSSEAU

Because Percy Bysshe Shelley chose Rousseau, in "The Triumph of Life" (1822), as the man who represented the direction in which Europe was rushing, and because Shelley was both an adamant and vociferous vegetarian as well as a utopian perfectibilist who expected the newly enlightened era rapidly to right all wrongs, we may well expect citizen Rousseau, as he loved to be called as a Genevese by birth and breeding, to have rejected all flesh. Indeed, he seems to do so in his writings, especially *Émile*. In fact, in the poem, Shelley's thoughts do not dwell for a moment on the fleshless diet, and Rousseau's regimen is not at all a topic. Shelley's concluding words to the unfinished poem were: "Fell, as I have fallen by the wayside." But he was not thinking of Rousseau's eating habits. If Shelley had not drowned before the poem's completion, we might have learned more. As it is, we know nothing from the pen of Shelley as to whether Rousseau was commonly thought to have been a practising vegetarian. Perhaps it would still not have helped if the poem were complete. As Edward Duffy wrote, Shelley's "Triumph of Life" verses constitute "one of the most baffling pieces of romantic literature."[123]

If, as we shall see, Rousseau ultimately failed to follow his own vegetarian advice, many in succeeding generations who thought of themselves as Rousseauians were adamant followers of the creed, and at least a few died at the guillotine for their radical faith, although not principally for the vegetarian aspect of it that some of them practised. To be fair to Rousseau, he never explicitly stated that he practised the vegetarian regimen himself. And it is *possible* to read Rousseau as affirming that the altruistic part of our fundamental nature calls for abstinence from flesh, whereas the self-preservation aspect allows for the killing of animals for sustenance. And we live by self-preservation! It was what he called "second nature" that triumphed.

Despite Shelley's silence, we have more pertinent information about the life of Rousseau than about any other eighteenth-century vegetarian advocate. And what we know about Rousseau seems representative of the type as a whole. In reply to Voltaire's 1755 letter offering milk and vegetables (cited above), Rousseau wrote in conclusion, making no reference to the vegetables, "I would rather drink the water of your fountain than the milk of your cows." Whether Rousseau intended to refer to anything other than frugality and simplicity is to be doubted. And the statement might be mere self-congratulatory rhetoric, especially given that, despite his stated preference for water, he was known to quaff a good bumper or two of country wine and of some better wine when finances or hospitality permitted. Perhaps the complete sincerity is also to be doubted, for he wished to be regarded as the quintessentially simple man and, as Maurice Cranston points out, both Voltaire and Rousseau "may have written their letters with an eye to publication."[124] To be sure, in general, Rousseau conscientiously pursued a life of austerity, at least for public consumption – although there are at least three portraits of him wearing fur trim, one by Gérard, one by Schellenberg, and one by Allan Ramsey. Nonetheless, as Cranston also wrote: "In principle, Rousseau objected to the luxury and splendour of Holbach's hospitality; in practice he enjoyed it."[125] Nor was Holbach alone in offering luxury to Rousseau. Certainly, Helvétius was one of numerous others. In fact, in the Paris period, "Rousseau alternated the frugality of a Bohemian existence in the rue de Grenelle with the luxury of rich friends' châteaux and *hôtels particuliers*."[126] With Rousseau, the frugal protestations – "it is by simplicity man distinguishes himself" – do not always conform to a frugal way of life.[127]

In the *Discourse on the Origin and Foundations of Inequality among Men* (1754) and *Émile* (1762), Rousseau, the noble savage, or "honest savage" as his friend Lord Keith usually called him, gives admirable indication of his respect and consideration for the animal realm, but it is in *Émile* alone that he addresses the issue of an appropriate dietary regimen.[128] There he advises: "One of the proofs that the taste for meat is not natural to man is the indifference which children exhibit for that kind of food, and the preference they all give to vegetable foods, such as dairy products, pastry, fruits, etc. It is above all important not to denature this primitive taste and make children carnivorous. If this is not for their health, it is for their character."[129]

It is notable here that Rousseau seems to employ an argument similar to that of Saint Thomas Aquinas and Immanuel Kant. That is, we ought to do good to animals in order to be better human beings rather than for the sake of the animals themselves. That, however, would be to misread Rousseau and render him an injustice. In Rousseau's view, our character is improved when we do what is right, but our duty is to the animals directly. In fact, he *liked* animals and kept pigeons, chickens, cats, and dogs as pets. A contemporary engraving by Monsiaux depicts Rousseau boating with a dog (perhaps his pet, Sultan), and with rabbit companions, along with two women, perhaps Thérèse Levasseur and the wife of his friend Engel, when he tried

in 1765 to colonize with rabbits an island on Lake Bienne – now called the
Isle de Rousseau. He was disconsolate when his dog Turc died of an accident in 1762, and he received several letters of condolence that bore witness
to the depths of his distress. Sultan accompanied Rousseau to exile in England, taking the arduous journey across Europe and the channel with him
– no mean reflection of Rousseau's attachment to the dog.

"For, however one explains the experience," continues Rousseau in *Émile*,
"it is certain that great eaters of meat are in general more cruel and ferocious than other men."[130] The erroneous belief that diet itself affects the
character – and hence that one is what one eats – has persisted over the centuries and is still believed by many eschewers of flesh today. Like Voltaire,
he must have thought of himself as a flesh eater subject to the same ferocity and cruelty if he had meant what he said. Even when Rousseau is not
writing about diet, the vegetarian vocabulary being absent, much of what
he says implies vegetarianism. Thus, for example, in the *Discourse on Inequality*, he writes: "as long as [one] does not resist the inner compulsion of
compassion, he will never do harm to another man, or even to another sentient being."[131] What Rousseau has to say about dietary habit in *Émile* is
more readily believed than what he says about the effect of flesh on character:

> The farther we are removed from the state of nature, the more we lose our
> natural tastes; or rather habit gives us a second nature that we substitute for
> the first to the extent that none of us knows this first nature any more. It fol-
> lows from this that the most natural tastes ought also to be the simplest ...
> Fruits, vegetables, herbs, and finally some meats [Rousseau does not mean
> flesh meats] grilled without seasoning and without salt, constituted the feasts
> of the first men ... Has anyone ever been seen to have a disgust for water or
> bread? That is the trace left by nature; that is, therefore, also our rule.[132]

"Trace left by nature" and "our rule" they may be in principle. But we
have no evidence Rousseau lived for any period of time by his own implied
rules and a great deal of evidence that he did not. After all, although he
esteemed the state of nature above all, he also insisted it was not possible to
return to the state of nature. Perhaps not even to its traces. To be sure, he
tells us "the convulsions of a dying animal will cause [Émile] an ineffable
distress."[133] But he made it abundantly clear the education he designed for
Émile, in which the boy could enjoy the natural sensibilities, was possible
only in a republic. And in France, Rousseau did not live in a republic. In
Switzerland, he lived in a republic that had betrayed its republican principles. Moreover, Rousseau does not seem to have been entirely consistent in

*Émile,* for one of the practical, mathematical tasks he sets the boy requires
him to want to fish in the moat from the window. In addition, the tutor
instructs the lad in the benefits of exercise to be had from hunting. The
slaughter of animals is not the purpose. It is to distract Émile from the dangers of sex.[134] But, surely, no authentic ethical vegetarian would ever consider consensual sex a more pernicious activity than the unnecessary killing
of sentient beings, even if the killing were not the primary purpose. Did
Rousseau live permanently in humanity's "second nature" while extolling
the first in abstract principle?

Whether he was with Louise de Warens at Les Charmettes in his youth,
with the bluestocking Mme. d'Épinay at the Hermitage, with the Comtesse d'Houdetot – "the first and only love of my whole life," albeit un-
requited – with his long-time semiliterate companion Thérèse Levasseur,
with whom he went through a form of marriage at Bourgoin in 1767, with
Mme. la Maréchale de Luxembourg at the Château de Montmorency, with
Mme. de Verdelin, with the Comtesse de Boufflers, as a fugitive for a short
time at Yverdon in the republic of Berne at the home of the banker Daniel
Roguin, temporarily resident in asylum as the guest of David Hume, or
renting Wootton Hall in Derbyshire from a Mr. Davenport, there is no indication of any fleshless diet.[135] In fact, while he was first living at Môtiers
in Neuchâtel, Rousseau dined as a paying guest with the Girardiers until
the arrival of Thérèse from France – apparently without requesting special
fare. In Môtiers, Thérèse was said to have charmed visitors "by her simplicity of manners as well as her skill as a French country cook" – a seemingly
improbable compliment if she had restricted herself to eighteenth-century
fleshless fare.[136] Indeed, among the items she was reported to have cooked
were gigot of mutton, trout, quail, and woodcock. As Cranston observes:
"Given Thérèse's skill in the kitchen and the poor reputation of the fare at
the local inn, it is hardly surprising that Rousseau always ate at home."[137] It
is difficult to believe that the mutton, fish, and game fowl were not
intended for Rousseau. Did he resist "the inner compulsion of compassion" he enjoined?

The Abbé de Morellet wrote to Rousseau that he could readily appreciate why, in the case of la Maréchale, he "had made an exception" of
"renouncing the world and its splendours."[138] In fact, there are many more
occasions when Rousseau seems not to have resisted "the world and its
splendours." At restored Montlouis, he entertained Mme. Luxembourg's
husband, the Maréchal de Luxembourg, as well as the Duc de Villeroy, the
Prince de Tingry, and many other persons of rank. What do we imagine
he served? We can perhaps hazard a guess from the so-called "simple" meal he

served to the Hungarian count, Joseph Teleki de Szek, in 1761, which included veal, rabbit, and paté. Are we to imagine Rousseau did not partake of the flesh himself? None of his guests or hosts ever said he ate different fare than they. Even if he did not partake, he would have been guilty, vicariously at least, of the conduct he deplores in *Émile*. Borrowing from Plutarch, he asks: "How could [a person] see a poor, defenceless animal bled, skinned, and dismembered? How could he endure the sight of quivering flesh? How did the animal smell not make him sick to his stomach?"[139] Apparently, it did not make Rousseau sick. It has been said that, on at least one occasion, Rousseau told a fairy story while he and his guests took turns rotating the meat on the spit.[140] On another occasion, on a walking tour from Môtiers with François-Louis d'Eschernay in 1764, they are reported to have taken with them "a picnic of patés, poultry, venison, and a good supply of wine – loaded on the back of a mule."[141] On James Boswell's visit to Rousseau at Môtiers in the same year, a biographer of Johnson reports Boswell to have said that "our" dinner included beef and veal stew, pork, and trout.[142] In 1758, Rousseau received a new year's gift of four Le Mans chickens – by contemporary repute the best – from his old friend Mme. de Créqui. We would have expected her to have known better than to present the gift if Rousseau always declined flesh or was even indifferent to the fare. Two of the chickens he gave away, and two of them he, or his household, ate. On receiving a copy of *Émile,* the celebrated author Charles-Marie de la Condamine beseeched Rousseau to let him come to Montmorency for a visit and bring a chicken for the pot. So little did Condamine imagine the words of *Émile* were to be transformed into practice. Someone else – possibly Mme. de Verdelin – sent Rousseau a capon. The Prince de Conti twice sent game, and the Maréchal – who knew him as well as did Mme. de Créqui – sent partridges. True, Rousseau did not appreciate the gifts, but that appears to be because he abhorred the practice of receiving gifts, which he thought deprived him of his independence, rather than because he disliked the gifts themselves. Hume said he had a fierce resistance to receiving charity.[143] Did he consult only the "individual will" when his philosophy would have recommended he consult "the general will"? Does Rousseau provide himself in *The Social Contract* with a convenient excuse for his flesh eating? There he wrote: "savage man" – of the Arcadian type, we presume he means – "when he has eaten, is at peace with the whole of nature."[144] The acquisition of food, then, seems to escape the provisions of the peaceful laws of primitive nature. Rousseau wrote explicitly to condemn adultery in *Lettres morales* – "illegitimate love" he called it – but he practised it nonetheless, if less frequently than he desired.[145] Did vegetarianism similarly belong to the category of the impractical, republican ideal? Perhaps Rousseau's practice is captured in his commentary in his edition of the Abbé de St. Pierre's *Project for Perpetual Peace:* "It is a sort of madness to be wise in a world of fools."[146]

On one occasion Mme. d'Épinay made Rousseau a gift of salt – the high tax on, and hence price of, salt was a major cause of the French Revolution. Was the purpose of the gift to cure flesh or preserve fish, as seems likely? It is certainly a commodity Rousseau thought in *Émile* we should do without – as did "the first feasts of men" do "without seasonings and without salt." He wrote a potential visitor to the Hermitage: "I shall have wine and rustic foodstuffs, and if my picnic does not suit you, you may bring your own."[147] On another occasion, he offered a different guest "a rustic meal."[148] Indeed, he was known as "the philosopher of rusticity."[149] On yet another date, a few years later, he wrote an invited guest to Petit Montlouis at Montmorency: "If it is necessary for me to agree to your bringing your own dish of food, I do so with pleasure."[150] Were the meals served to the Hungarian count and to James Boswell a momentary lapse, an aberration? In at least one instance, the dinner he served his guests moved straight from soup to dessert, although we are not told what was in the soup.[151] Was this poverty or principle? Simplicity or probity? Was it vegetarian fare he offered or peasant *saucisse* as opposed to bourgeois *cotelettes* duly sauced and seasoned? This was the age of urban culinary sophistication, in which just a half-century later Viscount Chateaubriand's chef invented "Chateaubriand" for the visit of the Duke of Wellington to the French Embassy in London, and Wellington's chef replied with "Beef Wellington" for the return invitation to Apsley House. Probably, Rousseau was merely contrasting his own simple cuisine with the luxuries of the *beau monde*. But if it was a fleshless meal Rousseau himself ate, did he consume vegetables at his cottage and flesh in the confines of the luxurious homes of his friends at which he so often dined? And without any comment being made? Clearly, we are left with far more questions than complete confidence in answers. But the balance of probabilities is very clear. It is not just that Rousseau deviated occasionally from a fleshless diet, but that meat was his regular fare.

On composing *La nouvelle Héloise*, Rousseau remarked: "In my continual ecstasy I intoxicated myself with the most delicious feelings that ever entered the heart of man. Entirely forgetting the human species, I invented societies of perfect beings, whose virtues were as celestial as their beauty."[152] Were the vegetarian virtues celestial and Rousseau a mere mortal? He wrote at great length to Diderot, explaining the considerable difficulties he would have in accompanying Mme. d'Épinay to Geneva, including his evacuation

problems, which would occasion frequent breaks in the journey, but without mentioning the difficulties of obtaining fleshless fare at the inns en
route. With reference to the theatre, Rousseau advises us: "In shedding our
tears for fiction, we satisfy all the duties of humanity without having to give
up anything further of ourselves."[153] *Émile* was fiction. Was the consumption of flesh one of those things he wept over but did not feel he had to
renounce? The opening sentence of the author's preface to *La nouvelle
Héloise* contains the words "romances are necessary to a corrupt people."[154]
In Rousseau's view, he inhabited a corrupt monarchy where republican
virtues were out of place. Mme. du Deffand said of the Comtesse de
Boufflers that she never allowed her principles to interfere with her pleasures. Could the same be said of Rousseau? It would appear so, at least on
fairly regular occasion, for, although Rousseau wrote on benevolent education for the young, he also consigned his five natural children with Thérèse
Levasseur to the Foundling Hospital in Paris for adoption. He was frequently brutally honest in his *Confessions* – "sometimes ... described as the
first true biography ever written" – even implying masturbation, although
he also indicated his disapproval of the practice.[155] He acknowledges having been a flesh eater in the *Confessions,* but the reader could be excused for
thinking of these times as momentary lapses from the customary regimen.
In writing to the physician Dr. Théodore Tronchin, Rousseau affirmed:
"There is not a single man in the world who in doing everything his heart
prompted to him would not soon become the worst of scoundrels."[156] Did
the promptings of his heart meet a declination of the will? On the balance
of probabilities, nay certainties, the answer has to be decidedly in the affirmative. In their common denial of flesh fare, Rousseau and Voltaire seem
to have taken the opportunity to condemn the cruel dietary practices of
a good part of the human race, at least of Western civilization, but to
have continued themselves to behave like the rest of humankind.[157] Yet
Rousseau's ideas were common currency in the forming of the culture of
the French Revolution, where his speculative "would-it-were-so's" encountered a formidable will to act. Quietism was defeated at the barricades.

In large part through the writings of Bernardin de Saint-Pierre, Rousseau soon came to be seen as the vegetarian voice of France – indeed, of the
whole of mainland Europe – and vegetarians soon came to follow in what
they saw as his footsteps, or at least his advocacy. Not only was Saint-Pierre
himself a vegetarian advocate and apostle of rustic simplicity, but, so far as
we can tell, unlike the master, he also practised what he preached, although
a skeptic might consider it probable that he was no more than a pesco-
vegetarian who dined on shellfish. It was certainly common enough in the

earlier nineteenth century – largely with acknowledgments to Rousseau but often via Saint-Pierre – to deem the human in nature and origin a herbivorous creature.

## ALPHONSE DE LAMARTINE, RICHARD WAGNER, AND ALFRED LORD TENNYSON

In addition to those who failed to live up to the dictates of their advocacy or even to try, there are also a few figures of some historical importance from a slightly later period who tried, in some manner or another, to follow their convictions but who failed in the attempt. Thus, for example, one of those influenced by Rousseau's precepts was Alphonse de Lamartine (1790-1869), briefly head of the provisional government after the February Revolution of 1848 in France. In *Les Confidences* (1848) Lamartine described his vegetarian predilections. Having explained the orientations of his early education from his mother, based on the principles of Rousseau and Bernardin de Saint-Pierre, he added:

> It was in accord with this system that she raised me. My education was a second-hand philosophical education corrected and softened by motherhood.
>
> In practice this education was derived substantially from Pythagoras and *Émile*.
>
> Accordingly, the greatest simplicity of dress and the most rigorous frugality of food constituted its foundation. My mother was convinced, a conviction I share, that killing animals in order to feed on their flesh and blood is one of the weaknesses of the human condition; that it is one of those curses inflicted on mankind, either by his fall from grace, or by the hardening of the heart through his own perversity. She believed, a belief I share with her, that the custom of hardening the heart towards the most gentle animals, our companions, our helpers, here on earth, our brethren in work and even in affection, that these sacrifices, blood lusts, and the sight of palpitating flesh, both brutalize the person and harden the instincts of the heart.

Especially in France, but not absent from Britain, this idea of animals as human helpers was quite common in the general culture, made famous after *Les Confidences* by Auguste Comte (1798-1857), often deemed the founder of sociology, in *Theory of the Great Being* and *Theory of the Future of Man* (both 1854).[158] It was a conception that influenced John Stuart Mill. Lamartine continued: "She believed, and I believe it too, that [flesh] food, appearing more succulent and remedial, contains irritants and putre-factions which turned the food sour and shortened man's life-span. As evidence in favour of abstinence from flesh, she would cite the numerous peoples of India, who denied themselves every living being, and the robust and healthy pastoral peoples, and even our industrious rural workers, who work more, live simpler and longer lives, and who eat meat perhaps ten times in their lives."

Marianne Stark noted that Lamartine's observation applied to Italy, too. Writing in *Letters from Italy, between 1792 and 1798* (1800), she stated that: "The most remarkable quality in the Florentine Peasant is their industry, for, during the hottest weather, they toil all day without sleep, and seldom retire early to rest: yet, notwithstanding this fatigue, they live almost entirely on bread, fruits, pulse, and the common wine of the country."[159]

As instances of rationalizations in favour of the side on which one is arguing, and without any confirmatory evidence for their statements, it is notable that Buffon deems the middle-class flesh eaters to live longer lives, whereas Lamartine states that the peasants, who rarely eat flesh, outlive their urban counterparts. Neither offers any evidence for his proposition but assumes his authority will be sufficient to obviate any further inquiry.

Lamartine continues his account of his childhood:

She never allowed me to partake [of flesh] until I was thrown pele-mele into school life. To rid my desire for it, if ever I had one, she did not reason with me but employed that instinct that resonates with us better than logic.

I had a lamb, a gift from a peasant from [the town of] Milly, which I had taught to follow me everywhere, like a most loving and faithful dog. We loved each other with that first passion which children and young animals naturally have for each other. One day the cook said to my mother in my presence "Madame, the lamb is fat; the butcher has come to ask for it; should I give it to him?" I cried out. I threw myself on the lamb. I demanded to know what the butcher wanted with it; and what was a butcher. The cook replied that he was a man who killed lambs, sheep, small calves, and lovely cows for money. I could not believe it. I begged my mother. And readily got mercy for my friend. Some days later, my mother, who was going into town, took me with her, and brought me, as if by accident, to the butcher's yard. I saw men with naked and bloody arms, who were slaughtering an ox; others were cutting the throats of calves and sheep; yet others were carving their still palpitating limbs. Rivulets of blood steamed here and there on the pavement. A profound compassion, mingled with horror, came over me, and I asked that we pass by quickly. The thought of those horrible and disgusting scenes, the obligatory foretaste of one of the meat platters that I saw served up at the table, caused me to loathe animal food and dread butchers. Despite the necessity of conforming to the customs of society, where [in my political career] I could be found eating what everyone else eats, I retained a rational repugnance for cooked flesh, and have always found it difficult not to view the butcher's trade as sharing something like that of bureaucrats. I thus lived until I was twelve years of age on bread, dairy products, vegetables and fruit. My health was no less robust, my growth no less rapid, and perhaps it was as a result of this diet that I acquired those pure traits, that refined sensibility, and that quiet serenity of humour that I have maintained to this day.[160]

It is perhaps surprising – but, based on experience, it should not surprise us – that a man of such self-described "profound compassion, tinged with horror," such "refined sensibility," should find it so easy, or even at all possible, to revert to flesh eating. If the emotions were truly as expressed by Lamartine, would not flesh have nauseated him in precisely the same way that the customary, unthinking, animal eater would be nauseated if expected to engage in cannibalism? If Lamartine truly felt as he says but returned to flesh for the remainder of his life because of "the necessity of conforming to the customs of society," then convention is even stronger than we have so far depicted it in these pages. Otherwise, we must conclude that Lamartine's political career was of far greater importance to him than the maintenance of a moral system in which he appears to have believed so passionately – at least until he was twelve years of age! It would appear there can be, at the same time, both a natural compassion that spurs one to deplore the eating of flesh and a natural compulsion, born of our genetic impulses, to continue to eat it. There is no likelihood that Lamartine returned to a vegetarian diet when he had retired from public service.

The German composer (Wilhelm) Richard Wagner (1813-1883) was one who saw the moral necessity of vegetarianism but, despite his will, could not bring himself personally to abandon flesh. He was undoubtedly committed to improvement of the animal's lot. In *Offener Brief über die Vivisektion* (Open Letter on Vivisection), addressed to Herr Ernst von Weber, author of *Die Folterkammern der Wissenschaft* (The Torture Chambers of Science), which letter was published in the *Bayreuther Blätter* in 1879, Wagner condemned the barbarity of animal experimentation. That we do not have the courage to abandon such atrocities, he claimed, was "the curse of our civilization."[161] He was no less committed in principle to overcoming the habit of dining on flesh. Even from an early age, he was appalled by the barbarity of killing food animals. When Wagner was a child, hewitnessed the slaughtering of an ox. "As the axe descended," writes Barry Millington in *Wagner*, "the boy would have rushed at the butcher had his friends not held him back. For some time after he refused all meat."[162] As an adult, he would discuss vegetarianism with his erudite wife, Cosima. Having been convinced by reading Gleizès that the impulses of his youth were correct, "this teaching," he wrote in *Religion and Art* (1880):

> (of the sinfulness of murdering and living on our fellow beings) was the result of a deep metaphysical recognition of a truth; and if the Brahman has brought us to the consciousness of the most manifold phenomena of the living world, with it is awakened the consciousness that the sacrifice of one of our near kin is, in a manner, the slaughter of one of ourselves: that the non-human animal is separated from man only by the degree of its mental endowment, and, what is of more significance than mental endowment, that it has the faculties of pleasure and pain, has the same desire for life as the most reason-endowed portion of mankind ... From the first, amidst the rage for predatory pursuits and for bloodshed, it has never been familiar to the consciousness of the true philosopher that the human race suffer from the disease which maintains them in a state of demoralisation.[163]

In the words of Barry Millington, Wagner maintained in *Religion and Art* that the "earliest people on earth were graziers and tillers of soil; only later did they kill animals for food and, acquiring a blood lust, turning to murdering each other ... Christ exhorted his followers to adopt vegetarianism, offering his own flesh and spilt blood. The primary cause of the decay of early Christianity was the failure of his followers to abstain from animal food." Moreover, Wagner averred, it would be possible to regain the lost purity if we were to retrace these steps. Millington reported further Wagner's statement that "a return to natural food is the only basis of a possible regeneration of mankind. Vegetarians and animal-lovers should join forces with the temperance societies and socialists to help bring this about ... the most effective way of communicating these ideas is through art, in particular the art of the tone-poet (i.e., music drama)."[164]

Yet Wagner himself failed to follow the path of the regeneration he thought necessary for humankind. The "deep metaphysical recognition" never advanced beyond the metaphysics. The widow of Siegfried Wagner, the composer's son, confirmed in 1972 the long attested fact that "Wagner would have liked to have been a vegetarian for ethical reasons, but his poor health prevented him from changing his diet. He suffered from a weak heart and eczema of the face."[165] Yet, when his health was far less of a concern, he failed equally to follow the regimen he prescribed with such moral fervour.

Although Alfred Lord Tennyson (1809-1892) is often referred to, usually a touch unkindly in intent, as the author of the memorable words "Nature, red in tooth and claw," he was also a vice president of the National Anti-Vivisection Society. In his 1820 notebook – he was eleven years of age – he described himself as letting wild animals out of traps to the fury of the gamekeepers. At home he had a pet owl, commemorated in verse, and at Cambridge University he kept a pet snake, and later a hedgehog. Toward the end of his life he kept a wolfhound, named Karenina, out of his respect for the vegetarian Leo Tolstoy. As an undergraduate, before Charles Darwin embarked on the *Beagle,* Tennyson subscribed to a Lamarckian theory of evolution. He brooded gloomily on evolution: "A monstrous eft was of old the Lord and Master"; now man "is first, but is he the last? is he not too base?"[166] His last Lincolnshire poem, "Owd Roä" (1887), is about a dying dog that rescued a child from a fire. Like William Blake, he adopted Swedenborgianism, with its, often ignored, vegetarian principles. Yet he did not become a lasting vegetarian (nor, it would appear, did William Blake, even temporarily). Tennyson's poem "To E. Fitzgerald" refers to his early attempt to become a vegetarian: "Once for ten long weeks I tried, / Your table of Pythagoras." Tennyson had the requisite animal sympathies but not the firmness of mind. Despite his deep admiration for Shelley, he failed in his attempt to emulate him. Over a century earlier than Tennyson, Lord Byron appears to have reached the same conclusions in favour of vegetarianism, if more for vainglory than for the animals. As Marian Scholtmeijer wrote aright in *Animal Victims in Modern Fiction:* "Byron practised vegetarianism only sporadically and largely out of vanity."[167] His conviction was not really a moral conviction at all.

What some of these accounts reflect is the considerable difficulty, but not impossibility, prior to the twentieth century of readily being served, or of readily obtaining year round, adequate vegetarian fare, especially if one was in public life or if one's regular activities entailed public dining. They reflect also the degree to which a number of individuals were first convinced of the ethical requirement to eschew flesh but managed to find arguments for the continued consumption, in the words of Lamartine, of "what everyone else eats." As Gandhi wrote so appositely, although not thinking of historical vegetarianism: "nothing is more common than to hear men warmly supporting a theory in the abstract without any intention of submitting to it in practice."[168] These words might stand as the emblem of much seventeenth- to nineteenth-century vegetarian advocacy. The histories indicate also the extent of rationalization present among a number of those who, in their more ethical moments or their poetical imagination, acknowledged the moral requirement of a vegetarian diet but felt more strongly the generally perceived obligation, again in the words of Lamartine, of "conforming to the customs of society." But if ethical vegetarianism's successes were quite modest in practice, many members of the medical profession, enthusiastically if sporadically, continued to promote the vegetarian diet among their patients for reasons of health.

Sometimes, for the literary figures – especially the poets – form and finesse outweighed substance in their compositions. There was an Enlightenment tradition of intellectual rhetoric in which the rhetoric far exceeded the material substance in importance. Whether for poet or not, the Golden Age often functioned as a convenient rhetorical device for proclaiming the moral necessity of a diet beyond the realm of reasonableness in the world as it had become. The perfect human created by God had become a haughty and corrupt being, so it was said. Many thought this corruption had received the warrant, even blessing, of God – and of society – and so in corruption humankind must live. Over the millennia the human constitution had changed. The human was now an irremediable carnivore. It is perhaps above all the human capacity to rationalize self-interest that lies at the root of omnivorousness.

Known as the "English Marcellus," the fine Cambridge classical scholar from Trinity, author of the brilliant *Prolusiones Juveniles* (1793), Northumbrian friend of William Wordsworth, and winner of four of the university's literary prizes, John Tweddell (1769-1799) was "persuaded we have no other right, than the right of the strongest, to sacrifice to our monstrous appetites the bodies of living things, of whose qualities and relations we are ignorant."[169] Engaged in archeological quests, he died suddenly in Greece of a mysterious fever at the tender age of thirty. If he had he lived, Tweddell would probably have been a valuable ornament in the vegetarian cause. As it is, his remark could stand as a monument to the reality of human greed fuelled everywhere by the Hobbesian lust for power. These words at the turn of the nineteenth century from this French Revolutionary sympathizer are representative of the change from the age of sentiment of the eighteenth century to its successor's age of implementation. Unfortunately, in general, the recognition of the moral case for vegetarianism seems to have preceded the perceived need to practise it.

It is certainly worthy of consideration how fortunate are contemporary vegetarians who can usually find something reasonably appealing in a regular grocery store and, naturally, in a vegetarian or organic-food specialty store – and vegetarian food that will not damage, but will enhance, good health. Moreover, most restaurants offer vegetarian, and a few offer vegan, alternatives – and, of course, there are numerous specialty vegetarian or vegan restaurants in the larger cities, at least in some countries. Vegetarians of prior centuries enjoyed none of that. Nor did those who affected to be vegetarian.

# 10

# Militant Advocates: From Oswald and Ritson to Shelley, Phillips, and Gompertz

If there were several who were eloquent in their proselytization but way-ward in putting the doctrine to the test, beginning in the 1790s, there began a movement, extremely articulate if very loose in organization – other than perhaps a small French-British coterie of John Oswald and his associates – that took its ethical dietary principles very seriously. It was they who made vegetarianism a viable moral cause and helped to create the public consciousness that resulted in the formation of the Vege-tarian Society a half-century later, although the vegetarian influences of Rousseau and Bernardin de Saint-Pierre in mainland Europe in particular should not be neglected. In fact, the jump from the eighteenth to the nine-teenth century was dramatic. It was not that ethical vegetarianism was declared much more frequently in the last decade of the eighteenth and early years of the nineteenth century than before but that many of those who professed the principle believed it applied to themselves directly in the here and now. Increasingly, those who were convinced of the appropriate-ness of the vegetarian diet were persuaded that vegetarianism was the path to uncircumscribed justice. The eighteenth-century advocates were "Men of Feeling" – a standard term of the century – whereas their successors were men (and women) of action. Of course, there are no convenient well-marked dividing lines in history. Not all eighteenth-century advocates failed to practise. Nor did all nineteenth-century advocates remain consis-tent in word and deed. But connected with 1789 is the decisive moment in which the balance tilts from thought to action.

The general questioning of authority unleashed by the revolutionary forces in France was sometimes extended to issues beyond the immediate. As Percy Bysshe Shelley rightly declared, the Revolution was "the master theme of the epoch in which we live."[1] It was the inauguration of democratic modernity. The apocalyptic expectation could be heard in Wordsworth's "Bliss was it in that dawn to be alive, / But to be young was very Heaven! ... When Reason seemed the most to assert her rights."[2] Or more prosaically, in William Cowper's lines about the Bastille: "There's not an Englishman's heart that would not leap / To hear that ye were fall'n at last."[3] It was a time of which the eccentric yet tender Charles Lamb could write that it was "our occupation ... to write treason."[4] If the histrionic Edmund Burke could say, as he did, that England was "not tainted with the French malady," he did not know the changing culture of his own country.[5] Wordsworth understood the times better when he recognized "shocks repeated day by day / And felt through every nook of town and field."[6] Later, even Burke acknowledged what he called "the Frenchified faction" among his compatriots. If the Revolution was French, it was not without numerous avid supporters across the channel, at least in its early stages. And for some, the object was to relieve animals as well as humans from tyranny.

From subject to citizen was a momentous leap; being a citizen meant that one could do and not merely be done to. The air was pregnant with promise. A new, just, and vibrant order was thought to be in the making. It was not merely a radical political innovation but also a jarring of the mind, now full of the most earnest imaginings. It was the practical fruition of Enlightenment Sensibility. As happened again in the late 1960s, the questioning of traditional authority promoted the vegetarian bloodless agenda. Indeed, it was no coincidence that principled, *practised* vegetarianism arose at the very instance of the French conflagration. Nor is it without significant relevance that, despite the Enlightenment Sensibility of the eighteenth century, the first wide-ranging attempts to legislate against animal cruelty arose at the turn of the nineteenth. Ideas of law as an instrument of social policy were as yet scarcely known, and relevant laws were very infrequently promulgated. Concomitantly, until now, there was no general recognition that the ways of the world were subject to change. Until now, the way things were socially was thought somehow irrevocably ordained. The poor, it had commonly been said, will always be with us. The same was true of oppressed animals.

If there was a continuity in British vegetarianism from the mid-seventeenth century, it had now reached its ethical and practical climax. Finally, fundamental change was no longer a utopian dream but an achievable goal. The culture of deference met the renunciation of privilege. The Revolution, if itself a failure, having been corrupted after the purge of the Girondins by the gross excesses of Robespierre and the Montagnards, managed nonetheless to change the public conception of unalterable providence into realizable potential.[7] The revolutionary conflict was rapidly becoming a contest between equally invidious alternatives, but the doctrines that the republicans espoused had a broader appeal. Vegetarianism, which in the hands of the revolutionaries was not merely a moral creed but also a resolute *non serviam,* could now be argued on its own grounds. The so-called Gagging Acts of 1795 (the Treasonable Practices Bill and the Seditious Meetings Bill) tempered the clamour for radical reform in England. But if the ardour was dampened, it was certainly not extinguished. The principal literary contributors to this culmination in British vegetarianism were John Oswald, George Nicholson, Joseph Ritson, William Lambe, John Frank Newton, Percy Bysshe Shelley, Sir Richard Phillips, Lewis Gompertz, and Thomas Forster. They are entitled to a place of honour in the annals of vegetarian history.

The eighteenth-century Enlightenment was the age of exorbitant optimism for the future and of skepticism of traditional religious and secular authority. Secular intellectuals imagined not only that rational men could solve all the puzzles of the universe – as, indeed, most thought the new breed of scientists was already doing – but also that the application of rational principles would solve all social, political, and ethical problems. There was, they thought, now nothing beyond human comprehension and, accordingly, nothing to hinder the human capacity to solve all the world's previous and present ills.

James Gillray's famous government-sponsored cartoon of 1798 for George Canning's *Anti-Jacobin* journal, lampooning the new intellectual class (including Samuel Taylor Coleridge, Robert Southey, Charles Lamb, William Wordsworth, Erasmus Darwin, Joseph Priestley, and John Thelwall – the last being the administration's principal target for his atheist radical republicanism), was entitled derisively the "New Morality." And it *was* new, and exciting, and, above all, benevolent. It heralded a new, if implausible, kind of wholly altruistic being. "The Jacobin school of poetry" was how the *Anti-Jacobin* termed the new Romantics. A few, including Rousseau, Edmund Burke, and several Dissenters, demurred, although from widely differing perspectives, but the prevalent view of the learned embraced the idea that this was the age of "perfectibility" – Coleridge, for example, referring to his dream of "trying the experiment of human Perfectibility on the banks of the Susquehanna."[8] However, as the Reign of Terror increasingly dimmed the expectations of a benevolent world-changing outcome of the Revolution, vegetarianism became less an integral part of a thoroughly radical worldview. Nonetheless, it continued to appeal most readily to those who were sympathetic to the republican and democratic culture first presaged by the Revolution but who were no longer confident of its imminent victory. Even the adamant supporters of the "New Morality," especially Coleridge, Southey, and Wordsworth, became far less sanguine about its promises, and many later abandoned their early radicalism. The most radical in each direction was Southey, who was already known while an undergraduate at Balliol College, Oxford, for his extreme republican views with strong French Jacobin sympathies and for prophesying violent revolution in England and who was later regarded as an archreactionary by Shelley and the like-minded. The matter was little different in Germany, where Hegel, Klopstock, and Goethe were among those who renounced their early adherence to the revolutionary cause. It is an unfortunate fact that no more than a few who espoused the "New Morality" became vegetarians but a notable fact that those who were persuaded intellectually were often also practitioners.

By the closing decades of the eighteenth century there was an overwhelming increase in the interest in Nature, although most naturalists, amateur and professional, still failed to recognize the reality of such events as bird migration and although mermaids were often claimed to be sighted. Still, the idea of the unity of life, as demonstrated by Giovanni Borelli in *De moto animalium* (On the Movement of Animals, 1680), namely that the same laws governed the wings of birds, the fins of fishes, and the legs of insects, began to percolate. The notion that there was one template for all of animated nature was an increasingly common recognition. Of course, a few continued to think that animals were intended for human use, but more of the educated now concurred with Henry More and John Ray that this belief was no more than a remnant of a bygone age – in Ray's words, "wise men nowadays think otherwise."[9] But if most of the well-educated no longer imagined animals were for human use, they continued to use them – and eat them – anyway.

If the naturalists were interested more in understanding and collecting than in appreciating, the stage was set nonetheless for a vibrant movement to declare that the eating of animals was an infringement on the rights of animals and was an activity incompatible with the nature of the properly conceived human constitution, as it was in the present, not merely in some idyllic past or some phantom future. Moreover, such recognition implied a *practical* refusal to eat the animals. Nor was the advocacy of the abandonment of flesh eating restricted to a few physician dietary reformers and the occasional animal advocate, for it reached out to some such as Robert

Owen (1771-1858) – described as a "utopian socialist" by Friedrich Engels –
who was the philanthropic industrial reformer of the spinning mills of
New Lanark in Scotland and, later, initiator of the utopian experiment of
New Harmony in Indiana. He advocated the adoption of vegetarianism by
the employees of his new visionary co-operative industrial system. It was
said that his workers treated Shelley's *Queen Mab* as their Bible, although,
presumably, more for its protosocialism than for the promoted vegetable
diet alone. Owen found industry reformist sympathizers in the vegetarian
Lewis Gompertz, secretary of the Society for the Prevention of Cruelty to
Animals (SPCA), and in William Thompson, the pioneering advocate of
co-operative socialism. In fact, many vegetarian advocates at this time saw
vegetarianism and socialism as inextricably linked ideologically. Yet the
spirit of reform was in the air generally. Even the Anglican priest William
Paley, whom we met earlier, was almost convinced of the case for vegetarianism.[10] He stated initially that we have a "right to the fruits or vegetable
produce of the earth" – for the "insensible parts of the creation are incapable of injury." He then gave the next section of his *Principles of Moral and
Political Philosophy* the title "A right to the flesh of animals" and continued:
"This is a very different right from the former. Some excuse seems necessary for the pain and loss which we occasion to brutes by constraining them
of their liberty, mutilating their bodies, and at last putting an end to their
lives, which we suppose to be their all, for our pleasure or conveniency."[11]
God's dispensation was enough for Paley to ignore the logical conclusions
of his analysis. He was adamant that "Wanton, and, what is worse, studied
cruelty to brutes, is certainly wrong." Only his God could convince him that
the slaughtering of animals for food was not wanton and studied cruelty.


## John Oswald

The first to enter the messianic fray on behalf of the animals was an Edinburgh Scot, one-time Grub Street journalist John Oswald (1760-1793),
later an army officer who was sent to India, learned its culture and its
mores, returned to England, visited France, and died a colonel in the French
volunteer army fighting the revolutionary cause on the killing grounds of
the Vendée campaign against the royalist sympathizers – although his rank
is disputed, the colonelcy being claimed by some, quite implausibly, to
belong to an American of the same surname.[12] To be precise, he fell at
Thouars in Poitou while leading his men in the bloody battle for the strate-
gically important Ponts-de-Cé. His two sons died in battle later in the

revolutionary wars. He was an habitué of the Hôtel d'Angleterre in Paris, along with other *engagé* compatriots, and was represented in Wordsworth's dramatic tragedy *The Borderers* as "the finest young man in the vale."[13] Before leaving the second time for France, Oswald wrote a short book, almost as much notes as text, titled *The Cry of Nature, or An Appeal to Mercy and to Justice on Behalf of the Persecuted Animals.* It was published in 1791 in London by J. Johnson of St. Paul's Churchyard, the most distinguished liberal publisher of the time. To be published by Johnson was a validation of Oswald's radical credentials, earned in Parisian political intrigue. The title page bore with obvious authorial pride the information that the writer was a member of the Jacobin Club. This membership reflected the author's fundamental discontent with the unreformed world – it was rumoured he was involved in a plot to assassinate George III – its politics, its societal codes, and its ethics. He was in earnest expectation of an early revolutionary revision of the reigning order. Indeed, Oswald was an enthusiastic volunteer in both the French and the Rousseauian Revolutions. And he lived in France at a time when rejection of flesh was recognized as a status symbol among some of the most ardent of the revolutionaries. Vegetarianism was also popular in England – perhaps, as before, more in advocacy than steady practice – during the years of the war with France but mainly on the grounds of health and economy rather than of humanitarianism. Oswald's practical experience, rather than mere book learning, of vegetarian India is evident throughout the book, although it is an idealization of Indian vegetarian lore he presents. Nonetheless, what the lessons of India taught many, of whom Oswald was a prime exemplar, is that it was quite possible to renounce flesh and live a life that was both healthy and innocent. Whereas many previous advocates thought of vegetarianism as the noble ideal, they also managed to persuade themselves that it was a diet unacceptable to the human constitution as it had developed over the millennia. Now the vegetarian ethic could be adapted to lessons from cultural experiences within India, although many still seemed to think the diet acceptable in the warm Orient but alien – indeed, dangerous – in the Occidental clime.

The temper of Oswald's book is summarized in the concluding paragraph:

May the benevolent system spread to every corner of the globe; may we learn to recognize and to respect in other animals the feelings which vibrate in ourselves; may we be led to perceive that those cruel repasts are not more injurious to the creatures whom we devour than they are hostile to our health, which delights in innocent simplicity, and destructive of our happiness, which is wounded by every act of violence, while it feeds as it were on the prospect of well being, and is raised to the highest summit of enjoyment by the sympathetic touch of social satisfaction.[14]

Perhaps there is no other paragraph that stands better as a symbol for the incipient movement than the following passage from Oswald, although the book as a whole is a call to engagement. He tells us that:

> From the practice of slaughtering an innocent animal to the murder of man himself the steps are not very remote ... from the texture of the very human heart arises the strongest argument in behalf of the persecuted creatures. Within us there exists a rooted repugnance to the shedding of blood, a repugnance which yields only to custom, and which even the most inveterate custom can seldom entirely overcome. Hence the ungracious task of shedding the tide of life, for the gluttony of our table, has, in every country, been committed to the lowest class of men, and their profession is, in every country, an object of abhorrence.

Yet, paradoxically, he was an emphatic supporter of the armed introduction of the French Revolution to British soil. Bloodshed against fellow humans in the honourable cause was justifiable, it would appear. Oswald would probably have faced difficulties with the British authorities once France and Britain were at war if he had survived. In fact, it was not always safe to be a vegetarian in those dark days. Publishers of vegetarian texts and vegetarian advocates often found themselves in prison – Johnson was sentenced to six months in 1798 – although far more for the radical republican views often associated with vegetarianism than for their espousal of ethical vegetarianism itself.

It is not only for the abstention from flesh that Oswald pleads but also for the abstention from vivisection, an issue he considers very close to that of vegetarianism:

> Vainly planted in our breast, is this abhorrence of cruelty, this sympathetic affection for every animal? Or, to the purpose of nature, do the feelings of the heart point more unerringly than all the elaborate subtlety of a set of men, who, at the shrine of science, have sacrificed the dearest sentiments of humanity?[15]

For most ethical vegetarians, the two matters are intertwined: respect for animals requires both a refusal to eat them and a refusal to treat them as appropriate beings for invasive animal experimentation. Interestingly, the nineteenth century spawned the first ever vegetarian society and a large number of opponents, almost successful opponents, one might add, of vivisection. The latter group consisted first and foremost of dissenting Christians, above all Methodists. Very few of those who opposed vivisection with such fervour, as we saw with the Anglican Samuel Johnson, were also vegetarians, even though the founder of the Methodist movement, John Wesley (1703-1791), was himself a vegetarian. "Thanks be to God," he wrote to the Bishop of London in 1747, "since the time I gave up flesh meals and wine I have been delivered from all physical ills." It is reflective of much in Western culture that abstention from wine became an intrinsic part of the Methodist nostrums, but nowhere has abstention from flesh played a Methodist role. And although the abstention from flesh was on medical advice from Dr. George Cheyne, we should not imagine it entirely health- or asceticism-related. Wesley claimed that animals had immortal souls and that there were considerable similarities between human and non-human animals. He was concerned to alleviate their ills – "how severely do they suffer," he remarked – and ultimately to allow them retribution for the evils bestowed upon them by replicating the Peaceable Kingdom of Isaiah 11:6-9.[16] It is logically strange that most of those who were appalled at the disgusting cruelty of vivisection did not find the slaughter of food animals equally repulsive. Even the redoubtable leader of the anti-vivisectionists, the Unitarian Frances Power Cobbe, was a confirmed flesh eater.

That the practise of vegetarianism was no longer as rare as before does not, of course, at all imply that a majority of animal advocates now refused to consume animal flesh. In fact, many striking apparent inconsistencies continued as before. For example, the renowned animal advocate and Oxford classicist Thomas Taylor (1758-1835) – but not an academic on account of his rejection of Christianity – was not a practising vegetarian. He was the translator of Porphyry's essay on the eating of flesh and of much other Greek into English as well as the author of a witty, if unsuccessful, refutation of his former tenant Mary Wollstonecraft's *The Rights of Woman,* entitled *A Vindication of the Rights of Brutes.* He has been claimed for Pythagoreanism by Joscelyn Godwin in the foreword to *The Pythagorean Sourcebook and Library.*[17] Perhaps more appropriate would be to describe Taylor as a neo-Platonist with a profound empathy for, and understanding of, the pagan idealist tradition, including respect for animals – a tradition that would include Pythagoras as commonly conceived. Coleridge referred to "Taylor, the English pagan," as though this were a fact commonly understood.[18] Yet on reading the piety expressed in his *The Life of William Cowper,* written just two years before his death, one would be inclined to deem the paganism in rapid retreat.

Are we to understand by Godwin's claim that Taylor was a vegetarian? Taylor had a significant influence on Blake, Shelley, Byron, Wordsworth, and Ralph Waldo Emerson, but none of them claimed Taylor to eschew flesh. To be sure, the translator of Porphyry and Iamblichus and commentator on Greek neo-Platonist vegetarians was often thought by his contemporaries to be a vegetarian and was of enduring importance to the vegetarian cause through his translations. But Taylor declared himself too active to lead a vegetarian life. Such a life was the ideal, he asserted, but was suitable only for the sedentary. Fortunately, there were now many no less active than Taylor – Oswald, for example – who decided that their actions must conform to their principles.

To understand the often incongruous relationship of the expression of deeply felt sensibility to animals and the continuance of eating their flesh, it is important to investigate where the linguistic expression seems to imply vegetarianism when, in fact, it is not at all practised. This is especially relevant in understanding Romanticism, in which the expressions are of the greatest sensibility. But whereas some were enticed by vegetarianism, most representatives of the "New Morality" continued as before.

Like Taylor, William Blake (1757-1827) was one who sounded as though he were a vegetarian. His poetry is full of wondrous phrases that we imagine only a vegetarian could have written. Like Oswald, he was sympathetic to the aims of the Revolution. And he believed, like Pythagoras apparently, in metempsychosis. He had, he said, once been Socrates and on another occasion mentioned "the books and pictures of old, which I wrote and painted in ages of Eternity before my mortal life."[19] Blake did not, however, mention any transmigrations into animals. He was a Swedenborgian in religion, and Swedenborg advocated vegetarianism, but Blake was not a vegetarian. For Blake, Swedenborgianism was, as Peter Ackroyd indicates, "a synthesis of occult and alchemical doctrine placed in the Christian context of redemption." It is doubtful Blake was truly interested in understanding Swedenborg doctrine. Rather, his concern was "to press Swedenborg's beliefs into the framework of his own concerns."[20]

Equally strange is the case of Arthur Schopenhauer (1788-1860), who had, in word at least, the greatest fellow-feeling with other species: "Boundless compassion for all living beings is the finest and surest guarantee of pure moral conduct."[21] And he was recognized as the "chief interpreter of Buddhist ideas in Europe."[22] Yet he continued to consume animal flesh. "Boundless compassion," indeed! Of no one could it be said more appropriately, with perhaps the exception of Oliver Goldsmith himself, in the words of Goldsmith: "They pity, and they eat the objects of their compassion." Still, it might be said that there was some kind of general movement in the air against flesh in the early nineteenth century. For example, in Chapter 3 of Elizabeth Gaskell's *Life of Charlotte Brontë* (1857), we are told that, earlier in the century, the father, Patrick Brontë, raised his children on a fleshless diet, serving them only potatoes for dinner. The intent, according to Gaskell, was to raise them to simplicity and hardiness. The passage from Gaskell has persuaded many vegetarians that Charlotte Brontë was one of their number. In fact, even as children, the Brontë siblings ate flesh, both according to the father and to their friends. Moreover, the diaries of the Brontë children refer to their meals and their menus, all of which contain a flesh component. But now the tables were turned. Now those who sounded as though they were vegetarian usually were vegetarian, despite the notable exceptions, in contrast with much of the eighteenth century, when those who praised the vegetarian ethic were most often not vegetarians themselves.

Nonetheless, there were many who were vegetarian, or almost vegetarian, by default, at least temporarily, and not just among the exceedingly poor. Thus Dorothy Wordsworth in 1794, writing to her Crackanthorpe kin, stated: "My supper and breakfast are of bread and milk, and my dinner chiefly of potatoes from choice."[23] Again, at a coaching inn in Brunswick in 1798, she was delighted to be served potatoes for her meal. But she did not decline flesh when it was readily available. Nor did her brother William. The "plain living and high thinking" that Wordsworth idealized did not include the rejection of flesh on moral principle. Still, when living at Racedown, Dorset, in the winter of 1797, they survived, William said, on "the essence of carrots, cabbage, turnips and other esculent vegetables not excluding parsley, the produce of my garden," adding "and in to cabbages we shall be transformed."[24] By contrast, Coleridge complained of the lack of vegetables served at his Christ's Hospital school – but then there was no flesh either![25] The West Country poor all around them when they were at Racedown were even less well off. Certainly, they were customarily vegetarian but not from any desire. The rural indigent population could not course the hares and eat the prey as did Dorothy and William on occasion at Racedown as guests of the Pinney brothers, their landlords. When Coleridge walked the hills and dales of Scotland, he survived on tea, porridge, ale, and oatcakes, but his everyday meals were otherwise. He enjoyed "beef and pudding" as the common fare of the Coleridge home at Ottery St. Mary and "meat and potato pie" at Nether Stowey. On the Harz Brocken in Germany it was bacon with schnapps in milk. The first meal Coleridge shared with the Napoleon-worshipping republican journalist William Hazlitt was "Welsh Mutton and turnips."[26] He treated leather with a compound of

"Mutton suet, Hog's Lard and Venetian Turpentine."[27] The Scotland tramp-
ing regimen was an exception. To be sure, the Wordsworth household was
more often without flesh, but as among the impoverished masses, it was
not a matter of choice. As Samuel Rogers observed, they were compelled
"to deny themselves animal food several times a week," being "in such dire
straitened circumstances."[28] Many revolutionary sympathizers – as were
the young Lake Poets – expressed the greatest compassion for the downtrodden animals without giving an apparent moment's thought to the need
to cease to eat them or kill them for their hides. Even in the projected
utopia, Southey refers without any apparent qualm to the pleasure of
"hunting a buffalo," presumably for the larder.[29] In formulating his ideals,
Coleridge wrote of "the Fraternity of universal Nature."[30] This fraternal
union he regarded as "One Life." Yet he continued to eat his brothers.
"Methinks it should have been impossible / Not to love all things," he
wrote in "The Eolian Harp," clarifying elsewhere that he means "a Thing
[that] has a Life of its own."[31] However impossible, the love included the
eating of the objects of adoration. "Arcadia" was a term the Romantics
often used to refer to their utopia. It was certainly not a bloodless Eden.
But not all revolutionary sympathizers were so careless of the rights of
animals. Given their language, one might have expected to encounter a
principled vegetarianism among the Lake Romantics. But one does not.
Fortunately, despite these Romantics' adherence to the practical norm,
there were others who followed in the steps of Oswald.

## GEORGE NICHOLSON

Six years after Oswald's volume, previously Bradford now Manchester
printer George Nicholson (1760-1825) – "among the least known [of vege-
tarians], but none the less among the most estimable," is Howard Williams's
sound opinion[32] – joined the Oswald cause in 1797 with a remarkable com-
pendium of prior vegetarian and animal-welfare thought and practice from
the earliest days of literature, entitled *On the Conduct of Man to Inferior
Animals*. This he expanded in 1801 into *On the Primeval Diet of Man; Arguments in Favour of Vegetable Foods; On Man's Conduct to Animals &c. &c.*
Nicholson included commentary from Porphyry, Plutarch, and Montaigne, through Cowper, Thomson, Lawrence, Young, Locke, Goldsmith,
Erasmus Darwin, and John Arbuthnot, to William Buchan, George
Cheyne, and John Elliott, among numerous others, adding a few snippets
of his own along the way. A supplement, *On Food*, was appended to the

1803 edition, offering numerous vegetarian recipes and enumerating "one hundred perfectly palatable substances, which may easily be procured at an expense much below the prices of the limbs of our fellow animals."[33] Because he often did not acknowledge his sources, it is sometimes difficult, where the pieces quoted are not well known, to determine precisely what comes from Nicholson himself and what he has borrowed from elsewhere. A substantial part, however, was a verbatim repetition of Oswald. And certainly, many of those he quoted, as he surely knew, were not vegetarians but wrote in opposition to cruelty both in the operating theatres and the abattoirs. In fact, Nicholson's interests were restricted not to vegetarianism alone but to all aspects of animal welfare, popular education, women's rights, abolition of slavery, and democratic government. Again, he was one of those for whom justice was indivisible.

Nicholson's argument in *On the Primeval Diet of Man* has five major components. Initially, he argues that the earliest human habits are the primary indicator of our natural diet, that if we are to live well we should live as nature intended – that is, he claimed, as our remote ancestors did. Second, he contends that if we live a vegetarian life, we will live a far healthier and longer life. Third, he claims that if we recognize how essentially similar in all relevant respects other species are to ourselves, we will treat them with a great deal more respect. Fourth, human conduct toward other species is frequently both unjust and inappropriate. Finally, he argues the pressing need for legislative protection of, and education concerning, the interests of other species.

One of those to whom Nicholson gave prominence was John "Walking" Stewart (1749-1822), so known because he had travelled through Europe, Canada, and North Africa mostly on foot. As an employee of the East India Company stationed abroad and from his sojourning in India afterward, the abrasive Stewart had learned to appreciate the benefits of vegetarianism, although in the first instance from a health perspective: "I am disposed to believe the aliment of flesh and fermented liquors to be heterogeneous to the nature of man in every climate. I have observed among nations, whose aliment is vegetable and water, that disease and medicine are equally unknown, while those whose aliment is flesh and fermented liquor, are constantly afflicted with disease, and medicine more dangerous than disease itself; and not only those guilty of excess, but others who lead lives of temperance."[34]

Stewart's exaggerated view of the simple path to ideal health *merely* by abstention from flesh and liquor reflects the customary contemporary distortion of reality produced by one's predilections. What is both illuminating and disturbing about Stewart's account is that he had ample opportunity to witness the reality of health outside his native Britain, and it was certainly no better than in the homeland. Such is the apparent force of rationalization. In India, early death from malaria, for example, was common, and deformity from leprosy had been a prevalent problem for two thousand years. A vegetable diet did not save the Hindus from these ills.

Despite his commonly noted abrasiveness, the pantheist Stewart became both an intimate of the industrialist vegetarian advocate Robert Owen and a friend of the essayist and fellow opium addict Thomas de Quincey, who greatly admired the vegetarian principles of Stewart without joining him in living them. De Quincey also thought him strictly honest in his accounts of his adventures, which suggests his interpretation of the health of the inhabitants' of vegetarian lands was no simple attempt to mislead. As E.M. Forster's *A Passage to India* indicates, British administrators met largely with one class of Indians and had a distorted view of the reality of the nation they governed. Although not as radical or as entirely *engagé* as Oswald, who could be numbered among the infamous *enragés,* Stewart was one of "the Frenchified faction" and was in Paris during the early years of the Revolution, where, according to de Quincey, he impressed the young Wordsworth (also in Paris) with his views on living in accord with nature.[35] For Stewart, the innocent diet was an integral aspect of the new world in the making.

In line with the age, Nicholson is convinced, perhaps a little too readily, that the "Primeval Diet of Man" – and, indeed, that of a later age – was wholly without sin. He cites Porphyry to tell us that the "ancient Greeks lived entirely on the fruits of the earth," as did "the ancient Syrians," and that "by the laws of Triptolemus, the Athenians were strictly commanded to abstain from all living creatures."[36] From Aelian, he derives the information that "the ancient Arcadians lived on acorns, the Argives on pears, the Athenians on figs."[37] Via the writings of Diodorus Siculus, we are informed how the fleshless diet of Pythagoras's followers made them "very strong and valorous."[38] From Gellius and Macrobius, we learn that the "Romans were fully persuaded of the superior effects of a vegetable diet, that besides the private examples of many of their great men, they publicly countenanced this mode of diet in their laws concerning food."[39] Like Montaigne, he pictured the Golden Age at around the time of the classical Greeks rather than prior to civilization. Such was the state of the vegetarian interpretation of the Golden Age as historical reality at the turn of the nineteenth century!

There are two sentences on which Nicholson lays particular stress, capitalizing them in the original. The first, "whatever we do by another we do ourselves," conveys his insistence that if we eat flesh, it as though we have done ourselves what the slaughterhouse butcher has done.[40] It is a doctrine reminiscent of the *Mahabharata,* although not informed by it.[41] The second adds his version of the Golden Rule: "Treat the animal which is in your power, in such a manner, as you would willingly be treated were you such an animal," in fact a paraphrase of the statement to similar effect by Humphry Primatt writing in 1776.[42] Nicholson explains the inconsistencies of flesh eaters and refutes most ably the customary defences of flesh eating, adding that "to take away the life of any happy being: to commit acts of outrage and depredation, and to abandon every refined feeling of sensibility, is to degrade the human kind beneath its professed dignity of character but to devour and eat any animal, is an additional violation of those principles, because 'tis the extreme of brutal ferocity."[43] He accounts for this immoral continuance of the shedding of blood by telling us that "education, habit, prejudice, fashion, and interest have blinded the eyes of men, and have seared their hearts."[44] Given the importance of Nicholson's book in the history of vegetarianism, it is unfortunate, even though it was reprinted more than once, that it appears to have been largely ignored, at least by vegetarians. The public was rather more impressed. On Nicholson's death, his obituary in the bourgeois *Gentleman's Magazine* amply recognized his merits, counting him "a man whose worth and talents entitle him to notice" and observing that his writings, which were numerous and varied, "already obtained the meed of praise from contemporary critics." Moreover, "in a Treatise 'on the Conduct of Man to inferior Animals' (which has already gone through four editions) we have evidence of his humanity of disposition; and numerous Tracts calculated to improve the morals, and add to the comforts of the poorer classes, are proofs of the same desire of doing good. In short, he possessed, in an eminent degree, strength of intellect, with universal benevolence and undeviating uprightness of conduct."[45] *Gentleman's Magazine* failed, however, to acknowledge Nicholson's vegetarianism.

## JOSEPH RITSON

Within a few months of the publication of Nicholson's revised tome, there appeared a volume from the cantankerous and caustic revolutionary sympathizer Joseph Ritson (1752-1803), an antiquarian of repute but one with numerous enemies and a smaller number of staunch and stalwart friends. The book was *An Essay on Abstinence from Animal Food as a Moral Duty.* After his death, Ritson's "incipient insanity" in advanced age was noted by the compilers of *The Dictionary of National Biography* – needless to say, the compilers were not among the firm friends! And the comment was unjust. But the source of the injustice was perhaps a friendly one. The obituary in the *Monthly Mirror* by his frequent companion, the philosopher William Godwin – dubbed "the Professor" by Charles Lamb for his verbosity – referred to Ritson being subject to fits, to his having lost his prodigious memory, and to rapidly advancing senility.[46] In addition, the judgment in *The Dictionary of National Biography* was probably based primarily on his declared atheism – according to Shelley, in the culture of the time atheism implied "immorality, social inferiority and unpatriotic behaviour" – on his animosity to others, and on his support for the French revolutionary cause. He liked to be called "citizen Ritson," and his home was decorated with pictures of Rousseau, Voltaire, and Paine. And he displayed a bellicose spirit in his revival of the legend of Robin Hood as an anti-establishment hero. He termed his fellow antiquarians "fool" and "liar." He attacked Thomas Warton's scholarship in his *Observations on Warton's History* (1782), a mordant critique of the Oxford professor of poetry's *History of English Poetry* (1774-1781). He disputed the originality of Bishop Percy's *Reliques* and was less than impressed by Dr. Samuel Johnson's edition of Shakespeare. The reception of the millenarian republican Ritson, if not of his work, has to be understood in the light of his perceived demeanour, a reflection in some part of the fact that in the early years of the conflict with France he feared for his life at the hands of English government agents. There was a conviction he would be arrested as a traitor. As to his work, Joseph Haslewood wrote a tribute in *Some Account of the Life and Publications of the Late Joseph Ritson,* and his publisher, Sir Richard Phillips, as well as Percy Bysshe Shelley, William Godwin, John Frank Newton, and Sir Walter Scott admired him greatly. Ritson even appears in favourable guise in some of Scott's Waverley novels. He claimed to derive his radical vegetarianism from Mandeville's *Fable of the Bees* and from the age of nineteen rejected all flesh, noting apologetically as an exception an occasion in Scotland when he ate a few potatoes "dress'd under the roast."[47] And he occasionally ate eggs, about which he also appeared a trifle guilty. Nonetheless, despite the occasional support, he was ridiculed in the socially conservative *Edinburgh Review* by an anonymous critic, probably Henry Brougham, Whig politician and co-founder of the *Review,* who was full of "disgust, pity, contempt, laughter, detestation" and who was distraught that beef and mutton eaters should be thought the equivalent of cannibals.[48]

In the opening chapter of *Abstinence from Animal Food,* concerning a defence of the state of nature as man's ideal, Ritson tells us: "Of all rapacious animals, man is the most universal destroyer. The destruction of

carnivorous quadrupeds, birds, and insects, is, in general, limited to particular kinds: but the rapacious capacity of man has hardly any limitation.
His empire over the other animals which inhabit this globe is almost universal."[49] Ritson's vilification of the human species – which is not to say
unjustifiable vilification – which he exemplifies at some length, sets the
tone for the remainder of the work, although he acknowledges, too, that
other species are equally rapacious: "there is neither benevolence nor intention in nature."[50] This tone continues to the final chapter, where he dis-
misses some of the customary justifications of flesh eating:

> "If god made *man*, or there be any *intention* in *nature*, the life of the *louse*,
> which is as natural to him as his frame of body, is equally sacred and invio-
> lable with his own ... there is neither evidence nor probability, that any one
> animal is "intended" for the sustenance of another, more especially by the
> privation of its life. The lamb is no more "intended" to be devour'd by the
> wolf, than the man by the tyger or other beast of prey, which experiences
> equally "the agreeable flavour of his flesh," and "the wholesome nutriment it
> administers to their stomachs"; nor are many millions of animals ever tasteëd
> by man; such reasoning is perfectly ridiculous! ... Man, in a state of nature,
> would, at least, be as harmless as an ourang-outang.[51]

In the second chapter, Ritson purports to show that neither human teeth,
nor intestines, nor other human body parts are appropriate for flesh consumption. He quotes the Scottish judge Lord Monboddo's view that "by
nature, and in his original state, [humankind] is a frugivorous animal, and
that he only becomes an animal of prey by acquir'd habit."[52] In the third
chapter Ritson aspires to demonstrate by numerous historical and geo-
graphical examples that a nonflesh diet is quite capable of providing the
strength and vigour necessary for hard labour, noting, for example, that the
"mineërs in Cornwall are remarkably strong, well made and laborious.
Their chief food is potatos."[53] This chapter is followed by one on animal
food being "the cause of cruelty and ferocity" in humans, which in turn is
succeeded by the claim that, historically, the eating of animal flesh led to
crimes against humans and ultimately to cannibalism.[54] In light of such
claims about cruelty and ferocity, one may not be surprised by the *Dictionary of National Biography*'s contention that Ritson was going mad, but then
it should equally be noted that the rather far-fetched claims of Ritson were
common currency among those who were advocates for the elimination of
flesh foods. Much of the remainder of the book is concerned to show that
animal food is pernicious and vegetable food healthy. Not only did flesh

eating lead to harm to the animals, but it also constrained people to engage in "barbarous and unfeeling sports" such as horseracing, shooting, bull- and bearbaiting, cockfighting, and boxing. Moreover, a plant-based diet was much less expensive than a flesh diet, and the labouring classes were turning toward a flesh-free regimen.

Despite the title of the book, only in the final chapter does Ritson turn his attention fully to the issue of justice toward the animal realm, although it is touched upon on occasion throughout the book. Postulating that each animal has a right to life in and of itself, Ritson offers an analysis that was able to elude the common critique of the vegetarian case that as long as ani- mals were killed instantly and without apprehension of their impending demise, no harm was done – no pain and suffering was inflicted. Of course, if life itself had a value, the force of this antivegetarian argument disap- peared. Implied in the argument is that it is remarkable how we treat human life as valuable, never venturing it acceptable to kill painlessly a human with a will to live but acceptable to kill a fellow animal provided it is a pain- less killing.

## WILLIAM LAMBE AND JOHN FRANK NEWTON

The eminent London physician of vegetarian conviction William Lambe (1765-1847) was fortunate enough to number among his eminent friends both Lord Erskine (1750-1823), brilliant defender of the accused radicals in the infamous treason trials of 1795 and author of *The Causes and Conse- quences of the Present War,* who led the parliamentary attempt in the early decades of the 1800s to provide England with animal-welfare legislation, and John Frank Newton (1770-1825), author of *Return to Nature,* who, hav- ing been converted to the innocent diet by Lambe, dedicated his important book on the vegetarian cause to him. Erskine also had a friendship with the vegetarian publisher Sir Richard Phillips. One is led to wonder whether Thomas Erskine was a silent adherent or a strong sympathizer of the vege- tarian cause. He made it clear in the Commons that he did not *champion* radical causes, but where his heart lay, and perhaps sometimes his knife and fork, we do not know. The lack of ribald derision for his diet by his parlia- mentary opponents may reflect his decision to have dined as they dined.

What we cannot be sure of about Erskine, we know with confidence about Lambe, who, after undergraduate studies at St. John's College, Cam- bridge, proceeded to become a physician of considerable merit and renown. Having been elected as Fellow to the College of Physicians, he was appointed to the Censorship and Croonian lectureship on several occasions and once to the office of Harleian orator. To be sure, he was considered an eccentric for his fleshless diet, but this apparent "eccentricity" in no wise hindered his career or reputation, the heights of his success coming well after he had changed to a fleshless diet. It was at the age of forty that he decided to confine himself totally to "vegetable food" – and a few years later he produced *Additional Reports on Regimen,* which argued the case for a fleshless diet almost entirely from the health perspective of a physician.[55] "The doctrine it seeks to establish," he announced retrospectively in 1838, "is in direct opposition to popular and deep-rooted prejudice. It is thought (most erroneously) to attack the best enjoyments and most solid comforts of life; and, moreover, it has excited the bitter hostility of a numerous and influential body in society – I mean that body of medical practitioners who exercise their profession for the sake of its profits mere, and who appear to think that disease was made for the profession and not the profession for the disease."[56] Although the benefits to the animal are scarcely ever raised in print by Lambe, we know from his association with Erskine, Phillips, and Shelley that they were there, even though he thought humans on a very different plane from other animals. Indeed, his position is almost identical to that of Aristotle: "In his nobler part, his rational soul, man is distinguished from the whole tribe of animals by a boundary, which cannot be passed. It is only when man divests himself of his reason, and debases himself by brutal habits, that he renounces his just rank among created beings, and sinks himself below the level of the beasts."[57]

If we are inclined to regard Lambe as, at best, a secondary figure in the history of ethical vegetarianism, he must nonetheless be acknowledged as a person of significance in playing a role in bringing about the first small, but not infrequent, semiformal gatherings of ethical vegetarians.

John Frank Newton was once a chronic invalid, who claimed the recovery and maintenance of his health were due entirely to William Lambe, who, Newton states in dedicating *Return to Nature* to him, was the author of "a medical discovery" – the value of distilled water, Lambe's primary nostrum, was almost certainly what was meant – "which, I am confident, will place your name at some future, and perhaps no distant period, at the head of your profession."[58] The return to nature that Newton advocated embraced vegetarianism, abstinence from alcohol, and possibly nudism (at least Shelley's friend Thomas Jefferson Hogg thought so, although others disagreed), the last of which was to become faddish in the early decades of the twentieth century among back-to-nature thinkers. He also entertained the strange notions that meat eating caused syphilis and that the signs of

the zodiac represented ancient symbols of vegetarianism.[59] Scarcely surprising is that vegetarians were often thought somewhat idiosyncratic! But
then this was the millenarian age.

It was at Newton's home that he, Lambe, Shelley, the protoanarchist and
revolutionary sympathizer William Godwin, probably Joseph Ritson (we
know he dined frequently with Godwin), and the "naturist" – or perhaps
merely libertine – Boinvilles (sister- and brother-in-law of Newton) met
for vegetarian dinners and like-minded radical conversation in the late
eighteenth century and early years of the nineteenth century – the Vegetarian Society in embryo![60] Perhaps included were Sir Richard Phillips and
a few others as yet unknown to us – and *maybe* even Mary Wollstonecraft,
at least as an occasional guest. Wolstonecraft left no evidence she was
attracted to the vegetarian diet. But we know she sometimes dined with her
husband-to-be William Godwin at the Newtons.[61] We know also that the
others were frequent dining companions of each other – although in
Phillips's case we know only of close associations rather than specifically of
dining together. But we do not know for certain that they dined together
as a group rather than in fours and sixes, although it is a distinct possibility.[62] Nor do we know whether William Godwin continued his fleshless
diet long after marriage to the second Mrs. Godwin. It is to be doubted
that he did so, at least consistently. And we know that Shelley and Newton
did not meet until the second decade of the nineteenth century. Mentioning only Lambe, Shelley, Newton and his family, and unknown others as
participants, Howard Williams refers to "these pioneers of the New Reformation [who] were accustomed to meet, and celebrate their charming
*réunions* with vegetarian feasts."[63] The festive group would surely also have
included the Boinvilles (mother and daughter), whose French officer hus-
band/father had died in the retreat from Moscow and with whom the Shelleys resided for a while in 1813, and other acknowledged vegetarians of the
Bracknell radical community. Shelley's companion from undergraduate
days Thomas Jefferson Hogg, who was also often around the Newton residence at Bracknell in Berkshire and probably for a very short time a practising vegetarian – when habituated to life as a lawyer, he evinced, in the
words of Mary Shelley, "an attachment to sporting" – called this throng,
memorably, "the vegetable church of Nature."[64]

"It is not man we have before us but the wreck of man," wrote Newton
in *Return to Nature* (1811).[65] The theme of the book is the rectification
through the medicine of William Lambe of the "wreck" of humankind's
fall from its natural state. Like Lambe, Newton devotes his attention and

efforts primarily to the health aspects of vegetarianism, although, as with Lambe, there are undeniable ethical undertones and the occasional explicit comment. His claim is that if human beings could be as healthy as the "wild animals, they would ... certainly exceed the age of one hundred and fifty years."[66] He understands the environmental benefit to the adoption of a fleshless diet, arguing against the necessity of the new and popular Malthusian pessimism that "no point can be demonstrated more clearly than that the earth might contain and support at least ten times the number of inhabitants that are now upon it."[67] More land devoted to agriculture and less to animal husbandry was becoming a favourite nostrum of the time, embraced, beyond Newton, by such diverse figures as Shelley, Godwin, William Paley, Adam Smith, and Erasmus Darwin. Shelley embellished Newton's view with his own conclusion that not only did animals suffer when land was devoted to animal husbandry but so did the human poor because the grain to feed the animals was at the expense of grain for the human needy. The customary Malthusian riposte to such animadversions was that the population would soon expand beyond the increased capacity of agricultural production to feed the increased number of people. But the moral value of decreasing animal suffering by turning away from animal husbandry was not dented by the Malthusian response.

Not until Newton is two-thirds through the book does he mention the ethical argument for eschewing flesh. He quotes John Ray, noting that "how much more innocent, sweet, and healthful, is a table covered with [vegetable foods] than with all the reeking flesh of butchered and slaughtered animals. Certainly, man by nature was never made to be a carnivorous animal, nor is he armed at all for prey and rapine, with jagged and pointed teeth, and crooked claws sharpened to rend and tear; but with gentle hands to gather fruit and vegetables, and with teeth to chew and eat them."[68] And he finally adds his own words: "So long as men are compassionate to such a degree that they cannot hear a fly struggling in a spider's web without emotion, it never can be maintained that it is their natural impulse to wound and kill the dumb animals [i.e., those who are without the capacity to speak], or to butcher one another in what is called the *field of honour*."[69] This sentence reveals the depth of Newton's concern for animals. We can presume with some confidence, if not with certainty, that animal interests were rarely mentioned by some of the vegetarian advocates, or rarely mentioned at length, not because they were thought irrelevant but because it was thought they would not resonate as effectively with the audience. Only an appeal to the maintenance of the reader's health could be fully persuasive.

## Percy Bysshe Shelley

Iconoclast Percy Bysshe Shelley (1792-1822) was not so pessimistic, or if he was, he appealed to the public conscience anyway. In fact, Shelley appeared the millenarian antithesis to pessimism in his writings. When William Godwin had written in the first edition of *An Enquiry Concerning Political Justice* (1793) that soon there would be "no war, no crime, no administration of justice as it is called, no government" – a prophecy he soon came to regret – the perfectibilist Shelley remained astounded throughout his short life that the prognosis had not proved immediately accurate.[70] He was the author *inter alia* of *Queen Mab* (1813), in which his radical philosophy is first expounded, and of *Prometheus Unbound* (1820), in which Prometheus was his symbol for the originator of the new Golden Age. If it was not truly a return to nature, it was what Wordsworth called "golden hours," "human nature being born again."[71]

Shelley was, by consensus, the "greatest rhetorician and most sublime lyricist of all the English Romantic poets."[72] A perusal of his verse might suggest an author with a greater love for love, beauty, politics, sex, and poetry itself than for animals, or perhaps even humans, although there are exceptions – for example, in *The Revolt of Islam* and when in *Queen Mab* he tells us: "no longer now / He slays the lamb that looks him in the face, / And horrible devours his mangled flesh." Still, his prose tells another story than much of the verse. Despite being expelled from University College, Oxford, for his declared religious disbelief – he composed a scabrous pamphlet, *The Necessity of Atheism* – it would appear that he learned enough there to spice his writings with evident erudition, even though Shelley himself deemed the college a fortress of mediocrity. He was equally disparaging of his previous education at Eton. In part, the extraordinary scholarship of the notes to *Queen Mab* undoubtedly came from private reading. The notes are almost as long as the nine-canto poem and contain lengthy quotations from Pliny, Lucretius, Holbach, Spinoza, Bacon, and Plutarch. And it is in these notes we encounter Shelley's first defence of the vegetable regimen. Shelley had a decided aversion to didactic poetry but none at all to didactic prose to elucidate the poetry.

Converted to vegetarianism by Newton, with whom he had a regular acquaintance (and secondarily by Lambe and Ritson), and to millenarianism by Rousseau and William Godwin, his mentor and later father-in-law (creeds that seemed to replace the discarded religion), he penned two pamphlets against the eating of flesh, the first being a part of the notes to *Queen Mab* and the second being lost until the twentieth century. In these pamphlets, he argued that vegetarianism was natural to humans, that it promoted health and longevity, and – with even greater emphasis – both that it permitted food animals to escape the consequences of their harmful domestication and that wild animals should be spared the cruelties inflicted upon them by human predators. By general repute, Shelley's exposition is the finest argument for ethical vegetarianism since Porphyry in the third century, so much so that George Bernard Shaw wanted to rename vegetarianism "Shelleyism." As a youth, Shaw was already a committed Shelleyian: "I read him, prose and verse, from beginning to end."[73] Shaw also related the story he heard from an old Chartist that "Queen Mab was known as the Chartists' Bible."[74] In short, it was a poem that announced the young Shelley's controversial and decidedly radical political agenda. In including the flesh diet as one aspect of the oppression and injustice he was determined to overcome, he shows himself, like Thomas Tryon, as one of those moralists for whom justice is indivisible. Injustice to the animals is as much an aspect of injustice as injustice to the human poor. Indeed, Shelley thought the intent of a writer must be to serve "the interests of liberty," and in his political writings in the year following the infamy of the Peterloo Massacre (1819), he sounds in his political analyses, especially in *A Philosophical View of Reform*, like a prescient Friedrich Engels. "Boldly but temperately written," Shelley wisely intoned about his *View of Reform*.[75] Poets and philosophers, he opined in his famous phrase from *A Defence of Poetry*, "are the unacknowledged legislators of the world." In *Defence*, poetry has a political and moral, rather than merely aesthetic, role. On first planning the lengthy *Queen Mab* in late 1811, he said it would be "by anticipation a picture of the manners, simplicity and delights of a perfect state of society: tho' still earthly."[76] It was his unacknowledged legislation for a just society. Newton and Godwin were perhaps joint catalysts for the vegetarian part of that agenda in *Queen Mab*, for at the time the poem was being written Godwin happened to meet Shelley (their first encounter) taking tea at Newton's and discussing the vegetable regimen.

In the first pamphlet, *A Vindication of Natural Diet: Being One of a Series of Notes to Queen Mab, a Philosophical Poem*, Shelley wrote:

Prometheus (who represents the human race) effected some great changes in the condition of his nature, and applied fire to culinary purposes, thus inventing an expedient for screening from his disgust the horrors of the shambles ... It is only by softening and disguising dead flesh by culinary preparation, that it is rendered susceptible of mastication or digestion, and that the sight of its bloody juices and raw horror does not excite intolerable

loathing and disgust. Let the advocate of animal food, force himself to a
decisive experiment on its fitness, and as Plutarch recommends, tear a living
lamb with his teeth, and plunging his head into its vitals, slake his thirst with
the steaming blood; when fresh from the deed of horror let him revert to the
irresistible instincts of nature that would rise in judgment against it, and say,
Nature formed me for such a work as this. Then, and only then, would he be
consistent ...

   Is it to be believed that a being of gentle feelings, rising from his meal of
roots, would take delight in sports of blood ...? [He who is] unvitiated by the
contagion of the world ... will hate the brutal pleasures of the chase by
instinct; it will be a contemplation full of horror and disappointment to his
mind, that beings capable of the gentlest and most admirable sympathies,
should take delight in the death-pangs and last convulsions of dying animals
... never take any substance into the stomach that once had life.[77]

The essay had enormous impact on succeeding generations of vegetarians
as a superb example of irrefutable justification for their cause.

   Timothy Morton, one of Shelley's biographers, points out that the idea
of the Golden Age in *Queen Mab* – "politics parading as poetry," another
of his biographers, Richard Holmes, calls it – is one where "animals forget
their animality and humans become more humane."[78] Shelley evidently
believed that recent experience of explorers with animals who had hitherto
been ignorant of humans demonstrated that animal nature would be quite
different if humans behaved amiably toward them – a remarkable conflu-
ence of an atheistic conception of the coming Golden Age with the Christian image of a regained paradise. As it was, animals were victims of the
human race, and we find the impoverished Shelley, somewhat reminiscent
of Leonardo da Vinci with the caged birds, buying expensive crawfish from
the Marlow hawkers and returning them to the river.

   It is unfortunate that Shelley's second and untitled piece, called by his
editors *On the Vegetable System of Diet* (also composed in 1813, probably
entirely on a visit to Scotland), remained unpublished until the twentieth
century and unfortunate, too, that it remains largely unknown, for it is
altogether an even more persuasive piece than the first. While Shelley repeats some of what he had argued in the first pamphlet, he adds a new
gloss: "It demanded surely no great profundity of anatomical research to
perceive that man has neither the fangs of a lion nor the claws of a tiger,
that his instincts are inimical to bloodshed, and that the food which is not
to be eaten with the most intolerable loathing until it is altered by the

action of fire and disguised by the addition of condiments, is not that food for which he is adapted by his physical conditions. The bull must be degraded into an ox, the ram into the wether by an unnatural and inhuman operation."

That is, they are altered by castration, an operation he also condemns in the first essay. Having noted the various tortures inflicted on food animals (e.g., chickens "are mutilated and imprisoned until they fatten" – those who condemn factory farming but are wistful of a return to traditional farming methods should take note!), Shelley proceeds to ask: "What beast of prey compels its victims to undergo such protracted, such severe and such degrading torments? The single consideration that man cannot swallow a piece of raw flesh would be sufficient to prove that the natural diet of the human species did not consist in the carcases of butchered animals ... Those who are persuaded of the point which is the object of this enquiry to establish, are bound by the most sacred obligations of morality to adopt in practice what he admits in theory."

Shelley seems to be alluding to what was suggested in Chapter 9, namely that there were some who accepted the arguments for a vegetarian diet but who seemed to think they applied only to the abstract people of the "state of nature" and certainly not in practice to themselves. The Golden Age was long in the past, and humans inhabited a "fallen" world to which the rules of the idyllic past no longer applied. Shelley's reasoning was quite different. He tried to practise what he preached and to proselytize, like Oswald and his ilk, on behalf of the persecuted animals. Some of those animals, he claimed, such as the Argali sheep, had been corrupted by domestication from their magnificent natural selves into a mere shadow of their true nature.

Shelley's biographer Richard Holmes, in decidedly less enthusiastic vein for Shelley's vegetarian compositions than were Shaw or Gandhi, describes the essay as "one of his most peculiar and crotchety productions," as being marked by "thin high-flown rhetoric," and as an instance of unphilosophical "speculative 'dietetics.'"[79] It is a haughty and unfounded judgment. Perhaps the evaluation says more about Holmes than Shelley, for the biographer regards vegetarianism as "the cranky" part of *Queen Mab*.[80] If there is anything hackneyed in the prose, it arises from the fact that Shelley had translated Plutarch's essays on flesh eating from Greek to English and had borrowed some of their flowery language.

Certainly, Shelley answered – in the manner intimated by James Boswell yet more stridently – John Hawkesworth's, Frances Hutcheson's, and Dr. Samuel Johnson's considerations about due recompense for existence:

The very sight of the animals in the fields who are destined to the axe must encourage obduracy if it fails to awaken compassion. The butchering of harmless animals cannot fail to produce much of that spirit of insane and hideous exaltation in which the news of a victory is related altho' purchased by the massacre of a thousand men. If the use of animal food be in consequence, subversive to the peace of human society, how unwarrantable is the injustice and barbarity which is exercised toward these miserable victims. They are called into existence by human artifice *that they may drag out a short and miserable existence of slavery and disease, that their bodies may be mutilated, their social feelings outraged.* It were much better that a sentient being should never have existed, than that it should have existed only to endure unmitigated misery.[81]

If Shelley stood firmly on the side of the animals, it must still be recognized, as Christine Kenyon-Jones perceptively observed, that although "animals are to be protected from human cruelty and even called 'brethren' – and Shelley's biographers cite several instances of his attempts to rescue animals from cruel treatment – the very process of showing such humanitarianism can be seen as one which distances the human from other species and ... seeks to legislate against cruelty to animals in order to render human beings less like 'the brutes' they might otherwise resemble."[82] It is a philosophical enigma faced by all animal activists. Benevolent action on behalf of other species seems prima facie to demonstrate human exclusivity. Still, Shelley would no doubt have replied that the very purported human superiority would be grounds not only for benevolence but also for absolute refusal to eat animal flesh.

The *Dictionary of National Biography* casts doubt on the consistency of Shelley's vegetarianism, telling us: "About this time [i.e., 1812] he adopted the vegetarian system of diet, to which he adhered with more or less constancy when in England, but seems to have generally discarded when abroad."

Bread and raisins was his common supper fare in his home with Mary at Marlow from 1815 – for a time, he kept a record of what he ate in grams – and at their lodgings at Livorno in 1819 it was grapes and figs; the Shelleys were constantly on the move, occupying eight residences in two years. But of course, when travelling and staying at inns at considerable distance from one's home, one would be constrained to accept whatever the inn had to offer. Still, we do not know on what basis the *Dictionary of National Biography* reached its conclusion, although it was a common enough opinion. Did Byron or one of the other guests at his regular Pisa dinners in 1822, at which Shelley was a constant presence and at which we know that wild boar was served on one occasion, report on a carnivorous Shelley? We have no record, and it seems unlikely, but we cannot be sure. We are given cause for concern when we find Shelley fishing with Edward Williams in the bay of Lerici in 1822 – they failed to catch any. Did fish not count as flesh for Shelley – despite his habit, noted above, of buying expensive crawfish only to release them – as they appeared not to count for the early Christians and the Cathars?

Certainly, flesh eaters, to assuage their unconscious guilt and justify their own practices, will often try to besmirch the reputation of vegetarians with stories of palpable dietetic failure. During a period of illness in the late 1930s, George Bernard Shaw was prescribed fifteen monthly injections of liver extract. Immediately, the *Daily Express* trumpeted "G. B. S. Takes Meat." "I do not," he told the *Vegetarian News*. "My diet remains unchanged."[83] In Shelley's case, the cynics were at least partly right, for Shelley had returned to flesh on two occasions in 1815, the year of Waterloo. It was the culmination of political events that would be a serious blow to the prospects for his radical idealism – even though later he would write, despondently, a sonnet celebrating Napoleon's defeat. Indeed, the Battle of the Nations at Leipzig two years earlier had already pointed the trend. To be sure, in the first instance the lapse was occasioned by the fact that his friend Thomas Peacock made it difficult for the Shelleys to obtain a vegetable meal, but Percy's lack of resistance reflects his state of ennui. On that occasion, exhausted from rowing and portage, Shelley was persuaded to eat three whole mutton chops. On a second boating trip a while later in the same year, Peacock fed him the same diet and attributed Percy's renewed enjoyment in life to it. Even earlier, on arrival at Holyhead from his abortive attempt to influence Irish politics in 1812, Percy startled his wife, Harriet, by ordering flesh at an inn. And later, in the final days of 1817, Mary, the second Mrs. Shelley, persuaded Percy to go on what proved to be a very temporary flesh diet because of his illness. Whether the illness was physical or a result of despondency over the political future and his publication ambitions is open to dispute.

But the return to flesh was never long-lived. In truth, Shelley complained that his household was in poor health, a situation not improved by the fact that in winter in England the only vegetables readily procurable were cabbage, carrots, potatoes, and turnips, a diet of insufficient variety easily to maintain health. The situation improved somewhat for Shelley from 1818 until his death when he was resident in Italy and a more appealing regimen was more readily available. In fact, throughout his adult life Shelley was frequently ill, especially when the weather was cold. And he suffered repeated and severe psychological depression. His illnesses clearly troubled his vegetarian conscience, for in 1817 he wrote to his fellow poet and publisher Leigh Hunt: "Do not mention that I am unwell to your nephew, for the advocate of a new system of diet is held bound to be invulnerable by disease" or else his regimen is deemed unpersuasive.[84] But perhaps political disappointments rather than ill-health occasioned the infrequent lapses. Certainly, Shelley himself thought his health benefited from his vegetable diet. Writing from his temporary home in Wales to his friend Hogg in 1813, he announced: "I continue vegetable. Harriet [who was pregnant] means to be slightly animal until spring."[85] Shelley was confident his own health was "much improved" by the vegetable diet yet realized that with the limited vegetation available, the damp and dreary winter did not sit well with his wife's pregnancy. By June, Harriet was stating that they had "all" – presumably "all" meant their extended household – "taken to the vegetable regimen again."[86] Certainly, Shelley continued to practise his vegetable diet for most of the rest of his life. Concerning a literary dinner at the Hampstead home of Hunt, the painter Benjamin Robert Haydon wrote sneeringly of Shelley "carving a bit of broccoli or cabbage on his plate, as if it had been the substantial wing of a chicken," while the others duly ate the flesh they had been served.[87] Shelley's vegetable diet was of sufficient significance to him to risk censure and mockery for his principle.

Keith Thomas is also dubious of Shelley's consistency and commitment: "Some doubt is thrown upon the seriousness of Shelley's conversion to the 'Pythagorean system' in 1812 by the tone of his wife's invitation to a friend: 'Mrs Shelley's comp[liment]s to Mrs Nugent and expects the pleasure of her company to dinner, 5 o'clock, as a murdered chicken has been prepared for her repast.'"[88] If anything, this note from Harriet during the Shelleys' residence in Ireland to Mrs. Nugent, an Irish republican sympathizer, serves to strengthen our conviction in the vegetarian regimen of the Shelleys at this time. It would certainly not be normal to refer to the meal as a "murdered" chicken unless one's feelings were somewhat intense. And it is noticeable that the chicken is for *her* repast. Surely, if the Shelleys were intending to partake, it would have been *our* repast or *the* repast. Moreover, a willingness to serve flesh to others seems to have been not uncommon among at least some vegetarians, although perhaps not as common among those as vehement as Shelley in their conviction. For example, according to William St. Clair in *The Godwins and the Shelleys,* after Godwin had opted for a "natural diet" he "still served meat to his guests and never scolded them for enjoying it."[89] Moreover, Lord Byron, in denigrating their meagre diet of "green fruit," indicates in 1820, just two years before Shelley's death,

that Claire Clairmont, the mother of Byron's daughter, and the Shelleys –
a different Mrs. Shelley by this time – were still practising a wholly vegetarian regimen in Italy, a fact that hints at the general error of the cynics as
well as of the misgivings of the doubting Thomas.[90]

Whether the mercurial Mary Shelley (1797-1851) was a long-term committed vegetarian, we do not know for certain. Nor, if she was thus committed, do we know whether she remained one after her husband's early
death, although there is no evidence for any change of heart or of any dispute with her husband or father, William Godwin, on the issue; yet there
was considerable dispute with Godwin on her elopement and subsequent
affair with Percy. Godwin's vegetarian proclivities are significant, for, as
Mary's latest (and best) biographer says: "It would be rash to underestimate
the degree to which Godwin, rather than Shelley, formed his daughter's
social and political views."[91] Nonetheless, on sending young Mary away to
boarding school in Ramsgate or to stay with Baxter Dissenters at Dundee,
no special dietary provisions appear to have been required, although the
Glassite Dissenters in Dundee, of which the Baxters were members, practised a quasi vegetarianism that, reminiscent of Clement of Alexandria,
they called "love feasts." Perhaps in his days of grave financial and paternal
distress, Godwin deemed diet too trivial a matter with which to be overly
concerned. Perhaps by this time Godwin himself no longer restricted his
diet to vegetables. Nonetheless, it should be acknowledged that as a young
man Godwin had been a disciple of the millenarian and egalitarian dissenter
John Glas (1695-1773) and may have acquired early proclivities toward vegetarianism from that source, later to be rediscovered and strengthened by
John Frank Newton. Perhaps the vegetarian leanings of the Baxters were at
the back of Godwin's mind in sending Mary to his friends in Scotland.

We know that Mary was sympathetic to the vegetarian cause and that,
apparently, she practised vegetarianism during much of the span of her
married life. For example, in the first days of her elopement with Percy in
1814, she refers to her Paris supper of fried leaves of artichoke. In the same
year at an inn near Troyes, the Shelley party had to resort to milk and sour
bread in the absence of appropriate fare. Their room in a Swiss inn where
they stayed housed a glass case of stuffed birds. Mary's and Percy's disapproval reflected their orientations. A short while later, in financial desperation at the Cross Keys Inn in London, Mary, her half-sister, and Percy were
constrained to dine on cake. We find Mary at Windsor in 1815 joining with
Percy in arguing the merits of a vegetable diet against the unsympathetic
Thomas Peacock. Snidely, John Keats asked after Mary in 1816: "Does Mrs
S[helley] cut Bread and Butter as neatly as ever?"[92] Comments on Mary's

fare are very infrequent, but when they are made there is no mention of flesh. Thus, for example, in Mary's journal we read that she and the Shelley household lunched during an expedition to Pompei in 1818 on oranges, figs, bread, and apples.

In her *Frankenstein* (1818), her daimon was an animal-respecting, compassionate vegetarian, although subject to malevolent influences – a clear indication of her own leanings. Indeed, given that Byron was also on the whole a vegetarian sympathizer, if an inconsistent one, and at the time in a vegetarian phase of his life, and given that Byron and the Shelleys were together, along with others, at Villa Diodati at Compegny, about three miles from Geneva, where the novel was written, at least thematically it is fair to say *Frankenstein* was born in a vegetarian spirit.[93] In *The Last Man* (1826), conceived the year after Percy's drowning, Mary Shelley displayed the same animal sensibilities and maintained the view, as in *Frankenstein,* that it is human deviation from Nature that has brought about *Homo sapiens'* demise. And a couple of years before her death, Mary said she preferred bread and cheese to luxurious living. Still, on social and political matters generally, she had softened her stance by the 1830s. She even tried to soften the public image of Shelley as the radical rebel. Certainly, he had moderated in some respects his extremes over the years, especially after Harriet's suicide.[94] But Mary overdid it. Ably abetted by her daughter-in-law, Jane St. John, she was so successful in portraying an anodyne Shelley that in the 1890s George Bernard Shaw wondered when the atheist poet would be depicted "in a tall hat, Bible in hand, leading his children on Sunday mornings to the church in his native parish."[95] No longer prompted by the utopianism of Percy or her father, Mary came to advocate slow progress. "I am not for violent extremes," she wrote, dismayed by the rumblings of the Chartists. Her very final journal entry was to copy out a quotation from Edmund Burke. Perhaps somewhere in the post-Percy period she abandoned the fleshless regimen. Perhaps she was never as fully committed as Percy, but certainly, as indicated by Byron of the household diet in 1820, she at least sometimes practised.

## LORD BYRON AND SIR RICHARD PHILLIPS

As noted, Lord Byron (1788-1824) appears to have been an inconsistent vegetarian and not one who proselytized in the vegetarian cause nor one for whom the interests of animals played a major role in the choice of vegetarian diet, despite his sensibilities to animals in general and his surrounding himself with them even more than Rousseau and Tennyson – for example, five monkeys, five cats, ten horses, eight dogs, and eleven birds, including five peacocks, at his home at Ravenna in 1821. As an undergraduate at Trinity College, Cambridge, he strolled King's Parade with his pet bear, whereas the less ostentatious Coleridge kept the more customary cat in his rooms at Jesus College. Byron's abstinence from animal flesh, when he was abstaining, was based on the preservation of his own character, not on ethics, or at least not predominantly so. An early biographer and personal associate of Byron, the Irish poet Thomas Moore, tells us of a particular prandial embarrassment:

> As we had none of us been apprised of his peculiarities with respect to food, the embarrassment of our host [the banker and poet Samuel Rogers] was not little on discovering that there was nothing on the table which his noble guest could eat or drink. Neither meat, fish, nor wine would Lord Byron touch; and of biscuits and soda water, which he asked for, there had been, unluckily, no provision. He professed, however, to be equally well pleased with potatoes and vinegar; and of these meagre materials contrived to make rather a hearty meal ... We frequently during the first months of our acquaintance dined together alone ... Though at times he would drink freely enough of claret, he still adhered to his system of abstinence in food. He appeared, indeed, to have conceived a notion that animal food has some peculiar influence on the character; and I remember one day as I sat opposite him, employed, I suppose, rather earnestly over a "beef-steak," after watching me for a few seconds, he said in a grave tone of inquiry – "Moore, don't you find eating beef-steak makes you ferocious."[96]

A more recent Byron biographer, Phyllis Grosskurth, describes Byron's regimen habits as "manic dieting" and "erratic eating" rather than as flesh-less dining.[97] Moreover, Rogers, when asked how long Byron would preserve his present diet, is reported to have replied: "Just as long as you continue to notice it."[98] His public persona masked his private character. Certainly, there were periods of his life when Byron was a consistent flesh eater.

This episode highlights the difficulties faced by vegetarians in the nineteenth and earlier centuries. But it also indicates a difficulty for the historian. If a person were successful in clandestinely avoiding flesh as a guest, did not dine in clubs or at inns, and did not indicate his or her own dietary habits, the vegetarian practice might be unknown, even though these contingencies are unlikely.

If Sir Richard Phillips (1767-1840) is less well known than Percy Bysshe Shelley in the vegetarian cause, he was certainly no less committed. He was a businessman, founder and owner of the *Leicester Herald* newspaper, and publisher of books, employing numerous respected authors, including Coleridge. In addition, he was a politician who was elected high sheriff of the City of London and County of Middlesex, a republican, and a prison reformer second only to John Howard (1726-1790) – who was himself a committed vegetarian, claiming that his diet gave him immunity from "gaol fever."[99] Phillips was dedicated to the vegetarian cause from the days of his youth. He was a consistent social reformer who remained convinced of the moral necessity of vegetarianism and wrote decisively in its favour. He was not, however, universally admired. In 1798, Phillips "invented and promulgated" – his words, from his tombstone – what he called "the interrogative system of education." The resulting substantial pamphlet *The Interrogative System* (1820) was a serious source of contention, several commentators claiming Phillips to be a scoundrel who synthesized and plagiarized existing educational writing. Perhaps this was little more than a reflection of the animosities of the age, for he also maligned as "a dirty little Jacobin" and was known, not endearingly, by the nickname "Pythagoras." Scoundrel or not, Jacobin or not – and he certainly retained much of his early radicalism – Phillips was sufficiently in favour to receive a knighthood in 1808.

In 1826, he composed *Golden Rules of Social Philosophy, Being a System of Ethics,* in which he adumbrated, *inter alia,* sixteen dietary principles that had fully informed his life. The first five should suffice to demonstrate the ethical nature of Phillips's conviction. He claimed the human should be committed to the flesh-denying cause:

1  *Because,* being mortal himself, and holding his life on the same uncertain and precarious tenure as all other sensitive beings, he does not find himself justified by any supposed superiority or inequality of condition in destroying the enjoyment of existence of any other mortal, except in the necessary defence of his own life.
2  *Because* the desire of life is so paramount, and so affectingly cherished in all sensitive beings, that he cannot reconcile it to his feelings to destroy or become a voluntary party in the destruction of any innocent living being however much in his power, or apparently insignificant.
3  *Because* he feels the same abhorrence from devouring flesh in general that he hears carnivorous men express against eating human flesh, or the flesh of Horses, Dogs, Cats, or other animals which, in some countries, it is not customary for carnivorous men to devour.

4 *Because* Nature seems to have made a superabundant provision for the
   nourishment of animals in the saccharine matter of Roots and Fruits, in
   the farinaceous matter of Grain, Seeds, and Pulse, and in the oleaginous
   matter of the Stalks, Leaves and Pericarps of numerous vegetables.
5 *Because* he feels an utter and unconquerable repugnance against receiving into his stomach the flesh or juices of deceased animal organization.[100]

The sixteen provisions of his manifesto as a whole could well have stood
as the ethical foundation of the Vegetarian Society founded twenty-one
years after the publication of *Golden Rules of Social Philosophy* and a mere
seven years after Phillips's death.


## Lewis Gompertz and Thomas Forster

To the best of existing knowledge, Lewis Gompertz (c. 1783-1861) had no
acquaintance with any of the other persons mentioned thus far in this chapter, other perhaps than Lord Erskine. Of distinguished German descent, he
was a Jewish philanthropist, inventor of numerous devices, some to mini-
mize the burden to animals, and advocate of the oppressed, whether en-
slaved, female, impoverished, or brute being. Like Tryon, Oswald, Nicholson,
and Shelley, he believed that justice was not divisible. He was a vegetarian
– indeed, effectively a vegan – who refused to eat eggs or drink milk, refused to wear leather or silk, would not ride in a coach on account of the
suffering to horses, and abominated hunting and animal experimentation.
He advocated developing alternatives to horse labour, believing it better
that humans should put their "own shoulders to the wheel" for important
tasks rather than oppress animalkind. In 1824, he wrote *Moral Inquiries on
the Situation of Man and of Brutes,* a short time after the passage of the first
British animal-welfare legislation since the Cromwellian Protectorate and
in the same year as the founding of the Society for the Prevention of Cruelty to Animals. In that year, under the auspices of the Irish member of Parliament Richard Martin – "Humanity Dick," as he was designated by
George IV – who had steered the legislation through the Commons, a public meeting was held that resulted in the formation of the SPCA, one of
whose purposes was to enforce the recently passed legislation. The first
secretary was the Reverend Arthur Broome, who proved incapable of handling the precarious finances of the fledgling society. He was replaced by
Gompertz, who held the post for six years before resigning, allegedly over
a dispute concerning the purported "Christian principles" that were

claimed to be the foundation of the society. Gompertz then founded the Animals' Friend Society, of which he remained president until ill health compelled his resignation in 1846. His vegetarianism had been at odds with many of the more prominent of the original society's honorary vice presidents and even of the general membership. No less a legislative promoter and SPCA co-founder than Richard Martin was a hunter and an angler. After all, the SPCA's founding statement rejected "all visionary and overstrained views" – and by the standards of the SPCA, Gompertz was undoubtedly a visionary.[101] If his so-called Pythagorean practices – a charge levelled at him by one who thought the SPCA's practices should be wholly Christian, which to him meant omnivorous – were in conflict with those of the SPCA, they stood a little closer to at least some of the practices of the members of the Animals' Friend Society.

In the *Moral Inquiries,* Gompertz provides what is perhaps the underlying ethical principle of the book in Axiom 5 of Chapter 4: "That we should never admit of the propriety of the will or volition of one animal being the agent of another, unless we should perceive its own good to come from it, or that justice should require it."[102] We must assume that Gompertz is thinking of human will over other species. As it stands, the axiom implies that there is a moral obligation of the fox to the chicken and of the lioness to the zebra. Among the other principles he espouses is that "every animal has more right to the use of its own body than others have to use it."[103] Most of the principles are versions of the utilitarian doctrine, summed up by the statement: "Our *first* duty is to *do as little harm as possible.* The *second* duty is *to do good.*"[104]

Perhaps the most interesting aspect of Gompertz's argument – and one that runs in total contrast with all those arguments for ethical vegetarianism we have encountered to date – is that he readily concedes that flesh food is valuable to human health. But this fact, Gompertz insists, does not provide humans with an entitlement to that flesh. Gompertz depicts a contest between two antagonists, Y and Z, with Z taking the part of the animal advocate:

> Z: First, how do you prove that mankind is invested with the right of killing [animals] and that brutes have been created [to be of service to mankind]? Secondly, it is to be observed that man himself possesses the same nourishing and palatable qualities. Are we then to become cannibals for that reason? I grant that the health of man requires animal food, and it is not to be expected that the strength and faculties of either the body or mind can be near as great with the privation of it, as with its aid, but that is nothing to the

animals; a robber would not be so rich if he were not to steal; it is not there-fore right to steal, when the laws can be evaded.[105]

Thus, in Gompertz's view, humans are deprived of some degree of health without flesh and are harmed in strength and intellectual capacity without flesh, but, still, the human has no right to that flesh. The animal owner of the flesh has a prior claim. There is a distinct emphasis on the equality of human and nonhuman animals: "It matters not whether the victim be fur-nished with two legs or with four, with wings, with fins, or with arms; where there is sensation, there is subject for cruelty, and in proportion to the degree of sensation will its actions operate."[106]

Thomas Forster (1789-1860) dedicated to Gompertz his book *Philozoa, or Moral Reflections, on the actual condition of the Animal Kingdom, and the means of improving the same.* Published in Brussels in 1839, the book was probably one of the thirty-four formally entered for the SPCA £100 prize for the best essay on humanity to animals.[107] The prize was won by the Reverend Dr. John Styles, DD, for *The Animal Creation: Its Claims on Our Humanity Stated and Enforced,* by modern standards of judgment inferior to at least three of the essays submitted. Forster was a rarity, at least for the time, being a nonmonastic Catholic vegetarian.[108] In the appendix to his *Animals' Rights Considered in Relation to Social Progress* (1892), Henry Salt gives a lengthy bibliography containing what he considered "a list of the chief English works, touching directly on" the subject of "Animals' Rights."[109] Salt ignored Styles's contribution. The book by Forster he describes as an "excellent treatise" by "a distinguished naturalist and astronomer who had taken an active part in the founding of the Animals' Friend Society."[110] No doubt wary of the carnivorous judgments of the SPCA's board of examin-ers, Forster was a little guarded in his statements but nonetheless subtly pressed the case for vegetarianism in his section on "The Cruelty Con-nected with the Culinary Art":

Some persons in Europe carry their notions about cruelty to animals so far as not to allow themselves to eat animal food. Many very intelligent men have, at different times of their lives, abstained wholly from flesh; and this too, with very considerable advantage to their health ... All these facts, taken col-lectively, point to a period in the progress of civilisation when men will cease to slay their fellow-mortals in the animal world for food ... The return of this paradisical state may be rather remote; but in the meantime we ought to make the experiment, and set an example of humanity by abstaining, if not from all, at least from those articles of cookery with which any particular cruelty may be connected, such as veal, when the calves are killed in the ordinary way.[111]

Whether guarded or not, the rather staid and conservative SPCA representatives on the examining board – the Right Honourable Earl of Carnarvon, the Honourable and Reverend B. W. Noel, and Mr. Sergeant Talfourd, MP – preferred a work, partly plagiarized, by a Church of England flesh-eating reverend doctor to one by a Catholic abstainer.[112]

If the eighteenth century was the age of preaching without practising and the first half of the nineteenth century was the era of advocacy coupled with practical responsibility, together with a minimal level of organization, although somewhat increasing as the decades progressed, the late 1840s onward witnessed the first large-scale coordination of ethical vegetarian advocacy and practice in recorded human history.

# 11

# The Victorians, the Edwardians, and the Founding of the Vegetarian Society

If the eighteenth century had been the age of Sensibility and the French Revolution had then given birth to the age of action, the middle of the nineteenth century witnessed the coming of the age of organization. Technological and economic innovation – the canals, railways, factory system of production, and urbanization, for example – had brought about effective communication among far larger numbers of people than ever before and the ability to co-operate over far greater distances than ever before. Modernity brought all the hitherto unknown ills of anomic novelty, but it also allowed for co-operative accomplishments on a scale hitherto beyond imagination.

Although numerous analysts have found the origins of the Vegetarian Society in 1847 to stem from Rev. William Cowherd (1763-1816) and the Salford Swedenborgians of the early years of the nineteenth century, it is appropriate also to look farther back to Shelley, Ritson, Lambe, Newton, Phillips, Gompertz, and the like in London and Bracknell of the same era. Decidedly, this secular orientation was decisive in the long run and likely had considerably greater influence even in the short run than is commonly recognized. This is not to say that Cowherd's co-religionists were without immediate relevance. Indeed, they were vital. But the burgeoning ethical aspects of the movement reflect the significant attitudinal changes that were underway in the Enlightenment-influenced cultural context of the early nineteenth century as witnessed particularly in the thought of Percy Bysshe Shelley and Sir Richard Phillips. Even the most evangelical of the numerous new religious denominations acquired an increasingly secular orientation, although, of course, they neither recognized nor acknowledged that orientation. In fact, many of the increasingly secular aspirations of the nineteenth century were expressed in organized religion. Of more immediate relevance to the foundation, alongside the Salford contingent, were the Alcott House followers of James Pierrepont Greaves (1777-1842), whose communal home was named for Bronson Alcott, himself a vegetarian and a respected transcendentalist resident visitor from the United States. Greaves had founded a vegetarian community on the outskirts of London, where he also promoted his radical educational and political ideals. Together, the Salfordians and the followers of Greaves were instrumental in the foundation of the new Vegetarian Society, although Greaves himself died a few years before the society came to fruition, as had Cowherd over a quarter-century earlier. It was left to their followers to conceive and construct the society. If Cowherd was, in religion, a devotee of Swedenborgian mysticism, he was not without an earnest secular reformist side, dispensing hot vegetable soup to the Salford poor and preaching the inadequacies of existing institutions and policies. In fact, the pantheist Cowherd and Pestalozzian educational reformer Greaves, known as the "sacred" socialist, were not unworthy followers of the radical tradition espoused by some of their immediate forerunners. Indeed, radical secular and nonconformist Christian opinion were fused in the origins of the society. Socialism was a common home for vegetarians. Along with Greaves and, of course, George Bernard Shaw, we find, for example, the classicist Henry Salt, the theosophist Annie Besant, and the utopian Edward Carpenter embracing the socialist and vegetarian causes simultaneously. The Fabian socialists Sidney and Beatrice Webb, joint authors of *History of Trade Unionism* (1894) and the nine-volume *English Local Government* (1906-29), were also vegetarians. Beatrice described herself as an "anti-flesh-fish-egg-alcohol-coffee-and-sugar eater."[1] She imposed her frugal diet successively on the reluctant Sidney and on their disappointed dinner guests. The fine poet and Fellow of King's College, Cambridge, Rupert Brooke, who was killed in the Aegean in the First World War, was also a Fabian whose "socialism," Margaret Lavington tells us, "was accompanied by a passing phase of vegetarianism."[2]

Cowherd and his fellows – a congregation of some four hundred at its height – reflect, however, in part an asceticism of a dying era, that of Swedenborg, whose concern was to achieve spiritual unity with the deity. It was not that asceticism was moribund, merely that the principles usually associated with asceticism were promoted increasingly on secular grounds – hence Methodist, Baptist, and Salvation Army opposition to alcohol because of its *practical* effects on health, enjoyment, employment, and ability to provide for one's family. Nor is this to say that no nominally Sweden-borgian inspiration lay behind the origins of the Vegetarian Society, merely that those inspirations were more secular than ascetic, even if the Sweden-borgian mystical system still appealed to some. To be sure, Joseph Brother-ton, Member of Parliament for Salford and an original member of Cowherd's Swedenborgian Bible-Christian Church, chaired the founding meeting of the Vegetarian Society at the Northwood Villa vegetarian hos-pital in Ramsgate in 1847, and James Simpson (1812-1859), likewise a mem-ber of the Bible-Christian Church, was elected the society's first president. But many of the other 140 present at the first convention had no connec-tion with the Bible-Christian Church. Choosing Ramsgate for the inaugu-ral meeting proved an early instance of the later common practice of holding conventions at seaside resorts. It lies on the Isle of Thanet in East Kent and was one of the most popular seaside towns of the nineteenth century. The town was a couple of hundred miles closer to Alcott House than to Salford, a long distance to travel in those days, and of greater convenience for the Greaves than the Cowherd contingent. Moreover, Cowherd, the vegetarian inspiration behind the church, was long dead, as we have noted. A number of his congregation, and indeed some of those most committed to vegetar-ianism, had left for America, and the influence of the Bible-Christian Church does not seem to have been at all pervasive in English vege-tarian circles. Moreover, any remnants of influence possessed by the Bible-Christian Church waned as the society became increasingly concerned with the ethical aspects of keeping animals free from harm. In his address to the assembled throng at the founding meeting, Brotherton argued that eating flesh was injurious to human happiness and health and that the con-tamination of flesh foods was likewise damaging to the body. Although it was not the most prominent part of his speech, he also pointed toward the future in indicating that it was unnecessary, and by implication unjust, to kill animals for food. If the ethical argument was not central at first, it already had its place, and it was a rapidly growing place. By 1883 when soci-ety member Howard Williams's 400-page volume on the history of contri-butions to vegetarianism was published, the title he gave it – *The Ethics of Diet* – was witness to the trend that had become the dominant reality.

That there was a significant remnant of Salford Bible-Christian influence is seen in the first annual meeting of the society in 1848, when there were 478 members; 232 attended the closing dinner held at Hayward's Hotel in Manchester (Salford and Manchester are contiguous), near which, in Altrin-cham, the society eventually established its permanent home. Salford's geo-graphical influence was significant as home to the Bible-Christians. However,

Brotherton died in 1857 and Simpson in 1859, thus diminishing most remaining ties with the Salford Swedenborgians, tenuous as they already were, other than notably through Brotherton's wife, author of *A New System of Vegetable Cookery* (1821), a Bible-Christian Church adherent, and a vegetarian advocate until her dying day. If the role of the Greaves contingent in the origins of the society had been the lesser role, it was nonetheless not negligible. In 1849, Isaac Pitman (1813-1897), the creator of a noted system of shorthand that remained in common secretarial use until the invention of the recording and dictation machines, spoke at the society's annual general meeting, declaring he had been a vegetarian for eleven years. On the other side of the Atlantic, the Bible-Christian Church remained extremely influential throughout the nineteenth century. William Metcalfe, along with his wife, Susanna, James Clark, and some forty others had emigrated to America in 1817, and the Bible-Christian Church they founded there contributed significantly to nascent organized vegetarianism in America. Indeed, Metcalfe, if he did not convert the primary figures of Sylvester Graham and William Alcott to the vegetarian alimentary program, at least confirmed them in it.

In general, on the part of the majority, the tendency was to think of vegetarians as decided misfits and oddballs, although more with begrudging admiration and supercilious condescension than with outright hostility – for example, Anna Bonus Kingsford, vice president of the Vegetarian Society, commented on the favourable European reception of her *Perfect Way in Diet* in the preface to an English edition.[3] Nonetheless, as Harriet Ritvo observed: "Rejection of the national diet smacked of profounder dissents; if beef-eaters were self-classified as British, abstainers might belong in more disturbing categories."[4] Vegetarianism thus smacked of being a little unpatriotic! And the more conservative, especially those whose interests and occupations were threatened, could still be quite antagonistic. Thus, the satirical magazine *Punch* remarked about the Vegetarian Society conference dinner in 1848:

> We do not quite understand the principle upon which these gentlemen object to animal food, but if health is their object, we do not think that will be promoted by the mixture of messes they sat down to the other day at Manchester ... There is something very infantile in the pretended simplicity of this fare, for none but a parcel of overgrown children would sit down seriously to make a meal upon sweetstuff. We look upon the Vegetarian humbug as a mere pretext for indulging a juvenile appetite for something nice, and we are really ashamed of those old boys who continue, at their time of life, to display such a puerile taste for pies and puddings.[5]

Nonetheless, a Victorian cartoon depicted what vegetarians were always fond of repeating: that many very large and robust animals were by their very nature vegetarian. Under a sketch of a caged zoo hippopotamus regarding a female visitor, the hippopotamus remarks, under the caption of "A Gentle Vegetarian": "Morning, Miss! Who'd ever think, looking at us two, that you devoured Bullocks and Sheep, and *I* never took anything but rice?"[6] Perhaps *Punch*'s defamatory remarks were more of an exception than the rule, although, in America, Sylvester Graham was accosted, ineffectively it would appear, by some irate butcher and baker apprentices, maddened (or given a convenient excuse for preexisting bellicose tendencies) that his "raw food" advocacy would deprive them of their livelihoods. It is to be noted that the writer of the *Punch* report had a misconception of the vegetarian diet, although it must be conceded that what passed for vegetarian fare in those days differs from the kinds of meals most vegetarians would prepare today. Moreover, the author seemed quite incapable of imagining that a member of the human species might eschew flesh out of respect for the interest of other species, even though this was the era in which animal experimentation was almost abolished in Britain. But then this was the age par excellence in which even altruistic ethics were commonly dressed in self-interested garb – enlightened self-interest was, as a philosophical principle, often the best that could commonly be hoped for. Perfectibility was being replaced by a doctrine dominated by the role of self-interest.

Health, environment, and animal ethics were on the agenda at that historical inaugural meeting in Ramsgate: flesh was harmful and vegetables were beneficial, a great deal more could be produced from land with vegetable production than that used for animal grazing, and Dr. Charles Lamb and his lay disciple John Frank Newton were quoted on health and Plutarch and Porphyry on animal ethics.[7] For the first decade or so, while Brotherton and Simpson were at the helm, the society prospered and increased in membership. But by 1870 the membership had declined to 125, in part because increasing bourgeois wealth made flesh more readily affordable. The era of conspicuous consumption and status through consumption and ostentation had arrived, even though stalwart traditionalists were appalled. And it was the bourgeoisie that provided the Vegetarian Society with its effective membership. The poor had little interest in an organization whose principles were those by which they lived predominantly and by necessity. A typical expression was that of North Welsh construction malcontents shortly before Waterloo: "we cannot work without meat and we cannot get meat without money."[8] As long as they could get sufficient money, they would use it to purchase flesh. Usually, there were insufficient funds. Around 1872 the British government conducted a study on the diet of agricultural labourers in Europe and determined that they ate very little flesh. Only in Pomerania and England were flesh foods commonly a part of the regimen, and then only sparsely, Pomeranians eating meat three times a week, England being noted for its regional differences. Success meant acquiring more of the desirable, not renouncing what one had. In Belgium and Scotland they ate a little bacon but otherwise no meat. In Prussia and Saxony they ate flesh only on feast days. In the Netherlands, they fed on a little fish but otherwise no meat. In Bavaria, Italy, Ireland, Sweden, and Russia no meat was consumed. In Spain and Switzerland flesh was a luxury.[9] By the beginning of the twentieth century the English working-class diet was a lot worse and the Scottish working-class diet certainly no better. While the apparent vigour and robustness of the labourers were something to which the vegetarian could point to demonstrate that flesh was unnecessary, they could at this early stage expect little support from the labouring class. On the whole, the workers desired to partake of the flesh they were denied, not to deride it. It is curious, then, to find that in 1853 the membership was said to be 889, half of whom were reported as labourers and tradesmen. It seems unlikely the proportion is accurate for so early a date, and perhaps it was broadcast to encourage diversity and expanse of membership. To the extent that the proportion might express a partial truth – and surely no accurate occupational figures were kept – it would be largely a consequence of associated membership in a religious or political congregation now drawn to the new society or because of the frugal economy or health benefits claimed for vegetarianism. Still, from the early years of the nineteenth century, the working men's movement stimulated some degree of interest in organizations, such as the Hampden clubs, designed to improve the labourer's lot. And the sixty thousand who marched at Peterloo in 1819 demonstrated an emerging consciousness.

### Francis William Newman

In 1873 new life was breathed into the ailing organization when Professor Francis William Newman (1805-1897), younger brother of Cardinal Henry Newman, became president of the Vegetarian Society, having become a member five years earlier. Professor of Latin and co-founder of Bedford College for women, later a part of the University of London, Francis Newman not only brought charismatic prestige and social status to the society – the novelist George Eliot, once a geometry student of Newman, referred to him as "our blessed St. Francis," whose "soul was a blessed yea," and thought him a "renowned" and "famous" author – but also infused this prestige and status with a decided orientation toward animal ethics, one that was never to wane.[10] Newman stated in his *Essays on Diet:*

> That the first thought on discovering a new creature should be "is it nice to eat?" is to me shocking and debasing. What is called the love of sport has become a love of killing for the display of skill, and converts man into the tyrant of all other animals; yet this arose out of a desire of eating their flesh – a desire which cannot be blamed on that state of barbarism in which little other flesh food was to be had. But when with the growth of civilization other food is easier to get, when bread has won upon flesh-meat, it is evil to struggle for the more barbarous state. Does not the love of flesh inflame the love of killing, teach disregard for animal suffering, and prepare men for ferocity against men?
>
> We cannot blame the butcher if he become perfectly callous to the sufferings of animals. His trade not only trains him to callousness, but demands it of him: and this is equally true of the vivisector: Hence no security whatever, in either case, is possible against any amount of wanton cruelty. The man who by practice steals his own heart *must* lose his discernment of animal suffering with his concern for it.
>
> We must admit into our moral treatises the question of the rights of animals; and not only the limits of our rights over them, but other topics hence arising.
>
> When a man must starve unless he kill a deer or a bison, no one blames the slaughter; but it does not follow that when we have plenty of wholesome food without killing, we are at liberty to kill for mere gratification of the palate. To nourish a taste for killing is morally evil; to be accustomed to inflict agony on harmless animals by wounding or maiming them without remorse, prepares men's hearts for other cruelty.[11]

With Newman, vegetarianism and animal protection are irremediably and indivisibly interrelated. He lectured to the society membership on the beneficial environmental effects of vegetarianism and complained to them of the grievous problems of turning arable to pastoral land, but first and foremost his concern was with vegetarianism's potential to curb suffering to animals.[12]

Newman's presidency resulted in renewed interest in the Vegetarian Society. By 1880, the membership had topped 2,000, and such impetus was instilled that, according to Vice President Anna Bonus Kingsford, the membership had climbed past 3,000 by around the turn of the century.[13] If this figure sounds high, it is given credence by Harriet Ritvo's equally surprising claim, based on the figure provided in Charles W. Forward's *Practical Vegetarian Recipes* (1891), that "three thousand members of the Vegetarian Society attended its conference in 1881."[14] This membership was in part, no doubt, due to the association of vegetarianism with other relevant causes and also due to overlapping memberships. For example, the president of the Food Reform Society in 1885, the Reverend W.J. Monk, was also a vice president of the Vegetarian Society. And as Hilda Kean has reported: "According to the feminist and socialist Charlotte Despard, giving her presidential address to the Vegetarian Society, 'Vegetarianism is pre-eminently a woman's question because it will do away with the most degrading part of her work.'"[15] One wonders to what extent the future development of vegetarianism was hindered by later technological developments in the kitchen that diminished "the most degrading part" of the work, which was then generally, and by some still is, thought to be "woman's work."

The early Vegetarian Society suffered from internal divisions. At first, the Manchester-based organization was the sole Vegetarian Society, although there were numerous individuals from the metropolis associated with the Manchester Vegetarian Society via such groups as the Dietetic Reform Society (1875) and the London (later National) Food Reform Society (1877), titular indications that some balked already at the "vegetarian" designation, however much Newman tried to dress the "vegetarian" title in acceptable guise with a spurious explanation of the term's "vigorous" origins.[16] The London Vegetarian Society became a branch of the Manchester Society in 1885, but it was not to last. As Colin Spencer described the breach, "Relations between London and Manchester became somewhat strained in the 1880s. London wanted to be a vigorous nationwide reforming society, while Manchester thought it had been that for some time and London should merely be a branch of the central society at Manchester. In 1888 the London group severed all ties with the original society and the London Vegetarian Society was founded."[17] The separation of the London and Manchester societies was to continue for almost a century, not to be reunited until 1969, their respective journals having become one a decade earlier.

Even a few from society's upper echelons were attracted to the vegetarian diet. The widow of the British ambassador to Vienna, Lady Paget, boasted of the beneficial effects of her vegetarian lifestyle on her mental health: "I have experienced a delightful sense of repose and freedom, a kind of superior elevation above things material."[18] The former foxhunter Lady

Florence Dixie (1857-1905) was converted to the cause, bemoaning her past shooting practices:

> What is it but deliberate massacre when thousands and tens of thousands of tame, hand-reared creatures are every year literally driven into the jaws of death and mown down in a peculiarly brutal manner? A perfect roar of guns fills the air; louder tap and yell the beaters, while above the din can be heard the heart-rending cries of wounded hares and rabbits, some of which can be seen dragging themselves away, with legs broken, or turning round and round in their agony before they die! And the pheasants! They are on every side, some rising, some dropping; some lying dead, but the great majority fluttering on the ground wounded; some with both wings broken and a leg; others merely winged, running to hide; others mortally wounded, gasping out their last breath amidst the hellish uproar which surrounds them. And this is called "sport"![19]

Vegetarian practice allowed Lady Dixie to expiate her guilt. Far from the unhealthy dishes reported of the Vegetarian Society annual meeting by *Punch,* Lady Dixie lived on two meals a day, consisting in the morning of watermelon, banana, almonds, raisins, and dates, together with milk and egg whites, followed by pineapple with milk and egg whites in the afternoon.[20]

## HOWARD WILLIAMS

One of the members of the London Vegetarian Society was Howard Williams (1837-1931), graduate of St. John's College, Cambridge, and author of *The Ethics of Diet* (1883). It can be seen from the very positive and commendatory remarks of Williams about Newman shortly before the breach between the London and Manchester societies became final that the separation was not irrevocable. Two factors were of considerable significance in the breach: one was the desire of mighty London not to be subordinated to provincial Manchester; the second was the fear that the reforms introduced by Newman of the Manchester society would weaken the principles of the organization, especially the category of associate membership for only partial vegetarians. The new Manchester president, elected in 1884, another Professor of Latin, this time J.E.B. Mayor from Cambridge University – whom Williams also admired – was not deemed likely to tread the more radical paths desired by the younger and less staid London contingent.[21]

(The words of Williams reflect the pervasive ethical orientation of the vegetarian movement by the later nineteenth century:)

> The principles of Dietary Reform are widely and deeply founded upon the teachings of (1) Comparative Anatomy and Physiology; (2) Humaneness in the two-fold meaning of Refinement of Living and what is commonly called "Humanity"; (3) National Economy; (4) Social Reform; (5) Domestic and Individual Economy; (6) Hygienic Philosophy ... To the present writer, the humanitarian argument appears to be of double weight; for it is founded upon the irrefragable principles of Justice and Compassion – universal Justice and universal Compassion – the two principles most essential in any system of ethics worth the name. That this argument seems to have so limited an influence [in society at large] – even with persons otherwise humanely disposed, and of finer feeling with respect to their own, and also, in a general way, to other species can be attributed only to the deadening power of custom and habit, of traditional prejudice, and educational bias. If they could be brought to reflect upon the simple ethics of the question, divesting their minds of the distorting media, it must appear in a light very different from that in which they accustom themselves to consider it ...
>
> The step which leaves for ever behind it the barbarism of slaughtering our fellow beings, the Mammals and Birds, is, it is superfluous to add, the most important of all.[22]

Williams followed Shelley in the belief that "the natural form and organisation of the original types, the parent stocks of the domesticated Ox, Sheep, Swine [are] now very remote from the native grandeur and vigour of the Bison, the Mouflon, and the wild Boar."[23]

Williams's humanitarian concern for animals is expressed in the fact that he was a co-founder of the Humanitarian League with Henry Salt and a board member of the Animal Defence and Anti-Vivisection Society, instituted by one of the leading anti-vivisectionists, Louise Lind-af-Hageby.[24] Assuming Williams to be representative of the London Vegetarian Society, and to all intents and purposes he seems to have been, if Manchester and London were now taking different steps toward vegetarian goals, it is clear that the ethical principle of protection of animals from suffering was the primary mover in both organizations, even though their principles were extended well beyond the concern with suffering to encompass a whole way of life. However, some of Newman's reforms did not sit well with the London contingent. Newman, as noted, had created a category of associate membership – that is, those who were moving toward vegetarianism. In addition, Newman wanted the society to restrict itself to abstention from flesh alone, whereas the London Dietetic Reform Society, for example, also required abstention from alcohol and tobacco. Some wished to require the use of no condiments. Newman and Manchester were seen to lack the requisite purity of both spirit and practice. One important change was taking place that was of significant interest to both Manchester and London: The lower middle class was blossoming, and the age of the self-improving working man was underway – the Education Act of 1871 was having an influence. The vegetarian societies had new classes to which they could appeal. The membership claims of a half-century earlier were now able to be realized.

## THE BOOTHS, ANNIE WOOD BESANT, ANNA BONUS KINGSFORD, AND EDWARD MAITLAND

In the spirit of economy, although never connected with the Vegetarian Society, the Salvation Army's founders and leaders, William (1829-1912) and Catherine Booth (1829-1890), became vegetarians – William in principle but not in fact – and abstainers from alcohol because they saw in the former a method by which the poor could be fed and in the latter a method by which the poor might escape their precarious position. Often travelling, a factor that was deleterious to a vegetarian regimen, William Booth forsook complete vegetarian practice but not its promotion. However, his son, Bramwell Booth, became a consistent devotee. Bramwell's wife, Florence Bramwell Booth, helped to eliminate flesh from the Salvation Army's meals and supported the Humanitarian League against Cruel Sports, a successor to the Animals' Friend Society. She also denounced vivisection.

Another prominent vegetarian not connected with the Vegetarian Society was Annie Wood Besant (1847-1933), who was portrayed as Raina in Shaw's *Arms and the Man*. Besant admired Shaw not for his socialism alone but because he "preferred starving his body to starving his conscience."[25] Reputedly a great orator, a controversial social and political reformer, separated from her clergyman husband, deprived of her children by the judicial system in 1879 as a consequence of her atheism and unconventionality, advocate of birth control (then illegal), she embraced theosophy in 1889. She moved to India, founded the Central Hindu College at Benares, became president of the Theosophical Society, instituted the Indian Home Rule League, and became president of the Indian National Congress. A formidable woman! And one who was an earnest advocate for animals, embracing the transmigration of souls and castigating the sin of flesh consumption: "[Those who eat meat] are responsible for all the pain that grows out of meat-eating, and which is necessitated by the use of sentient animals as food; not only the horrors of the slaughterhouse, but also the preliminary horrors of the railway traffic, of the steamboat and ship traffic; all the starvation and the thirst and the prolonged misery of fear which these unhappy creatures have to pass through for the gratification of the appetite of man ... All pain acts as a record against humanity and slackens and retards human growth."[26]

Anna Bonus Kingsford (1846-1888), a vice president of the Vegetarian Society, as previously mentioned, was educated in Paris as a physician and, much to the consternation of her professors, was able to complete her studies successfully without having participated in vivisection. Her thesis was in effect a vegetarian manifesto. It was translated into English, by Kingsford herself, as *Perfect Way in Diet: A Treatise Advocating a Return to the Natural and Ancient Food of Our Race*. She did not, she wrote, study medicine for the benefit of humankind: "I do not love men and women. I dislike them too much to care to do them any good. They seem to me to be my natural enemies. It is not for them that I am taking up medicine and science, not to cure their ailments, but for the animals, and for knowledge generally. I want to rescue the animals from cruelty and injustice, which are for me not the only sins. And I can't love the animals and those who systematically ill-treat them."[27] If she was horrified by vivisection, she was no less inimical to flesh consumption:

No man who aims at making his life an harmonious whole, pure, complete, and harmless to others, can endure to gratify an appetite at the cost of the daily suffering and bloodshed of his inferiors in degree, and of the moral degradation of his own kind. I know not which strikes me most forcibly in the ethics of this question – the *injustice,* the *cruelty,* or the *nastiness* of flesh-eating. The injustice is to the butchers, the cruelty is to the animals, the nastiness concerns the consumer. With regard to this last in particular, I greatly wonder that persons of refinement – aye, even of decency – do not feel insulted on being offered as a matter of course, portions of corpses as food!

Such comestibles might possibly be tolerated during sieges, or other privation of proper viands in exceptional circumstances, but in the midst of a civilised community able to command a profusion of sound and delicious foods, it ought to be deemed an affront to set dead flesh before a guest.[28]

Despite her claimed lack of interest in humanity, Kingsford declared it her duty to civilization through the advocacy of vegetarianism to raise those, such as butchers and drovers, out of their moral degeneracy.

A speaker at a meeting of the Food Reform Society noted the incongruence of omnivorous habits among animal advocates and reformers of animal-welfare legislation: "It seems to me absurd to prosecute a poor uneducated donkey driver for ill treating his beast and complacently to sit down day after day to sirloin of beef and legs of mutton."[29] No doubt Kingsford would have concurred wholeheartedly, as would have her collaborator, Edward Maitland (1824-1897). With Kingsford, as with Besant, Williams, Newman, and the like, we hear a thoroughly modern voice. Edward Maitland was equally convinced that humans ate meat in defiance of their nature and their morality, even if his voice was in a little more antiquated mode than that of some of his fellows:

> We hold that neither by his physical nor his moral constitution does man belong to the order of the carnivora or of the omnivora, but is purely frugivorous; and in this we have the assent of all competent physiologists ... Hence we consider that in accepting the conditions of Nature as our guide, we do act but rationally. Adding to reason, experience, we have on our side, first the profoundest wisdom of all ages and countries from the remotest antiquity – the wisdom, namely, of all those really radical reformers, of whom a Trismegius, a Pythagoras, and a Buddha are typical examples, whose aim it has been to reform, not institutions merely, but men themselves, and whose first steps toward the perfectionment of their disciples was to insist on a total renunciation of flesh as food, on the ground that neither physically, intellectually, morally, nor spiritually can man be the best that it is in him to be save when nourished by the purest substances, taken at first hand from Nature, and undeteriorated by passage through organisms, and eschewing violence and bloodshed as a means of sustenance or gratification.[30]

Reading Maitland is almost like reading a representative of the mid-eighteenth rather than the late nineteenth century, but it is a matter more of style and tone than of substance that differentiates a Maitland from a Kingsford.

## HENRY SALT

An outstanding classics scholar at King's College, Cambridge, Henry Stephens Shakespear Salt (1851-1939) went on to teach at Eton – "cannibals in cap and gown," he termed his colleagues – until he met with disfavour for his advocacy not merely of the poetry and prose of Percy Bysshe Shelley but also of "Shelleyism," a doctrine that, for Salt, included his protosocialist anarchism as much as his vegetarianism.[31] Three years earlier, fellow socialist, vegetarian, and Eton teacher J.L. Joynes was also made unwelcome at Eton for publishing a book in which he confessed to having been arrested, unjustifiably, in Ireland as a suspected revolutionary Fenian. The headmaster of Eton, Dr. Warre, attributed his resignation to a subversive amalgam of socialism and *légumes*. Salt was closely connected with Joynes, having married his sister, Kate, in 1879.

Salt retired voluntarily from Eton in 1885 to a life of simplicity in Surrey, where he wrote some forty books, twelve of which were on animal rights and vegetarianism, the most memorable being *Seventy Years among Savages* (1921). The savages were his fellow Europeans. He also wrote *A Plea for Vegetarianism* (1886), which, along with Shelley's first vegetarian essay, was instrumental in persuading Gandhi to become an ethical rather than a cultural vegetarian, and his pièce de résistance, *Animals' Rights Considered in Relation to Social Progress* (1892). Gandhi acknowledged, in a talk he gave to the Vegetarian Society, at which Salt was present, that "it was Mr Salt's book, *A Plea for Vegetarianism,* which showed me why, apart from a hereditary habit, and apart from my adherence to a vow administered to me by my mother, it was right to be a vegetarian. He showed me why it was a moral duty incumbent on vegetarians not to live upon fellow-animals."[32] Gandhi was of Vaishnava caste from Gujarat, and on returning to India was accused by fellow Hindus of trying to impose Western ethical norms on traditional Hindu vegetarian lore.

Salt's arguments for vegetarianism were those that have been rehearsed frequently in these pages, but he parades them always with a novel banner. What distinguishes Salt *inter alia* from so many others is his eloquence. In *Seventy Years among Savages,* he displays his attitude toward harming any other being, whether for food or otherwise: "All sentient life is akin ... he who injures a fellow being is doing injury to himself." This is a fact of which he reminds his readers in verse:

The motive that you'll find most strong,
The simple rule, the short and long,
For doing animals no wrong.
Is this, *that you are one.*[33]

In *The Logic of Vegetarianism* (1899) he comments:

Behind the mere name of the reformed diet, whatever name be employed (and, as we have seen, "vegetarian" at present holds the field), lies the far more important reality. What is the *raison d'être,* the real purport of vegetarianism? Certainly not any *a priori* assumption, that all animal substances, as such, are unfit for human food; for though it is quite probable that the movement will ultimately lead us to the disuse of animal products, vegetarianism is not based on any such hard and fast formula, but on the conviction, suggested in the first place by instinctive feeling, but confirmed by reason and experience, that there are certain grave evils inseparable from the practice of flesh-eating. The aversion to flesh food is not chemical, but moral, social, hygienic. Believing as we do that the grosser forms of diet not only cause a vast amount of unnecessary suffering to the animals, but also react most injuriously on the health and morals of mankind, we advocate their gradual discontinuance: and so long as this protest is successfully launched, the mere name by which it is called is a matter of minor concern. But here on this practical issue, as before on the nominal issue, we come into conflict with the superior person who, with a smile of supercilious compassion, cannot see *why* we poor ascetics should thus afflict ourselves without cause.

Thereafter occurs a conversation between the so-called superior person and a vegetarian that covers the distinctions between eating egg and eating roast beef and between eating nonhuman animals and cannibalism, as well as the appreciation of "the superior person" for the consistency of what we would now call a vegan, but rather less for the inconsistency of the customary vegetarian, culminating in the assumption by the superior person that the reasons for vegetarianism are ascetic. Salt proceeds to debunk the idea that has played a prominent role in vegetarianism in previous centuries, especially the Middle Ages:

Asceticism! Such is the strange idea with which, in many minds, our principles are associated. It would be impossible to take a more erroneous view of modern vegetarianism; and it is only through constitutional or deliberate blindness that such a misconception can arise. How can we convey to our flesh-eating friends, in polite yet sufficiently forcible language, that their diet is an abomination to us, and that our "abstinence," far from being ascetic, is much more nearly allied to the joy that never palls? Is the farmer an ascetic because looking over into his evil-smelling pigsty, he has no inclination to swill himself from the same trough as the swine? And why, then, should it be counted asceticism on our part to refuse, on precisely the same grounds, to eat the swine themselves? No; our opponents must clearly recognize, if they wish to form any correct notion of vegetarianism, that it is based, not on asceticism, but aestheticism, not on the mortification, but the gratification of the higher pleasures.

We conclude, then, that the cause which vegetarians have at heart is the outcome, not of some barren academic formula, but out of practical reasoned conviction that flesh food, especially butcher's meat, is a harmful and barbarous diet ... The *raison d'être* of vegetarianism is the growing sense that flesh-eating is a cruel, disgusting, unwholesome, and wasteful practice, and that it behoves humane and rational persons, disregarding the common cant about "consistency" and "all or nothing," to reform their diet to what extent and with what speed they can.[34]

Increasingly, even the "superior persons" came to realize that modern vegetarianism customarily grows out of the horror of slaughtering innocent animals for human consumption rather than out of any desire for self-denial in and for itself. Moreover, Salt is concerned to express, in line with Newman's preferences for the Vegetarian Society in Manchester, the increasingly modern view that vegetarianism can involve a process toward a goal. During the *fin de siècle* years, "aestheticism" was the new watchword. According to Oscar Wilde, the informal leader of the aesthetic movement, aestheticism implied a world that was "judged by the beauty of its artifice rather than by its moral value." For a man like Salt, aestheticism existed within the realm of the moral.

## EDWARD CARPENTER

Born into an upper-middle-class family in Brighton, East Sussex, Edward Carpenter (1844-1929) attended Cambridge University and took holy orders in 1869. In 1874 he renounced both orthodox religion and civilized society. In their place he proposed a simple, primitive way of life that he sketched in the delightfully entitled *Civilisation: Its Cause and Cure,* which went through seventeen editions between 1889 and 1921. Indeed, Carpenter, known as the "Noble Savage," a second Rousseau but far more consistent in his abstinence from flesh, became a minor cult figure with a primitivist coterie of followers. But he also had his detractors. This "celebrated apostle of sandals," as Michael Holroyd called him, was thought by George Bernard Shaw to be far from a "Noble Savage." Instead, he was described by Shaw as "an ultra-civilized impostor."[35] But then Shaw was riled that Salt's wife, Kate, showed a decided preference for Carpenter over himself.

The essence of Carpenter's Rousseauian argument lay in the advocacy of living a rural, vegetarian lifestyle in which we would learn to live slowly and simply, in accord with our natural animal being, as do other animals. In *Civilisation: Its Cause and Cure,* one of several books he wrote, Carpenter shows how the life of nonhuman animals is superior to that of humans, and he advocates a vegetarian diet with inclinations toward a quasi-fruitarian regimen:

> It may be noted, too, that food of the seed kind – by which I mean all manner of fruits, nuts, tubers, grains, eggs etc. (and I may include milk in its various forms of butter, cheese, curds, and so forth), not only contain by their nature the elements of life in their most condensed forms, but have the additional advantage that they can be appropriated without injury to any living creature – for even the cabbage may inaudibly scream when torn up by the roots and boiled, but the strawberry plant *asks* us to take of its fruit, and paints it red expressly that we may see and devour it![36]

Carpenter seems to believe that modern civilization is an intermediate stage, perhaps a necessary one, between the Golden Age of the past and a perhaps even significantly grander Golden Age of a not too distant future. His is as much a millenarian dream as those of the *philosophes* during the Enlightenment:

> And when the Civilisation period has passed away, the old Nature-religion – perhaps greatly grown – will come back. The immense stream of religious life which beginning far beyond the horizon of earliest history has been deflected into metaphysical and other channels – of Judaism, Christianity, Buddhism, and the like – during the historical period, will once more gather itself together to float on its bosom with all the arks and sacred vessels of human progress. Man will once more *feel* his unity with the animals, with the mountains and the streams, with the earth itself and the slow lapse of the constellation, not as an abstract dogma of Science and Theology, but as a living and ever-present fact.[37]

The primitivist radicalism of the Carpenter kind has been both beneficial and detrimental to vegetarianism: beneficial in that it added a novel and persuasive dimension to the vegetarian cause; and detrimental in that it gave sustenance to the view of the vegetarian as a strange, unkempt, sandle-clad breed beyond the pale of normal society.

The notion of the sentience of vegetables raised by Carpenter was also addressed by Samuel Butler in his utopian novel *Erewhon* (1872), Butler reaching very different conclusions from Carpenter. In successive chapters on the rights of animals and the rights of vegetables, Butler explains that the Erewhonians had tried vegetarianism, but as the arguments for vegetarianism could be applied equally to plants, they argued, they resumed flesh eating. Moreover, Butler adds a friendly warning to vegetarians: "Those ... who preached to them about the enormity of eating meat, were an unattractive academic folk, and though they overawed all but the bolder youths, there were few who did not in their hearts dislike them."[38] Perhaps today's vegetarians are a little fortunate that many of today's "unattractive academic folk" seem concerned more with ecology than with justice for animals.

## George Bernard Shaw and Leo Tolstoy

Apart from some significant but generally considered second-rank figures in cultural history – such as Francis William Newman, William Bramwell, and Catherine Booth; Henry Salt, Edward Carpenter, and Howard Williams; Annie Wood Besant and the theosophists; and Anna Bonus Kingsford and Edward Maitland – the second half of the nineteenth century produced two vegetarians of the highest literary rank and public presence: George Bernard Shaw (1856-1950) and Leo Tolstoy (1828-1910). It is astonishing, and a reflection of the deeply entrenched nature of flesh eating in the human consciousness, that they did not have significantly greater influence than their prominence would have warranted.

George Bernard Shaw's interest in animal ethics ranged from vegetarianism to vivisection – on which much of his attention was focused – to the wearing of fur and feathers, and to evolution. "Creative Evolution," he called it, which was quite distinct from Darwinian natural selection, which he castigated as "no selection at all, but mere dead accident and luck."[39] The most popular of all anglophone dramatists – the sole exception being Shakespeare – Shaw described himself as "a vegetarian on purely humanitarian and mystical grounds" who had "never killed a flea or a mouse vindictively or without remorse."[40] It was Shelley's *The Revolt of Islam* (1818) that persuaded him of the virtue of both socialism and vegetarianism: "I was a cannibal for twenty-five years. For the rest I have been a vegetarian. It was Shelley who first opened my eyes to the savagery of my diet," recording "Never again may blood of bird or beast / Stain with its venomous stream a human feast."[41] At the age of twenty-five he became a vegetarian, and at the age of twenty-eight he declared wryly: "I am a species of savage and cannot be entertained like a civilized man. In short, I am a vegetarian."[42] With tongue still in cheek, he observed: "My objection to meat is that it costs too much and involves the slavery of men and women to edible animals that is undesirable."[43] When invited out, he told his hosts: "Do not kill anything for me. I simply won't eat it."[44] From the beef and mutton dining habit, whose "reek of the slaughterhouse ... convicted us all of being beasts of prey, I fled to the purer air of the vegetarian restaurant."[45] He listed nine inexpensive vegetarian restaurants worth frequenting that had recently opened in London, adding:

> To-day people are brought up to believe that they cannot live without eating meat, and associate the lack of it with poverty. Henry Salt, a champion vegetarian, said that what was needed in London were vegetarian restaurants so expensive that only the very rich could afford to dine in them habitually, and people of moderate means only once a year, as a very special treat, as in Paris, where British tourists brag of having dined at So and So's with a European reputation for high prices and exquisite cookery.
>
> What you have to rub in is that it is never cheap to live otherwise than as everybody else does; and that the so-called simple life is beyond the means of the poor.[46]

Apple, cheese, macaroni, and salad with milk and soda was a typical meal for Shaw and his guest when dining at The Queen's Restaurant in Sloane Square.

On one occasion, recuperating from illness, he returned to flesh for a short while, whereafter his illnesses were often attributed by the ill-will of others to his vegetarian diet, whereas he claimed his good health to be attributable to his vegetarian diet. However much he was chided by his friends, never again did he willingly eat flesh. In his nineties he lived mainly from soups, eggs, milk, honey, cheese, fruits, cream, biscuits, and lemon juice – together with sugar spooned furtively from the bowl and large slices of iced cake or chocolate when no one was supposed to be looking.[47]

He described his literary "pastime as writing sermons in plays, sermons preaching what Salt practised."[48] In fact, Shaw's "sermons" are to be found rather less in the plays themselves than in their extraordinary prefaces, which are often wordier than the plays. Still, they are not absent from the plays. In the *Devil's Disciple* (1897) we learn: "The worst sin toward animals is not to hate them, but to be indifferent to them. That's the essence of inhumanity." In *The Admirable Bashville* (1901) Shaw castigated both vivisection ("Groping for cures in the tormented entrails / Of friendly dogs") and the wearing of animal products ("Oh, your ladies / seal skinned and egret feathered; all defiance / to Nature"). Flesh eating, he observed, was "cannibalism with the heroic dish omitted."[49] In *Back to Methuselah* (1922) Shaw shows his ironic and sarcastic contempt for those who claim flesh eating a prerequisite of strength, courage, and valour. One of Adam's sons, he says, "invented meat-eating. The other was horrified at the innovation." Franklyn Barnabas summed up what followed as: "With the ferocity which is still characteristic of bulls and other vegetarians, he slew his beefsteak-eating brother, and thus invented murder. That was a very steep step. It was so exciting that all the others began to kill one another for sport, and thus invented war, the steepest step of all. They even took to killing animals as a means of killing time, and then, of course ate them to save the long and difficult labor of agriculture."[50]

Shaw was convinced of the value of the alcohol-free and vegetarian diet to a well-functioning body. For a while, he was an avid cyclist, which complemented his idea of his vegetarian fitness. Following a rather nasty cycling mishap, he observed: "I am not thoroughly convinced yet that I was not killed. Anyone but a vegetarian would have been. Nobody but a teetotaller would have faced a bicycle again for six months."[51]

So little was vegetarianism generally accepted as a viable alternative to flesh eating during Shaw's lifetime that popular commentators claimed it was only the secret consumption of liver that kept him alive.[52] The prevailing view was that it was simply not possible to live without flesh. It was odd that, much as the literary Shaw was revered, he remained ineffective in persuading more than a few to follow the vegetarian banner. The same remains true today. A Shaw Festival is held annually at Niagara-on-the-Lake, Ontario. His plays, and those of a few others, can be seen from late March or early April to November. They are viewed not merely by many thousands of visitors from elsewhere in Canada but also by many from the United States, by some from Japan, and by a few from Europe. Very few of the playgoers are aware that Shaw was a vegetarian. The festival's organizers do nothing at all to commemorate – or even recognize – the fact. And the restaurants in Niagara-on-the-Lake have very few, if any, vegetarian options. They are less vegetarian-friendly than restaurants in general. Indeed, upon my asking restaurateurs and servers in Niagara-on-the-Lake whether they were aware of Shaw's vegetarianism, not one responded in the affirmative.

The continued difficulty vegetarians face is perhaps exemplified by H.G. Wells in *Anna Veronica* (1909), where he caricatures and pillories "the Higher Thought, the Simple Life, Socialism, Humanitarianism" and counts vegetarianism among them.[53] As Hilda Kean reports of *Anna Veronica*:

"Miss Minerva, who lives on movements and fourpence a day, and her friend the Groopes are ridiculed for their diet of fruitarian refreshments of chestnut sandwiches buttered with nutter, accompanied by lemonade and unfermented wine."[54] Resurrected here is the image of the esoteric, "little old lady" vegetarian who has nothing better to do and is not to be taken too seriously. Even Shaw's commitment was not always taken with the earnestness with which it was felt. That vegetarianism was not acknowledged by some as an altogether serious and worthy ethical commitment is exemplified in the treatment of Shaw by the otherwise laudable William Morris. Morris and Shaw often dined together at a London vegetarian restaurant, even though Morris was not a vegetarian. So Morris would have known the depth of Shaw's commitment. Yet the Morrises chided Shaw for his diet, and on one occasion, while dining at the Morrises, Shaw was clandestinely but intentionally given suet to eat. After he had eaten it, Janey Morris said: "That will do you good, there is suet in it."[55] Suet is the hard white fat on the kidneys and loins of cattle, sheep, and other mammals. It does not seem to have crossed the Morrises' minds that, for Shaw, to consume such food would have constituted a serious breach of ethical principle. Shaw's reaction is unknown but can be readily imagined.

Leo Tolstoy, one of the world's great novelists, wrote such masterpieces as *The Cossacks* (1863), *War and Peace* (1865-69), and *Anna Karenina* (1875-77). Although Tolstoy's sensibilities to animals were not absent from his novels, they are far more pronounced in his later primitive Christian writings, after he had become a vegetarian fairly late in life. According to one of his biographers, William Shirer, he gave up "hunting, smoking and drinking and, in time, he became a vegetarian."[56] Vegetarianism seems to have been the most difficult virtue to acquire. In the end, he was as opposed to vivisection as he had become to flesh eating. In a letter of July 1909 he wrote: "What I think of vivisection is that if people admit that they have the right to take or endanger the life of living beings for the benefit of many, there will be no limit to their cruelty."[57] Tolstoy's primary vegetarian statement is in "The First Step" (1892), written as an introduction to a Russian edition of Howard Williams's *The Ethics of Diet:*

> I had wished to visit a slaughter-house in order to see with my own eyes the reality of the question raised when vegetarianism is discussed. But at first I felt ashamed to do so, as one is always ashamed of going to look at suffering which one knows is about to take place but which one cannot avert; and so I kept putting off my visit.
>
> But a little while ago I met on the road a butcher returning to Túla

after a visit to his home. He is not yet an experienced butcher and his duty is to stab with a knife. I asked him whether he did not feel sorry for the animals that he killed. He gave me the usual answer: "Why should I feel sorry? It is necessary." But when I told him that eating flesh is not necessary but only a luxury, he agreed; and then he admitted he was sorry for the animals. "But what can I do?" he said, "I must earn my bread. At first I was *afraid* to kill. My father, he has never even killed a chicken in all his life." The majority of Russians cannot kill; they feel pity, and express the feeling by the word "*fear.*" This man had been afraid but he was no longer ...

Not long ago I also had a talk with a retired soldier, a butcher, and he too was surprised at my assertion that it was a pity to kill, and said the usual thing about it being ordained. But afterwards he agreed with me: "Especially when they are quiet, tame cattle. They come, poor things! trusting you. It is very pitiful."

Once when walking from Moscow, I was offered a lift by some carters who were going from Sérpoukhov to a neighbouring forest to fetch wood. It was the Thursday before Easter. I was seated in the first cart with a strong, red, coarse carman, who evidently drank. On entering the village we saw a well-fed, naked, pink pig being dragged out of the first yard to be slaughtered. It squealed in a dreadful voice, resembling the shrieking of a man. Just as we were passing they began to kill it. A man gashed its throat with a knife. The pig squealed still more loudly and piercingly, broke away from the men, and ran off covered with blood. Being nearsighted I did not see all the details and watched closely. They caught the pig, knocked it down, and finished cutting its throat. When its squeals ceased the carter sighed heavily. "Do men not really have to answer for such things?" he said.

So strong is man's aversion to all killing. But by example, by encouraging greediness, by the assertion that God has allowed it, and above all by habit, people entirely lose this natural feeling.

On Friday I decided to go to Túla, and, meeting a meek, kind acquaintance of mine, I invited him to accompany me.

"Yes, I have heard the arrangements are good, and have been waiting to go to see it; but if they are slaughtering I will not go in."

"Why not? That's just what I want to see! If we eat flesh it must be killed."

"No, no, I cannot."

It is worth remembering that this man is a sportsman and himself kills animals and birds.[58]

Tolstoy then describes the conditions of the abattoir in gruesome and distressing detail, before concluding:

> But why, if the wrongfulness – i.e., the immorality – of animal food was known to humanity so long ago, have people not yet come to acknowledge this [moral] law? will be asked by those who are accustomed to be led by public opinion rather than by reason.
>
> The answer to this question is that the moral progress of humanity – which is the foundation of every other kind of progress – is always slow; but that the sign of true, not casual, progress is its uninterruptedness and its continual acceleration.[59]

This slaughterhouse statement from Tolstoy speaks loudly to me. As confirmed flesh eaters some sixteen years ago, my co-author and I stated in *Animal Welfare and Human Values:* "We know from respected colleagues of the unbridled terror of the slaughterhouse and we know, and we are told, we must go to see for ourselves. But we won't. We simply don't have the stomach for it."[60] By the time the book was published, we were vegetarians. Had we visited a slaughterhouse we would probably have been vegetarians many years before seeing a documentary on stockyard "downers" persuaded us to take the step that in our hearts we knew we should have taken long before. It now pains me, puzzles me, and shames me to think that dedicated animal protectionists, myself included – to repeat Oliver Goldsmith again – could continue to eat the objects of their compassion. But such is the paradoxical nature of humankind.

# 12

# Vegetarians and Vegans in the Twentieth Century

The early decades of the twentieth century were a period of decline for vegetarianism in general and for the Vegetarian Society in particular, perhaps best symbolized by the fact that shortly after the October Revolution in 1917 Russia, the vegetarian movement was declared illegal and dozens of vegetarian restaurants and several vegetarian societies were compelled to close their doors, although in the 1930s George Bernard Shaw's wife, Charlotte, was under the impression that "there are plenty of vegetarian restaurants in Moscow."[1] Of course, nowhere else at that time was there proscription, but there was retrenchment. The late-Victorian gains that had been made in Britain, especially among the less affluent, were being eroded as working-class and petit-bourgeois living standards declined. And the First World War made the prospects of the fleshless diet even dimmer. Labourers who had volunteered or had been conscripted for the armed forces found they enjoyed the "luxury" of the unhealthy army regimen with, for them, copious amounts of flesh they had been unable to afford as civilians and without which they would have been unable to survive on the otherwise meagre military rations. Young women at home on a far leaner diet had no desire to abstain but wished to obtain a modicum of what the men at the front were given. And the overarching approach of the Victorian era disintegrated as new and specialist organizations came into existence, although members of the Vegetarian Society and the former Humanitarian League could now be found in co-operation in, for example, the League for the Prohibition of Cruel Sports.

After the war several private schools – some Quaker establishments, for example – adopted a fleshless diet with the earnest, if utopian, aspiration of abolishing conflict, war, and bloodshed. But, of course, such private schools were beyond the reach and pocket of the poorer classes. Moreover, however well-intentioned, they were also unrealistic in their goals. Vegetarian restaurants retained the appeal they had acquired in the last quarter of the nineteenth century, but they were frequented far more by those who wanted a pleasant, inexpensive alternative to their regular fare rather than a moral or even dietary commitment. However, the perceived nutritional value of fruit and vegetables was on the rise, and a few were tempted by raw food diets but primarily out of a concern for health and economy, not a serious concern for the animals. Raw food was, of course, an aspect of the return-to-nature movement that had early beginnings, had never died out entirely, and was now enjoying a period of renewed popularity.[2]

## ROMAIN ROLLAND AND ALBERT SCHWEITZER

Intellectual vegetarian advocacy was not in quite the same doldrums as the vegetarian movement. In France, Romain Rolland (1866-1944), the popular pacifist, novelist, playwright, and biographer of both Tolstoy and Gandhi, used his novel *Jean-Christophe,* which won Rolland the 1915 Nobel Prize for Literature, to state the case for animals. It was a study of contemporary French and German civilization through the life of a German-born musician who

> could not think of the animals without shuddering in anguish. He looked into the eyes of the beasts and saw there a soul like his own, a soul which could not speak: but the eyes cried for it:
> "What have I done to you? Why do you hurt me?"
> He could not bear to see the most ordinary sights that he had seen hundreds of times – a calf crying in a wicker pen, with its big protruding eyes, with their bluish whites and pink lids, and white lashes, its curly white tufts on its forehead, its purple snout, its knock-kneed legs: – a lamb being carried by a peasant with its four legs tied together, hanging head down, trying to hold its head up, moaning like a child, bleating and lolling its gray tongue: – fowls huddled together in a basket: the distant squeals of a pig being bled to death: – a fish being cleaned on the kitchen-table ... The nameless tortures which men inflict on such innocent creatures made his heart ache. Grant animals a ray of reason, imagine what a frightful nightmare the world is to them: a dream of cold-blooded men, blind and deaf, cutting their throats,

slitting them open, gutting them, cutting them into pieces, cooking them alive, sometimes laughing at them as they writhe in agony ... To a man whose mind is free there is something even more intolerable in the sufferings of animals than in the sufferings of men. For with the latter it is at least admitted that suffering is evil and that the man who causes it is a criminal. But thousands of animals are uselessly butchered every day without a shadow of remorse. If any man were to refer to it, he would be thought ridiculous. – And that is the unpardonable crime ... If God is good only to the strong, if there is no justice for the week and lowly, for the poor creatures who are offered up as a sacrifice to humanity, then there is no such thing as goodness, no such thing as justice.[3]

It is doubtful anyone has portrayed the psychology of an ethical vegetarian along with the psychology of the food animals with greater insight and pathos.

Of equal empathy with the animals, and winner of the 1952 Nobel Prize for Peace, was Albert Schweitzer (1875-1965). Born in Alsace, he became a medical missionary, establishing a field hospital in 1913 at Lambaréné, Gabon, then French Equatorial Africa, where he remained, apart from frequent European fundraising trips and one visit to the United States, for the remainder of his working life. An authority on Bach and organ music, he developed a Christian ethic he called "reverence for life." Already as a child he had great fellow-feeling with animals. Recalling one childhood memory, he exclaimed: "One thing that especially saddened me was that the unfortunate animals had to suffer so much pain and misery. The sight of an old limping horse, tugged forward by one man while another kept beating it with a stick to get it to the knacker's yard at Colmar [in Alsace], haunted me for weeks."[4] At night he prayed silently: "O, heavenly Father, protect and bless all things that have breath; guard them from all evil, and let them sleep in peace."[5] As an adult, he developed the theme of "reverence for life" in three major works: *The Decay and Restoration of Civilization, Civilization and Ethics,* and *Reverence for Life.* It is in *Civilization and Ethics* that he developed the idea of reverence for life with respect to animals most fully, arguing that such an ethic would reconcile the drives of altruism and egotism by requiring a respect for all other beings and by requiring simultaneously the development of the individual's resources. There he tells us:

Ethics ... consists in this, that I experience the necessity of practising the same reverence for life toward all [who possess] the will-to-live, as toward my own [life]. Therein I have already the needed fundamental principle of morality. It is *good* to maintain and cherish life; it is *evil* to destroy and to check life ... A man is really ethical only when he obeys the constraint laid on him to help all life which he is able to succor, and when he goes out of his way to avoid injuring anything living. He does not ask how far this or that life deserves sympathy as valuable in itself, nor how far it is capable of feeling. To him life as such is sacred.[6]

The maintenance of such an ethic, Schweitzer realizes, is difficult, but necessary, for the progress of civilization and justice. Indeed, if we take Schweitzer's position in the strict sense, as referring to all life rather than just to animal life, the doctrine requires one to be a fruitarian. Since plants also have life, it is necessary, if one is not to starve, to live from the fruit of the plant in such a manner that the host plant itself does not die. But Schweitzer did not intend his doctrine to be so interpreted, for he made it clear that his reference to life is to that which possesses the will to live. He states that the person who holds reverence for life principles

is not afraid of being laughed at as sentimental. It is indeed the fate of every truth to be an object of ridicule when it is first acclaimed. It was once considered foolish to suppose that colored men were really human beings and ought to be treated as such. What was once foolishness has now become a recognized truth. Today it is considered an exaggeration to claim constant respect for every form of life as being the serious demand of a rational ethic. But the time is coming when people will be amazed that the human race was so long before it recognized that thoughtless injury to life is incompatible with real ethics. Ethics is in its unqualified form extended responsibility to everything that has life.[7]

## GANDHI

After his awakening to the justice of vegetarianism, primarily by his reading of Henry Salt, Gandhi devoted himself to the vegetarian ideal with a similar dedication to that which he brought to the other causes he espoused. Mohandas Karamchand (Mahatma) Gandhi (1869-1948) was educated as a barrister and promoted political change through *satyagraha*, literally "holding to the truth," but generally understood as civil disobedience. He led India toward independence from Britain, promoting a primitivist message, symbolized by the spinning wheel *(charkha)* rather than by industrialization. In the later 1920s he gave a talk to the London Vegetarian Society in which the primitivist return-to-nature message was repeated but with an emphasis on animal ethics:

What I want to bring to your notice is that vegetarians need to be tolerant if they want to convert others to vegetarianism. Adopt a little humility. We should appeal to the moral sense of the people who do not see eye to eye with us. If a vegetarian became ill, and a doctor prescribed beef-tea, then I would not call him a vegetarian [if he followed the doctor's advice]. A vegetarian is made of sterner stuff. Why? Because it is for the building of the spirit and not of the body. Man is more than meat. It is the spirit in man for which we are concerned. Therefore vegetarians should have that moral basis – that a man was not born a carnivorous animal, but born to live on the fruits and herbs that the earth grows. I know we must all err. I would give up milk if I could but I cannot. I have made that experiment times without number. I could not after a serious illness, regain my strength unless I went back to milk. That has been the tragedy of my life. But the basis of my vegetarianism is not physical, but moral. If anybody said that I should die if I did not take beef-tea or mutton, even under medical advice, I would prefer death. That is the basis of my vegetarianism.[8]

And if that sounds somewhat extreme, the omnivores need only ask themselves how they would feel and behave if asked to eat human flesh. The difference between the ethical vegetarian and the omnivore is that, by and large, the vegetarian considers humans as animal *in the same way* that other animals are animal. The omnivore recognizes humans as animal but imagines them subject to a very different ethic than that which ought to govern humans. For the omnivore, humans are animals who escape all the negative ethical implications of being animal by being different in some special way.

## ADOLF HITLER AND NAZISM

Historically, as we have seen throughout this book, vegetarianism has frequently been associated with primitivism – that is, the return-to-nature ideas that predominated among those who believed humans were vegetarian in origin. Even Nazism, which came to power in 1933, represented a version of the primitivist movement, at least some of the time, although never consistently, a version evidenced in many of the medieval spectacles at the Nuremberg rallies. And it has frequently been suggested that Hitler was a vegetarian.[9] Indeed, taking the socialism in the "Nazi" name – from National Social Democratic Party – at its face value, both Gandhi and Shaw expressed an early sympathy for the beneficial potential in Hitler's regime.

Certainly, Hitler boasted frequently of his abstention from flesh, sometimes even presenting himself as a raw-food advocate. There would appear to have been periods when Hitler, and a number of his senior henchmen, promoted with pride their vegetarian predilections. At other times, it was less prominent or simply disregarded. In his *Animals in the Third Reich*, Boria Sax postulates that one "possible explanation [of the vegetarianism of the Nazi leaders] is that the leading Nazis used abstinence from meat to signify their elite status. Throughout most of history only elites could readily afford to eat meat on a regular basis. Many Christians, Buddhists and Hindus have refrained from eating meat to signify their regard for but also their elevation above animal life."[10] It is notable that in Hitler's *Mein Kampf* (My Struggle) of 1926 and in *H.J. Marschiert: Das neue Hitler-Jugend-Buch* (Hitler Youth on the March: The New Book for the Hitler Youth), full of advice on attitudes and behaviour appropriate for the new Germans and published within a year of the meteoric Nazi rise to power, there is not a word of vegetarian advocacy.[11] If vegetarianism was appropriate for the Nazi leadership, it was not recommended to the masses. Whatever the reasons, Third Reich animal orientation is nonetheless suggested both by the pronouncements on treating animals with respect and by the fact the Nazis had an aversion to animal experimentation – although ultimately they only hindered it rather than prevented it – and they had something approximating a policy of environmental awareness. They proved more successful in influencing their weaker neighbours with regard to opposition to animal experimentation, especially Liechtenstein in the mid-1930s.

But probably, for Hitler, vegetarianism was far more boast and aspiration than reality. Hitler revered the music (and the racism) of Richard Wagner, who also had vegetarian ambitions, but seemingly he was ultimately no more successful than his mentor in fully achieving them. Not only did the Nazis outlaw and persecute Germany's vegetarian societies, but several of Hitler's biographers and chefs have referred to Hitler's consistent deviation from vegetarianism in his liking for sausage meats. One former chef mentioned his favourite meal as stuffed squab. In 1945 Symon Gould of the *American Vegetarian* derided the vegetarian who was so solely on health grounds: "Like Hitler, he sneaks a pig's knuckle every time he feels better."[12] To the extent that Hitler desired to be a vegetarian, it would appear to be primarily on ascetic or perhaps aesthetic grounds rather than there being serious and consistent ethical dimensions. Unfortunately, discussions of Hitler's purported vegetarianism are often coloured by the fact that many antivegetarians are predisposed to find a vegetarian Hitler, while many vegetarians are loath to find a loathsome man professing a loathsome ideology counted among their number. Perhaps a little less heat might shed a little more light. Currently, hostile attitudes to Hitlerism, rather than objective interpretation of the evidence, play a decisive role in determining the outcome of the debate. With less ideologically oriented investigation, a measure of truth might be found. As it is, it is clear that Hitler's professed vegetarianism was a far from consistent practice but something of a Nazi leadership ideal nonetheless.

## Between the World Wars

In the period between the two world conflicts, vegetarianism continued to suffer, now in part from its association with conscientious objection in the First World War. The COs (conscientious objectors), whether pacifist, religious, or vegetarian, or all three, were still treated with disdain and without understanding or sympathy by the general public. Much of the vegetarianism there was, and there was a fair amount, was not ethical vegetarianism in that the vegetarian concern arose primarily from grounds other than the elimination of animal suffering: among those prescribing a fleshless diet were the Order of the Cross (a pacifist and vegetarian informal Christian fellowship founded by Rev. John Todd Ferrier in 1904), Mazdaznanism (an offshoot of Zoroastrianism with hints of Buddhism), Seventh Day Adventists, and Quakers – the last of which approximated the ethical ideal more than the others. The ascetic vegetarians were concerned instead with the purity of their souls. The secular vegetarians, even among those of religious bent, thought it a part of their moral duty to pursue justice for animals. The English vegetarian societies continued to exist, most visibly in the weekly meetings of the cycling brotherhood, although the societies did not flourish as they had at the turn of the century. They showed their sympathy with the miners during the Jarrow-inspired general strike of 1926, sending food parcels to the marchers. There were a few vegetarian Members of Parliament but no palpable vegetarian successes. By and large, the terrors of the wars and the humility of the Great Depression turned attention away from animal suffering and toward human suffering. Human suffering had always held prominence. Now, it was almost entirely exclusive. The agenda had many priorities ahead of the animals: class justice, gender suffrage, antifascist organization, economic and social reform. Precisely those most likely to support the animal causes usually found a human cause about which they could feel far more strongly.

When there are burning questions of human injustice to humans – and there always seem to be – it is very difficult to divert the attention of the morally outraged from human issues, often leading to the common jibe against animal advocates: "why concern yourself with lesser animal problems when there is so much human suffering in the world requiring our undivided attention?" The retort of the animal advocate is that justice is not divisible, animal issues are just one of the issues of injustice that must be addressed. To ignore any one grievous injustice is to leave the whole tarnished. Indeed, it is precisely when one looks to the animal advocate that one is likely to see a person embroiled in many ethical issues, nonhuman animal, human, and environmental alike. And how arrogantly presumptuous, the vegetarian opines, to imagine human suffering to be ipso facto of a higher order than animal suffering!

In and after the Second World War, food rationing in Britain meant that everyone was deprived equally of flesh – at least everyone without significant social and economic influence! Meat in very small quantities was allowed by the rationing formula but was very scarce and very hard to acquire. The result was not that people accustomed themselves to a vegetarian diet but instead that they yearned longingly for the day when once again flesh would be readily available. Even horse and whale flesh were not to be despised, although, in fact, whale flesh in particular, Spam second, came to be abominated as the symbol of the years of deprivation. Moreover, as flesh slowly became once more available, status was very largely invested in the quantity of flesh, how often it could be obtained, and its quality. The government tried to persuade the population to turn to vegetables, but that very fact made vegetables less palatable.

## DONALD WATSON, ELSIE SHRIGLEY, AND THE VEGAN SOCIETY

There was during the war years one event of monumental significance for the vegetarian movement. In November 1944, in the city of Leicester in the English midlands, the Vegan Society found its origins in the concerns of Donald Watson and Elsie Shrigley (d. 1978). Watson was a conscientious objector and woodwork teacher, who had ceased to eat flesh at the age of fifteen and who died at the age of ninety-five in 2005. The organization's head office is now at St. Leonard's on Sea in East Sussex. If the vegetarian diet was essential to a cruelty-free way of life, veganism was the path to even greater elimination of animal suffering. For the vegans, it was not only important to abstain from flesh but equally vital that chickens and cows should be spared the cruelties of egg, milk, butter, and cheese production and that all animals be spared being killed for their hides, pelts, or skins and being mistreated for their wool. For some vegans no animal produce was to be worn or eaten; no animal was to be exploited for human benefit. In December 1943 Watson gave a talk on vegetarianism and dairy products to the Vegetarian Society, of which a summary was published in *The Vegetarian Messenger* the following March. In August, Watson and Shrigley discussed the formation of a subgroup of nondairy vegetarians. Unfortunately, the Vegetarian Society declined to give the fledgling group special status or to advertise their proposal in the pages of the journal, feeling that, although sympathetic to the group, promoting the program of what they saw as an extreme wing might diminish the commitment of the existing vegetarians to their cause by seeming to designate them as less completely pure. Nonetheless, in November 1944 Elsie Shrigley, Donald Watson, and five others met at the Attic Club in Holborn, London, to discuss the formation of the new association. From several proposals, the new name was chosen, apparently by Watson alone, by taking the first three and last two letters from vegetarian, because, Watson said, "veganism starts with vegetarianism and carries it through to its logical conclusion." In the same month, the Vegan Society published its manifesto, which ran as follows:

The aims of the Vegan Society are:

1   To advocate that man's food should be derived from fruits, nuts, vegetables, grains and other wholesome non-animal products and that it should exclude flesh, fish, fowl, eggs, honey, and animals' milk, butter, and cheese.
2   To encourage the manufacture and use of alternatives to animal commodities.

The Vegan Society seeks to abolish man's dependence on animals, with its inevitable cruelty and slaughter, and to create instead a more reasonable and humane order of society. Whilst honouring the efforts of all who are striving to achieve the emancipation of man and of animals, The Vegan Society suggests the results must remain limited so long as the exploitation in food and clothing production is ignored.

The Vegan Society is eager that it should be realised how closely the meat and dairy produce industries are related. The atrocities of dairy farming are, in some ways, greater than those of the meat industry but they are more obscured by ignorance. Moreover, The Vegan Society asserts that the use of milk in any form after weening is biologically wrong and that, except when taken directly from the mother, it becomes polluted and unsafe. The Society, therefore, sees no honourable alternative but to challenge the traditions of orthodoxy by advocating a completely revised diet based on reason and humane principle and guided by science to meet physiological requirements.

It is not suggested that Veganism alone would be sufficient to solve all the problems of individual and social well-being, but so close is its philosophy linked with morality, hygiene, aesthetics and agricultural economy that its adoption would remedy many unsatisfactory features of present-day life. Thus, if the curse of exploitation were removed, spiritual influences, operating for good, would develop conditions assuring a greater degree of happiness and prosperity for all.

According to Elsie Shrigley, the day at the Attic Club was "a Sunday, with sunshine and a blue sky – an auspicious day for the birth of an idealistic movement" – a movement that was also clearly optimistic, for the Second World War was still in progress, although the ultimate victory of the Allies seemed increasingly assured. Over a half-century after the inception of the Vegan Society, the principles on which it was founded are finally beginning to permeate significant numbers within the animal advocacy community.

## THE 1960S AND THE PROMOTION OF ANIMAL RIGHTS

In the early 1960s the Quaker vegetarian Ruth Harrison began the effective synthesization of the concepts of animal rights and vegetarianism in Britain. After Harrison, the espousal of animal rights implied, more often than not, a refusal to eat animal flesh. Her book on *Animal Machines* (1964) demonstrated that modern methods of animal husbandry were, beyond all shadow of a doubt, a moral nightmare for the animals. In 1965 Brigid Brophy wrote a full-page article entitled "The Rights of Animals" in the London *Sunday Times,* advertising a concept that seemed wholly new to the readers, although in fact the epithet had been in use for many years, a book including those very words prominently in its title having appeared over a century and a quarter earlier – never mind its author's view that flesh consumption and even hunting are morally acceptable![13] Moreover, the first uses with regard to animals had been recorded, a trifle circuitously, and *perhaps* not in a discussion of animals at all, by the Quaker George Fox in 1673 and, directly, by the Pythagorean Thomas Tryon in 1683.[14] Following Harrison and Brophy, Oxford replaced Cambridge as the British spiritual home of the promotion of animal interests. In 1969 a group of intellectuals, primarily academic philosophers, devoted themselves to the promotion of animal rights. The group included Stanley and Roslind Godlovitch, John Harris, Richard D. Ryder, and others, soon to be joined by Stephen Clark, Andrew Linzey, Peter Singer, and others – a disparate group of generally excellent minds with competing religious and secular orientations. High on the agenda was vegetarianism. Rightly, the animal-rights advocates observed it was not possible truly to claim to care for animals with one breath and to consume them with the next. The idea of a meeting to discuss measures to protect animals at which ham and beef sandwiches were served seemed increasingly oxymoronic – indeed, downright immoral! In fact, Singer makes precisely this point at the very beginning of the book that is widely viewed as the original book of the animal-ethics revival: *Animal Liberation*.[15] Slowly, beginning with Harrison, animal-rights advocacy and vegetarianism became almost synonymous in Britain, spreading rapidly to mainland and Nordic Europe and to Australasia, whence Singer came, and a little more slowly but no less effectively to North America. Or at least almost as effectively. I was astonished when I gave a talk at an academic literature conference on animals in Ottawa in 2005 to be asked privately afterward why I had mentioned vegetarianism more than once. The questioner did not seem to imagine that vegetarianism and animal ethics were inextricably related!

Although there had always been some vegetarians, until the second half of the twentieth century flesh deniers were almost chimerical creatures. As Andrew Linzey explained:

> When that theologian, Dean Inge, deeply committed to animal rights as he was, argued as recently as 1926 that we could not give up flesh because "we must eat something,"[16] I do not believe that he was being disingenuous. He really believed, as did many of his compassionate forebears, that one could not live without eating animals. Rumours of vegetarians existed but like the rumours themselves they did not – it was thought – persist. Most people until comparatively recently were incredulous that real vegetarians both existed *and* flourished.[17]

The merit of what is called loosely the animal-liberation movement is that vegetarianism is now a visible and perceptible reality. Moreover, the new proponents of vegetarianism have been able to dismiss effectively the age-old saws that vegetarianism was essentially unhealthy, that all supposed vegetarians cheated sometimes, and that the only real protein was animal protein. In the Victorian and later periods, as Harriet Ritvo has reported of a Victorian cookbook, it "was widely acknowledged that ... 'animal food satisfied hunger more completely and for a longer time than vegetables,' and that 'beef and mutton were the most nutritious of meats.'"[18] Nor did such a view disappear with the Victorian era. Quite to the contrary of the earlier suppositions, the original animal liberationists now demonstrated that vegetarianism was not only the moral course but also in reality even a healthier course, that better health was derived from nonflesh foods than from flesh.

Besides those explicitly concerned to promote the rights of animals, there were also significant proportions of the counterculture – from flower power to peacenik – who turned to vegetarianism in part as a means to protest the establishment and its values but also because animal issues were seen as legitimate aspects of the cause itself, even the *New Left Review* eventually coming to see animal rights as a legitimate part of the crusade. The traditional radical-authoritarian-"left" view had been quite unsympathetic. Marx and Engels deemed "members of societies for the prevention of cruelties to animals" on a par with "organisers of charity, temperance fanatics, [and] hole-and-corner reformers of every imaginable kind,"[19] a judgment with which many radical animal advocates, with their rabid denunciations of "welfarists," would seem to concur. In *On the History of Early Christianity,* Friedrich Engels referred disparagingly to vegetarians and "anti-vivisectionists."[20] Leon Trotsky wrote of "vegetarian-Quaker prattle."[21] This *New Left Review* reorientation, then, was quite a shift from the traditional Marxist view, but it has not been followed in general by the far left. In fact, vegetarians remain in general very wary of the current "new left," the green movement, as quite unaware of – and, in general, unconcerned about – the plight of animals, other than from an ecological perspective, and also wary of it as a movement that puts the holistic interests of the environment above the interests of nonhuman animals but not above those of human animals. Indeed, many animal-rights advocates for whom vegetarianism is an included necessity regard the customary holism of ecology as a subterfuge. Their view is that if the ecologists truly believed that the rights of the whole are greater than those of the parts, they would advocate the culling not just of animals occasionally but also of a good part of the human population. If not, and of course in reality they are not expected to, they are implicitly acknowledging the human is not an animal in the same way that other animals are animal. The human animal is subject to different ethical criteria. Like the other conventional political parties, the Greens, as a few of their most avid supporters claim explicitly, are acknowledging that the ends of political action are the promotion of human interest alone. Even action to promote the interests of the environment are ultimately about making it as appropriate a place as possible for humans to live.

Given the successes of Ruth Harrison with *Animal Machines,* Peter Singer with *Animal Liberation,* Andrew Linzey with *Animal Rights: A Christian Perspective,* Stephen Clark with *The Moral Status of Animals,* Richard Ryder with *Animal Revolution,* and the report of the Brambell Committee of 1965-66, instituted as a response to Ruth Harrison's revelations, with the intent to portray effectively the unacceptability of modern farming methods, it is a little disappointing that there remain, even among the vegetarian and animal-rights advocates, significant misconceptions, or at least exaggerations, of what has happened in the years since *Animal Machines.* Some have exaggerated the successes by imagining there is now a general sense of shame among the flesh eaters. To the minor extent that this is true, it is not a new phenomenon. Thus the literary critic and essayist William Hazlitt in 1823 preferred not to have his sensibilities ruffled, declaring that "animals that are made use of as food should either be so small as to be imperceptible, or else we should ... not leave the forms standing to reproach us with our gluttony and cruelty. I hate to see a rabbit trussed, or a hare brought to table in the form which it occupied while living."[22] In reality, by far the majority today is quite able to ignore the former sentience of the pork chops now being consumed, although neither quite as easily nor in quite the same proportions as before. In addition, there have long been some whose sensibilities balked but who continued to consume nonetheless. Those who imagine the changes in sensibility to have been significant believe that people now prefer to ease their consciences by shopping in supermarkets rather than at the butcher's. In supermarkets the animal form of the flesh they are purchasing is less readily recognized as animal. But in reality, people purchase those items that resemble their living form (e.g., fish, lobster, whole poultry) just as readily as those whose animal identity is less easily noticed. The changes that have taken place with the advent of the supermarkets is for the profit of the purveyor and the convenience of the customer, not to hide that we are eating flesh.

Nonetheless, the promoters of vegetarianism have done a great deal to ensure that the wellbeing of animals is now a far higher priority than in the immediate past. Thus Peter Singer, by far the best known of the vegetarian animal advocates, has argued persuasively to many for a metamorphosis in our attitudes toward other species and for a kind of human-animal equality: "If we wish to avoid being numbered amongst the oppressors, we must be prepared to re-think even our most fundamental attitudes. We need to reconsider them from the point of view of those most disadvantaged by our attitudes, and the practices that follow from these attitudes." "All animals are equal," he writes, and the "basic principle of equality ... is equality of consideration; and equal consideration for different beings may lead to different treatment and different rights."[23] Of course, it has been said that if the rights are to be quite different, there is no real equality at all. What if one concludes the human has the right to life but the nonhuman animal no such right? Yet Singer's statement implies, in fact, that historically the animals' rights have not been considered and are entitled to be considered as morally relevant in the same manner that all humans are entitled to have their rights considered.

The philosopher Stephen Clark approaches the matter in a different way in demonstrating that many of the antivegetarian objections miss the point:

What is the evidence that [other species] feel less distress than we do or that their desires are "of another sort" than ours? Doubtless there are all sorts of distresses, at the way the country is going to the dogs, or at Jones's new car, or the like, which beasts are fortunately spared – though the fact that they most probably do not appreciate our idiosyncratic problems might raise the question as to whether *they* have idiosyncratic problems too. It does not follow, however, from their lack of these distresses that calves cannot be acutely distressed at the absence of their mothers, nor that chickens are not distressed when unable to stretch their wings ... Animals, maybe, take as little thought for the morrow ... unless perhaps they're squirrels. But this can hardly excuse our inflicting present distress on them, merely because they cannot foresee a future *end* of such distress ... We do not, emotionally at least, have much understanding of death: my absence from the world is strictly unimaginable to me ... Cattle taken to the slaughter are similarly terrified.[24]

Outside the realm of academe, others contributed to the elaboration of the vegetarian ideal. Thus publisher and author Jon Wynne-Tyson explored what he called "dietethics" – that is, the ethics of diet – although he was concerned the matter should be seen from a practical, not merely philosophical, perspective and from one that the food industry should not itself fear in the immediate future:

To turn to practicalities, what feasible alternative is there to the present dominant stock-farming economy governing our eating patterns in the West? I suggest there is no doubt that the only alternative in the long term (and it is the long term we must keep constantly in mind) is vegan farming. This is not to suggest that it is practicable to bring orthodox farming policies to a halt overnight as some of the more hysterically anti-progress lobbies seem to fear. Today's butchers and farmers need not fear for their livelihoods now or in the future. Fundamental change invariably comes slowly. But they, with us, should face the fact that the only ethical and lastingly workable future economy must be based on farming methods which are solely directed to the growing and consuming of plant foods. There can be no eventual place in such an economy for animals bred under man's control to satisfy his acquired taste for eating their bodies.[25]

It is quite misleading to assert, as does Colin Spencer, that "a large majority of people who turn to vegetarianism do so because they believe meat to be unhealthy."[26] Certainly, vegetarians *do* usually believe that meat is unhealthy, but today ethics come before health in the vegetarian public mind. As Henry Salt and Lewis Gompertz demonstrated, there is no necessity for the vegetarian to assert that flesh is unhealthy.[27] Nor are health concerns the primary reason for becoming vegetarian. As we saw in the introduction, 72 percent of American vegetarians gave animal ethics as their reason for becoming vegetarian, and the figure would probably be higher in Europe.[28] In a survey of 1,000 vegetarians conducted by the English Vegetarian Society in 2005, the most popular reasons for choosing a vegetarian diet were "disgust at the treatment of farm animals" and "moral or spiritual conviction that taking life is wrong." In fact, the first four answers were all ethical. Only the fifth ground was "consider a vegetarian diet to be healthier than eating meat." If, in the early centuries of vegetarianism, asceticism played the predominant role and only later did health become an overriding criterion for the dietary choice, today the grounds for vegetarianism are, above all, of an ethical nature. Avoidance of the injury involved in the eating of sentient creatures outweighs all other considerations in the choice of a vegetarian diet.

It is certainly true that health becomes inextricably intertwined with ethics, in large part because those who are convinced of the justice of the eschewing of animal flesh find that it is easier to persuade others who are not already convinced of the great injustices perpetrated on animals to abstain from flesh by appealing to their self-interest in their own health. And vegetarians, having become such, find health a good, if incomplete, ground for remaining so. Moreover, increasing awareness of the unhealthy nature of what is usually called factory or intensive farming has turned numerous individuals – small a percentage of the whole as it is – completely away from flesh foods and has occasioned others to be a great deal more selective and abstemious in their choices.

Genetic engineering is likewise seen as a serious cause for concern, as are potential diseases, such as bovine spongiform encephalopathy (BSE), popularly known as mad cow disease. In fact, the concern with BSE replicated a prior worry in the 1890s when there was a common fear that tuberculosis might be spread from cattle to humans, a fear that engendered calls to ban the import to Britain of cattle from Ireland and the United States. Much of the argument about genetic engineering is technical and comprehensible only by those trained in the natural sciences. Nonetheless, Greenpeace International has succeeded admirably in reducing the daunting complexities to issues readily understood by the scientifically untutored mind. Molecular biology, they concede, has the potential to promote medical advances and increase our knowledge of the operations of the natural world while having an equal potential to turn the environment into a vast genetic experiment operated in the interests of commercial enterprise rather than the public good. Moreover, such enterprise, they argue, will be at the expense of the biodiversity and environmental integrity on which the future of the world and its food supply depends. Genetic engineering, Greenpeace points out, enables scientists to create artificial plants, animals, and micro-organisms that can spread throughout the environment and interbreed with natural organisms in an unforeseeable and uncontrollable manner. Once introduced into the environment, these genetically modified organisms (GMOs) cannot be recalled. This "genetic pollution" is seen as a major threat to future safety, especially through the potential limitation of natural diversity. Accordingly, they argue, these GMOs should not be released into the environment because there is totally inadequate scientific understanding of their effects. As an interim measure, Greenpeace insists, all genetically engineered ingredients must be segregated from natural ingredients and duly labelled as such on all products. Greenpeace opposes all patenting of plants, animals, humans, and their genes on the grounds that "life is not an industrial commodity." Although they acknowledge the efforts of governments to address the threat of genetic engineering through such international regulations as the Biosafety Protocol, they emphasize the necessity of recognizing that biological diversity must be protected if the earth's very survival is not to be put at risk. The only addition the animal advocate would make to the Greenpeace proposals is that the concept of "public interest" must include the interests of the nonhuman animals, both as species and as individuals.

## VEGETARIANISM GOES MAINSTREAM

Following the creation of the English Vegetarian Society in 1847, many other nations instituted such societies in rapid succession, among them the United States in 1850, Germany in 1867, France in 1879, Australia in 1886, and India in 1889. In 1908 the International Vegetarian Union was founded as the unifying body of territorial vegetarian societies, holding a World Vegetarian Congress every two or three years – customarily now two – the first of which was held at Dresden, Germany, in the year of the union's founding. Whereas national and international societies remain vibrant today, contact between vegetarians is kept more readily via the Internet than via any other medium. There are numerous vegetarian e-mail groups covering such diverse factors as region (e.g., Derbyshire vegetarians), race and region together (e.g., black vegetarians of Georgia), nation (e.g., vegetarians in Canada), religion (e.g., Christian vegetarian association), relational context (e.g., vegetarian parents' organization), orientation (e.g., vegetarian history), type of food (e.g., living and raw foods), and promotional services (e.g., Vegetarian Resource Group). There is even a group for conservative vegetarians. Together, all serve to provide an integrational basis for vegetarian association on a more frequent and less formal basis than at any time in the past. The natural consequence is that those who are tempted to return to their previous habits have a very convenient support base readily at hand – a vegetarian AA, so to speak.

If vegetarianism has not as yet succeeded in gaining a high proportion of converts, it has undoubtedly succeeded in making itself a part of the societal mainstream. Vegetarians are no longer merely tolerated but, by and large, welcomed. This welcome is especially noticeable in those countries – such as Britain, but far from Britain alone – where, almost invariably, restaurant menus have either a green "V" next to the several vegetarian items or, less frequently, a special page devoted to vegetarian options. Airlines now offer a half-dozen vegetarian alternatives (e.g., Asian vegetarian, ova-lacto vegetarian). Not merely specialty shops but also large grocery stores offer a significant variety of prepared vegetarian items. Even those who are not committed to a vegetarian lifestyle will now happily choose a vegetarian meal in a restaurant not merely to avoid the dangers brought to light by the avian flu and other potential illnesses but also because the vegetarian items are usually every bit as succulent and tasty as the flesh alternatives.

Naturally, many vegetarians object when these grocery store items are designed to replicate the taste of turkey (e.g., Tofurky®, or tofu turkey), beef, chicken, pork sausage (e.g., soy Bratwurst), and the like, as such imitations maintain the notion that one is eating something akin to the "real" thing, and thus the desire for the taste of flesh is maintained. And the idea that the vegetarian is being deprived of something worthwhile is encouraged. George Bernard Shaw was among those who thought such food choices a capitulation: "do not be seduced by messy pies, entrées, or such weak concessions to the enemy as 'vegetable rabbit,' 'vegetable sausage' and the like."[29] Nonetheless, such imitations ease the path for the new vegetarian to find foods that are as palatable as those they have renounced, and such foods are very convenient to prepare for those whose busy lifestyles hinder them from preparing tasty vegetarian meals from scratch. Moreover, such imitations encourage the visits of omnivorous relatives, who are likely to find the fare quite pleasant, thus helping to maintain associations that are threatened through the choice of a vegetarian regimen – and to save the lives of a few more animals into the bargain.

# 13

# Vegetarianism in North America

---

## UNITED STATES

It is certainly presumptuous to attempt to cover the American vegetarian experience in a few pages, especially when vegetarian societies in the United States, although interrupted, have a history almost exactly as long as that of Britain. Indeed, a fine book on American vegetarian history – *Vegetarian America: A History*, by Karen and Michael Iacobbo – already exists, the authors finding it took 267 pages to deal adequately with the topic.[1] Although it is quite incorrect to say, as does Andrew Linzey in the foreword to the Iacobbos's book, that this "is one of the few – perhaps even the first – history of vegetarianism written from the perspective of vegetarians" (what of prior authors such as Howard Williams, Michael Allen Fox, Daniel Dombrowski, Kerry S. Walters and Lisa Portmess, or Colin Spencer?), it does far more than this present book to put the totality of American vegetarian history into perspective.[2] Nonetheless, it would be a grievous error to omit the American experience entirely from a general book on the history of ethical vegetarian thought such as this.

The temporary vegetarianism of Benjamin Franklin, prompted by Thomas Tryon, has already been mentioned.[3] But there are more vegetarians of the same period of a far more permanent nature, at least one of whom Franklin knew, the German immigrant Johann Beissel, a founder in 1732 of the Seventh Day Baptists, known as Dunkers. Franklin probably knew several more, perhaps including the membership of the sect. These Baptists were vegetarian, perhaps vegan, primarily for ascetic reasons but seem to have believed also in kindness to animals. Another vegetarian of the early eighteenth century was Joshua Evans, of Jersey, who claimed that all animals love life and that it is a sin to take that life from them. In addition, there were "the Dorrelites" toward the end of the eighteenth century, founded by William Dorrell, an English immigrant, who were probably also vegan and largely ascetic and who also seemed to respect the rights of animals. Unfortunately, the historical record is too skimpy to say much more about these early American recusants from the dietary norm.

In the same year that William Cowherd was founding the vegetarian Bible-Christian Church in England, an American, L. Du Pre, was arguing that to eat animal flesh, specifically that of the cow, was to breach a covenant with God. Around the same time, perhaps a few years earlier, John Chapman of Massachusetts – the folk hero Johnny Appleseed – was practising vegetarianism as a follower of the teachings of Emmanuel Swedenborg but with an even greater respect for the animals than Swedenborg seemed to possess.

Apart from such uncommon individuals and sects, we have to look to the immigrants from Cowherd's Salford Bible-Christian Church to find the origins of vegetarianism, certainly of organized vegetarianism, in America. Even then the level of organization was, at first, very limited. With some forty fellow church members, William Metcalfe, his wife Susanna, and James Clark crossed the Atlantic. From the hardship of the journey, only eighteen remained vegetarian by the time America was reached. These immigrants established the Bible-Christian Church in Pennsylvania and began the task of proselytization. However, because of unemployment in the area, several of the original congregation sought work elsewhere, including Clark, and some returned to flesh as well as to alcohol, which was also banned. Still, the faithful persisted, above all Rev. Metcalfe, who was convinced his principles were ordained by God and His Son, arguing that the "fish" that Jesus was supposed to have eaten referred in fact to some nonflesh food. Indeed, as we have already seen, even if the food *was* fish, perhaps it was regarded as a nonflesh food.[4] In his booklet *Abstinence from the Flesh of Animals*, Metcalfe argued there was no human limitation to the precept "Thou shalt not kill." He suffered the inevitable derision but one that was accompanied by a degree of admiration, Metcalfe even being offered the ministry of a more affluent and respectable church provided he adopt the same mores as his parishioners – which, of course, he refused to do. It has been hinted that offers of assistance accompanied by the requirement to abandon the vegetarian and temperance principles may have had some devious motives.[5] In fact, there appear to have been no nefarious ulterior motives, no conspiracy, no threat. These "rich friends" were merely concerned to see Metcalfe as, from their perspective, a responsible Christian leader coming to share "regular" Christian values. To be sure, his abolitionist, pacifist, abstinence principles were anathema to many, but the ridicule directed at him was matched by the friendship of numerous others. In fact, he and his church continued, albeit with considerable difficulty on occasion, and in 1850 he was instrumental – indeed, the prime mover – in the establishment of a national Vegetarian Society, just three years after the founding of the Vegetarian Society in England. In fact, Metcalfe kept in touch with developments in Britain that influenced him to do the same in the United States. Moreover, somewhat akin to Mrs. Brotherton in England, Susanna Metcalfe collected vegetarian recipes from church members and published them as the Bible-Christian cookbook.

The momentous step forward took place already in 1830 when a temperance advocate, the Presbyterian minister Sylvester Graham (1794-1851), came to lecture and to meet members of the Bible-Christian Church. Whether Graham was already a vegetarian is unclear, although it is clear he had already developed Graham crackers, but from then on, the already popular Sylvester Graham became the principal advocate of the vegetarian and anti-alcohol causes in America – and this at a time when flesh and alcohol, even drugs such as opium (laudanum), were not only considered "normal" fare but were also widely recommended as a medicinal cure for almost all ailments. During the cholera epidemic of 1832 local authorities and even the US Board of Health attempted to restrict the consumption of vegetables. Flesh, alcohol, and prayer to combat what was seen as a divinely ordained illness, a punishment for sin, were the most common nostrums. Graham prescribed the very reverse of the popular and "official" view, achieving a considerable degree of support. He achieved some notoriety, too, especially among the medical fraternity, because Graham insisted that the prevailing unhealthy diet was the *cause* of the illness rather than, through an increase of the harmful foodstuffs, a *remedy* for it. Frequent bathing – a novel idea given that until the seventeenth century in Europe, even annual bathing was a rarity, and that by the nineteenth, regular bathing was still uncommon – drinking water rather than alcohol, outdoor exercise, and a plant-based diet with whole grain bread would, Graham claimed, restore health, eradicate illness, and prevent recurrence. Many responded favourably to Graham's eloquent pleas with the result that American vegetarians were known for quite some time not by the confusing epithet "vegetarian" but as "Grahamites."

Like many of his British and other European counterparts, as we have seen, Graham told his audiences that Genesis represented a vegetarian Golden Age when the population lived on a wholly beneficial natural diet, that the human body was not designed for a flesh diet, or for condiments, and that by nature the human was a frugivore. Like Lewis Gompertz before him and Henry Salt later, Graham agreed that humans could derive adequate nourishment from flesh, but he went further than Gompertz and Salt in pointing out what he saw as its negative attribute of stimulating lust and the desire for alcohol. Nonetheless, whereas Gompertz and Salt considered the protection of animals the primary reason for the vegetarian diet, Graham appears to have taken the primary ground to be human health. For Graham, raw foods were best, unadulterated foods came second, and flesh and alcohol were entirely detrimental and to be avoided. Nonetheless, abstinence from flesh alone would not suffice, Graham warned. A poorly prepared and poorly chosen vegetable regimen would be worse than a modest mixed diet of vegetable and flesh.

Whereas the age of perfectibilty had arisen a little earlier in Europe, this was the millenarian age in the United States. From prison reform to industrial democratization to gender questions, all aspects of American life were put in question with the prevailing belief that every social, economic, and political ill had a ready remedy. Human reason, aided by God – or at least by some unknowable deity – would show the way. To be sure, the idea was already present at the time of the Declaration of Independence, but now it reached its zenith. The appropriate diet and the surest road to health were among the historical questions that could now, it was felt, be answered definitively. In light both of the large meals that were served and of the prominence of flesh in those meals, not only Graham but also many visitors to the United States noted the excesses in the American regimen. For Graham, one of the excesses was white flour, which should, he argued, be replaced with coarsely ground whole wheat flour – hence "Graham flour" and, made from that flour, "Graham crackers." The Iacobbos summed up the Grahamite regimen: "Graham advised those seeking health to abandon all medicine, liquor, coffee, tea, butter, and milk (the latter not preferred but allowed only in small quantities and diluted). They were to drink water, toast water, or water gruel; eat food in its natural state, unspiced; and especially eat boiled wheat bread and fruit for regularity. Cleaning and exercising the skin with a brush was also advised."[6] Many thousands attended Graham's lectures – as many as two thousand at a time, several hundred being common. Many were convinced and converted. Perhaps at no time prior to the Progressive Era at the turn of the twentieth century, that Gilded Age of optimism, has Western vegetarianism, albeit a vegetarianism

based predominantly on health concerns, had a larger hearing and gar-
nered more success – along with vehement opposition. Grahamite America offered great potential for the vegetarian cause. Moreover, with rather
more culinary wisdom than is suggested by the diet served at early meetings of the English Vegetarian Society, Graham urged his followers to avoid
puddings and pastry – the diet of which *Punch* had been so derisive.[7] Graham's *Lectures on the Science of Human Life,* published in two volumes in
1839, provided the essence of his teachings for a welcoming public.

William Alcott (1780?-1854), not to be confused with his cousin Bronson
Alcott, was also a dietary reformer, preaching his message in the same era as
Graham. His success was not as great as that of Graham but was considerable nonetheless. He was already a noted health-reform physician when he
turned to the vegetarian regimen, claiming, like Graham, the human to be
a natural frugivore, designed to live on fruit and nuts. In 1837, Alcott joined
Sylvester Graham in the newly formed – and primarily "Grahamite" –
American Physiological Society, which focused on the teaching of physiology, anatomy, and the diet that should result from the correct understanding
of the first two. The society and its women's branch, the Ladies' Physiological Society, became a voice for vegetarianism and a natural forerunner of
the American Vegetarian Society, founded just over a decade later. The Ladies'
Physiological Society was also prominent in the promotion of greater independence of, and rights for, women. As in Britain, until the twentieth century
vegetarianism was promoted together with other radical and reformist causes
that were seen to be of a progressive nature.

Alcott wrote numerous books, one of which was *Vegetable Diet: As Sanctioned by Medical Men, and by Experience in all Ages* (1848). His grounds for
the recommendation of the vegetarian diet consisted of the experiences of
early history, including the Pythagoreans and Essenes, and mentioned the
Bible-Christian Church, George Cheyne, William Lambe, and Baron Cuvier's
work on teeth; environmental and personal economy, health, human physiology, and anatomy; and finally, but most important for the future, moral
reasons, namely the unnecessary and unconscionable slaughter of animals.
If Graham did more than anyone else to bring vegetarianism – indeed,
"Grahamism" – to the attention of the American public, it was William
Alcott who moved American vegetarianism more rapidly toward its appropriate animal-ethical base. It was not that Graham had entirely ignored the
ethical base by emphasizing the primarily ethological factors – for example,
he stated explicitly that he sympathized with the animals in their plight –
but that he had given greater prominence to other factors. In an 1838 edition of the *Graham Journal of Health and Longevity* he quoted, unattributed

and slightly incorrectly, from Erasmus Darwin on regard for "Our brother emmets and our sister worms" and mentioned favourably, without indicating their source other than "Northern India," austere and, for Graham, "extreme" Jaina practices.[8] Nonetheless, Alcott stressed the ethical rather more, condemning hunting and fishing as well as stating:

> Nearly every argument which can be brought to show the superiority of a vegetable diet over one that includes flesh or fish, is a moral argument ... The destruction of animals for food, in its details and tendencies, involves so much cruelty as to cause every reflecting individual – not destitute of the ordinary sensibilities – to shudder ...
>
> ... the world, I mean our own portion of it, sometimes seems to me like one mighty slaughterhouse – one grand school for the suppression of every kind, and tender, and brotherly feeling – one grand process of education to the entire destruction of all moral principle – one vast scene of destruction to all moral sensibility, and all sympathy with the woes of those around us. Is it not so?
>
> ... How can the Christian with the Bible in hand, and the merciful doctrines of its pages for his text, "Teach me to feel another's woe,"[9] – the beast's not excepted – and yet, having laid down that Bible, go at once from the domestic altar to make light of the convulsions and exit of a poor domestic animal?[10]

If the moral argument was becoming the predominant argument for vegetarianism in Britain by the mid-nineteenth century, its arrival in the United States was perhaps a fraction earlier.

Another physician who became a vegetarian advocate – indeed, also a distinguished future president of the American Medical Association – was Reuben Dimond Mussey (1780-1866). He believed that humans bore much similarity to the great apes and, thus, that humans lived most appropriately on the similar vegetarian diet on which he thought the apes all thrived. Mussey regarded ancient civilizations – where, he opined, humans had lived longer – to have been vegetarian, and he persuaded many of his medical students at Dartmouth to adopt his flesh-abstaining practices. Two rumours were prevalent at large: first, that the Grahamites had all died from cholera as a consequence of their weak constitutions resulting from the abstinence from animal flesh; and second, that the vegetarians were planning to introduce legislation to outlaw flesh consumption. Mussey's presence was perhaps enough to dispel the first – although rumour is frequently unresponsive to evidence – but the second was so increasingly common that he felt compelled to refute it in public. It is certainly worthy of note that Mussey's reputation as a vegetarian did not prevent him from being elected president of the American Medical Association.

Despite the relative successes of Graham, Alcott, Mussey, and others, a flesh diet remained the norm. But the very stridency of most of the medical establishment in heaping a measure of ridicule on the reformers, mixed occasionally with a modicum of goodwill in recognizing the force of some of the vegetarian argument, reflected the positive public response to the vegetarian appeal that was frequently heard. It is only when the advocates of change are somewhat successful that they need to be opposed so aggressively.

In 1843 social reformer Bronson Alcott (1799-1888), a dedicated Pythagorean and cousin of William Alcott, teamed with British visitors to inaugurate a Massachusetts vegetarian community. He had been a vegetarian, almost vegan, since 1835, considering the wearing of leather "an invasion of the rights of animals." He was one of the leaders of the transcendentalists – Romantic idealists – centred on Concord, Massachusetts, and the only one to be a committed vegetarian, writing of the horrors of butchery in a style reminiscent of Alexander Pope.[11] Yet whereas the horror was sufficient to turn Alcott away from flesh forever, the horror served only to stimulate rhetorical flourish in Pope.

Karen and Michael Iacobbo write correctly, but with the potential to be misinterpreted, that another transcendentalist, "Henry David Thoreau ... wrote about vegetarianism in Walden, perhaps reflecting on his friendship with [Bronson] Alcott."[12] First, as "Walden" is not here italicized, it might be thought there was a vegetarian community at Walden Pond, which, of course, there was not. Second, and more important, Thoreau's comments on diet in *Walden, or Life in the Woods* (1854) reflect more his fascinatingly paradoxical nature than any association with Alcott, although he had tried the Grahamite diet. His being was a synthesis of Eden and Arcadia.[13] In Thoreau the two are inextricably intertwined. When he was in Maine, we find him eating pork, moose, and fish rather than the Grahamite diet. It is important to the appropriate understanding of one of the most enigmatic yet interesting figures in the intellectual history of America that the impression not be left that Thoreau was a vegetarian, as many have imagined him to be. Thus, he stated: "As I came through the woods with my string of fish, trailing my pole, it being now quite dark, I caught a glimpse of a woodchuck stealing across my path, and felt a strange thrill of savage delight, and was strongly tempted to seize and devour him raw ... Once or twice ... while I lived at the pond, I found myself ranging the woods, like a half-starved hound, with a strange abandonment, seeking some kind of venison

which I might devour, and no morsel could have been too savage for me."
After much in the same Arcadian vein, but then quoting Chaucer on
hunters not being holy men (although getting the facts and words from
*The Canterbury Tales* wrong), he determines:

> It may be vain to ask why the imagination will not be reconciled to flesh and
> fat. I am satisfied that it is not. Is it not a reproach that man is a carnivorous
> animal? True, he can and does live, in great measure, by preying on other ani-
> mals, but this is a miserable way, as any one who will go to snaring rabbits,
> or slaughtering lambs, may learn, – and he will be regarded as a benefactor
> to his race who shall teach man to confine himself to a more innocent and
> wholesome diet. Whatever my own practice may be, I have no doubt that it
> is a part of the destiny of the human race, in its gradual improvement, to
> leave off eating animals, as surely as the savage tribes have left off eating each
> other when they came in contact with the more civilized.[14]

This is the Edenic aspect of his persona. It sounds rather reminiscent of
the "thy will be done, o lord, but, please, not just yet" attitude we encountered among certain British vegetarian advocates in Chapter 9. Only when
the nature of humanity has changed will it be appropriate to become vegetarian, he seems to say like his forerunners. But on Thoreau's own interpretation, the contradictions are an inherent part of the human character.
Indeed, a correct comprehension of Thoreau will allow us to understand
both the desirability of vegetarianism and the great difficulties present in
the human character that hinder its achievement. Unfortunately, the complex aspect of the Thoreau character is usually not recognized, and even as
fine a scholar as Angus Taylor is led to state, quite incorrectly, that "Henry
David Thoreau ... stuck primarily to a vegetarian diet."[15] Nonetheless, it
is notable that W.E.H. Lecky's later famous idea of continuous moral
progress toward the improved treatment of animals is already conceived by
Thoreau and that Thoreau understood full well – an idea he may indeed
have adopted from Bronson Alcott – that the ground for abstaining from
animal flesh is ultimately a moral one.[16] Bronson Alcott may well have
been the source also of Thoreau's theory of nonviolent resistance to the
state as expressed in Thoreau's ever-popular essay on "Civil Disobedience,"
but it was not a nonviolence he extended to the animal realm. Nonetheless,
the essay confirmed Mahatma Gandhi in the path of nonviolence, in which
animals were included. Bronson Alcott also tried to persuade another
transcendentalist, Ralph Waldo Emerson, of the moral equivalence, or at
least significant similarity, between cannibalism and the consumption of

nonhuman flesh, an argument, it is rumoured, strong enough to persuade Emerson to try the vegetarian diet but without any continued success.

## The Origins of Organized American Vegetarianism

All along, the Bible-Christian Church had continued to operate in Philadelphia and, indeed, continued to do so until it ceased to exist some time in the 1920s, advocating reform in general with regard to diet, temperance, tobacco, pacifism, and the abolition of slavery. But vegetarianism was its primary advocacy as the cornerstone of all other reforms. In 1842 the secretary of the Kensington Physiological Society, directly associated with the church, argued that abstention from flesh foods was the prerequisite of reform in general, a claim to be perpetuated later by the American Vegetarian Society: "Abstinence from Murdered Animals as Food" – this was capitalized by the society – was "the first step" in reform, a dictum reminiscent of Tolstoy, who also wrote at a later date of vegetarianism as the "first step" in reform.[17] Equally, the Massachusetts animal advocate George Angell wrote later of reform in animal ethics in terms of steps. Yet vegetarians were not all united in their desired overall reforms. Most were abolitionist, but some were more wary. Most were Christian and some avowedly, even stridently, secular. Some were conventional Christians and some radically evangelical. What was needed was an organization dedicated to the common cause that could unite all the "Grahamites."

Shortly before the Physiological Society lecture, Metcalfe had published a thirty-five-page booklet that aroused considerable comment well beyond the confines of Philadelphia: *Bible Testimony on Abstinence from the Flesh of Animals as Food, being an Address delivered at the Bible-Christian Church, North Street, West Kensington, on the Eighth of June 1840, being the Anniversary of said Church*. Metcalfe announced that the Bible proscribed flesh consumption not merely in Genesis and the prophesies of Isaiah but also in Romans 14:21: "It is good neither to eat flesh nor drink wine." Of course, he rehearsed the customary arguments, including the claim that Jesus neither ate nor provided fish as well as other flesh. He mentioned the abstinence experience of his own church over two decades. Although some reviewers were dubious about the validity of the arguments, they were not entirely unfavourable. Apparently, the church's consistency impressed them. Most important, the booklet brought Sylvester Graham, William Alcott, and William Metcalfe together again in common cause.

In the belief that an organization devoted solely to the vegetarian message was necessary, William Metcalfe organized a convention in New York as a harbinger of an American Vegetarian Society. The triumvirate of Metcalfe,

Alcott, and Graham, the latter long ill and shortly to die at the age of fifty-eight, were present, accompanied by William's cousin Bronson Alcott, who was to become a preeminent voice for American vegetarianism. The number present at Clinton Hall was quite modest, but commendations from numerous well-wishers who were unable to attend were read to the assembly, at least one of which was worthy of comment. Whereas one of the reputed founders of sociology, the Frenchman Auguste Comte, had looked forward to the benevolent use of "higher" animals for human ends once technological advances had rendered oppressive animal power unnecessary, and although the London Zoological Society (Regent's Park Zoo) thought one of its tasks to be the domestication of animals likely to be of human use – the zoo succeeded only in domesticating the golden hamster! – Dr. David Prince of St. Louis regarded the elimination of animal service "rendered by steam and galvanization" as a future victory in itself.[18] Animal use would be increasingly less necessary. The convention repeated the litany of vegetarian arguments, the attendees referring to the supporting evidence of Wesley, Swedenborg, Franklin, Shelley, Pope, and Isaac Newton – only half of whom had been vegetarians for any duration – but it was agreed to form the American Vegetarian Society, at least one of those present objecting to the use of the word "vegetarian" on the customary grounds. In September 1850 the newly founded society met at the Chinese Museum in Philadelphia to celebrate the First Annual Meeting. It was a good day for the animals, as the founding of the American Vegetarian Society was accompanied – in fact, if not causally – by an increase of the recognition of certain, confessedly limited, rights for animals and by their promotion by the society, as was occurring also in Britain and Ireland. With the meetings in New York and Philadelphia, the American Vegetarian Society had been born, even though the birth pangs would prove painful for the society and, indeed, would lead to infant mortality. But unlike the society, the movement managed to prosper.

At this time, vegetarianism was often associated with what now seem strange panaceas to cure the sick or those who were afraid of becoming sick. The water cure, or hydropathy, was the most popular of these cure-alls, one that required the immersion of the patient in water. Such cures remained popular until the close of the nineteenth century. These treatments were conducted at specially designed spas and were sometimes associated with a vegetarian diet. Consequently, by showing what might comprise a sound and pleasurable vegetarian regimen, these cures were sometimes a valuable antidote against the prevalent myths that the vegetarian diet consisted entirely of whole wheat bread and water and that it rendered the practitioner enfeebled or insane. Indeed, such myths were sufficiently widespread that the American Vegetarian Society and its members felt compelled to make strenuous efforts to extinguish the misconceptions. Among the common claims of members of the Vegetarian Society in its early years – as also of its English counterpart – were that the vegetarian cuisine should release women from the repressive roles imposed upon them by society. Notably, women outnumbered men in the fledgling society but not in its leadership. It was notable, too, that most American vegetarians were Christians who regarded their chosen diet as an intrinsic aspect of their religion. One of the most common Christian vegetarian claims, by then common among European Christians as well, was that the "dominion" of Genesis imposed an obligation on humans to care for their charges. It is remarkable how long the contrary opinion has pervaded the arguments of vegetarianism's secular promoters. Perhaps the most commonly repeated erroneous view was that a flesh diet promoted aggressive and bellicose tendencies among the partakers. But the most significant fact was that the wellbeing of animals was now foremost on the agenda.

One of the greatest tragedies for the spread of vegetarianism was the early death in 1851, the year after the society was founded, of Sylvester Graham. If the greatest and best-known promoter of the creed had died so early, this was surely evidence, so it was thought, of the inappropriateness of a vegetarian diet. It was a common conviction that was hard for vegetarians to overcome. By 1854 Sylvester Graham and William Alcott were dead, and William Metcalfe had returned to England. The triumvirate was gone. The new guard was not yet ready. The Vegetarian Society ran out of funds and ceased to function. But if the society was moribund, the vegetarian cause, judging by the writings in its favour, was not about to join its organizational parent.

Once again, the Bible-Christian Church came to the rescue, although not effectively until three decades later, after other attempts to salvage vegetarian ideals had met with little success. This time the rescue came in the person of an immigrant from England, Henry Clubb. In 1855 he had founded the Vegetarian Settlement Company, one of numerous attempts to organize a utopian commune in the New World, the two best known being the short-lived quasi-transcendentalist commune of Brook Farm (1841-1847) and the Pantisocracy (from Greek *pant-isocratia,* meaning government by all) beside the Susquehanna River envisaged, but never realized, by Samuel Taylor Coleridge and Robert Southey. Of somewhat greater success was Joseph Priestley's scientific academy at Northumberland, Pennsylvania, which lasted from 1794 until Priestley's death a decade later. Like the Pantisocracy of the English Romantics, the Vegetarian Settlement Company never got off the ground. After his utopian failure, Clubb became a journalist but never lost his interest in the cause of the vegetarian community, waiting to reorganize a national society when the time was ripe. But the time was not ripe for Mr., now Rev., Clubb until 1886, when the Vegetarian Society of America was instituted. A lengthy hiatus! Despite the lack of a national organization – the New York Vegetarian Society had also become temporarily defunct – the vegetarian ideal was still preached and practised. After the founding and then demise of the Vegetarian Society of America, Clubb continued his association with the Philadelphia Bible-Christian Church and as late as 1922 was a member of the committee that wrote the 192-page *History of the Philadelphia Bible-Christian Church for the First Century of its Existence*.[19] Unfortunately for the vegetarian cause, the Bible-Christian Church was also soon to cease to exist.

Meanwhile, many of the late-nineteenth-century water-cure establishments opted for a vegetarian diet. Thus, for many Americans, especially those not wedded to traditional mores, vegetarianism and health were closely associated. Indeed, the recruitment successes of the water-cure and vegetarianism advocates were sufficient that the allopathic (i.e., "regular") physicians joined in a somewhat concerted effort to combat the vegetarian advances. The result was a standoff. If the vegetarians did not succeed in making America fleshless, the allopathics likewise failed to convince those of a doubting nature to return to what the physicians saw as "normalcy." In fact, the Hygienist movement advocating drugless cures and a vegetarian diet became popular throughout both the United States and Europe, especially the former.

Among those drawn to the water cure were Ellen and James White. In 1863 the Whites established a new denomination, the Seventh Day Adventists, whose name reflects that they regarded Saturday as the Sabbath and that they awaited the second coming. They also advocated (and the church still advocates but does not require) vegetarian practices. Because of the difficulties that have occurred for travelling vegetarians throughout recorded history, Ellen White did not entirely renounce flesh until later in her ministry, but she was nonetheless steadfast throughout in her advocacy. The Seventh Day Adventists were successful in their proselytization, made many converts, and expanded, although Ellen White and her church did little to advocate the moral cause on behalf of animals. Today, approximately 50 percent of Adventists are estimated to be vegetarian. The Nutrition Council of the denomination recommends the vegetarian diet on both health and scriptural grounds, declaring it to be appropriate "because of their belief in the holistic nature of humankind." The interests of the animals receive no attention.

With considerable degree of contrast, immediately preceding the Civil War, the Bible-Christian Church, continuing its perennial advocacy, listed seven compelling grounds for abstinence from flesh, none of which were mutually exclusive. The biblical teachings, the investigations of science, and justice for the animals headed the list. As was to be expected, however, the American Civil War (1861-1865) interrupted vegetarian advances. Indeed, neither the North nor the South provided vegetarian meals for its warriors. The vegetarian soldier was perforce compelled to return to flesh or to starve. As always, as we have seen before, war, animal ethics, and vegetarianism did not mix well.

Still, the Civil War at an end, a few nonconformists persisted in their hortative endeavours during Reconstruction, and even the allopathic physicians felt compelled again to recognize the success of the vegetarian appeal. But, on balance, the orthodoxy of the flesh-eating regimen prevailed. Not only was it difficult for the tempted to conquer their own ingrained habits and the persuasive force of the practices of their companions and acquaintances, but it was also an almost insuperable task to make themselves outsiders among the members of their own families. As Lawrence Grunland, an opponent of vegetarianism, asserted, in a debate in the Chicago Vegetarian Society's magazine, it was not desirable for a social being to differ from most others and to be deemed one of the peculiar people.[20] It is an argument that has proven a thorn to all advocates of unconventional change in human history. And vegetarianism was especially prone to such a critique.

In 1872, seeing their advocated reform in some jeopardy, Mr. and Mrs. White of the Seventh Day Adventists hired the nutrition expert Dr. John Kellogg of breakfast-cereal fame to take vegetarian practices beyond, it would appear, even the heady days under the popularity of Sylvester Graham. Vegetarianism spread, through Kellogg and others, from the Northeast into parts of the United States that it had never ventured before.

## The Rebirth of Organized American Vegetarianism

Despite the popularity of nutritional vegetarianism, a national, specifically vegetarian, organization had not existed since the mid-1850s. Rev. Henry Clubb now recognized, as we have noted, both the need and the opportunity to bring one into existence, and naturally, as he was a Bible-Christian Church minister in the city where the church had its roots, Philadelphia became the home of the new Vegetarian Society of America, despite the Chicago Vegetarian Society's attempt to persuade the fledgling organization to make its home in the windy city. Whereas dissenting Christianity in Britain had readily turned to a version of animal rights and was in the forefront of the crusade against vivisection, Christianity in the United States turned more readily than its transoceanic counterpart to vegetarianism. Nonetheless, in line with the increasing skepticism of the times, the vegetarian movement embraced the principles of other faiths and philosophies, especially theosophy, under the influence of which the ethical aspects of the creed prospered even further.

An increasing connection became evident in the later nineteenth century between such animal issues as vivisection and vegetarianism as well as between some members of humane organizations and vegetarian practice, although, in some instances, there was a surprising lack of it. For example, one of the most influential and radical animal advocates, George Thorndike Angell (1823-1909), co-founder of the Massachusetts Society for the Prevention of Cruelty to Animals (1867) and founder of the Bands of Mercy (1882) and of the American Humane Education Society (1889), was an abolitionist on issues of animal experimentation. His motto for the Human Education Society was: "Glory to God, Peace on Earth, Kindness, Justice and Mercy to Every Living Creature." He stated: "I am sometimes asked, 'Why do you spend so much of your time and money in talking about kindness to animals, when there is so much cruelty to men?' And I answer, 'We are working at the roots. Every humane publication, every lecture, every step in doing or teaching kindness to them, is a step to prevent crime, – a step in promoting those qualities of heart which will elevate human souls.'"[21] Yet although an abolitionist on experimentation, there seems no evidence Angell joined his even more radical colleagues in eschewing flesh. Of course, and this remains true of SPCAs today, fledgling humane societies were loath to associate themselves with the vegetarian cause directly, in fear that they may alienate many of their flesh-eating, fund-contributing, support-rendering members. They would not be able to continue to promote the more commonly acknowledged protection of animals if they openly advocated what were seen as radical programs. Nonetheless, the turn of the twentieth century seemed to augur well for the final defeat of flesh and the elimination of cruelty to animals, even if not in immediate prospect. America saw itself as the symbol and reality of progress, and the elimination of cruelty in all its modes and dietary reform were viewed by many Americans as essential aspects of that progress. Many in the women's suffrage movement saw animals as entitled to a world of greater justice, just as they saw the same with even greater conviction for themselves. And refrigeration in transport vehicles was making fruits and vegetables available, and at lower prices, to many more people for far longer portions of the year than hitherto.

Of the greatest importance was that the promise of John Kellogg's engagement with the Seventh Day Adventists' vegetarian cause was bearing fruit. He was now acknowledged as the prime proponent of healthy vegetarian nutrition. Kellogg had been working on producing nutritious substitutes for flesh at the Battle Creek Sanitarium Health Food Company since the 1870s, more than ably aided most of the time by his accomplished wife, Ella Eaton Kellogg. By the turn of the century his primarily nut-based products were achieving tremendous acclaim, and Kellogg was reminding those who benefited that their diet was also to the great advantage of the animals who were spared. Kellogg's successes were broadcast widely in the press, and vegetarianism became both respectable and popular, prompting the flesh-eating defenders to take up arms against promoters of dietary change. Each side vied with the other in offering, sometimes irrelevant, sometimes simply spurious, examples of armies, athletes, and scientific experiments to demonstrate the superiority of their chosen regimen. Following the lead of the Booths in Britain, the American Salvation Army joined the battle on the vegetarian side; several journalists and, naturally, the meat industry itself carried the cudgel for flesh. The tide began to turn against the promoters of animal interests in the early years of the twentieth century, when animal experimentation, long practised but previously a perennial failure in providing medical benefits, began to succeed, as its promoters had always proclaimed would come to pass. Animal experimentation was convincing the public of its legitimacy with far greater success than before and was now seen to be immensely beneficial in the promotion of human health. The claim of the opponents that similar successes could have been readily achieved without animal experimentation fell on increasingly deaf ears. The altruists were put on the defensive by the ever-prominent promoters of human self-interest. Still, perhaps more from high prices than from any concern with dietary reform, flesh consumption – apart from the composition of the military regimen – diminished into the 1920s.

With the First World War and the Great Depression – the Regressive Era to follow the Progressive Era, the Rusted Age to succeed the Gilded Age – human problems, and they were legion and oppressive, were the preeminent concern. Exclusively human interests, not animal interests, were the content of the mind. The dust bowl that was the Midwest proved incapable of providing adequate vegetarian fare. Many Americans were desperately undernourished and were compelled to eat whatever they could get. The Depression forced even the Battle Creek Sanitarium into receivership.

Vegetarians reverted once more to being regarded as cranks. Even the discovery of the great benefits of the soybean could not dim the revival of the desirability of flesh, if and when flesh could be obtained, and hunger and scarcity made flesh even more desirable – this despite Henry Ford's advocacy of the benefits of the bean. Many who were vegetarian from religious conviction maintained their diet, but they had little success in persuading others to join them. In the Second World War vegetarianism fared no better. Other than for military personnel, flesh was rather scarce – a fact that made it more desirable, not less. But if vegetarianism was in decline, the ethical orientation of those who remained true to the faith was not. More and more, flesh eating was regarded by vegetarians as morally barbaric.

## The American Vegetarian Party and the American Vegan Society

In 1948 Symon Gould of the *American Vegetarian* founded the American Vegetarian Party with John Maxwell as presidential candidate, far less to make any serious incursions into the dominant two-party system of the United States and far more to advertise the vegetarian agenda to the American public. The ploy worked. Newspapers covered the presidential candidates and reported on the vegetarian program, including Maxwell's adamant opposition to the killing of animals for food, fun, or fashion. The presidential candidate for the party in 1952 was former military general Herbert Holdridge, whose platform seemed more generally pacifist than vegetarian. If vegetarianism did not increase rapidly as a consequence of the publicity, at least the political party seems to have been successful in gaining vegetarianism a modicum of support, again at least sufficient support that the medical profession took the opportunity once more to deride the "food fadists."

But at least as a portent of the direction in which vegetarians were moving, or wished to move, in 1960 the American Vegan Society was founded in New Jersey by Indian-born Jay Dinshah (1933-2000), who promoted the principles of Jainism through *ahimsa* (the principle of nonharm). In *Out of the Jungle* (1967) he wrote: "Man cannot pretend to be higher in ethics, spirituality, advancement, or civilization than other creatures, and at the same time live by lower standards than the vulture or hyena. The Pillars of Ahimsa indisputably represent the clearest, surest path out of the jungle, and toward the attainment of that highly desirable goal."[22]

In *Ahimsa* (1971) he developed a philosophy of reverence for life itself that bore considerable similarity to the reverence-for-life philosophy of Albert Schweitzer:

To anyone who believes that life itself has some purpose – or is even its own reason for being – one should not wantonly destroy even plants. The destruction of any life is thus an act not to be taken lightly, or presumed to be isolated in the scheme of things. It is to be preceded by careful consideration of the responsibilities and the possible alternatives involved, and accompanied by an understanding that one is indeed doing the right thing according to the present state of existence...The ethical vegetarian is seriously interested in lessening the suffering that he may be causing in the world – even inadvertently afflicted upon relatively low forms of life.[23]

By including plants in the vegetarian concern, Dinshah, like Edward Carpenter in England earlier, gave vegetarian adversaries an opportunity to cast vegetarians once again as irrelevant eccentrics.

## From New Vegetarianism to Environmentalism

The revolution that was about to change much of the orientation of America in the 1960s and 1970s was both cultural and intellectual but primarily the former. Even at its mildest it was the age of the questioning of authority. This period saw the beginnings of the mass-market publicity stunts that began to broadcast the vegetarian message to a far wider audience – an audience that, on the whole, disparaged the stunts but could not avoid the message. The new vegetarianism, as many of its participants saw it, intended both to spare the animals their suffering and to end world hunger, claiming that wheat rather than cattle as the primary food source would readily feed the whole world. Feeding the world's grain to people rather than food animals would solve the world-hunger problem, wrote Frances Moore Lappé in *Diet for a Small Planet* (1971). The book has sold 3 million copies and has influenced, if not always converted, almost as many minds. Vegetarian food, said many of the hippies, did not have to be boring and dull. It could be so readily nutritious, inexpensive, far more enjoyable than beef burgers or pork tenderloins, and overcome a whole history of cruelty into the bargain. Vegetarian cookbooks abounded, especially by the later 1970s. Thoreauian simplicity was the watchword of the new advocates, both in cuisine and lifestyle. Suddenly, vegetarianism was "in" – not with the average American perhaps but among many of the California and New York actors and media gurus as well as among those who were alienated from America's seemingly unidimensional capitalist and acquisitive values.

In 1975 *Vegetarian World* indicated that the grounds for practising vegetarianism among the American people were environmental, health-based, ethical, aesthetic, religious, and physiological, but as the proportions were not given, the information told us very little about recent changes. However, one might surmise that the ethical grounds were primary, or at least becoming ever more dominantly so, that environmental reasons were increasing, that religious groups opposed to eating flesh remained about the same, and that health reasons would often be mixed with other reasons. The ground that humans were vegetarian by physiological nature – despite being decidedly in decline as the primary reason – remained a useful justification for having become a vegetarian but almost never a motive to become one. And the aesthetic ground – that flesh eating is in and of itself a disgusting and ugly activity – was now rarely considered, although it had been a common ground given for vegetarianism in the nineteenth century. In addition, the high cost of meat apparently persuaded some to try a vegetarian diet in order to save money. Such opportunistic vegetarians would eat the occasional piece of flesh when the opportunity arose and revert to an omnivorous diet when finances allowed.

American intellectuals were rather latecomers on the scene. The seemingly solitary J. Howard Moore (1862-1916), Chicago author of at least five books on evolutionary biology and animal ethics, became a vegetarian, probably around the age of thirty, in ignorance of any vegetarian advocacy.[24] He tells us, "I became a vegetarian by my reflection. I did not know at the time of the vegetarian movement, and hence, supposed myself alone among republics of carnivora. Nearly every doctrine came to me as a trembling contraband ... I became a vegetarian for ethical considerations."[25] This was written in 1897. By 1906 he was able to inform his English correspondent Henry Salt – they had immense admiration for each other – that there were four vegetarian restaurants in Chicago "that serve together many hundreds of people daily." In 1910 he told Salt that "Over here, we are in the midst of a mild crusade against meat-eating." But he had to confess: "As usual, the impelling motive is a selfish one – the desire to save a few cents ... How primitive. How sad. In one sense, how contemptible."[26] He argued that the same general moral code applied "not to the black man and the white woman alone, but to the sorrel horse and the grey squirrel as well. Yes, do as you would be done – not to creatures of your own anatomy or your own guild only, but to all creatures."[27] Like Thomas Tryon and others before him, Moore believed justice to be indivisible. Suffering a debilitating illness, he shot himself at the age of fifty-four in 1916. He seems to have been well ahead of his time, for there is no evidence his vegetarian advocacy had any direct influence on the American intelligentsia. His two major works, *The Universal Kinship* (1906) – "the best ever written in the human-itarian cause," according to Henry Salt – and *The New Ethics* (1907), seem to have remained largely unknown to his own generation.

Upton Sinclair's *The Jungle* (1905), describing *inter alia* the horrors of the slaughterhouse, did rather more to promote the vegetarian message among intellectuals. Yet despite the vegetarian message toward the end of *The Jungle*, Sinclair still treated the human, rather than the slaughtered ani-mal, as the dupe of the slaughterhouse operators. Humans, not animals, were the victims.[28] Indeed, the socialist Sinclair demonstrated his orienta-tion by attending, the year before his death, the presidential signing of the Wholesome Meat Act in 1967. In fact, the vegetarian cause was not promi-nent among intellectuals until the 1960s and 1970s, and then only periph-erally, arising effectively much later than the counterculture, mainly in the 1980s and 1990s with such thinkers as Tom Regan, Daniel Dombrowski, and Carol J. Adams, and culminating in *Food for Thought: The Debate over Eating Meat* (ed. Steve F. Sapontzis, 2004) – a book that presents argu-ments maintained by vegetarian proponents and adversaries, with valuable contributions from numerous philosophers and others, including, on the vegetarian side, in addition to the above-mentioned scholars, James Rachels, Evelyn Pluhar, Bart Gruzalski, Roberta Kalechofsky, and Val Plumwood. The inclusivist position advanced by Tom Regan, one consistent with the views of most modern ethical vegetarians, is expressed by Regan as follows:

> In its simplest terms the animal rights position I uphold maintains that such diverse practices as the use of animals in science, sport, and recreational hunting, the trapping of fur-bearing animals for vanity products, and the practice of raising animals for human consumption are wrong because they systematically violate the rights of animals involved. Morally, these practices ought to be abolished. This is the goal of the social struggle for animal rights. The goal of our individual struggle is to divest ourselves of our moral and economic ties to these injustices – for example, by not wearing the dead skin of animals and by not eating their decaying corpses.[29]

Carol J. Adams added the eco-feminist dimension to the debate, argu-ing that "the sexism in meat eating recapitulates the class distinctions with an added twist: a mythology permeates all classes that meat is a masculine food and meat eating a male activity."[30]

The primary success of the 1980s was in getting the message to many more Americans than had heard it before: everyone was now made aware of vegetarianism and animal rights. If relatively few were convinced, none

could escape the barrage of information. If the 1980s began in some ignorance, a far greater ignorance than in the early years of the century, it ended
with awareness. But those years also brought the problems of opulence and
the desire to have the best – people became proud to have acquired a passion for food, especially gourmet cuisine. Often the best was seen to be
shrimp, scallop, or frog-leg appetizers, together with salmon, filet mignon,
veal, or lobster entrées, all prepared in specialty sauces. And if one had a
surfeit of the "best," there were always the increasingly popular ethnic
cuisines to savour.

Portentously, 1980 was the year of the founding of People for the Ethical
Treatment of Animals (PETA) by Alex Pacheco, who retired after twenty
years at the helm, and Ingrid Newkirk, for many always the primary voice
of the organization. Their outrageous but effective propaganda was (and
still is) disparaged by many, including many vegetarians themselves. But no
one could doubt the success in bringing animal ethics constantly to public
attention. Moreover, PETA's educational work had an extensive and direct
impact on all who were willing to inquire. Animal rights activism and vegetarian, even vegan, promotion were now seen as one and the same. From
now on, those who did not know the plight of food animals had chosen not
to know, or not to care, about the cruelties they were inflicting, even if vicariously. A similar approach, but entirely vegan, was taken by Alex Her-
shaft, founder in 1981 of the Farm Animal Reform Movement (FARM),
which was similarly concerned with outrageous but effective propaganda.
Unfortunately, sometimes, when one has heard the message too often or
too stridently, one becomes deaf to the appeal – stone deaf if one is too selfish to lend an ear. Yet the idea remains among so many, although rarely
voiced, that we would of course be vegetarians in an ideal world, but in this
vale of woe and tears we will carry on much as before. This is an evil world,
so it is okay for us to be somewhat evil, too.

Heir to the Baskin and Robbins ice cream empire and bred to direct the
company, John Robbins renounced his inheritance and published *Diet for
a New America* in 1987, a book that, even if notoriously inaccurate in some
of its detailed evidence and argument, persuaded many that there were
overwhelming economic, environmental, and animal-rights arguments for
adopting a vegetarian diet. Despite the invincible environmentalist arguments for adopting a vegetarian diet, even if they are not as one-sided as
vegetarians sometimes make out, most environmentalists continue their
flesh-consuming ways, a clear indication that whatever primary concern
one has is likely to outweigh all other considerations. Some environmentalists look to the environment alone and do not raise issues that involve

consideration for factors not immediately relevant to their overriding belief in ecological holism, failing to recognize that in such a system nonhuman animals have a right to be considered as individual ends in themselves in the same manner that humans are usually treated as such, especially when individual human lives are at stake. Environmentalists have managed to catch one ear of government, a factor that gives immense prestige and legitimacy, and some consequence, to their cause. Until the animal advocates can catch the other ear of government, or the ear of a sizable and influential group within bureaucracies or legislative bodies, they are likely to remain criers in the wind, even though they may succeed in persuading reasonable numbers of the public that their cause is just. It remains as true today as in the past that power and interest talk far more loudly than justice. And the animal advocates must persuade those in authority not only that they are right but also that their cause is a matter of priority. For that, given the nature of influence in government, animal advocates must relate their goal to a human cause. With considerable justice, vegetarians delight in portraying themselves as uncompromising radicals, believing emphatically that right is on their side, but if the animal advocates are to achieve the success of the ecologists, a wing of the vegetarians must present themselves in moderate guise. Although Edmund Burke is bound to be one of their least admired political philosophers, they must learn from Burke that what is morally right may be politically wrong. Whether the vegetarian advocates want to be pristinely pure or politically effective is a question they must ask of themselves in far more serious than rhetorical vein.

Earthsave, founded by John Robbins in 1989, fulfils the role perhaps better than any other organization of attempting to combine the potentially divisive environmental and vegetarian causes, however similar their ends may appear to be on the surface. Earthsave attempts to show how each can contribute through justice for the environment and for the animals to the individual's health, but the organization seems to have greater effect in persuading animal advocates to acknowledge the merits of the environmental cause than in attracting ecologists to animal rights.

Similarly, PETA, which had attracted 325,000 members by 1990, argued persuasively how the vegetarian and ecology causes could be in unison. Again, however, the effect was far more to put an extra arrow in the vegetarian quill with which to state the vegetarian case than to persuade environmentalists to give consideration to the lives of individual animals of all species. Rather, on the whole, the environmentalists seemed quite willing to subordinate animal interests to the environmental interest and willing, say, to cull large numbers of deer to protect Carolinian forests. Animals mattered when species were endangered. Individual nonhuman – but not human – lives were expendable when no such threats existed. More than anything else, the vegetarian found the need to counter well-healed hordes of those whose wealth and pleasure were derived from the destruction of animal lives, aided by occasional academics more concerned to further their careers through the publication of yet another article than to face squarely a moral issue of considerable magnitude. To be sure, such individuals – whether rancher, hunter, or academic – recognize the human as an animal, but somehow the human animal never appears as an animal in quite the same manner that other animals are animal – a point that has been stressed frequently in this book. Almost never are the criteria thought appropriate for the consideration of human rights the same criteria as those thought appropriate for the consideration of nonhuman rights. Other than a few hidebound relics of a previous era, physicians seem no longer willing to portray a flesh diet as essential to human health, although they tend to deviate from recommending an omnivorous diet only when there are compelling immediate health reasons for a particular patient to eschew flesh. Certainly, physicians now warn against the dangers of the excesses of flesh, especially trans fats, but despite the increasing scientific evidence they are loath to advocate the final step, especially when the eating of fish is declared to be so beneficial to the human race. It is a damning indictment of the human species, which prides itself on its much vaunted moral sense, that it is able to escape the opprobrium of killing and torturing sentient beings. There appears to be little recognition of the validity of the argument that, *even if* animal food were advantageous to human health, this fact would not give humans the right to deprive other animals of their lives. Even the former cattle rancher turned animal advocate Howard Lyman, of *Voice for a Viable Future,* is unable to persuade his former colleagues of their cruelty and lack of consideration, although, undoubtedly, he provides valuable grist to the animal advocacy mill in showing from experience how inexcusable is the behaviour of his former colleagues.

The greatest advantage the modern vegetarian possesses over those of previous centuries is the significant number and variety of vegetarian organizations that help to further the cause. The modern vegetarian is far more impervious to the dangers of backsliding, of feeling alone, of feeling "different" and isolated, for even if family – sometimes even spouse or parents, friends and associates – continue to consume flesh, there is always a friendly and supportive voice on a website or at a conference able and willing to comfort and give strength and added validation to the ethical choices. There is always an organization with meetings to attend that help to reinforce the commitment as well as provide new and alternative friends. More and more grocery stores have substantial vegetarian sections that further the recognition that one does not stand entirely outside the community. More and more restaurants offer multiple vegetarian options, not just a dish from which the flesh portion has been omitted. Less and less are vegetarians considered oddballs; perhaps they are not yet deemed "normal," but increasingly this is so. Perhaps the worst-treated vegetarians are American Christian vegetarians – at least to judge from the complaints one hears from them about the derision heaped upon them by their fellow Christians – except in the few churches committed to the vegetarian diet. In establishment American Christianity, one still hears frequently the absurd claim that God commanded humans to eat flesh – which shows how little they know of the teachings of their own religion. It may be that certain segments of American Christianity are among the final bastions of ignorance and prejudice waiting to be overcome in this changing world.

## Canada

Canada's climate and the great difficulty of providing a year-round vegetarian diet will undoubtedly have inhibited any serious spread of vegetarian practice before the development of refrigeration in the twentieth century that could keep vegetables fresh over the hot summer months and that could assist trucks and trains to transport chilled vegetables from regions with far milder climates further south during the cold winters and in early spring. Indeed, traditionally, the Inuit diet was an almost entirely flesh diet, a fact reflective of horticultural impossibility in the Far North, which is also to be found, with only degrees of lesser difficulty beyond the fertile spring and summer months, somewhat further to the south. To be sure, wedded as English-speaking Canada was, prior to the mid-twentieth century, to British thought and tradition, with American influence increasing rapidly from the Edwardian era on, the vegetarian arguments will have been known well enough but will not have been seen to have a ready application in the Canadian context. The Canadian winter climate was a powerful argument against vegetarianism until well into the twentieth century.

In fact, organizationally, little or nothing happened on behalf of ethical vegetarianism in Canada prior to the founding of the Toronto Vegetarian Association in 1945. No doubt, there were individual secular vegetarians before that time, and of course, there were the Doukhobors and other religious vegetarian sects. But individual Canadians had to look to European and American vegetarian groups for comradeship and information on the latest developments. Vegetarianism perhaps got its start in Canada with the Doukhobors, who had originally been a communal Russian religious group prominent in Eastern Europe in the eighteenth and nineteenth centuries and subject to frequent persecution. They were befriended by Tolstoy, who enabled them to emigrate to Canada in 1898-99, some 7,400 of them moving to what is now Saskatchewan. Predominantly, they were "naturists," practising nudism and vegetarianism and believing fiercely in their own independence from all authority, whether secular or religious. Even when still in Russia, not all Doukhobors were entirely vegetarian, although in 1895 they determined to become so. In Canada, they were at first vegetarian, but today, whereas many of the remaining Doukhobors on communal farms remain vegetarian, many of those who began independent farms also began raising livestock and eating flesh. Today, the Doukhobors who moved to British Columbia – 5,000 bought land and resettled in British Columbia in 1908 after much of their donated Saskatchewan land was confiscated when the Doukhobors refused to swear the oath of allegiance – are more likely to be vegetarian than their Saskatchewan counterparts. In both provinces, they are today in serious decline in numbers.

With some similarity to the United States, there was also a Swedenborgian church in Canada founded at Kitchener, then called Berlin, in 1842, but neither the church, nor any of the other Swedenborgian churches that followed throughout the country, especially in the West, seemed especially interested in the vegetarianism within Swedenborgian doctrine. Ironically, the Berlin church claimed as a member J.M. Schneider, the butcher who founded the J.M. Schneider flesh-foods company in 1890.

The founding of the Toronto Vegetarian Association in 1945, a society that has continued uninterrupted to today, was followed shortly by the Calgary Vegetarian Association, which at some point faltered, a new Calgary association being instituted in 1993. The Canadian Vegetarian Union (CVU) was acknowledged in the 1950 minutes of the Congress of the International Vegetarian Union, where confirmation of the membership application of the CVU was also recorded. Members of the International Vegetarian Union from the Toronto and Calgary associations were recorded in 1960, from the Winnipeg association in 1993, and from the Atlantic association in 2003. The membership of the Toronto association, which began with 20 members, had become 150 a year later. By 1965, it became increasingly involved in animal-rights activities when it had some 500 members. Membership grew further to 1,000 members in 1993 and to 1,400 in 1995. By the turn of the century, the number was said to be 1,700.

Apart from the Toronto Vegetarian Association, with its only modest historical lineage, it would appear that continued interest in vegetarian ideals in Canada was decidedly late in its arrival. Nonetheless, vegetarianism in Canada is today very much on the upswing and includes among its adherents a substantial proportion of vegans.

## THE NORTH AMERICAN VEGETARIAN SOCIETY, THE VEGETARIAN UNION OF NORTH AMERICA, AND THE INTERNATIONAL VEGETARIAN UNION

The Vegetarian Society of America having long been defunct, probably since 1922 when Rev. Henry Clubb passed away, it was considered important to give the North American vegetarian movement an organizational base. Thus was the North American Vegetarian Society founded in 1974 to act as an umbrella group for more regionally based organizations and to help institute new organizations. There are today numerous American and several Canadian affiliates. Its first major function was to host the World Vegetarian Congress at the University of Maine in 1975, co-organized by the vegan Jay Dinshah, the largest congress put on yet for the International Vegetarian Union. The International Vegetarian Union was instituted in 1908 with the intent to provide an avenue for promotion of the vegetarian ideal throughout the world. By 1914 there was an associated vegetarian society in almost all the European countries, several of them, together with New Zealand and Australia, joining at the founding. By 1960, Asia outside of India – India was a fairly early member – was represented, as was Africa. Latin America and the Caribbean followed in 1975. In 1985 the International Vegetarian Union created the regional council of the European Vegetarian Union; in 1987 the Vegetarian Union of North America, formed in Toronto, followed as a regional council; and in 1999 came the equivalent Asian Vegetarian Union, all serving as liaisons with the worldwide vegetarian movement. The International Vegetarian Movement holds world congresses, usually every two years, as has been noted, whereas the regional councils hold regional conferences, usually in the year between the two world congresses.

# Postscript: Prospects

In the May 2001 edition of *Enroute,* Air Canada's inflight magazine directed largely to the business traveller, the opening article included an interview with Pierre Lacombe, the former executive vice president of a chain of vegetarian restaurants. The article implied that foot-and-mouth disease and the mad cow scare were primary factors in the contemporary increasing popularity of vegetarianism but speculated, with somewhat potential to be misunderstood, that "this trend is a return to the norm, a reminder that a predominantly vegetarian diet has historically been the rule rather than the exception for most of the world's population."[1] In the interview Lacombe reported that the "number of people who include vegetarian meals in their weekly menus is rising fast. In Canada, the health food sector is growing by about 25 percent a year, compared with 2 percent for the food sector as a whole. Per capita meat consumption peaked in the late 1980s and is now on the decline."[2] Although vegetarian food and what is commonly regarded as health food should certainly not be equated, vegetarian food constitutes a fair proportion of health food. The factors reported by Lacombe with perhaps a little exaggeration are probably replicated elsewhere in the Western world. It should perhaps also be noted that Lacombe regards the "percentage of strict vegetarians in the developed world to be about the same everywhere: 5 percent," a rather higher figure than has been deemed probable in this book.[3]

As we have seen, vegetarianism was extremely well argued in classical Greece and the Roman Empire without it ever becoming a predominant Western viewpoint. In early and medieval Christianity, vegetarianism was again espoused by a decided minority. It became popular and somewhat respectable, at least among the intelligentsia, at the turn of the nineteenth century and again in the middle and toward the end of that century, before going into a decline. Vegetarianism has now become increasingly popular, albeit slowly, ever since the 1960s. Is there likely to be any difference this time? Is vegetarianism just another "fad," awaiting its inevitable decline as circumstances alter? Is vegetarianism now permanently mainstream? What are the differences between the current increasing popularity of vegetarianism and previous periods of popularity? We might suggest the relevant factors in favour of vegetarian advances to be that: (1) increased awareness of the deleterious effects of interventions in food production by big business has resulted in legitimate health fears and some consequent flesh avoidance; (2) the legitimacy of the vegetarian diet has increased, as exemplified by media and medical-journal treatment of the issues; (3) in light of increasing medical knowledge, physicians now only rarely tell their patients of the necessity of flesh for health, except in certain exceptional cases and even then without adequate justification; (4) at one time, the flesh food industry would proclaim the unhealthiness of a vegetarian diet, whereas today it is compelled to resort, on the whole, to spurious and unconvincing claims that flesh food can be equally as healthy as a vegetarian regimen; (5) increased general education has resulted in a willingness to question traditional authority on issues of diet and has consequently made vegetarianism a more likely option for many individuals, especially the well-educated; (6) increased awareness in the public as a whole of issues relating to animal rights has put vegetarianism on the moral agenda in a way that was not possible in the past when education, especially higher education, was restricted to an elite; (7) increased use of Internet sites and Internet e-mail has served to maintain the interest and commitment of those who have been convinced by the vegetarian arguments; (8) increased, if not a great amount of, publicity for the vegetarian and animal-rights causes in college and university courses and through books, at frequent conferences, and by other means of regular communication have increased significantly the attention given to animal ethics; (9) as a greater variety of easy-to-prepare, precooked, appetizing, vegetarian options has become available in grocery stores, the easier it has become for working couples, especially those couples with children, to turn to a vegetarian diet; a precondition of this practice increasing will be a diminution of a certain amount of vegetarian purist prejudice against fleshless meals that resemble their meat counterparts (e.g., tofu "chicken" and soy "meatballs"); (10) the acknowledgment by significant segments of the medical profession that a vegetarian diet is perfectly healthy – a fact they once denied – has increased its acceptability; (11) there have been considerable advances in nutritional knowledge, so it is far easier than previously to avoid the deleterious health consequences sometimes faced in the past; (12) vegetarian cuisine is now far more appealing and enjoyable than at any time in the past.

Nonetheless, several limits to potential vegetarian advances might be noted. (1) The decreased cost of certain flesh foods makes them more affordable than in the past and perhaps more affordable than many healthy vegetarian items. (2) The continued importance of flesh for all the social reasons outlined in the Introduction has persisted in the context of family and collegial dinners, particularly on special occasions such as first dates, weddings and funerals, religious festivals, and occasions that once had a religious origin. (3) Genesis 9:3 supersedes the earlier vegan edict by legitimizing a flesh diet following the flood: "Every moving thing that liveth shall be meat for you." It is a justification of flesh consumption that is still used, especially in the United States, to suggest that a vegetarian diet is unholy and contrary to God's will – even as a command – which, of course, is not the case. Such religious legitimization diminishes the vegetarian appeal for a considerable number of practising Christians. Nonetheless, there are a few churches that advocate vegetarian or vegan diets, including perhaps the most radical of all, the Universal Equalitarian Church of Missouri, whose motto reads: "Where All Species Are Created Equal." (4) The increased wealth, both personal and national, throughout much (but by no means all) of the world arising from general economic development has encouraged, and is encouraging, the counting of flesh consumption as a mark of success, a fact readily notable in the Caribbean, India, and China, for example. (5) The ability of the organized business forces of intensive farming to spend vast sums of money to make their products popular and appealing has continued. Such publicity makes their claims difficult to counter. However, the successes of very well-funded groups, such as People for the Ethical Treatment of Animals (PETA), enable these groups to retaliate against, although not yet to defeat, such business strength. (6) There has been a rise in regressive and ultraconservative political trends in the United States and Europe. (7) There has been a concomitant rise of religious fundamentalism in both Christianity and Islam during the same period. (8) Finally, and most important, the evolutionary need shown in Chapter 1 to find some replacement for the hunt, most easily achieved through some kind of sporting activity, in order to satisfy the idea of conquest in the human, especially the male, psyche remains a vital factor. This has already occurred to some significant degree: witness the gradual decline in hunting over the decades as the felt need for hunting has declined and sports activities have increased. Now, fewer than 10 percent of the populations of Western nations engage in hunting. But more needs to be done immediately to associate vegetarianism with athletic activity as the English Vegetarian Society once did with cycling. Such activities promote the vegetarian cause to individuals who otherwise might be impervious to the vegetarian appeal. Moreover, such activities serve to associate pleasurable events with something seen prima facie as a burden and thus make the latter more desirable, even something directly associated with the former. At the very least, social gatherings – and there are already more than a few – on a rather more local basis than the biennial meetings of the International Vegetarian Union would encourage a greater sense of belonging and commitment among the converted. To date, however, there are few notable successes.

Although the prospects for immediate and large increases in the number of vegetarians is not especially encouraging, a critical mass embracing vegetarianism would nonetheless offer genuine possibilities. If such a critical mass comprised say 15 or 20 or perhaps even as little as 10 percent of the population of complex Western economies – that is, those that are not likely to experience rapid economic development in the foreseeable future of the type now affecting China and India – we could be confident that the very normality of vegetarianism would encourage many more to take the ethical step. We are such mimetic creatures! Almost always, we do what most of our associates do. If, prehistorically, cannibalism was replaced by the ritual eating of animals, other rituals can surely be conceived to satisfy the imaginary need for flesh, presumed by so many to be a necessary part of being truly human. Above all, it will be when others find the vegetarian life not merely morally superior but also preferable as a way of life that vegetarianism will succeed. When vegetarians receive not just respect for their morals but also envy for their status, vegetarianism will make the inroads that have for so long eluded it. It is not an impossible dream. And instances of it are being witnessed. After all, not too many years in the past, smoking conferred status on the smoker. Now, the reverse is true. Today, it is the wastrel and the underachiever who are depicted as smokers. A higher status is conferred on the nonsmoker. And the proportion of nonsmokers in society has increased dramatically. Vegetarianism will succeed when more and more people *aspire* to be vegetarians, taking their inspiration from more and more vegetarian role models.

Ironically, the greatest prospect for vegetarianism arises precisely because of a condition all animal advocates deplore: greater human dominance over other species than at any prior time in history. Today, we no longer live in fear of other species in the West. There is little fear of dangerous predatory carnivores or slithering creatures of deadly venom, little fear of plague- and disease-spreading rodents. The animal – the "other" – is no longer viewed as our natural enemy. Animals are no longer quite so "other." Animals are no longer a serious threat to our very lives or the food supply on which our lives depend, as they once were. They are no longer intrinsically "alien." It is precisely because we no longer live in dread that we can afford to respect. Once, at best, we felt awe for the megafauna – and awe is originally based in fear. Now, we can feel a measure of a bond. And when there is respect and bonding, there is no desire to seek the revenge from which our substantial flesh eating probably originally arose.

Still, one sometimes despairs at the possibility of any long-term success at all. Perhaps the human being is congenitally incapable of species improvement. After all, *Homo sapiens* is the only species one could conceive to be so oblivious of its own reality as to devise terms for itself – humanity, humane, humanitarian – that refer to the very antithesis of the reality of human behaviour throughout recorded history. Humanity has never, as a rule, practised humanity, acted humanely, or been a humanitarian species. May such unjustified self-glorification not last in perpetuity. Even better, and even more unlikely, would it be if the ethical self-glorification were to become justified.

# Notes

ACKNOWLEDGMENTS

1. Although the title of this book is an allusion to the sixteenth-century *Catechism* in the *Book of Common Prayer* of the Anglican Church, I do not pretend that sixteenth-century Anglicanism was at all vegetarian in its outlook, merely that many early vegetarians deemed the desire to eat animal flesh to have arisen from the same aspects of human character as the "sinful lusts of the flesh" warned against in the catechism.

## INTRODUCTION: BILL OF FARE TO THE FEAST

1. Henry Fielding opened the Contents page of *Tom Jones* with the words: "The introduction to the work, or bill of fare of the feast." How much more appropriate are such words to open a tome concerned with the ethics of diet rather than with the occasional lack of ethics of an engagingly roguish foundling. The phrase "Wisdom's Bill of Fare" was used by the seventeenth-century Pythagorean Thomas Tryon to refer to a vegetarian diet. Mary McCarthy, *The Group* (1963; reprint, Franklin Center, PA: Franklin Library, 1978), 4, 5.

2. In his *Introduction to the Principles of Morals and Legislation,* ed. J.H. Burns and H.L.A. Hart (1789; reprint, London: Methuen, 1982), Jeremy Bentham famously argued, in favour of the application of moral principles to animals, that "the question is not, can they *reason,* nor can they *talk,* but can they *suffer?*" (sec. 17, subsec. 4b, 282, original emphasis). In *The Principles of Penal Law* (1811), in *The Works of Jeremy Bentham,* vol. 10 (1843; reprint, New York: Russell, 1962), however, he averred: "It ought to be lawful to kill animals, but not to torment them" (549-50). Of course, one could argue that Prothero, as a hunter, tormented as well as killed them.

3. On William Karkeek, see Rod Preece, ed., *Immortal Animal Souls: Joseph Hamilton's Animal Futurity (1877), together with the Debate among Karkeek, Spooner and Manthorp*

on *"The Future Existence of the Brute Creation" (1839-1840)* (Lampeter: Mellen, 2005); see also William Youatt, *The Obligation and Extent of Humanity to Brutes, Principally Considered with Reference to the Domesticated Animals,* ed. Rod Preece (1839; reprint, Lampeter: Mellen, 2003).

4. Rabbi Alfred S. Cohen, "Vegetarianism from a Jewish Perspective," in Roberta Kalechofsky, ed., *Judaism and Animal Rights* (Marblehead, MA: Micah, 1992), 176.

5. Hilda Kean, *Animal Rights: Political and Social Change in Britain since 1800* (London: Reaktion Books, 1998), 204, citing Realeat and Oxford surveys in 1994 of 11,000 people, as quoted in Emma Haughton, "The Fruit and Nut Case," *Guardian* (London), 3 June 1997, 13.

6. Sushil Mattal and Gene Thursby, eds., *The Hindu World* (New York: Routledge, 2004), 367.

7. James Gaffney, "Eastern Religions and the Eating of Meat," in Steve F. Sapontzis, ed., *Food for Thought: The Debate over Eating Meat* (Amherst, NY: Prometheus Books, 2004), 233.

8. Jan Dodd et al., *The Rough Guide to Japan* (London: Rough Guides Limited, 2001), 9.

9. As reported by BBC World News, 15 February 2005.

10. As stated in Lorna Chamberlain, *Pawsitive News* (London, ON), Summer 2004, 1-5.

11. Bernard Shaw, *Three Plays* (Franklin Center, PA: Franklin Library, 1979), 16.

12. Mary Midgley, *Animals and Why They Matter* (Athens: University of Georgia Press, 1983), 27.

13. Roger Scruton, "The Conscientious Carnivore," in Sapontzis, ed., *Food for Thought*, 81-91.

14. George Salmon, *Introduction to the New Testament*, ch. 11, 243, as quoted under "vegetarian" in the *Oxford English Dictionary*.

15. See, for example, Dan Murphy, *Meatingplace.com*, 10 September 2004, reproduced by Doug Powell on *Food Safety Network*, same date.

16. Voltaire, *Candide*, trans. Tobias Smollett (1759; reprint, Franklin Center, PA: Franklin Library, 1978), 3.

17. In fact, the Hebrew word *rādā,* which is translated as "dominion," allows for authority over animals but with a corresponding obligation toward them. See Rod Preece and David Fraser, "The Status of Animals in Biblical and Christian Thought: A Study in Colliding Values," *Society and Animals: Journal of Human-Animal Studies* 8, 3 (2000): 245-63, esp. 247. An explanation at greater length is to be found in this book at pages 120-21.

18. Henry Fielding, *The History of Tom Jones: A Foundling* (1749; reprint, Franklin Center, PA: Franklin Library, 1980), 8.

19. Ibid., 11.

20. Émile Zola, *Nana,* trans. George Holden (1880; reprint, Franklin Center, PA: Franklin Library, 1981), 78.

21. Ibid., 164.

22. William Minto, *Logic: Inductive and Deductive* (London: John Murray, 1909), 51.

23. Quoted in James A. Maxwell, ed., *America's Fascinating Indian Heritage* (Pleasantville, NY: Pegasus, 1978), 315.

24. George Nicholson, *On the Primeval Diet of Man,* ed. Rod Preece (1801; reprint, Lampeter: Mellen, 1999), 18.

25. See Howard Williams, *The Ethics of Diet: A Catena of Authorities Deprecatory of the*

*Practice of Flesh-Eating,* ed. Carol J. Adams (1883; reprint, Urbana: University of Illinois Press, 2003), 162-63.

26. F.R. Cowell, *Cicero and the Roman Republic* (Harmondsworth: Penguin, 1956), 54.

27. On *Larry King Live,* CNN, 1 July 2005.

28. Emily Klassen, quoted in the *London Free Press* (London, ON), 22 September 2004, D2.

29. See Richard Schwartz, *Judaism and Vegetarianism,* rev. ed. (New York: Lantern, 2000), esp. 15-16 and 109-10.

30. Plato, *Apology of Socrates,* 38A.

31. Clement of Alexandria, *Miscellanies VII,* in *The Writings of Clement of Alexandria,* trans. W. Wilson (London: Hamilton and Co., 1867), quoted in Colin Spencer, *Vegetarianism: A History,* 2nd ed. (New York and London: Four Walls Eight Windows, 2002), 120.

32. As late as 1814, Percy Bysshe Shelley encountered stories of cannibalism in France occasioned by the ravages of the postrevolutionary wars.

## Chapter 1: The Human in Prehistory

1. See page 104.

2. George Nicholson, *On the Primeval Diet of Man,* ed. Rod Preece (1801; reprint, Lampeter: Mellen, 1999), 23-24.

3. Keith Thomas, *Man and the Natural World: Changing Attitudes in England, 1500-1800* (London: Penguin, 1984), 289.

4. For example, see Mathias Guenther, *Tricksters and Trancers: Bushman Religion and Society* (Bloomington: Indiana University Press, 1999), where he refers to items of Bushman practice: "stuffs gathered by the women: roots, seeds, leaves, nuts, and melons, on occasion with a few click beetles, lizards, fledgling birds, or the odd tortoise thrown in, to round out the food groups" (148). Such foods are classified together in one distinctive category and contrasted with "the 'male' game antelopes and predatory felines" (152) hunted by the men, which are classified in a distinctive category.

5. See, for example, Genesis 9:4.

6. Jean de La Fontaine, *Discours à Madame de la Sablière* (written before 1679), cited by George Boas, *The Happy Beast in French Thought of the Seventeenth Century* (1933; reprint, New York: Octagon Books, 1966), 153.

7. Thomas Hobbes, *The English Works of Thomas Hobbes of Malmesbury,* vol. 5, ed. Sir William Molesworth (London: G. Bohn, 1839), 187-88.

8. Desmond Morris, *The Animal Contract* (London: Virgin, 1990), 85; Jared Diamond, *The Third Chimpanzee: The Evolution and Future of the Human Animal* (San Francisco: HarperPerennial, 1992), 4-5, 36, and elsewhere.

9. Randall Collura, "What Is Our Natural Diet, and Should We Really Care?" in Steve F. Sapontzis, ed., *Food for Thought: The Debate over Eating Meat* (Amherst, NY: Prometheus Books, 2004), 36.

10. See Nicholson, *Primeval Diet.*

11. Collura, "What Is Our Natural Diet?" 36.

12. Although the idea is from Genesis, the exact phrase comes from Milton, *Paradise Lost,* bk. 1, 1.1.

13. Collura, "What Is Our Natural Diet?" 42.

14. Donna Hart and Robert W. Sussman, *Man the Hunted: Primates, Predators, and Human Evolution* (New York: Westview, 2005), 16.

15. M. Teaford and P. Ungar, "Diet and the Evolution of the Earliest Human Ancestors," *Proceedings of the National Academy of Science* 97 (2000): 13, 508-13, 509.

16. Hélène A. Guerber, *Myths and Legends of the Middle Ages: Their Origins and Influence in Literature and Art* (1909; reprint, London: G.G. Harrap, 1926), 241.

17. Quoted in Francis Ween, *How Mumbo-Jumbo Conquered the World* (London: Harper-Perennial, 2004), x.

18. Ibid., 10.

19. Voltaire, *Candide*, trans. Tobias Smollett (Franklin Center, PA: Franklin Library, 1978), 23.

20. Gustave Flaubert, *Madame Bovary: A Story of Provincial Life* (New York: Oxford University Press, 1985), 179.

21. Pliny the Elder, *Natural History: A Selection*, trans. John F. Healy (London: Penguin, 1991), 104.

22. See Rod Preece, *Brute Souls, Happy Beasts, and Evolution: The Historical Status of Animals* (Vancouver: University of British Columbia Press, 2005), ch. 4.

23. Elijah D. Buckner, *The Immortality of Animals,* ed. Rod Preece (1903; reprint, Lampeter: Mellen, 2003), 23, 24. See also John Wesley, "The General Deliverance," in *Sermons on Several Occasions*, 2nd ser., sermon 60, in *The Works of John Wesley*, vol. 6 (1872; reprint, Grand Rapids, MI: Zondervan, n.d.), 240ff.

24. Hesiod, *Theogeny and Works and Days,* ed. and trans. M.L. West (Oxford: Oxford University Press, 1988), 42, 40.

25. Ibid., xix.

26. Ovid, quoted in Arthur O. Lovejoy and George Boas, *Primitivism and Related Ideas in Antiquity* (1935; reprint, Baltimore: Johns Hopkins University Press, 1977), 46-47.

27. Empedocles, via Diels, *Fragmente der Vorsokratiker*, 4th ed., vol. 1, 271-72, quoted in ibid., 33.

28. Scholiast to Nicander, *Theriaca*, 452, quoted in Jonathan Barnes, *Early Greek Philosophy* (London: Penguin, 1987), 199.

29. See Mircea Eliade, *The Myth of the Eternal Return, or Cosmos and History* (Princeton: Princeton University Press, 1974).

30. Joseph Campbell, *Historical Atlas of World Mythology,* vol. 2, *The Way of the Seeded Earth*, pt. 3, "Mythologies of the Primitive Planters: The Middle and Southern Americas" (New York: Harper and Row, 1989), 331.

31. Joseph Campbell, *Historical Atlas of World Mythology,* vol. 1, *The Way of the Animal Powers,* pt. 1, "Mythologies of the Primitive Hunters and Gatherers" (New York: Harper and Row, 1988), 14.

32. Nicholson, *Primeval Diet,* 20.

33. Maynard Mack, *Alexander Pope: A Life* (New York: Norton, 1985), 31.

34. Richard Erdoes and Alfonso Ortiz, "Great Medicine Makes a Beautiful Country," in Richard Erdoes and Alfonso Ortiz, eds., *American Indian Myths and Legends* (1984; reprint, London: Pimlico, 1997), 111-14. The story is based on a 1905 account by George A. Dorsey that is entirely consistent with the accounts collected in 1899 by the American Museum of Natural History.

35. Ibid.

36. Collura, "What Is Our Natural Diet?" 44.

37. The Jungian element will be readily recognized. I claim it to be also Wordsworthian because of, for example, the words in "Ode: Intimations of Immortality from Recollections of Early Childhood" (1807), stanza 10: "the primal sympathy! Which having been must ever be."

38. Some pet-food stores offer vegetarian food specially prepared for companion animals, which many animal advocates, as evidenced by claims on vegetarian webpages, claim to succeed in providing a healthy diet for their charges. And although I am skeptical and dubious, I have sufficient respect for two such raisers of animals that I am not prepared to dismiss their claims out of hand, at least not for dogs, although cats are much more complete carnivores who would, at the very least, require a diet that included a taurine supplement. The story is related in Johanna Angermeyer, *My Father's Island: A Galapagos Quest* (London: Viking, 1989), of how it was a common South American belief in the 1920s that an ocelot reared as a pet could be rendered harmless by being fed a vegetarian diet. The "common belief" was not verified in practice. Moreover, Howard Williams, *The Ethics of Diet: A Catena of Authorities Deprecatory of the Practice of Flesh-Eating*, ed. Carol J. Adams (1883; reprint, Urbana: University of Illinois Press, 2003), 8, appears to hold to the same view when he tells us that "there are well-authenticated instances, even in our own times, of true *carnivora* that have been fed, for longer or shorter periods, upon the non-flesh diet." It would appear he believed *carnivora* could readily become successful herbivores by a change in diet.

39. See Preece, *Brute Souls*, ch. 6.

40. Charles Darwin, quoted in Adrian Desmond and James Moore, *Darwin: The Life of a Tormented Evolutionist* (New York: Warner, 1992), 449.

41. "The Sayings of the Fathers," in Helen Waddell, ed. and trans., *The Sayings of the Desert Fathers* (New York Vintage Books, 1998), 160. The saying is derived from Isaiah 11:9: "They shall not hurt nor destroy in all my holy mountain."

42. Porphyry, *On Abstinence from Animal Food*, excerpted in Kerry S. Walters and Lisa Portmess, eds., *Ethical Vegetarianism: From Pythagoras to Peter Singer* (Albany, NY: State University of New York Press, 1999), 45.

43. Collura, "What Is Our Natural Diet?" 37.

44. Daniel Dombrowski, *The Philosophy of Vegetarianism* (Amherst: University of Massachusetts Press, 1984), 19.

45. Dostoevsky, *The Devils*, vol. 2, 21, quoted in Joseph Frank, *Dostoevsky: The Miraculous Years, 1865-1871* (Princeton: Princeton University Press, 2002), 26.

46. See, for example, Hans Kruuk, *Hunters and Hunted: Relationships between Carnivores and People* (Cambridge, UK: Cambridge University Press, 2002).

47. As noted in Barbara Ehrenreich, *Blood Rites: Origins and History of the Passions of War* (New York: Henry Holt, 1997), 43.

48. Ibid., 44.

49. William Godwin, from a letter to Mary Wollstonecraft.

50. In fact, in Ontario (the largest province) only seven persons have been killed by black bears since 1916. There is a population of between 75,000 and 100,000 black bears in Ontario.

51. Hart and Sussman, *Man the Hunted*, 74.

52. Colin Campbell, quoted in ibid., 229.

53. Porphyry, *On Abstinence from Animal Food*, ed. E.W. Tyson, trans. Thomas Taylor (1793; reprint, Fontwell, UK: Centaur, 1965), 53.

54. Plato, *The Trial and Death of Socrates: Four Dialogues* (New York: Dover, 1992), 12.
55. James Serpell, *In the Company of Animals: A Study of Human-Animal Relationships* (Oxford: Blackwell, 1988), 5.
56. Ehrenreich, *Blood Rites,* 26-27.
57. René Girard, *Violence and the Sacred* (Baltimore: Johns Hopkins University Press, 1979).
58. See Hans-Peter Schmidt, "The Origins of Ahimsa," in *Mélanges d'Indianisme à la mémoire de Louis Renou* (Paris: Éditions E. Boccard, 1968), 644-45.
59. Ehrenreich, *Blood Rites,* 83.

## CHAPTER 2: EASTERN RELIGIONS AND PRACTICE

1. Mircea Eliade, *Yoga: Immortality and Freedom,* 2nd ed., trans. Willard R. Trask (Princeton: Princeton University Press, 1969), viii.
2. See Rod Preece, *Animals and Nature: Cultural Myths, Cultural Realities* (Vancouver: University of British Columbia Press, 1999), esp. 12-13.
3. Voltaire, quoted in Archibald Ballantyne, *Voltaire's Visit to England* (1893; reprint, Geneva: Slatkine Reprints, 1970), 169.
4. See D.N. Jha, *The Myth of the Holy Cow* (London and New York: Verso, 2002), 39-40.
5. Ibid., 29.
6. See ibid., 34ff.
7. See the quotations from Professor Lal on page 64.
8. Jha, *Myth of the Holy Cow,* 116-17.
9. Steven J. Rosen, *Holy Cow: The Hare Krishna Contribution to Vegetarianism and Animal Rights* (New York: Lantern Books, 2004), 27.
10. James Gaffney, "Eastern Religions and the Eating of Meat," in Steve F. Sapontzis, ed., *Food for Thought: The Debate over Eating Meat* (New York: Prometheus Books, 2004), 226.
11. *Mahabharata,* 109.10, quoted in Rosen, *Holy Cow,* 29.
12. *Pancatantra* 13, 14, quoted in G. Naganathan, *Animal Welfare and Nature: Hindu Scriptural Perspectives* (Washington, DC: Center for Respect of Life and Environment, 1989), 10, 15.
13. Vishnu Sarna, ed., *The Pancatantra,* trans. Chandra Rajan (London: Penguin, 1993).
14. Naganathan, *Animal Welfare,* 2.
15. R.C. Zaehner, trans., *Hindu Scriptures* (London: J.M. Dent, 1966), 185.
16. Juan Mascaró, ed. and trans., *The Upanishads* (London: Penguin, 1973), 49.
17. See Introduction, note 17.
18. *Mahabharata,* 12, quoted in Naganathan, *Animal Welfare,* 9.
19. *Mahabharata,* 13, quoted in ibid., 15.
20. *Bhagavad Gita,* bk. 10, 20, quoted in, Zaehner, trans., *Hindu Scriptures,* 325.
21. *Mahabharata,* quoted in Jon Wynne-Tyson, ed., *The Extended Circle: A Commonplace Book of Animal Rights* (New York: Paragon House, 1989), 122. For a lengthy list of relevant passages from the *Mahabharata,* see Christopher Key Chapple, *Nonviolence to Animals, Earth and Self in Asian Traditions* (Albany: State University of New York Press, 1993), 16-17.
22. *Hitopadesa,* quoted in Wynne-Tyson, ed., *Extended Circle,* 121.

23. *Bhagavatam*, 6, quoted in Naganathan, *Animal Welfare*, 5.
24. Rosen, *Holy Cow*, 22.
25. Mohandas K. Gandhi, *An Autobiography: The Story of My Experiments with Truth* (1947; reprint, Boston: Beacon Press, 1993), 235.
26. Joseph Campbell, *Baksheesh and Brahman: Indian Journal, 1954-1955*, ed. Robert Larsen, Stephen Larsen, and Anthony van Couvering (New York: HarperCollins, 1995), 42-43.
27. Mohandas K. Gandhi, *How to Serve the Cow* (1934), quoted in Marvin Harris, *Cows, Pigs, Wars and Witches: The Riddles of Culture* (1974; reprint, New York: Vintage Books, 1989), 26.
28. Campbell, *Baksheesh and Brahman*, 144.
29. Rosen, *Holy Cow*, 23.
30. *Laws of Manu*, 5.53, quoted in ibid., 23.
31. See Jha, *Myth of the Holy Cow*, 34.
32. *Laws of Manu*, 5.27, quoted in John Mackenzie, *Hindu Ethics: A Historical and Critical Essay* (1922; reprint, New Delhi: Oriental Books Reprint Corporation, 1971), 59.
33. *Laws of Manu*, quoted in ibid., 60.
34. Basant K. Lal, "Hindu Perspectives on the Use of Animals," in Tom Regan, ed., *Animal Sacrifices: Religious Perspectives on the Use of Animals in Science* (Philadelphia: Temple University Press, 1986), 200.
35. Ibid., 205.
36. Jha, *Myth of the Holy Cow*, 91, 143.
37. Mackenzie, *Hindu Ethics*, 60, in reference to the *Laws of Manu*.
38. Ranchor Prine, *Hindu Ecology: Seeds of Truth* (London: Cassell, 1992), 11. Prine is here paraphrasing the words of Salish Kumar.
39. See ibid. For a balanced view of the influence of the British on the Raj, see the interviews with Maharajah Raj Singh of Dungarpur, Ali Ahmed Broli, and Zulfiqar Jamote in Christopher Ondaatje, *Sind Revisited* (Toronto: HarperCollins, 1996), 72-74, 125-26, 184-87.
40. Mohandas K. Gandhi, *Young India*, 18 November 1926.
41. Idanna Pucci, ed., *Bhima Swarga: The Balinese Journey of the Soul* (Boston: Little, Brown, 1992), 84, 98.
42. Charles Wei-Hsun Fu and Gerhard E. Spiegler, eds., *Movements and Issues in World Religions* (New York: Greenwood, 1987).
43. See Jha, *Myth of the Holy Cow*, 63ff.
44. See ibid., 65.
45. Ibid., 67.
46. Ibid., 69
47. Ibid., 70.
48. Ibid., 71.
49. See ibid., x.
50. *Dhammapada*, 129, in Juan Mascaró, ed. and trans., *The Dhammapada* (London: Penguin, 1973), 54. Section 130 is identical to that of 129, with the exception that the words "life is dear to all" replace "all fear death."
51. *Dhammapada*, 270, in ibid., 74.
52. *Dhammapada*, 405, in ibid., 91.
53. See Jha, *Myth of the Holy Cow*, x.
54. See Michael Holroyd, *Bernard Shaw*, vol. 3 (Harmondsworth: Penguin, 1990), 288-90.

55. Surendra Botha, ed., *The Yoga Shastra of Hemchandracharya: A Twelfth Century Guide to Jain Yoga*, trans. A.S. Gopani (Jaipur: Prakrit Bharti Academy, 1989), 11-12.

56. Ibid., 39.

57. Heinrich Zimmer, *Philosophies of India* (1951; reprint, Princeton: Princeton University Press, 1989), 255.

58. Ibid., 279.

CHAPTER 3: PYTHAGOREANISM

1. Those who have presented Pythagoras as the father of Western philosophical vegetarianism include Tom Regan, "McCloskey on Why Animals Cannot Have Rights," *Philosophical Quarterly* (July 1976): 251; and Daniel Dombrowski, *The Philosophy of Vegetarianism* (Amherst: University of Massachusetts Press, 1984), 35.

2. Apollonius, *Marvellous Stories*, 6, cited in Jonathan Barnes, *Early Greek Philosophy* (London: Penguin, 1987), 85.

3. Isocrates, *Busiris*, 28-29, cited in ibid., 84.

4. Annie Besant, "Introduction," in Florence M. Firth, ed., *The Golden Verses of Pythagoras and Other Pythagorean Fragments* (Kila, MT: Kessinger, n.d.), ix.

5. William H. Drummond, *The Rights of Animals and Man's Obligation to Treat Them with Humanity* (London: John Maldon, 1838), 29.

6. Martin West, "Early Greek Philosophy," in John Boardman, Jasper Griffin, and Gwyn Murray, eds., *The Oxford History of the Classical World* (Oxford: Oxford University Press, 1993), 114.

7. Edouard Schure, *Pythagoras and the Delphic Mysteries* ([1907?]; reprint, Kila, MT: Kessinger, n.d.), 65.

8. Charles Kahn, *Pythagoras and the Pythagorean Way of Life* (Indianapolis: Hackett, 2001), 4.

9. Golden Verses, nos. 70 and 71, quoted in Firth, ed., *Golden Verses*, 6.

10. Plutarch, *Table Talk*, quoted in Barnes, *Early Greek Philosophy*, 74.

11. Kahn, *Pythagoras*, 5.

12. Colin Spencer, *Vegetarianism: A History*, 2nd ed. (New York: Four Walls Eight Windows, 2002), 51.

13. Howard Williams, *The Ethics of Diet: A Catena of Authorities Deprecatory of the Practice of Flesh-Eating*, ed. Carol J. Adams (1883; reprint, Urbana: University of Illinois Press, 2003), 8. Frequently in these pages, rather than referring to the 1883 edition, to which I referred in *Brute Souls, Happy Beasts, and Evolution*, and sometimes, rather than referring to the difficult-to-obtain original works that are quoted in Williams, I have given the Illinois reprint pages where the relevant quotations are to be found so that the reader may more easily locate them.

14. Kahn, *Pythagoras*, 5.

15. Eduard Zeller, *Philosophie der Griechen in ihrer geschichtlichen Entwicklung* (Leipzig, 1892), cited in ibid., 2.

16. Diogenes Laertius, on Xenophanes, quoted in Barnes, *Early Greek Philosophy*, 82.

17. Erich Frank, *Platon und die sogennanten Pythagoreer* (Halle, 1923), vi, quoted in Kahn, *Pythagoras*, 2.

18. Ibid., 38n.

19. Porphyry, *Vita Pythagorae,* quoted in ibid., 105.

20. Williams, *Ethics of Diet,* 5.

21. Dominic J. O'Meara, *Pythagoras Revived: Mathematics and Philosophy in Late Antiquity* (Oxford: Clarendon, 1992), 5.

22. On Plato in this respect, see page 98.

23. West, "Early Greek Philosophy," 113.

24. Heraclitus, quoted by Diogenes Laertius, in Barnes, *Early Greek Philosophy,* 82.

25. Kahn, *Pythagoras,* 2.

26. Jonathan Barnes, *The Presocratic Philosophers,* 2 vols. (London: Routledge and Kegan Paul, 1979).

27. See Kahn, *Pythagoras,* 70. See also Barnes, *Early Greek Philosophy,* 206.

28. See the biographies in Kenneth Sylvan Guthrie, comp. and trans., *The Pythagorean Sourcebook and Library* (Grand Rapids, MI: Phanes, 1988), 137, 130.

29. Athenaeus, quoted in Barnes, *Early Greek Philosophy,* 207.

30. Plutarch, *Table Talk,* via Aulus Gellius, *Attic Nights,* bk. 4, xi, quoted in ibid.

31. Williams, *Ethics of Diet,* 8.

32. Golden Verses, no. 167, quoted in Firth, ed., *Golden Verses,* 6.

33. Porphyry, quoted in Williams, *Ethics of Diet,* 7.

34. See Richard Sorabji, *Animal Minds and Human Morals: The Origins of the Western Debate* (Ithaca, NY: Cornell University Press, 1993), 131.

35. Diodorus, *Universal History,* bk. 10, sec. 6, 1-3, quoted in Barnes, *Early Greek Philosophy,* 87.

36. Williams, *Ethics of Diet,* 10.

37. Spencer, *Vegetarianism,* 54.

38. Thomas Aquinas, *Summa contra gentiles,* vol. 4, trans. Charles J. O'Neil (Grand Bend: Notre Dame University Press, 1975), sec. 3, 42.

39. Aristotle, via Aulus Gellius, *Attic Nights,* bk. 4, xi, quoted in Barnes, *Early Greek Philosophy,* 205-6.

40. See Kahn, *Pythagoras,* 70.

41. Aristoxenus, via Aulus Gellius, *Attic Nights,* bk. 4, xi, quoted in Barnes, *Early Greek Philosophy,* 206.

42. Cicero, *On Divination,* via Aulus Gellius, *Attic Nights,* bk. 4, xi, quoted in ibid.

43. Spencer, *Vegetarianism,* 64.

44. Barnes, *Early Greek Philosophy,* 81.

45. Isocrates, *Busiris,* 28-29, quoted in ibid., 84.

46. See page 47.

47. Ovid, *Metamorphoses,* trans. Mary Innes (London: Penguin, 1955), 228.

48. Barnes, *Early Greek Philosophy,* 81.

49. Schure, *Pythagoras and the Delphic Mysteries,* 94.

50. Ibid., 107.

51. Ibid., 84.

52. Sextus Empiricus, *Against the Mathematicians,* 9, 127-29, quoted in Barnes, *Early Greek Philosophy,* 200.

53. Kahn, *Pythagoras,* 11.

54. Porphyry, *Life of Pythagoras,* 19, quoted in Barnes, *Early Greek Philosophy,* 86.

55. As per Plutarch, via Aulus Gellius, *Attic Nights,* bk. 4, xi, quoted in ibid., 207.

56. O'Meara, *Pythagoras Revived,* 215.

57. Ibid., 28.
58. Empedocles, via Hippolytus, *Refutation of All Heresies*, bk. 7, xxix, 14-23, quoted in Barnes, *Early Greek Philosophy,* 195.
59. Scholiast to Nicander, *Theriaca*, 452, quoted in ibid., 199.
60. Aristotle, *Rhetoric*, 1373b, 6-9, 14-17, quoted in ibid., 199-200.
61. Voltaire, quoted in Archibald Ballantyne, *Voltaire's Visit to England* (1893; reprint, Geneva: Slatkine, 1970), 124.

CHAPTER 4: GREEK PHILOSOPHY AND ROMAN IMPERIUM

1. Oswyn Murray, "Life and Society in Classical Greece," in John Boardman, Jasper Griffin, and Oswyn Murray, eds., *The Oxford History of the Classical World* (Oxford: Oxford University Press, 1986), 217.
2. Howard Williams, *The Ethics of Diet: A Catena of Authorities Deprecatory of the Practice of Flesh-Eating*, ed. Carol J. Adams (1883; reprint, Urbana: University of Illinois Press, 2003), 20.
3. On George Nicholson, see pages 242-45.
4. Marcus Tullius Cicero, *Tuscan Disputations,* rev. ed., trans. J.E. King (Cambridge, MA: Harvard University Press, 1945), 435.
5. See Rod Preece, *Awe for the Tiger, Love for the Lamb: A Chronicle of Sensibility to Animals* (Vancouver: University of British Columbia Press, 2002), ch. 2.
6. Xenophon, *Memorabilia,* cited in Arthur O. Lovejoy and George Boas, *Primitivism and Related Ideas in Antiquity* (1935; reprint, Baltimore: Johns Hopkins University Press, 1997), 389.
7. Plato, *Statesman,* trans. J.B. Skemp (Indianapolis: Bobbs-Merrill, 1962), 230.
8. See Rod Preece, *Brute Souls, Happy Beasts, and Evolution: The Historical Status of Animals* (Vancouver: University of British Columbia Press, 2005), 77-83, 85-87.
9. See page 72.
10. See Richard Sorabji, *Animal Minds and Human Morals: The Origins of the Western Debate* (Ithaca, NY: Cornell University Press, 1993), 192-93.
11. Charles Kahn, *Pythagoras and the Pythagorean Way of Life* (Indianapolis: Hackett, 2001), 51.
12. Plato, *Phaedo,* in *The Trial and Death of Socrates: Four Dialogues,* trans. Benjamin Jowett ([1875?]; reprint, New York: Dover, 1992), 63, original emphasis.
13. See Kahn, *Pythagoras,* 50; and Plato, *Gorgias: A Revised Text with Introduction and Commentary by E.R. Dodds* (Oxford: Clarendon, 1959), 303, 381.
14. See Plato, *Republic,* trans. H. Spens (Glasgow, UK: Robert and Andrew Foulis, 1763), 427-28.
15. See Daniel Dombrowski, *The Philosophy of Vegetarianism* (Amherst: University of Massachusetts Press, 1984), 62-63.
16. Williams, *Ethics of Diet,* vi.
17. Plato, *Republic,* 373b, in *The Great Dialogues of Plato,* trans. W.H.D. Rouse (New York: Mentor, 1956), 169.
18. Plato, *Republic,* 371a, in ibid., 169.
19. Williams, *Ethics of Diet,* 8.
20. For example, in the *Republic,* Plato allows for freedom of movement between the

classes of society, based on intellectual potential. Yet the age at which intellectual training of the guardian class is to begin effectively bars children among the ranks of the
artisans from taking their rightful place.

21. Aristotle, *Politics*, 1.8, 11-12, ed. and trans. Ernest Barker (London, UK: Oxford University Press, 1952), 21.
22. Ibid., 1.2 and 1.5, ed. and trans. Barker, 10-11, 9.
23. Aristotle, *Parts of Animals*, 10, 2, in Louise Ropes Loomis, ed., *Aristotle: On Man in the
Universe* (1943; reprint, New York: Gramercy Books, 1971), 62.
24. Aristotle, *Parts of Animals*, 1.4, in ibid., 49-50.
25. See Dombrowski, *Philosophy of Vegetarianism*, 66; and Preece, *Brute Souls*, 58.
26. Aristotle, *Politics*, ch. 1, sec. 2, ed. and trans. Barker, 11.
27. Aristotle, *Parts of Animals*, bk. 2, in Loomis, ed., *Aristotle*, 52.
28. Aristotle, *Nicomachean Ethics*, ed. and trans. Roger Crisp (Cambridge, UK: Cambridge University Press, 2000), ch. 7, sec. 1, 120.
29. Porphyry, *De Abstinentia*, quoted in Lovejoy and Boas, *Primitivism*, 94-95.
30. Cicero, *De officiis*, quoted in ibid., 96.
31. Dombrowski, *Philosophy of Vegetarianism*, 84.
32. Seneca, *Ad Lucilium Epistolae Morales*, vol. 3, trans. Richard M. Gummere (New York:
G.P. Putnam's Sons, 1925), 241-43.
33. Ibid., 245.
34. Colin Spencer, *Vegetarianism: A History*, 2nd ed. (New York: Four Walls Eight Windows, 2002), 96-97.
35. Plutarch, "On the Use of Reason by 'Irrational' Animals," in *Plutarch's Moralia*, vol. 12,
trans. Harold Cherniss and William Helmbold (1927; reprint, London: William
Heinemann, 1957), 355.
36. Plutarch, "Life of Marcus Crato," in Arthur Hugh Clough, trans., *Plutarch's Lives: The
Dryden Plutarch*, vol. 1 (London: J.M. Dent, 1910), 520-21.
37. Plutarch, "On the Eating of Flesh," in ibid., vol. 1, 547, 550-51.
38. Ibid., 551.
39. D. Shackleton Bailey, trans., *Cicero's Letters to His Friends* (London: Penguin, 1967), 81.
40. Porphyry, *Life of Plotinus*, cited in Sorabji, *Animal Minds*, 172.
41. Perhaps Porphyry is referring to the *Historia Animalium*, 588: A8. See page 103.
42. This kind of thinking played a significant role in the Middle Ages, when animals were
sometimes deemed criminally responsible for their actions and prosecuted in courts of
law. See Edward Payson Evans, *The Criminal Prosecution and Capital Punishment of
Animals* (1906; reprint, London: Faber and Faber, 1987).
43. Porphyry, *On Abstinence from Animal Food*, ed. E.W. Tyson, trans. Thomas Taylor
(1793; reprint, Fontwell, UK: Centaur, 1965), 110, 140-41, my emphasis.

CHAPTER 5: JUDAISM AND THE EARLIER CHRISTIAN HERITAGE

1. Thomas Young, *An Essay on Humanity to Animals*, ed. Rod Preece (1798; reprint, Lampeter: Mellen, 2001), 75.
2. William Paley, *The Works of William Paley, D.D., Archdeacon of Carlisle,* (1785; reprint,
Philadelphia: Chrissy Markley, 1850), 44.
3. Tertullian, quoted in Howard Williams, *The Ethics of Diet: A Catena of Authorities*

*Deprecatory of the Practice of Flesh-Eating,* ed. Carol J. Adams (1883; reprint, Urbana: University of Illinois Press, 2003), 52.

4. Roberta Kalechofsky, "Judaism and Vegetarianism: In the Camp of Kibroth-Hatavah," in Roberta Kalechofsky, ed., *Judaism and Animal Rights* (Marblehead, MA: Micah, 1992), 195ff.

5. See George Boas, *Primitivism and Related Ideas in the Middle Ages* (1948; reprint, Baltimore: Johns Hopkins Press, 1997), 17.

6. Clement of Alexandria, quoted in Williams, *Ethics of Diet,* 60.

7. Book of Enoch, quoted in Boas, *Primitivism,* 188.

8. Eusebius, *Ecclesiastical History,* 5.1.25, 2-6, in Philip Schaff and Henry Wace, eds., *The Church History of Eusebius* (Grand Rapids, MI: William B. Erdmann, 1961), 214.

9. Rabbi Kook, cited in Richard Schwartz, "Questions and Answers," in Kalechofsky, ed., *Judaism,* 224.

10. Edward Payson Evans, *Evolutional Ethics* (New York: D. Appleton, 1897); Lynn White Jr., "The Historical Roots of Our Ecologic Crisis," *Science* 155 (1967): 1203-7; Peter Singer, *Animal Liberation,* 2nd ed. (New York: New York Review of Books, 1990); Roderick Frazier Nash, *The Rights of Nature: A History of Environmental Ethics* (Madison: University of Wisconsin Press, 1984).

11. Andrew Linzey, *Christianity and the Rights of Animals* (New York: Crossroad, 1991), 25-28.

12. Elijah Judah Schochet, *Animal Life in Jewish Tradition: Attitudes and Relationships* (New York: KTAV, 1984), 46-79. The "delicate tool" is mentioned at page 63.

13. Lord Erskine, quoted in William Youatt, *The Obligation and Extent of Humanity to Brutes, Principally Considered with Reference to the Domesticated Animals,* ed. Rod Preece (1839; reprint, Lampeter: Mellen, 2003), 41. The matter is dealt with at greater length and with substantially more evidence in Rod Preece, *Brute Souls, Happy Beasts, and Evolution: The Historical Status of Animals* (Vancouver: University of British Columbia Press, 2005), 104-7.

14. William H. Drummond, *The Rights of Animals and Man's Obligation to Treat Them with Humanity* (London: John Mardon, 1838), 2, 167.

15. Rabbi Solomon Ganzfried, *Code of Jewish Law* (New York: Hebrew Publishing Company, 1977), bk. 4, ch. 19, 184, quoted in Lewis G. Regenstein, *Replenish the Earth: A History of Organized Religion's Treatment of Animals and Nature – Including the Bible's Message of Conservation and Kindness toward Animals* (New York: Crossroad, 1991), 184. Compare also Isidore Epstein, *Judaism* (London: Penguin, 1990), 27, 153.

16. Quoted in Richard Schwartz, "Tsa'ar Ba'alei Chayim: Judaism and Compassion for Animals," in Kalechofsky, ed., *Judaism,* 61. The Hebrew phrase is the mandate not to cause pain to any living creature.

17. *Shabbat,* 151b, via Alan Herzberg, "The Jewish Declaration on Nature," World Wildlife Conference statement, Assisi, September 1986, cited in Regenstein, *Replenish the Earth,* 190; and *Yerushalmi Keturot,* Yevanot 15, via *Encyclopedia Judaica,* cited in Regenstein, *Replenish the Earth,* 191.

18. *Sefer Hassidim,* 13c, no. 142, 54, via *Encyclopedia Judaica,* quoted in Regenstein, *Replenish the Earth,* 191.

19. Via Richard Schwartz, "Judaism and Animal Rights" (distributed by Concern for Helping Animals in Israel, Alexandria, VA), quoted in Regenstein, *Replenish the Earth,* 184.

20. *Even HaEzer,* 5:14, quoted in Ronald Isaacs, *Animals in Jewish Thought and Tradition* (Northvale, NJ: Jason Aaronson, 2000), 85.

21. *Orech Chayyim*, 223:6, quoted in ibid.

22. *Mechilta to Exodus*, 23:12, quoted in ibid., 86.

23. *Kitzur Schulchan Aruch*, 186:1, quoted in ibid., 87.

24. Flavius Josephus, *Antiquities of the Jews*, pt. 1, ch. 4, sec. 8, quoted in Youatt, *Obligation*, 16.

25. *Shabbat*, 77b, via Barry Feundel, "The Earth is the Lord's: How Jewish Tradition Views Our Relationship to the Environment," *Jewish Action* (Summer 1990): 24-25, quoted in Regenstein, *Replenish the Earth*, 189.

26. In Judges 14:5 Solomon tears a young lion apart with his bare hands, but this could be excused as a possible act of self-defence.

27. Roberta Kalechofsky, "Jewish Law and Tradition on Animal Rights," in Kalechofsky ed., *Judaism*, 49.

28. W.E.H. Lecky, *History of European Morals*, quoted in ibid.

29. See Regenstein, *Replenish the Earth*, 201.

30. For such a view of the Essenes, see, for example, Colin Spencer, *Vegetarianism: A History*, 2nd ed. (New York: Four Walls Eight Windows, 2002), 109.

31. David Winston, ed. and trans., *Philo of Alexandria: The Contemplative Life* (New York: Paulist Press, 1981), 249, 54.

32. See Keith Akers, *The Lost Religion of Jesus: Simple Living and Nonviolence in Early Christianity* (New York: Lantern, 2000), 24ff., 233.

33. Stephen H. Webb, *Good Eating* (Grand Rapids, MI: Brazos, 2001), 119.

34. Blake Leyerle, "Clement of Alexandria on the Importance of Table Etiquette," *Journal of Early Christian Studies* 3, 2 (Summer 1995): 125-41, quoted in ibid., 153.

35. Clement of Alexandria, quoted in Williams, *Ethics of Diet*, 60.

36. Benedicta Ward, ed. and trans., *The Sayings of the Desert Fathers* (Kalamazoo: Cistercian, 1975), xxiv.

37. Spencer, *Vegetarianism*, 110.

38. Ward, ed. and trans., *Sayings of the Desert Fathers*, 81.

39. Saint Athanasius, *The Life of St. Anthony the Great*, vol. 2 (Willis, CA: Eastern Orthodox Books, n.d.), 72, 74, 96.

40. "History of the Monks of Egypt," in Helen Waddell, ed. and trans., *The Desert Fathers* (New York: Vintage Books, 1958), 51.

41. The abbot Moses, quoted in "The Sayings of the Fathers," in ibid., 160.

42. "The *Pratum Spirituale* of John Moschus," in ibid., 173-74.

43. H.V. Morton, *Through Lands of the Bible* (London: Methuen, 1938), 8, 12.

44. See Boas, *Primitivism*, 1-14.

45. "The *Monasticon Scoticum* of Brockie" – presumably, as it is not absolutely clear from the Boas text – quoted in Boas, *Primitivism*, 115.

46. Ibid.

47. Ibid., 116.

48. Andrew Linzey, "Christianity and the Rights of Animals," *Animals' Voice*, August 1989, 45. For a list of such saints and the animal-friendly acts for which they were known, see Preece, *Brute Souls*, 131-32.

49. Webb, *Good Eating*, 29.

50. Saint Isaac the Syrian, via Vladimir Lossky, *The Mystical Theology of the Eastern Church* (1973), 111, quoted in Andrew Linzey, *Animal Theology* (Urbana: University of Illinois Press, 1995), 56.

51. Saint Basil, quoted by C.W. Hume, in *Universities Federation for Animal Welfare Theological Bulletin,* no. 2 (1962): 3.
52. Saint Basil, via Saint John Chrysostom, "Homily 19: The Liturgy of St. Basil," in *Homilies of John Chrysostom on the Epistles of St. Paul to the Romans,* quoted by Hume, in ibid., 3.
53. Williams, *Ethics of Diet,* 77. Spencer, *Vegetarianism,* 124, repeats the figure.
54. Saint John Chrysostom, quoted in Williams, *Ethics of Diet,* 77.
55. Chrysostom, quoted in ibid., 79-80.
56. Tertullian, quoted in ibid, 53.
57. On Fludd and Milton, see Preece, *Brute Souls,* 131-32.
58. Novation, *De cibis Judaicis,* ch. 2, quoted in Boas, *Primitivism,* 26.
59. Ibid., 94.
60. See Webb, *Good Eating,* 154.
61. Tertullian, quoted in Elijah D. Buckner, *The Immortality of Animals and the Relation of Man as Guardian from a Biblical and Philosophical Hypothesis* (Philadelphia: George W. Jacobs, 1903), 89.
62. Williams, *Ethics of Diet,* 78.
63. Saint Augustine, *Of the Morals of the Catholic Church,* via Blake Leyerle, "Clement of Alexandria on the Importance of Etiquette," *Journal of Early Christian Studies* 3, 2 (Summer 1995): 125-41, quoted in Webb, *Good Eating,* 153.
64. Saint Augustine, *Concerning the City of God against the Pagans,* 4th ed., trans. Henry Betterson (Harmondsworth: Penguin, 1980), bk. 19, ch. 16, 870. It is worth noting that Augustine, who relies primarily on Plato among the classics, refers to animals as "meant for our use," a doctrine customarily attributed to Aristotle. Yet Aristotle's work had been lost by this time – to be rediscovered from Arab sources in the twelfth century. Either the doctrine was far more pervasive than sometimes thought or ideas of the Aristotelian type were being imbibed via others, perhaps Xenophon, who had argued in *Memorabilia* earlier than Aristotle that animals were for our use. Moreover, as we have already seen, Plato had implied the same, although he never used the phrase "meant for our use."

## Chapter 6: Bogomils, Cathars, and the Later Medieval Mind

1. Howard Williams, *The Ethics of Diet: A Catena of Authorities Deprecatory of the Practice of Flesh-Eating,* ed. Carol J. Adams (1883; reprint, Urbana: University of Illinois Press, 2003), 82-3.
2. Malcom Lambert, *The Cathars* (Oxford: Blackwell, 1998), 56.
3. René Weis, *The Yellow Cross: The Story of the Last Cathars' Rebellion against the Inquisition* (New York: Vintage Books, 2002), xxi; and Lambert, *Cathars,* 11.
4. Peter, tsar of Bulgaria, quoted in Colin Spencer, *Vegetarianism: A History,* 2nd ed. (New York: Four Walls Eight Windows, 2002), 145.
5. Lambert, *Cathars,* 29.
6. Ibid., 34.
7. Pierre Maury, quoted, at greater length, in Weis, *Yellow Cross,* 168.
8. Ron Baxter, *Bestiaries and Their Users in the Middle Ages* (London: Sutton Publishing and Courtauld Institute, 1998), 209.

9. Richard Rolle of Hampole, "The Nature of the Bee," in Kenneth Siam, ed., *Fourteenth Century Verse and Prose* (1921; reprint, Oxford: Oxford University Press, 1985), 41-42.

10. John of Salisbury, *De Nugis Curialium*, pt. 1, ch. 4, quoted in Dix Harwood, *Love for Animals and How It Developed in Great Britain* (New York: privately printed, 1928), 65-66.

11. Walter Map, *De Nugis Curialium: Courtiers' Trifles,* ed. and trans. M.R. James (Oxford: Clarendon, 1983), 5, 7.

12. Richard de Wyche, via Alban Butler, *Lives of the Saints,* revised and supplemented by Rev. Herbert Thurston and Donald Attwater, vol. 2 (New York: P.J. Kennedy and Sons, n.d.), 362, quoted in Don Ambrose Agius, *God's Animals* (London: Catholic Study Circle for Animal Welfare, 1973).

13. Brigit of Sweden, quoted in Arthur Helps, *Animals and Their Masters* (London: Chatto and Windus, 1883), 124; Franciscan Bernardine of Siena, quoted in Michael W. Fox, *St. Francis of Assisi, Animals and Nature* (Washington, DC: Center for Respect of Life and Environment, 1989), 3.

14. William Langland, *Piers the Ploughman,* translated into modern English by J.F. Goodridge (Harmondsworth: Penguin, 1959), bk. 12, pt. 2, 138.

15. Saint Francis of Assisi, *Admonitions,* in *Francis and Clare: The Complete Works,* trans. Regis J. Armstrong and Ignatius C. Brady (New York: Paulist Press, 1982), 29.

16. Thomas of Celano, *First Life of St. Francis,* in Marion A. Habig, ed., *St. Francis of Assisi: Writings and Early Biographies* (Chicago: Franciscan Herald Press, 1983), bk. 1, ch. 21, 228; see also bk. 1, ch. 29, 297.

17. Saint Bonaventure, *Life of St. Francis,* in *Bonaventure: The Soul's Journey into God, The Tree of Life and The Life of St. Francis,* trans. Ewert Cousins (Malwah, NJ: Paulist Press, 1978), 254.

18. Michael Allen Fox, *Deep Vegetarianism* (Philadelphia: Temple University Press, 1999), 13.

19. Keith Thomas, *Man and the Natural World: Changing Attitudes in England, 1500-1800* (London: Penguin, 1984), 153.

20. Henry Chadwick, "The Early Christian Community," in John McManners, ed., *The Oxford History of Christianity* (Oxford: Oxford University Press, 2002), 42.

21. The full text is contained in Priscilla Barnum, ed., *Dives et Pauper* (New York: Kraus, 1973). This section is at 1.2, 35. "Sap. V" is Book of Wisdom, 5.

CHAPTER 7: THE HUMANISM OF THE RENAISSANCE

1. Francis Petrarch, quoted in Michael Seidlmayer, *Currents of Medieval Thought, with Special Reference to Germany* (Oxford: Blackwell, 1960), 157. The classic discussion of the topic is Jacob Burkhardt, *The Civilization of the Renaissance in Italy* (1860).

2. Seidlmayer, *Currents of Medieval Thought,* 108.

3. Percy Bysshe Shelley, quoted in Richard Holmes, *Shelley: The Pursuit* (1974; reprint, New York: New York Review of Books, 1994), 644.

4. Howard Williams, *The Ethics of Diet: A Catena of Authorities Deprecatory of the Practice of Flesh-Eating,* ed. Carol J. Adams (1883; reprint, Urbana: University of Illinois Press, 2003), 89.

5. Joseph Addison, "On Temperance," *The Spectator,* 13 October 1711, 195, in Alex Chalmers, ed., *The Spectator: A New Edition, Corrected from the Originals, with a Preface, Historical and Biographical,* vol. 4 (New York: E. Sargent and M. & W. Ward, 1810), 12.

6. Ibid., vol. 4, 14.

7. Joseph Addison, "Meditations on Animal Life," *The Spectator*, 25 October 1712, 519, in ibid., vol. 9, 33.

8. Luigi Cornaro, quoted in Williams, *Ethics of Diet*, 88.

9. W. Moffat, *Health's Improvement*, quoted ibid., 307.

10. Andrea Corsali, quoted in Jean Paul Richter, ed., *The Literary Works of Leonardo da Vinci*, 1st ed. (1883; reprint, London: Phaidon, 1970), 365.

11. Serge Bramley, *Leonardo: The Artist and the Man* (London: Penguin, 1994), 240.

12. Leonardo da Vinci, *Quaderni d'Anatomia*, bk. 2, 14 (housed in the Royal Library at Windsor). This was kindly brought to my attention by David Hurwitz.

13. Da Vinci, *Codex Atlantica*, 76 v a, quoted in Bramly, *Leonardo*, 240.

14. Giorgio Vasari, *The Great Masters*, ed. Michael Sonino, trans. Gaston C. Du Vere (1550; reprint, New York: Park Lane, 1988), 93-94.

15. Irma A. Richter, ed., *Selections from the Notebooks of Leonardo da Vinci* (Oxford: Oxford University Press, 1977), 245.

16. Ibid.

17. Jean Paul Richter and Irma A. Richter, eds., *The Literary Works of Leonardo da Vinci*, 2nd ed., vol. 2 (1883; reprint, London: Phaidon, 1970), 293.

18. Ibid., 302.

19. See *Catholic Encyclopedia*, www.catholic.org/encyclopedia.

20. Thomas More, *Utopia: Latin Text and English Translation*, ed. and trans. George M. Logan, Robert M. Adams, and Clarence H. Miller (Cambridge, UK: Cambridge University Press, 1995), 171.

21. Thomas More, quoted in Williams, *Ethics of Diet*, 93.

22. Montaigne, via Florio, trans., *Essays of Montaigne*, bk. 2, 126, quoted in Keith Thomas, *Man and the Natural World: Changing Attitudes in England, 1500-1800* (London: Penguin, 1984), 159.

23. Michel de Montaigne, "Apology for Raymond Sebond," in *Selected Essays*, trans. Donald M. Frame (New York: Oxford University Press, 1982), 357.

24. Montaigne, *Essais*, bk. 2, 12, quoted in Williams, *Ethics of Diet*, 99.

25. Giordano Bruno, *Cause, Principle and Unity: Five Dialogues*, trans. Jack Lindsay (New York: International Publishers, 1962), 81.

26. See Rod Preece, *Animals and Nature: Cultural Myths, Cultural Realities* (Vancouver: University of British Columbia Press, 1999), 261.

27. Francis Quarles, via *Century* 2, 100, quoted in Richard D. Ryder, *Animal Revolution: Changing Attitudes towards Speciesism* (London: Blackwell, 1989), 51, spelling modernized.

28. Francis Quarles, via *Century* 3, 23, quoted in ibid., 51, spelling modernized.

29. Colin Spencer, *Vegetarianism: A History*, 2nd ed. (New York: Four Walls Eight Windows, 2002), 172.

CHAPTER 8: THE CARTESIANS AND THEIR ADVERSARIES IN THE SEVENTEENTH AND EIGHTEENTH CENTURIES

1. Gary Francione, "Animals – Property or Persons," in Cass R. Sunnstein and Martha C. Nussbaum, eds., *Animal Rights: Current Debates and New Directions* (Oxford: Oxford University Press, 2004), 110.

2. René Descartes, *Discourse on the Method of Rightly Conducting the Reason and Seeking for Truth in the Sciences*, in *Philosophical Works* (1931; reprint, Franklin Center, PA: Franklin Library, 1981), 117.

3. René Descartes, *Meditations on the First Philosophy*, in ibid., 162.

4. See John Cottingham, *A Descartes Dictionary* (Oxford: Blackwell, 1993); A. Denny, *Descartes' Philosophical Letters* (Oxford: Clarendon, 1970); and Gary Steiner, "Descartes on the Moral Status of Animals," *Archiv für Geschichte de Philosophie* 80, 3 (1998): 268-91.

5. Hester Hastings, *Man and Beast in French Thought of the Eighteenth Century* (1936; reprint, New York: Johnson Reprint Corporation, 1973), 22.

6. Nicolas Malebranche, *De La Recherche de la Verité* (Paris, 1678), vi, 2, vii, quoted in Dix Harwood, *Love for Animals and How It Developed in Great Britain* (New York: privately printed, 1928), 98.

7. Pierre Gassendi, *Exercises in the Form of Paradoxes in Refutation of the Aristoteleans*, 2.6, 2, in *The Selected Works of Pierre Gassendi*, trans. Craig B. Bush (New York: Johnson Reprint Corporation, 1972), 86.

8. Pierre Gassendi, *Metaphysical Colloquy, or Doubts and Rebuttals Concerning the Metaphysics of René Descartes*, "Rebuttal to Meditation 2, Doubt 7," in ibid., 197-98.

9. Pierre Gassendi, quoted in Howard Williams, *The Ethics of Diet: A Catena of Authorities Deprecatory of the Practice of Flesh-Eating*, ed. Carol J. Adams (1883; reprint, Urbana: University of Illinois Press, 2003), 103-4.

10. Pierre Gassendi, "De Virtutibus," in *Physics*, bk. 2, quoted in ibid., 104.

11. Henry More, "Epistola Prima H. Mori ad Renatum Cartesium" [First letter of Henry More to René Descartes], in *Collection of Several Philosophical Works* (London, 1712), quoted in Harwood, *Love for Animals*, 102.

12. De Sévigné, quoted in the original French in George Boas, *The Happy Beast in French Thought of the Seventeenth Century* (1933; reprint, New York: Octagon Books, 1966), 141, my translation.

13. Lord Bolingbroke, *The Works of Henry St. John, Lord Viscount Bolingbroke*, vol. 5 (1754; reprint, London: D. Mallet, 1809), 344.

14. Bernard Fontenelle, quoted in the original French in Boas, *Happy Beast*, 141, my translation.

15. John Norris, *An Essay towards the Theory of the Ideal or Intelligible World*, vol. 2 (London, 1701), 44, quoted in Harwood, *Love for Animals*, 104.

16. Robert Boyle, *A Free Inquiry into the Vulgarly Receiv'd Notion of Nature* (London, 1686), 18-19, quoted in Peter J. Bowler, *The Norton History of the Environmental Sciences* (New York: Norton, 1993), 89.

17. See letter to Princess Elizabeth, in René Descartes, *Oeuvres de Descartes*, vol. 4 (Paris: Charles and Paul Tannery, 1897), 292.

18. Joseph Addison, *The Spectator*, 18 July 1711, 120, in Alex Chalmers, ed., *The Spectator: A New Edition, Corrected from the Originals, with a Preface, Historical and Biographical*, vol. 11 (New York: E. Sargent and M. & A. Ward, 1810), 284.

19. Alexander Pope, via Joseph Spence, *Anecdotes, Observations and Characters* (London, 1858), 222, quoted in Harwood, *Love for Animals*, 297.

20. George Nicholson, *On the Primeval Diet of Man*, ed. Rod Preece (1801; reprint, Lampeter: Mellen, 1999), 178.

21. *Monthly Review*, September 1770, quoted in ibid., 179, original emphasis.

22. Samuel Johnson, via Samuel Johnson, ed., *The Plays of William Shakespeare*, vol. 7 (London, 1765), 279, quoted in John Vyvyan, *In Pity and in Anger* (Marblehead, MA: Micah, 1988), 26. Johnson was commenting on the rebuke against the Queen in *Cymbeline*, when she proposed an experiment with poison on animals. Justifiably, in all likelihood, Johnson assumed opposition to animal experimentation to be Shakespeare's own view, as later did Bernard Shaw.

23. Samuel Johnson, *The Idler*, no. 17, 5 August 1758, in *The Idler* (London: W. Sullaby, 1810), microform.

24. Williams, *Ethics of Diet*, 209.

25. Jean Antoine Gleizès, quoted in ibid., 214.

26. Keith Thomas, *Man and the Natural World: Changing Attitudes in England, 1500-1800* (London: Penguin, 1984), 292.

27. See ibid., 289-90.

28. Ibid., 290.

29. Ibid.

30. Thomas Edwards, *Gangraena*, bk. 1, 20, quoted in ibid., 166.

31. Jakob Bauthumley, quoted in ibid., 301.

32. Nicholson, *On the Primeval Diet*, 87.

33. John Evelyn, quoted in Williams, *Ethics of Diet*, 109.

34. Thomas Tryon, *Wisdom's Dictates*, quoted in Jon Wynne-Tyson, ed., *The Extended Circle: An Anthology of Humane Thought* (London: Cardinal, 1990), 545.

35. Thomas Tryon, *Friendly Advice to the Gentleman Planters of the East and West Indies*, quoted in ibid. Tryon had lived in Barbados and was aghast at the horrendous conditions in which slaves were compelled to labour.

36. Thomas Tryon, *The Country-Man's Companion* (London, 1683), sig. A2, quoted in Thomas, *Man and the Natural World*, 171.

37. Thomas Tryon, *The Way to Health*, quoted in Williams, *Ethics of Diet*, 313.

38. Thomas Tryon, *Complaints of the Birds and Fowls of Heaven to Their Creator* (1684), 146, quoted in Rod Preece and Lorna Chamberlain, *Animal Welfare and Human Values* (Waterloo, ON: Wilfrid Laurier University Press, 1993), 73.

39. Benjamin Franklin, *The Autobiography and Other Writings*, ed. Kenneth Silverman (London: Penguin, 1986), 73.

40. Antonio Celestina Cocchi, quoted in Williams, *Ethics of Diet*, 158.

41. Cocchi, quoted in ibid., 159.

42. Emanuel Swedenborg, *Angelic Wisdom Concerning the Divine Law and the Divine Wisdom* (New York: Swedenborg Foundation, 1960), 27.

43. Martin Lamm, *Emanuel Swedenborg: The Development of His Thought* (1915; reprint, West Chester, PA: Swedenborg Foundation, 2000), 17.

44. Swedenborg, *Angelic Wisdom*, 184.

45. Lamm, *Emanuel Swedenborg*, 37.

46. Ibid., 40.

47. Emanuel Swedenborg, *Arcana Coelestia: The Heavenly Arcana Which Are Contained in the Holy Scripture, or Word of the Lord Disclosed* (London: Swedenborg Society, 1934), 145.

48. Swedenborg, quoted in Lamm, *Emanuel Swedenborg*, 22, 67.

49. Philippe Hecquet, quoted in Williams, *Ethics of Diet*, 317.

50. George Cheyne, *Essay on Regimen with Five Discourses, Medical, Moral and Philosophical &c.* (London, 1740), 54, 70, quoted in Williams, *Ethics of Diet*, 123-24.

51. Cheyne, quoted in Williams, *Ethics of Diet,* 124.

52. Joseph Ritson, *The World,* no. 61, 19 August 1756, quoted in Williams, *Ethics of Diet,* 140; the remainder of the essay from the *World* is at pages 320-21.

53. William Wordsworth, *The Prelude,* bk. 3, line 524.

54. William Langland, *Piers the Ploughman,* translated into modern English by J.F. Goodridge (Harmondsworth: Penguin, 1959), bk. 2, pt. 2, 136-38.

55. D.H. Lawrence, "Introduction to These Paintings," quoted in Jeffrey Meyers, *D.H. Lawrence: A Biography* (New York: Vintage Books, 1992), 368.

56. Thomas Hobbes, *Leviathan,* ed. C.B. Macpherson (London: Penguin, 1981), pt. 1, ch. 6, 124.

57. François Fénelon, *Traité de l'existence de Dieu,* vol. 2, 5, quoted in Arthur O. Lovejoy, *The Great Chain of Being: A Study in the History of an Idea* (1933; reprint, New York: Harper, 1960), 162.

58. William Hinde, *A Faithful Remonstrance of the Happy Life and Death of John Bruen* (London, 1641), 31-32, quoted in Thomas, *Man and the Natural World,* 157-58.

59. For the relevant liberties, see Rod Preece, *Awe for the Tiger, Love for the Lamb: A Chronicle of Sensibility to Animals* (Vancouver: University of British Columbia Press, 2002), 121.

60. Christopher Smart, via Callan, ed., *The Collected Poems of Christopher Smart,* vol. 1, 290, quoted in Thomas, *Man and the Natural World,* 176.

61. Richard Steele, *The Tatler,* no. 113, 27 December 1709, in *The Tatler and Guardian* (New York: Bangs Brothers, 1852), 221-22.

62. John Locke, *An Essay Concerning Human Understanding,* vol. 2 (1690; reprint, London: H. Hills, 1710), bk. 3, 49.

63. John Locke, *Some Thoughts Concerning Education* (1693), in John William Adamson, ed., *Educational Writings of John Locke* (Cambridge, UK: Cambridge University Press, 1922), 91.

64. Lord Shaftesbury, *An Inquiry Concerning Virtue or Merit* (1711), in Lawrence E. Klein, ed., *Characteristics of Men, Manners, Opinions, Times* (Cambridge, UK: Cambridge University Press, 1999), bk. 2, pt. 2, sec. 3, 226.

65. David Hume, *A Treatise of Human Nature,* ed. L.A. Selby-Bigge and P. H. Nidditch (1739-40; reprint, Oxford: Clarendon, 1978), bk. 2, pt. 2, sec. 12, 397.

66. Edmund Burke, *A Philosophical Enquiry into the Origin of Our Ideas of the Sublime and Beautiful* (1756; reprint, London: F.C. and J. Rivington, 1812), pt. 1, sec. 10, 66-67.

67. Frances Hutcheson, *A System of Moral Philosophy,* vol. 1 (London, 1755), 314, quoted in Thomas, *Man and the Natural World,* 179.

68. Hutcheson, *A System of Moral Philosophy,* vol. 2 (London, 1755), ch. 6, sec. 4, quoted in Harwood, *Love for Animals,* 163.

69. Soame Jenyns, *A Free Inquiry into the Nature and Origins of Evil,* 2nd ed. (1757; reprint, New York: Garland, 1976), 21-22, 36.

70. Henry Fielding, *Champion,* 22 March 1739-40.

## CHAPTER 9: PREACHING WITHOUT PRACTISING

1. Earl of Chesterfield, quoted in Keith Thomas, *Man and the Natural World: Changing Attitudes in England, 1500-1800* (London: Penguin, 1984), 298.

2. Margaret Cavendish, Marchioness of Newcastle, *Poems, and Fancies* (London: J. Martin and J. Allestrye, 1653), 184, spelling modernized.

3. Cavendish, quoted in Douglas Grant, *Margaret the First: A Biography of Margaret Cavendish, Duchess of Newcastle, 1623-1673* (Toronto: University of Toronto Press, 1957), 138.
4. Ibid., 100.
5. Duke of Newcastle, quoted in ibid., 149.
6. Margaret Cavendish, *Natures Pictures* (1656), quoted in ibid., 115.
7. Walter Charleton, quoted in ibid., 222.
8. Margaret Cavendish, *Orations* (1662), quoted in ibid., 166.
9. Cavendish, *Poems, and Fancies*, 104, spelling modernized.
10. Cavendish, quoted in Grant, *Margaret the First*, 122.
11. Richard Cumberland, quoted in James Sambrook, *James Thomson, 1700-1748: A Life* (Oxford: Clarendon, 1991), 64.
12. Samuel Johnson, quoted in ibid., 209.
13. William Howitt, *Homes and Haunts of the British Poets* (London: George Routledge, n.d.), 147.
14. Sambrook, *James Thomson*, 25.
15. Ibid., 107.
16. Ibid., 250.
17. Andrew Mitchell, quoted in ibid., 208.
18. James Boswell, quoted in ibid., 209.
19. Helen M. Fox, "Foreword," in John Evelyn, *Acetaria: A Discourse of Sallets* (1699; reprint, Brooklyn: Women's Auxiliary, Brooklyn Botanical Gardens, 1937), unpaginated; Howard Williams, *The Ethics of Diet: A Catena of Authorities Deprecatory of the Practice of Flesh-Eating*, ed. Carol J. Adams (1883; reprint, Urbana: University of Illinois Press, 2003), 107-10.
20. Evelyn, quoted in John Bowle, *John Evelyn and His World* (London: Routledge and Kegan Paul, 1981), 23.
21. Evelyn, quoted in ibid., 34.
22. Evelyn, quoted in ibid., 43.
23. Evelyn, quoted in ibid., 51.
24. Ibid., 55.
25. Evelyn, quoted in ibid., 57.
26. Ibid., 58.
27. Ibid., 87.
28. Evelyn, quoted in ibid., 87.
29. Evelyn, quoted in ibid., 148; and in E.S. de Beer, ed., *The Diaries of John Evelyn*, vol. 3 (Oxford: Clarendon, 1955), 549.
30. The relevant book he published in 1664 was entitled *Sylva, or A Discourse of Forest Trees and the Propagation of Timber in his Majestie's Dominions, as it was delivered to the Royal Society on the 15th of October, 1662, Upon occasions of Certain Quaeries compounded to that Illustrious Assembly by the Honorable the Principal Officers and Commissioners of the Navy.* Also in 1664, he published his *Kalendarium Hortense, or The Gard'ner's Almanack, what he is to do throughout the year and what Fruits and Flowers are in Prime.*
31. Evelyn, quoted in Bowle, *John Evelyn*, 222.
32. Evelyn, quoted in ibid., 126.
33. Evelyn, quoted in ibid., 190.
34. Ibid., 233.

35. John Hawkesworth, *The Adventurer,* no. 17, 1752.
36. Williams, *Ethics of Diet,* 168.
37. Hawkesworth, quoted in John Lawrence Abbott, *John Hawkesworth: Eighteenth Century Man of Letters* (Madison: University of Wisconsin Press, 1982), 58. The version in Williams, *Ethics of Diet,* 168, does not quite correspond to that of Abbott.
38. Abbott, *John Hawkesworth,* 23.
39. Hawkesworth, quoted in ibid., 25.
40. Ibid., 15.
41. Samuel Johnson, quoted in James Boswell, *The Life of Samuel Johnson, D.D.,* vol. 2 (1791; reprint, London: J.M. Dent, 1906), 36.
42. Ibid.
43. John Lawrence, *Horses,* vol. 1, 122, quoted in Thomas, *Man and the Natural World,* 298.
44. Boethius, quoted in Maynard Mack, *Alexander Pope: A Life* (New York: Norton, 1988), 134.
45. Alexander Pope, *Guardian* (London), 21 May 1713.
46. Pope, quoted in ibid., 73.
47. Mack, *Alexander Pope,* 141.
48. Peter Ackroyd, *Albion: The Origins of the English Imagination* (London: Chatto and Windus, 2002), 202.
49. Pope, *Guardian* (London), 21 May 1713, original emphasis.
50. Quoted from *The Philanthropist,* in Kenneth R. Johnston, *The Hidden Wordsworth: Poet, Lover, Rebel, Spy* (New York: Norton, 1998), 445.
51. For example, Arbuthnot says: "Of alimentary leaves, the olea, or pot-herbs, afford an excellent nourishment, amongst these are the cole or cabbage kind ... proper in cases of acidity. Red cabbage is reckoned a medicine in consumptions and spittings of blood. Amongst the pot-herbs are some latescent plants as lettuce, endive and dandelion, which contain a most wholesome juice ... useful in all diseases of the liver ... There may a stronger broth be made of vegetables than of any gravy soup ... I know more than one instance of irascible passions being much subdued by a vegetable diet." Quoted from the 1736 edition of *The Nature of Aliments and the Choice of Them* (1731), in George Nicholson, *On the Primeval Diet of Man,* ed. Rod Preece (1801; reprint, Lampeter: Mellen, 1999), 42-44, where several further examples are to be found.
52. Alexander Pope, *Essay on Man,* bk. 1, sec. 10, line 294.
53. Jonathan Swift, from a letter quoted in Mack, *Alexander Pope,* 411.
54. Archibald Ballantyne, *Voltaire's Visit to England* (1893; reprint Geneva: Slatkine, 1970), 39.
55. Lord Bathurst, quoted in Mack, *Alexander Pope,* 591; and Lady Mary Wortley Montagu, quoted in ibid.
56. Pope, quoted in ibid., 621.
57. William Kent, quoted in ibid.
58. Pope, quoted in ibid., 757.
59. Ibid., 752.
60. John Gay, from a letter quoted in Phoebe Fenwick Gaye, *John Gay: His Place in the Seventeenth Century* (London: Collins, 1938), 401.
61. Pope, quoted in ibid., 116.
62. Gay, quoted in ibid., 167.
63. Ibid., 205-6.
64. From a letter quoted in ibid., 277.

65. Ibid., 293.
66. David Nokes, *John Gay: A Profession of Friendship* (Oxford: Oxford University Press, 1995), 267.
67. Gaye, *John Gay*, 40.
68. Gay, quoted in ibid., 302.
69. Swift, quoted in ibid., 350.
70. Ibid., 463.
71. John Gay, *Trivia, or The Art of Walking the Streets of London* (1716), original emphasis. "Samian" because Pythagoras was born at Samos in Asia Minor.
72. Bernard Mandeville, *The Fable of the Bees, or Private Vices, Publick Benefits* (1714-28; reprint, Oxford: Clarendon, 1924), Remark P, 178.
73. Ibid., 181.
74. Benjamin Franklin, quoted in Richard I. Cook, *Bernard Mandeville* (New York: Twayne, 1974), 20.
75. Basil Willey, *The Eighteenth Century Background: Studies in the Idea of Nature in the Thought of the Period* (1940; reprint, London: Chatto and Windus, 1946), 97.
76. Ibid.
77. Ibid., 99.
78. Prima facie, associationism would appear a mechanistic doctrine, but as Hartley (and Priestley) recognized, it would be untenable without some additional elements.
79. See Richard C. Allen, *David Hartley on Human Nature* (New York: SUNY, 1999), 23.
80. David Hartley, *Observations on Man, His Frame, His Duty, and His Expectations,* vol. 2 (1748; reprint, Gainesville, FL: Scholars' Facsimiles and Reprints, 1966), ch. 3, sec. 2, proposition, 50, 222-23.
81. Ibid., vol. 2, ch. 3, sec. 2, prop. 52, 224.
82. Whiston succeeded Newton as Lucasian Professor of Mathematics in 1701 but was dismissed from the university in 1710 for his unorthodox religious views. Thereafter, he derived an income from giving lectures in London coffeehouses.
83. David Hartley, from his correspondence, quoted in Allen, *David Hartley,* 42.
84. See Charles Dickens, "Inhumane Humanity," *All the Year Round,* vol. 15, 17 March 1866, 239.
85. Oliver Goldsmith, "The Hermit: A Ballad," in *The Poetical and Prose Works of Oliver Goldsmith* (Edinburgh, UK: Gall Inglis, n.d.), 37 (as a separate ballad), 219 (as a part of *The Vicar of Wakefield*).
86. Oscar Sherwin, *Goldy: The Life and Times of Oliver Goldsmith* (New York: Twayne, 1961), 82.
87. Oliver Goldsmith, *The Citizen of the World,* letter 15, in *The Citizen of the World, The Bee* (London: J.M. Dent, 1934), 38-39.
88. Sherwin, *Goldy,* 65.
89. Ibid., 175.
90. Ibid., 199-200.
91. Richard Cumberland, quoted in ibid., 226.
92. Ibid., 256.
93. From a poem about himself that Goldsmith read to his club at The Sign of the Broom near Islington.
94. Williams, *Ethics of Diet,* 358.
95. Sherwin, *Goldy,* 110.

96. See, for example, representative quotations from Voltaire in Rod Preece, *Awe for the Tiger, Love for the Lamb: A Chronicle of Sensibility to Animals* (Vancouver: University of British Columbia Press, 2002), 162-63.

97. Voltaire, *Traité sur la tolérance* (1763; reprint, Paris: Flammarion 1989), 170-71, my translation.

98. Voltaire, quoted in Williams, *Ethics of Diet,* 149-50, original emphasis.

99. Samuel Taylor Coleridge, quoted in Richard Holmes, *Coleridge: Early Visions, 1772-1804* (New York: Pantheon, 1989), 304.

100. Norman L. Torrey, *The Spirit of Voltaire* (New York: Columbia University Press, 1938), 54.

101. Voltaire, quoted in Jon Wynne-Tyson, ed., *The Extended Circle: An Anthology of Humane Thought* (London: Cardinal, 1990), 557.

102. Torrey, *Spirit of Voltaire,* 19.

103. Voltaire, quoted in ibid., 21.

104. Ballantyne, *Voltaire's Visit,* 2, 3, 10, 4.

105. Wagnière, quoted in Torrey, *Spirit of Voltaire,* 34.

106. Voltaire, quoted in ibid., 83.

107. Voltaire, quoted in ibid., 170.

108. Voltaire, quoted in ibid., 28.

109. Voltaire, quoted in ibid., 67.

110. Voltaire, *Works,* vol. 33, 162, quoted in Ballantyne, *Voltaire's Visit,* 171.

111. Voltaire, *Works,* vol. 23, 306, quoted in ibid., 175.

112. Torrey, *Spirit of Voltaire,* 189, 191.

113. Ibid., 211.

114. Voltaire, quoted in Ballantyne, *Voltaire's Visit,* 279.

115. Samuel Sharpe, quoted in ibid., 307.

116. Voltaire, quoted in Torrey, *Spirit of Voltaire,* 147.

117. Later, Voltaire called Jean-Jacques "that arch-fool." Rousseau said Voltaire had "corrupted Geneva."

118. Voltaire, quoted in Maurice Cranston, *Noble Savage: Jean-Jacques Rousseau, 1754-1762* (Chicago: Chicago University Press, 1991), 9.

119. Voltaire, quoted in ibid., 44.

120. R.S. Ridgway, *Voltaire and Sensibility* (Montreal and Kingston: McGill-Queen's University Press, 1975), 244.

121. Georges Louis Leclerc, quoted in Williams, *Ethics of Diet,* 166, original emphasis.

122. Ibid., 167.

123. Edward Duffy, *Rousseau in England: The Context for Shelley's Critique of the Enlightenment* (Berkeley: University of California Press, 1979), 106.

124. Cranston, *Noble Savage,* 10.

125. Ibid., 2.

126. Ibid., 14.

127. Rousseau, quoted in ibid., 149.

128. On Rousseau's consideration for animals, see Preece, *Awe for the Tiger,* 162-63.

129. Jean-Jacques Rousseau, *Émile, or On Education,* ed. and trans. Allan Bloom (New York: Basic, 1979), bk. 2, 153.

130. Ibid.

131. Jean-Jacques Rousseau, *Discourse on the Origin and Foundations of Inequality among Men in Rousseau's Political Writings,* ed. Allan Ritter and Julia Conaway Bondanella, trans. Julia Conaway Bondanella (New York: Norton, 1998), 7.

132. Rousseau, *Émile*, bk. 2, 151.

133. Ibid., bk. 4, 222.

134. Ibid., bk. 4, 321.

135. Rousseau, quoted in Cranston, *Noble Savage*, 58. On the increasingly embittered relationship between Hume and Rousseau, see Rousseau, *Discourse on the Origin*, 195-99.

136. Maurice Cranston, *The Solitary Self: Jean-Jacques Rousseau in Exile and Adversity* (Chicago: University of Chicago Press, 1997), 25.

137. Ibid.

138. Morellet, quoted in Cranston, *Noble Savage*, 225.

139. Rousseau, *Émile*, 154.

140. Cranston, *Solitary Self*, 45.

141. Ibid., 89-90.

142. Ibid., 99.

143. Ibid., 138.

144. Rousseau, *The Social Contract*, quoted in Cranston, *Noble Savage*, 305.

145. Rousseau, *Lettres morales*, quoted in ibid., 74.

146. Rousseau, quoted in ibid., 27.

147. Rousseau, quoted in ibid., 46.

148. Rousseau, quoted in ibid., 56.

149. Ibid., 171.

150. Rousseau, quoted in ibid., 145.

151. See ibid., 207.

152. Rousseau, *La nouvelle Héloise*, quoted in ibid., 32.

153. Rousseau, quoted in ibid., 109.

154. Jean-Jacques Rousseau, *Eloisa: A Series of Original Letters* (London: John Harding, 1810), v.

155. Cranston, *Solitary Self*, 180.

156. Rousseau, quoted in Cranston, *Noble Savage*, 46.

157. Peter Singer, *Animal Liberation*, 2nd ed. (New York: New York Review of Books, 1990), 203, recognizes the continued carnivorous habits of Voltaire and Rousseau but offers neither evidence nor explanation because he was concerned at that point only to indicate the limitations to Enlightenment sensibilities.

158. See Preece, *Awe for the Tiger*, 251-53.

159. Marianne Stark, *Letters from Italy, between 1792 and 1798* (1800), 2 vols., letter 14, quoted in Nicholson, *On the Primeval Diet*, 80.

160. Alphonse de Lamartine, *Les Confidences* (1848; reprint, Paris: Hachette, 1893), 77-79.

161. Richard Wagner, "Against Vivisection (an Open Letter to Herr Ernst von Weber)," in M.R.L. Freschel, ed., *Selections from Three Essays by Richard Wagner* (Rochester, NH: Millennium Guild, 1933), 8-9.

162. Barry Millington, *Wagner*, rev. ed. (Princeton: Princeton University Press, 1992), 5.

163. Richard Wagner, *Religion and Art*, quoted in Williams, *Ethics of Diet*, 373.

164. Millington, *Wagner*, 104.

165. Quoted in Colin Spencer, *Vegetarianism: A History*, 2nd ed. (New York: Four Walls Eight Windows, 2002), 264.

166. Alfred Lord Tennyson, quoted in Peter Levi, *Tennyson* (New York: Charles Scribner's Sons, 1993), 223.

167. Marian Scholtmeijer, *Animal Victims in Modern Fiction: From Sanctity to Sacrifice* (Toronto: University of Toronto Press, 1993), 29.

168. Mohandas K. Gandhi, *Diet and Diet Reform* (Ahmadebad: Navajivan, 1949), 8.
169. John Tweddell, *Remains of John Tweddell* (1815), ed. Robert Tweddell, 215, quoted in Thomas, *Man and the Natural World*, 299.

## CHAPTER 10: MILITANT ADVOCATES

1. Percy Bysshe Shelley, quoted in Richard Holmes, *Shelley: The Pursuit* (1974; reprint, New York: New York Review of Books, 1994), 346.
2. William Wordsworth, *The Prelude*, bk. 11, 108-9, 113.
3. William Cowper, *The Task*, bk. 5, 5.
4. Charles Lamb, quoted in Kenneth R. Johnston, *The Hidden Wordsworth: Poet, Lover, Rebel, Spy* (New York: Norton, 1998), 249. Lamb himself objected to Coleridge's description of him as "gentle-hearted Charles"; "sober" was his preferred epithet.
5. Burke's histrionics were in evidence when he debated in the Commons in 1792 the apprehended threat to the British. Having left the Whigs to join Pitt on the Tory benches, Burke melodramatically threw a concealed knife on the floor of the House. Thereupon, he was assailed by his former Whig allies with the demand that he reveal his secreted forks and spoons as well.
6. Wordsworth, *Prelude*, bk. 9, 182-83.
7. The common view on the Revolution's measure of success was, for example, expressed in Samuel Taylor Coleridge, *Collected Letters of Samuel Taylor Coleridge*, vol. 1, ed. E.L. Griggs (Oxford: Clarendon, 1971), 527, where he refers to "the complete failure of the French Revolution." Even many of those who found excuses for the Terror became disenchanted when France attacked neutral Switzerland.
8. Coleridge, quoted in Richard Holmes, *Coleridge: Early Visions, 1772-1804* (New York: Pantheon, 1989), 66.
9. John Ray, *The Wisdom of God Manifested in the Works of Creation* (1691; reprint, New York: Garland, 1979), 129.
10. For the earlier discussion of Paley, see pages 117-18.
11. William Paley, *Moral and Political Philosophy*, in *The Works of William Paley, D.D., Archdeacon of Carlisle* (1785; reprint, Philadelphia: Crissy Markley, 1850), 43-44.
12. "Vendée" was a term used loosely to refer to areas of royalist insurrection throughout western France, including Brittany and Normandy, not just to the Vendée proper.
13. Wordsworth, *The Borderers*, quoted in David V. Erdman, *Commerce des Lumières: John Oswald and the British in Paris, 1790-1793* (Columbia, MI: University of Missouri Press, 1986), 104.
14. John Oswald, *The Cry of Nature, or An Appeal to Mercy and to Justice on Behalf of the Persecuted Animals*, ed. Jason Hribal (1791; reprint Lampeter: Mellen, 2000), 41.
15. Ibid., 24-26. The same passages are to be found in Howard Williams, *The Ethics of Diet: A Catena of Authorities Deprecatory of the Practice of Flesh-Eating*, ed. Carol J. Adams (1883; reprint, Urbana: University of Illinois Press, 2003), 181. The discrepancies between these texts and the originals point up a continuous problem with Williams's quotations. Williams adds after animal "of another species" without indicating that these words are not in the original. He substitutes "nature" for "texture." He replaces "creatures" with "beings." He has "the" table instead of "our" table. He introduces brackets where there are none in the original. He omits "to the purpose of

nature." Frequently, he changes punctuation to suit his fancy. Frequently, although not here, he adds italics where he thinks the words should be emphasized. None of this ever affects the meaning of the original passages, but those interested in precisely the words of the original author should refer to the original wherever possible and not rely entirely on Williams's text. It is very fortunate that Williams collected most of the material relevant to the history of vegetarianism and made it available in one place. It is rather less fortunate that the material there provided is not completely reliable. Nonetheless, it is amusing to read those authorities whose notes claim they are quoting from rather obscure original works but whose quotations retain exactly the same errors of interpolation or excision as those of Williams.

16. John Wesley, "The General Deliverance" (1788), in *Sermons on Several Occasions*, vol. 6, ser. 2, sermon 60, in *The Works of John Wesley* (1872; reprint, Grand Rapids, MI: Zondervan, n.d.), 251; see also 240-51.

17. Joscelyn Godwin, "Foreword," in Kenneth Sylvan Guthrie, comp. and trans., *The Pythagorean Sourcebook and Library* (Grand Rapids, MI: Phanes, 1988), 13.

18. Coleridge, quoted in Holmes, *Coleridge,* 130.

19. William Blake, quoted in James King, *William Blake: His Life* (London: Weidenfeld and Nicholson, 1991), 145.

20. Peter Ackroyd, *William Blake* (London: Sinclair-Stevenson, 1995), 102.

21. Arthur Schopenhauer, *On the Basis of Morality,* 2nd ed., trans E.F.J. Payne (Indianapolis: Bobbs-Merrill, 1965), 152.

22. Williams, *Ethics of Diet,* 268.

23. Dorothy Wordsworth, quoted in Johnston, *Hidden Wordsworth,* 407.

24. William Wordsworth, quoted in ibid., 477, 490.

25. Holmes, *Coleridge,* 25.

26. Coleridge, quoted in ibid., 179.

27. Coleridge, quoted in ibid., 342.

28. Samuel Rogers, quoted in Paul Johnson, *The Birth of the Modern World Society, 1815-1830* (London: Phoenix, 1991), 408.

29. Robert Southey, quoted in Holmes, *Coleridge,* 75.

30. Coleridge, quoted in ibid., 82.

31. Coleridge, *Collected Letters,* vol. 2, 864.

32. Williams, *Ethics of Diet,* 180.

33. George Nicholson, *On the Primeval Diet of Man,* ed. Rod Preece (1801; reprint, Lampeter: Mellen, 1999), iii.

34. John Stewart, quoted in ibid., 91-92.

35. Johnston, *Hidden Wordsworth,* 365-66.

36. Nicholson, *On the Primeval Diet,* 14.

37. Ibid., 13.

38. Ibid., 18.

39. Ibid.

40. Ibid., 183.

41. See page 61.

42. Ibid., 223.

43. Ibid., 98. The version of this quotation in Williams, *Ethics of Diet,* 192, corresponds almost exactly with the original, apart from the addition of italics on two occasions, the change of "'tis" to "it is," and the omission of a comma (see note 15). Throughout

this book, where I have not had the original to hand and have been unable to procure it, I have *faute de mieux* followed the Williams version, with the exception of omitting italics where I am confident they have been added.

44. Ibid., 99; also quoted in Williams, *Ethics of Diet*, 193.

45. *Gentleman's Magazine and Historical Chronicle*, no. 95, pt. 2, July-December 1825, 642.

46. *Monthly Mirror*, May 1805. See William St. Clair, *The Godwins and the Shelleys* (New York: Norton, 1989), 261.

47. Joseph Ritson, *An Essay on Abstinence from Animal Food as a Moral Duty* (London: Richard Phillips, 1802), 201. Incorrectly, Williams, *Ethics of Diet*, 186, gives the quotation as "dressed under roasted flesh."

48. Quoted in Harriet Ritvo, *The Platypus and the Mermaid and Other Figments of the Classifying Imagination* (Cambridge, MA: Harvard University Press, 1995), 199.

49. Ritson, *Essay on Abstinence*, 30-33. If four pages seem excessive for the number of words in the quotation, this is because three of the four pages have only two lines of text, the rest being consumed by footnotes.

50. Ibid., 37.

51. Ibid., 231-33, original emphasis. Ritson has an opening quotation mark before "sustenance" with no closing mark, which anyway seems superfluous. I have omitted it.

52. Lord Monboddo, quoted in ibid., 43.

53. Ibid., 77.

54. Ibid., 85.

55. William Lambe, quoted in Williams, *Ethics of Diet*, 199.

56. Lambe, quoted in ibid., 203.

57. Lambe, *Additional Reports on Regimen*, 226-27, quoted in Christine Kenyon-Jones, *Kindred Brutes: Animals in Romantic Period Writing* (Aldershot: Ashgate, 2001), 112.

58. John Frank Newton, *Return to Nature, or A Defence of the Vegetable Regimen; with some account of an experiment made the last three or four years in the author's family* (London: T. Cadell and W. Davies, 1811), iv.

59. St. Clair, *Godwins*, 263.

60. Ibid.

61. Ibid.

62. Sizable dinner parties were not uncommon in this period. Thus, for example, at a dinner at the Wordsworth residence at Alfoxden in 1797, fourteen persons sat down to eat.

63. Williams, *Ethics of Diet*, 202.

64. Mary Shelley, quoted in Holmes, *Shelley*, 273.

65. Newton, quoted in Williams, *Ethics of Diet*, 66.

66. Newton, quoted in ibid., 63-64.

67. Newton, quoted in ibid., 67.

68. John Ray, quoted by Newton, in ibid., 99.

69. Newton, quoted in ibid., 154, original emphasis.

70. William Godwin, *An Enquiry Concerning Political Justice* (1793), quoted in St. Clair, *Godwins*, 106.

71. Wordsworth, *Prelude*, bk. 6, 353-54.

72. Holmes, *Shelley*, 563.

73. George Bernard Shaw, quoted in Michael Holroyd, *Bernard Shaw*, vol. 1 (Harmondsworth: Penguin, 1990), 39.

74. Ibid., 208.

75. Shelley, quoted in Holmes, *Shelley,* 593.

76. Shelley, quoted in ibid., 97.

77. Percy Bysshe Shelley, *The Complete Works of Percy Bysshe Shelley,* vol. 6, ed. Roger Ingpen and Walter E. Peck (New York: Gordian, 1965), 6, 8, 11, 17, 18.

78. Richard Holmes, quoted in ibid., 157; and Timothy Morton, *Shelley and the Revolution in Taste: The Body and the Natural World* (Cambridge, UK: Cambridge University Press, 1994), 75-76, quoted in Kenyon-Jones, *Kindred Brutes,* 112.

79. Holmes, *Shelley,* 220.

80. Ibid., 201.

81. Shelley, *Complete Works,* vol. 6, 338, 339, 340-41, 343-44, original emphasis. On Boswell, see page 199.

82. Kenyon-Jones, *Kindred Brutes,* 112. The biographers she has in mind are Timothy Morton, *Shelley and the Revolution in Taste: The Body and the Natural World* (Cambridge, UK: Cambridge University Press, 1994); and Thomas Jefferson Hogg, *Life of Percy Bysshe Shelley,* 2 vols. (London: Edward Moxon, 1858).

83. Holroyd, *Bernard Shaw,* vol. 3, 363.

84. Shelley, quoted in Holmes, *Shelley,* 373.

85. Shelley, quoted in ibid., 184.

86. Harriet Shelley, quoted in ibid., 180.

87. Benjamin Robert Haydon, quoted in ibid., 360-61.

88. Keith Thomas, *Man and the Natural World: Changing Attitudes in England, 1500-1800* (London: Penguin, 1984), 296.

89. St. Clair, *Godwins,* 261.

90. See Phyllis Grosskurth, *Byron: The Flawed Angel* (Toronto: Macfarlane, Walter and Ross, 1997), 366. The letter from Byron on which the information is based is also quoted in Holmes, *Shelley,* 599.

91. Miranda Seymour, *Mary Shelley* (New York: Grove, 2002), 54.

92. John Keats, quoted in Holmes, *Shelley,* 361.

93. For the inception of Frankenstein, see Seymour, *Mary Shelley,* 283.

94. Arguably, there are occasional exceptions, such as the brilliant political pamphlet *On the Death of Queen Charlotte* (1817), and although *The Revolt of Islam* (1818) was, as published, *relatively* harmless, its original as *Laon and Cynthia* gave cause to fear government reprisal. In addition, Shelley's reaction to "the massacre of Peterloo" in 1819 was less than moderate, but then so was that of everyone else of even mildly liberal vein. And his 1820 economic and political writings are undoubtedly as radical as anything he ever wrote.

95. Shaw, via Newman Ivey White, *Shelley,* vol. 2 (1947), 416, quoted in Seymour, *Mary Shelley,* 555.

96. Thomas Moore, *Life, Letters and Journals of Lord Byron* (1860 ed.), quoted in Williams, *Ethics of Diet,* 331.

97. Grosskurth, *Byron,* 134, 194.

98. Samuel Rogers, quoted in ibid., 143.

99. Colin Spencer, *Vegetarianism: A History,* 2nd ed. (New York: Four Walls Eight Windows, 2002), 214.

100. Sir Richard Phillips, *Golden Rules of Social Philosophy, being a System of Ethics* (1826), quoted in Williams, *Ethics of Diet,* 240.

101. Arthur Broome, *SPCA Founding Statement* (London, 1824), 2, quoted in Hilda Kean,

*Animal Rights: Political and Social Change in Britain since 1800* (London: Reaktion Books, 1998), 36.

102. Lewis Gompertz, *Moral Inquiries on the Situation of Man and of Brutes,* ed. Peter Singer (1824; reprint, Fontwell, UK: Centaur, 1992), 68.
103. Ibid., 110.
104. Ibid., 140, original emphasis.
105. Ibid., 84-85.
106. Ibid., 150.
107. See William H. Drummond, *The Rights of Animals and Man's Obligation to Treat Them with Humanity,* ed. Rod Preece and Chien-Hui Li (1838; reprint, Lampeter: Mellen, 2005), xiv-xv.
108. Thomas, *Man and the Natural World,* 279.
109. Henry S. Salt, *Animals' Rights Considered in Relation to Social Progress* (1892; reprint, Clark Summit, PA: Society for Animal Rights, 1980), 136.
110. Ibid., 156.
111. Thomas Forster, quoted in ibid., 157-58.
112. On plagiarism, see Rod Preece and Chien-Hui Li, "Introduction," in Drummond, *Rights of Animals,* xxv-xxvi; and Rod Preece, "The Prodigous Mr. Youatt: Some Unanswered Questions," *Veterinary History* n.s. 12, 3 (2004): 261-72. It should be recognized, however, that plagiarism was not considered so serious a matter in the nineteenth century as now. Coleridge was a noted plagiarist, especially in *Biographia Literaria.*

## CHAPTER 11: THE VICTORIANS, THE EDWARDIANS, AND THE FOUNDING OF THE VEGETARIAN SOCIETY

1. Beatrice Webb, quoted in Michael Holroyd, *Bernard Shaw,* vol. 1 (Harmondsworth: Penguin, 1990), 269.
2. Margaret Lavington, "Rupert Brooke: A Biographical Note," in Rupert Brooke, *The Collected Poems of Rupert Brooke* (New York: Dodd, Mead and Company, 1940), 181.
3. Anna Bonus Kingsford, *Perfect Way in Diet: A Treatise Advocating a Return to the Natural and Ancient Food of Our Race* (Kila, MT: Kessinger, n.d.), vii.
4. Harriet Ritvo, *The Platypus and the Mermaid and Other Fragments of the Classifying Imagination* (Cambridge, MA: Harvard University Press, 1995), 198.
5. Quoted at greater length in Colin Spencer, *Vegetarianism: A History,* 2nd ed. (New York: Four Walls Eight Windows, 2002), 248.
6. The cartoon is reproduced in Ritvo, *Platypus,* 201.
7. Mistakenly, in *Vegetarianism: A History,* Colin Spencer has Newton with a doctorate, both in the text, at 231, and the index, at 380.
8. Quoted in Richard Holmes, *Shelley: The Pursuit* (1974; reprint, New York: New York Review of Books, 1994), 179.
9. The report is given with more details of the actual diet in Kingsford, *Perfect Way,* 37-38.
10. George Eliot, quoted in Frederick Karl, *George Eliot: Voice of a Century* (New York: Norton, 1995), 141.
11. Francis William Newman, *Essays on Diet,* quoted in Jon Wynne-Tyson, ed., *The Extended Circle: An Anthology of Humane Thought* (London: Cardinal, 1990), 338-39, original emphasis.

12. Howard Williams, *The Ethics of Diet: A Catena of Authorities Deprecatory of the Practice of Flesh-Eating,* ed. Carol J. Adams (1883; reprint, Urbana: University of Illinois Press, 2003), 93, 292.

13. Kingsford, *Perfect Way,* 37.

14. Ritvo, *Platypus,* 198.

15. Henry Amos, ed., *Food Reformers' Year Book* (London, 1909), 18, quoted in Hilda Kean, *Animal Rights: Political and Social Change in Britain since 1800* (London: Reaktion Books, 1998), 122.

16. See page 12.

17. Spencer, *Vegetarianism,* 258.

18. Lady Paget, "Foreword," in Charles W. Forward, *Food of the Future* (London, 1904), 97, quoted in Kean, *Animal Rights,* 126.

19. Lady Florence Dixie, quoted in Wynne-Tyson, ed., *Extended Circle,* 108-9.

20. *Food Reformers' Year Book* (1906), 6, and *Humane Review,* April 1905, cited in Kean, *Animal Rights,* 126.

21. On Williams's admiration of Mayor, see Williams, *Ethics of Diet,* 305.

22. Ibid. (1883 ed.), viii-ix, xii. I have here quoted from the 1883 edition because there seems to be some problem with the printing of pages xxvii-xxviii and xxix of the preface in the 2003 reprint.

23. Ibid. (1883 ed.), x-xi.

24. On Salt and on Lind-af-Hageby, see Rod Preece, *Awe for the Tiger, Love for the Lamb: A Chronicle of Sensibility to Animals* (Vancouver: University of British Columbia Press, 2002), 341-44 and 352-53, respectively.

25. Annie Wood Besant, quoted in Holroyd, *Bernard Shaw,* vol. 1, 168.

26. Besant, quoted in Philip Kapleau, *To Cherish All Life* (Rochester, NY: Zen Center, 1986), 81.

27. Kingsford, quoted in Edward Maitland, *Anna Kingsford: Her Life, Letters, Diary and Work,* 3rd ed. (London: G. Redway, 1913), 45-46.

28. Anna Bonus Kingsford and Edward Maitland, *Addresses and Essays on Vegetarianism* (1912; reprint, Kila, MT: Kessinger, n.d.), 65, original emphasis.

29. Quoted in Kean, *Animal Rights,* 123.

30. Kingsford and Maitland, *Addresses and Essays,* 170. "Trismegius," or "Trismegistus," means thrice-great Hermes and is the title given by the Greeks to the Egyptian god Thoth. By legend, Trismegius was the source of Egyptian priestly asceticism.

31. Henry Salt, quoted in Ritvo, *Platypus,* 199.

32. Mohandas K. Gandhi, *Diet and Diet Reform* (Ahmadebad: Navajivan, 1949), 35.

33. Salt, quoted in Richard D. Ryder, *Animal Revolution: Changing Attitudes towards Speciesism,* rev. ed. (Oxford: Berg, 2000), 123, original emphasis.

34. Henry S. Salt, "The Raison d'Être of Vegetarianism," from *The Logic of Vegetarianism,* in *The Savour of Salt: A Henry Salt Anthology,* ed. George Hendrick and Willene Hendrick (Fontwell, UK: Centaur, 1989), 24-28.

35. George Bernard Shaw, quoted in Holroyd, *Bernard Shaw,* vol. 1, 222.

36. Edward Carpenter, *Civilisation: Its Cause and Cure, and Other Essays* (1883; reprint, London: Allen and Unwin, 1919), 39.

37. Ibid., 45, original emphasis.

38. Samuel Butler, *Erewhon, or Over the Range,* 10th ed. (1872; reprint, London: Page and Company, 1923), 284.

39. George Bernard Shaw, "Preface" to *The Doctor's Dilemma,* in *The Doctor's Dilemma, Getting Married, and The Shewing-up of Blanco Posnet* (London: Constable, 1911), lviii-lix.
40. Shaw, quoted in Holroyd, *Bernard Shaw,* vol. 1, 87.
41. George Bernard Shaw, *Fifteen Self Sketches* (London: Constable, 1949), 53.
42. Shaw, quoted in Holroyd, *Bernard Shaw,* vol. 1, 84.
43. Shaw, quoted in ibid., vol. 1, 86.
44. Shaw, quoted in ibid., vol. 1, 88.
45. Shaw, quoted in ibid., vol. 1, 85.
46. Shaw, quoted in ibid., vol. 1, 87.
47. Ibid., vol. 3, 457.
48. Shaw, quoted in ibid., vol. 3, 214.
49. Shaw, quoted in ibid., vol. 1, 86.
50. Franklyn Barnabas, quoted in ibid., vol. 3, 45.
51. Shaw, quoted in ibid., vol. 1, 268.
52. Andrew Linzey, *Animal Theology* (Urbana: University of Illinois Press, 1995), 83.
53. H.G. Wells, *Anna Veronica* (1909; reprint, London: n.p., 1984), 109, quoted in Kean, *Animal Rights,* 126.
54. Wells, *Anna Veronica,* 110-11, cited in ibid., 126-27.
55. Janey Morris, via Fiona McCarthy, *William Morris* (London: Faber and Faber, 1994), 492, quoted in ibid., 127. Neither Kean nor McCarthy records Shaw's response, although McCarthy adds enigmatically: "In the subtle war between G.B.S. and Mrs Morris, perhaps this was his revenge."
56. William L. Shirer, *Love and Hatred: The Stormy Marriage of Leo and Sonya Tolstoy* (New York: Simon and Schuster, 1994), 106.
57. Leo Tolstoy, quoted in Wynne-Tyson, ed., *Extended Circle,* 376.
58. Leo Tolstoy, "The First Step," in *Recollections and Essays by Leo Tolstoy,* 4th ed., trans. Aylmer Maude (London: Oxford University Press, 1961), sec. 9, 124-26, original emphasis.
59. Ibid., sec. 10, 134.
60. Rod Preece and Lorna Chamberlain, *Animal Welfare and Human Values* (Waterloo, ON: Wilfrid Laurier University Press, 1992), 211.

## CHAPTER 12: VEGETARIANS AND VEGANS IN THE TWENTIETH CENTURY

1. Charlotte Shaw, quoted in Michael Holroyd, *Bernard Shaw,* vol. 3 (Harmondsworth: Penguin, 1990), 234.
2. See Rod Preece, *Brute Souls, Happy Beasts, and Evolution: The Historical Status of Animals* (Vancouver: University of British Columbia Press, 2005), ch. 4.
3. Romain Rolland, *Jean-Christophe,* trans. G. Cannan (New York: Random House, 1938), 327-28.
4. Albert Schweitzer, "Feeling for Animal Life," in *A Treasury of Albert Schweitzer,* ed. Thomas Kiernan (New York: Gramercy, 1994), 15.
5. Ibid.
6. Albert Schweitzer, *Civilization and Ethics* (London: A. & C. Black, 1923), 255.
7. Ibid., 256.

8. Mohandas K. Gandhi, *Diet and Diet Reform* (Ahmadebad: Navajivan, 1949), 35-36.
9. For example, by Colin Spencer, *Vegetarianism: A History,* 2nd ed. (New York: Four Walls Eight Windows, 2002), 283ff; and by Boria Sachs, *Animals in the Third Reich: Pets, Scapegoats, and the Holocaust* (New York: Continuum, 2000), 35.
10. Joyce Salisbury, *The Beast Within: Animals in the Middle Ages* (New York: Routledge, 1994), 170, cited in Sachs, *Animals in the Third Reich,* 35.
11. *H.J. Marschiert: Das neue Hitler-Jugend-Buch* (Berlin: Paul Franke Verlag, n.d.).
12. Symon Gould, quoted in Karen Iacobbo and Michael Iacobbo, *Vegetarian America: A History* (Westport, CT: Praeger, 2004), 159.
13. William H. Drummond, *The Rights of Animals and Man's Obligation to Treat Them with Humanity,* ed. Rod Preece and Chien-hui Li (1838; reprint, Lampeter: Mellen, 2005).
14. See Rod Preece, *Awe for the Tiger, Love for the Lamb: A Chronicle of Sensibility to Animals* (Vancouver: University of British Columbia Press, 2002), 108, 109.
15. Peter Singer, *Animal Liberation,* 2nd ed. (New York: New York Review of Books, 1990), i-ii.
16. W.R. Inge, "The Rights of Animals," in *Lay Thoughts of a Dean* (London: Knickerbocker, 1926), 199.
17. Andrew Linzey, *Animal Theology* (Urbana: University of Illinois Press, 1995), 83.
18. Harriet Ritvo, *The Platypus and the Mermaid and Other Fragments of the Classifying Imagination* (Cambridge, MA: Harvard University Press, 1995), 199.
19. Robert C. Tucker, ed., *The Marx-Engels Reader* (New York: Norton, 1978), 496. I am indebted to Renzo Llorente and John Sanbonmatsu for the information on which this and the following two references are based.
20. Friedrich Engels, *On the History of Early Christianity,* in *Marx and Engels on Religion* (New York: Schocken Books, 1964), 322.
21. Leon Trotsky, quoted in Steven Lukes, *Marxism and Morality* (Oxford: Oxford University Press, 1985), 23.
22. William Hazlitt, *The Plain Speaker,* quoted in Keith Thomas, "The First Vegetarians," in Kelly Wand, ed., *The Animal Rights Movement* (San Diego: Greenhaven Press, 2003), 32.
23. Peter Singer, "All Animals Are Equal," *Philosophic Exchange* 1 (Summer 1974): 103-9, excerpted at much greater length in Kerry S. Walters and Lisa Portmess, eds., *Ethical Vegetarianism: From Pythagoras to Peter Singer* (Albany, NY: State University of New York Press, 1999), 166, 167. Singer repeats essentially the same message in *Animal Liberation* and even has a chapter there entitled "All Animals Are Equal," but the article in *Philosophic Exchange* is the earliest printed statement of his position.
24. Stephen Clark, *The Moral Status of Animals* (Oxford: Clarendon, 1977), 40-41, excerpted in Daniel Dombrowski, *Not Even A Sparrow Falls: The Philosophy of Stephen R.L. Clark* (East Lansing: Michigan State University Press, 2000), 163-64.
25. Jon Wynne-Tyson, "Dietethics: Its Influence on Future Farming Patterns," in Richard Ryder and David Patterson, eds., *Animal Rights: A Symposium* (London: Centaur, 1979), excerpted at much greater length in Walters and Portmess, eds., *Ethical Vegetarianism,* 235-36.
26. Spencer, *Vegetarianism,* 303.
27. On Henry Salt, see page 281; on Lewis Gompertz, see pages 264-65.
28. See pages 17-18.
29. George Bernard Shaw, quoted in Holroyd, *Bernard Shaw,* vol. 1, 85.

CHAPTER 13: VEGETARIANISM IN NORTH AMERICA

1. Karen Iacobbo and Michael Iacobbo, *Vegetarian America: A History* (Westport, CT: Praeger, 2004).

2. Andrew Linzey, "Foreword," in ibid., x.

3. See page 174.

4. See page 28.

5. Colin Spencer, *Vegetarianism: A History*, 2nd ed. (New York: Four Walls Eight Windows, 2002), 256.

6. Iacobbo and Iacobbo, *Vegetarian America*, 30.

7. See page 270.

8. Erasmus Darwin, *The Temple of Nature*, vol. 4, 428, via Sylvester Graham, *Graham Journal of Health and Longevity* (1838), quoted in ibid., 49, and see note 78 therein. The quotation is slightly incorrect in that Graham has substituted "our" for "his" twice.

9. Alexander Pope, "Universal Prayer," stanza 11, line 1.

10. William A. Alcott, *Vegetable Diet: As Sanctioned by Medical Men, and by Experience in All Ages* (New York: Fowlers and Wells, 1848), 264-65.

11. Compare Odell Shepard, *The Journals of Bronson Alcott* (Boston: Little, Brown, 1938), 115, quoted in Iacobbo and Iacobbo, *Vegetarian America*, 57, with Alexander Pope, *Guardian* (London), 21 May 1713, especially the paragraph beginning: "But if our sports are destructive."

12. Iacobbo and Iacobbo, *Vegetarian America*, 58.

13. See pages 37-43.

14. Henry David Thoreau, *Walden, or Life in the Woods, together with Civil Disobedience*, ed. Philip Van Doren Stern (New York: Barnes and Noble, 1970), 339, 346.

15. Angus Taylor, *Magpies, Monkeys and Morals: What Philosophers Say about Animal Liberation* (Peterborough: Broadview, 1999), 71. The statement is still included in the 2003 revised edition with a different title: *Animals and Ethics: An Overview of the Ethical Debate*, 93.

16. On Lecky, see pages 123, 315.

17. Secretary of the Kensington Physiological Society, "A Lecture on the First Step in Physical and Moral Reform Delivered before the Kensington Physiological Society, in the Bible-Christian Church, on the Evening of the 14th of April, 1842" (Philadelphia, PA: William Metcalfe, 1842), 21, quoted in Iacobbo and Iacobbo, *Vegetarian America*, 62.

18. On Auguste Comte, see Rod Preece, *Awe for the Tiger, Love for the Lamb: A Chronicle of Sensibility to Animals* (Vancouver: University of British Columbia Press, 2002), 251-53.

19. Committee of the Philadelphia Bible-Christian Church, *History of the Philadelphia Bible-Christian Church for the First Century of its Existence* (Philadelphia: J.L. Lippincott, 1922). According to the preface, one member of the committee was ninety-two years of age, perhaps Clubb himself, who died in the same year the book was published.

20. See Iacobbo and Iacobbo, *Vegetarian America*, 120.

21. George T. Angell, *Autobiographical Sketches and Personal Recollections* (Boston: AHES, [1892?]), Appendix, 32. There was an earlier, but less complete, edition in 1884.

22. Jay Dinshah, *Out of the Jungle* (1967), quoted on the International Vegetarian Union website at www.ivu.org.

23. Dinshah, *Ahimsa* (1971), quoted at ibid.

24. See J. Howard Moore, *The New Ethics* (London: E. Bell, 1907); and J. Howard Moore,

*The Universal Kinship*, ed. Charles Magel (1906; reprint, Fontwell, UK: Centaur, 1992).

25. J. Howard Moore, "Why I am a vegetarian," *Chicago Vegetarian*, September 1897, 5. This was one of a series of five 1897 articles Moore wrote for the *Chicago Vegetarian*. To the best of my knowledge, he did not write directly on vegetarianism elsewhere.

26. Moore, correspondence with Henry Salt, quoted in Charles Magel, "Introduction," in Moore, *Universal Kinship*, ix, xiv.

27. Moore, "Why I am a Vegetarian," 10.

28. For a valuable analysis of Upton Sinclair's *The Jungle* and a comparison with Roald Dahl's "The Pig," see Marian Scholtmeijer, *Animal Victims in Modern Fiction: From Sanctity to Sacrifice* (Toronto: University of Toronto Press, 1993), 150-57.

29. Tom Regan, "Christians Are What Christians Eat," in Steve F. Sapontzis, ed., *Food for Thought: The Debate over Eating Meat* (Amherst, NY: Prometheus Books, 2004), 177. The same argument was presented by Regan both in *Liberating Life: Approaches to Ecological Theory*, ed. Jay B. McDaniel (Maryknoll, NY: Orbis, 1990), and in *The Three Generations* (Philadelphia: Temple University Press, 1991).

30. Carol J. Adams, "The Sexual Politics of Meat," in Sapontzis, ed., *Food for Thought*, 249. The argument is repeated from her *The Sexual Politics of Meat: A Feminist-Vegetarian Critical Theory* (New York: Continuum, 1990).

### POSTSCRIPT: PROSPECTS

1. *Enroute,* May 2001, 25.
2. Ibid., 26.
3. Ibid.

# Selected Bibliography

Abbott, John Lawrence. *John Hawkesworth: Eighteenth Century Man of Letters.* Madison: University of Wisconsin Press, 1982.

Ackroyd, Peter. *Albion: The Origins of the English Imagination.* London: Chatto and Windus, 2002.

–. *William Blake.* London: Sinclair-Stevenson, 1995.

Adams, Carol J. "The Sexual Politics of Meat." In Steve F. Sapontzis, ed., *Food for Thought: The Debate over Eating Meat,* 248-60. Amherst, NY: Prometheus, 2004.

–. *The Sexual Politics of Meat: A Feminist-Vegetarian Critical Theory.* New York: Continuum, 1990.

Agius, Don Ambrose. *God's Animals.* London: Catholic Study Circle for Animal Welfare, 1973.

Akers, Keith. *The Lost Religion of Jesus: Simple Living and Nonviolence in Early Christianity.* New York: Lantern, 2000.

Alcott, William A. *Vegetable Diet: As Sanctioned by Medical Men, and by Experience in All Ages.* New York: Fowlers and Wells, 1848.

Allen, Richard C. *David Hartley on Human Nature.* New York: SUNY, 1999.

Angell, George T. *Autobiographical Sketches and Personal Recollections.* Rev. ed. Boston: AHES, [1892?].

Angermeyer, Johanna. *My Father's Island: A Galapagos Quest.* London: Viking, 1989.

Aquinas, Thomas. *Summa contra gentiles.* 4 vols. Trans. Charles J. O'Neil. Grand Bend: Notre Dame University Press, 1975.

Aristotle. *Nicomachean Ethics.* Ed. and trans. Roger Crisp. Cambridge: Cambridge University Press, 2000.

–. *Politics.* Ed. and trans. Ernest Barker. Oxford: Oxford University Press, 1952.

Bailey, D. Shackleton, trans. *Cicero's Letters to His Friends.* London: Penguin, 1967.

Ballantyne, Archibald. *Voltaire's Visit to England.* 1893. Reprint, Geneva: Slatkine, 1970.

Barnes, Jonathan. *Early Greek Philosophy.* London: Penguin, 1987.

–. *The Presocratic Philosophers.* 2 vols. London: Routledge and Kegan Paul, 1979.

Barnum, Priscilla, ed. *Dives et Pauper*. New York: Kraus, 1973.

Baxter, Ron. *Bestiaries and Their Users in the Middle Ages*. London: Sutton Publishing and Courtauld Institute, 1998.

Bentham, Jeremy. *Introduction to the Principles of Morals and Legislation*. Ed. J.H. Burns and H.L.A. Hart. 1789. Reprint, London: Methuen, 1982.

–. *The Principles of Penal Law* (1811). In *The Works of Jeremy Bentham*. Vol. 10. 1843. Reprint, New York: Russell, 1962.

Besant, Annie. "Introduction." In Florence M. Firth, ed., *The Golden Verses of Pythagoras and Other Pythagorean Fragments,* vii-ix. Kila, MT: Kessinger, n.d.

Boardman, Jonathan, Jasper Griffin, and Gwyn Murray, eds. *The Oxford History of the Classical World*. Oxford: Oxford University Press, 1993.

Boas, George. *The Happy Beast in French Thought of the Seventeenth Century*. 1933. Reprint, New York: Octagon, 1996.

–. *Primitivism and Related Ideas in the Middle Ages*. 1948. Reprint, Baltimore: Johns Hopkins University Press, 1997.

Bolingbroke, Lord. *The Works of Henry St. John, Lord Viscount Bolingbroke*. 5 vols. 1754. Reprint, London: D. Mallet, 1809.

Borwick, Robin. *People with Long Ears*. London: Cassell, 1965.

Boswell, James. *The Life of Samuel Johnson, D.D.* 1791. Reprint, London: J.M. Dent, 1906.

Botha, Surendra, ed. *The Yoga Shastra of Hemchandracharya: A Twelfth Century Guide to Jain Yoga*. Trans. A.S. Gopani. Jaipur: Prakrit Bharti Academy, 1989.

Bowle, John. *John Evelyn and His World*. London: Routledge and Kegan Paul, 1981.

Bowler, Peter J. *The Norton History of the Environmental Sciences*. New York: Norton, 1993.

Bramley, Serge. *Leonardo: The Artist and the Man*. London: Penguin, 1994.

Bruno, Giordano. *Cause, Principle and Unity: Five Dialogues*. Trans. Jack Lindsay. New York: International Publishers, 1962.

Buckner, Elijah D. *The Immortality of Animals and the Relation of Man as Guardian from a Biblical and Philosophical Hypothesis*. Philadelphia: George W. Jacobs, 1903.

–. *The Immortality of Animals*. Ed. Rod Preece. 1903. Reprint, Lampeter, UK: Mellen, 2003.

Burke, Edmund. *A Philosophical Enquiry into the Origin of Our Ideas of the Sublime and Beautiful*. 1756. Reprint, London: F.C. and J. Rivington, 1812.

Burkhardt, Jacob. *The Civilization of the Renaissance in Italy*. 1860. Reprint, London: Phaidon, 1960.

Butler, Samuel. *Erewhon, or Over the Range*. 10th ed. 1872. Reprint, London: Page and Company, 1923.

Campbell, Joseph. *Baksheesh and Brahman: Indian Journal, 1950-1955*. Ed. Robert Larson, Stephen Larson, and Anthony Van Couvering. New York: HarperCollins, 1995.

–. *Historical Atlas of World Mythology*. Vol. 1, *The Way of Animal Powers*. New York: Harper and Row, 1988.

–. *Historical Atlas of World Mythology*. Vol. 2, *The Way of the Seeded Earth*. New York: Harper and Row, 1989.

Carpenter, Edward. *Civilisation: Its Cause and Cure, and Other Essays*. 1883. Reprint, London: Allen and Unwin, 1919.

Cavendish, Margaret, Marchioness of Newcastle. *Poems, and Fancies*. London: J. Martin and J. Allestrye, 1653.

Chadwick, Henry. "The Early Christian Community." In John McManners, ed., *The Oxford History of Christianity*, 21-69. Oxford: Oxford University Press, 2002.

Chalmers, Alex, ed. *The Spectator: A New Edition, Corrected from the Originals, with a Preface, Historical and Biographical*. 11 vols. New York: E. Sargent and M. & W. Ward, 1810.

Chamberlain, Lorna. *Pawsitive News* (London, ON), a publication of the London Humane Society, Summer 2004, 1-5.

Chapple, Christopher Key. *Nonviolence to Animals, Earth and Self in Asian Traditions*. Albany: State University of New York Press, 1993.

Cicero, Marcus Tullius. *Tuscan Disputations*. Rev. ed. Trans. J.E. King. Cambridge, MA: Harvard University Press, 1945.

Clough, Arthur Hugh, trans. *Plutarch's Lives: The Dryden Plutarch*. 2 vols. London: J.M. Dent, 1910.

Cohen, Alfred S. "Vegetarianism from a Jewish Perspective." In Roberta Kalechofsky, ed., *Judaism and Animal Rights*, 176-94. Marblehead, MA: Micah, 1992.

Coleridge, Samuel Taylor. *Collected Letters of Samuel Taylor Coleridge*. 4 vols. Ed. E.L. Griggs. Oxford: Clarendon, 1971.

Collura, Randall. "What Is Our Natural Diet and Should We Really Care?" In Steve F. Sapontzis, ed., *Food for Thought: The Debate over Eating Meat*, 36-45. Amherst, NY: Prometheus, 2004.

Cook, Richard I. *Bernard Mandeville*. New York: Twayne, 1974.

Cottingham, John. *A Descartes Dictionary*. Oxford: Blackwell, 1993.

Cowell, F.R. *Cicero and the Roman Republic*. Harmondsworth: Penguin, 1956.

Cranston, Maurice. *Noble Savage: Jean-Jacques Rousseau, 1754-1763*. Chicago: University of Chicago Press, 1991.

–. *The Solitary Self: Jean-Jacques Rousseau in Exile and Adversity*. Chicago: University of Chicago Press, 1997.

De Beer, E.S., ed. *The Diaries of John Evelyn*. 6 vols. Oxford: Clarendon, 1955.

De Lamartine, Alphonse. *Les Confidences*. 1848. Reprint, Paris: Hachette, 1893.

De Montaigne, Michel. "Apology for Raymond Sebond." In Donald M. Frame, trans., *Selected Essays*, 309-482. New York: Oxford University Press, 1982.

Denny, A. *Descartes' Philosophical Letters*. Oxford: Clarendon, 1970.

Descartes, René. *Oeuvres de Descartes*. 6 vols. Paris: Charles and Paul Tannery, 1897.

–. *Philosophical Works*. 1931. Reprint, Franklin Center, PA: Franklin Library, 1981.

Desmond, Adrian, and James Moore. *Darwin: The Life of a Tormented Evolutionist*. New York: Warner, 1992.

Diamond, Jared. *The Third Chimpanzee: The Evolution and Future of the Human Animal*. San Francisco: HarperPerennial, 1992.

Dickens, Charles. "Inhumane Humanity." *All the Year Round*, vol. 15, 17 March 1866.

Dodd, Jan, et al. *The Rough Guide to Japan*. London: Rough Guides Limited, 2001.

Dombrowski, Daniel. *Not Even a Sparrow Falls: The Philosophy of Stephen R.L. Clark*. Fort Lansing: Michigan State University Press, 2000.

–. *The Philosophy of Vegetarianism*. Amherst: University of Massachusetts Press, 1984.

Drummond, William H. *The Rights of Animals and Man's Obligation to Treat Them with Humanity*. London: John Maldon, 1838.

–. *The Rights of Animals and Man's Obligation to Treat Them with Humanity.* Ed. Rod Preece and Chien-hui Li. 1838. Reprint, Lampeter, UK: Mellen, 2005.

Duffy Edward. *Rousseau in England: The Context for Shelley's Critique of the Enlightenment.* Berkeley: University of California Press, 1979.

Ehrenreich, Barbara. *Blood Rites: Origins and History of the Passion of War.* New York: Henry Holt, 1997.

Eliade, Mircea. *The Myth of the Eternal Return, or Cosmos and History.* Princeton: Princeton University Press, 1974.

–. *Yoga: Immortality and Freedom.* 2nd ed. Trans. William R. Trask. Princeton: Princeton University Press, 1969.

Epstein, Isidore. *Judaism.* London: Penguin, 1990.

Erdman, David W. *Commerce des Lumières: John Oswald and the British in Paris, 1790-1793.* Columbia: University of Missouri Press, 1986.

Erdoes, Richard, and Alfonso Ortiz, eds. *American and Indian Myths and Legends.* 1984. Reprint, London: Pimlico, 1997.

Evans, Edward Payson. *The Criminal Prosecution and Capital Punishment of Animals.* 1906. Reprint, London: Faber and Faber, 1987.

–. *Evolutional Ethics.* New York: D. Appleton, 1897.

Evelyn, John. *Acetaria: A Discourse of Sallets.* 1699. Reprint, Brooklyn, NY: Brooklyn Botanical Gardens, 1937.

Fielding, Henry. *The History of Tom Jones: A Foundling.* 1749. Reprint, Franklin Center, PA: Franklin Library, 1980.

Firth, Florence M., ed. *The Golden Verses of Pythagoras and Other Pythagorean Fragments.* Kila, MT: Kessinger, n.d.

Flaubert, Gustave. *Madame Bovary: A Story of Provincial Life.* 1865. Reprint, New York: Oxford University Press, 1985.

Fox, Michael Allen. *Deep Vegetarianism.* Philadelphia: Temple University Press, 1999.

Fox, Michael W. *St. Francis of Assisi, Animals and Nature.* Washington, DC: Center for Respect of Life and Environment, 1989.

Francione, Gary. "Animals – Property or Persons." In Cass R. Sunnstein and Martha C. Nussbaum, eds., *Animal Rights: Current Debates and New Directions,* 108-42. Oxford: Oxford University Press, 2004.

Frank, Joseph. *Dostoevesky: The Miraculous Years, 1865-1871.* Princeton: Princeton University Press, 2002.

Franklin, Benjamin. *The Autobiography and Other Writings.* Ed. Kenneth Silverman. London: Penguin, 1986.

Freschel, M.R.L., ed. *Selections from Three Essays by Richard Wagner.* Rochester, NH: Millennium Guild, 1933.

Gaffney, James. "Eastern Religions and the Eating of Meat." In Steve F. Sapontzis, ed., *Food for Thought: The Debate over Eating Meat,* 223-35. Amherst, NY: Prometheus, 2004.

Gandhi, Mohandas K. *An Autobiography: The Story of My Experiments with Truth.* 1947. Reprint, Boston: Beacon Press, 1993.

–. *Diet and Diet Reform.* Ahmadebad: Navajivan, 1949.

Gassendi, Pierre. *The Selected Works of Pierre Gassendi.* Trans. Craig B. Bush. New York: Johnson Reprint Corporation, 1972.

Gaye, Phoebe Fenwick. *John Gay: His Place in the Seventeenth Century.* London: Collins, 1938.

Girard, René. *Violence and the Sacred.* Baltimore: Johns Hopkins University Press, 1979.

Goldsmith, Oliver. *The Citizen of the World, The Bee.* London: J.M. Dent, 1934.

—. *The Poetical and Prose Works of Oliver Goldsmith.* Edinburgh: Gall Inglis, n.d.

Gompertz, Lewis. *Moral Inquiries on the Situation of Man and Brutes.* Ed. Peter Singer. 1824. Reprint, Fontwell, UK: Centaur, 1992.

Grant, Douglas. *Margaret the First: A Biography of Margaret Cavendish, Duchess of Newcastle, 1623-1673.* Toronto: University of Toronto Press, 1957.

Grosskurth, Phyllis. *Byron: The Flawed Angel.* Toronto: Macfarlane, Walter and Ross, 1997.

Guerber, H.A. *Myths and Legends in the Middle Ages: Their Origins and Influence in Literature and Art.* 1909. Reprint, London: G.G. Harrap, 1926.

Guenther, Mathias. *Tricksters and Trancers: Bushman Religion and Society.* Bloomington: Indiana University Press, 1999.

Guthrie, Kenneth Sylvan, comp. and trans. *The Pythagorean Sourcebook and Library.* Grand Rapids, MI: Phanes, 1988.

Habig, Michael A., ed. *St. Francis of Assisi: Writings and Early Biographies.* Chicago: Franciscan Herald Press, 1983.

Harris, Marvin. *Cows, Pigs, Wars and Witches: The Riddles of Culture.* 1974. Reprint, New York: Vintage, 1989.

Hart, Donna, and Robert W. Sussman. *Man the Hunted: Primates, Predators and Human Evolution.* New York: Westview, 2005.

Hartley, David. *Observations on Man, His Frame, His Duty, and His Expectations.* 1748. 3 vols. Reprint, Gainesville, FL: Scholar's Facsimiles and Reprints, 1966.

Harwood, Dix. *Love for Animals and How It Developed in Great Britain.* New York: privately printed, 1928.

—. *Love for Animals and How It Developed in Great Britain.* Ed. Rod Preece and David Fraser. 1928. Reprint, Lampeter, UK: Mellen, 2002.

Hastings, Hester. *Man and Beast in French Thought of the Eighteenth Century.* 1936. Reprint, New York: Johnson Reprint Corporation, 1973.

Haughton, Emma. "The Fruit and Nut Case." *Guardian* (London), 3 June 1997, 13.

Helps, Arthur. *Animals and Their Masters.* London: Chatto and Windus, 1883.

Hesiod. *Theogony and Works and Days.* Ed. and trans. M.L. West. Oxford: Oxford University Press, 1988.

Hobbes, Thomas. *The English Works of Thomas Hobbes of Malmesbury.* Vol. 5. Ed. William Molesworth. London: G. Bohn, 1839.

—. *Leviathan.* Ed. C.B. Macpherson. London: Penguin, 1981.

Holmes, Richard. *Coleridge: Early Visions, 1772-1804.* New York: Pantheon, 1989.

—. *Shelley: The Pursuit.* 1974. Reprint, New York: New York Review of Books, 1994.

Holroyd, Michael. *Bernard Shaw.* 4 vols. Harmondsworth: Penguin, 1990.

Howitt, William. *Homes and Haunts of the British Poets.* London: George Routledge, n.d.

Hume, David. *A Treatise of Human Nature.* Ed. L.A. Selby Bigge and P.H. Nidditch. 1739-40. Reprint, Oxford: Clarendon Press, 1978.

Iacobbo, Karen, and Michael Iacobbo. *Vegetarian America: A History.* Westport, CT: Praeger, 2004.

*The Idler.* London: W. Sullaby, 1810.

Isaacs, Ronald. *Animals in Jewish Thought and Tradition.* Northvale, NJ: Jason Aaronson, 2000.

Jenyns, Soame. *A Free Inquiry into the Nature and Origins of Evil.* 2nd ed. 1757. Reprint, New York: Garland, 1976.

Jha, D.N. *The Myth of the Holy Cow.* London and New York: Verso, 2002.

Johnston, Kenneth R. *The Hidden Wordsworth: Poet, Lover, Rebel, Spy.* New York: Norton, 1998.

Johnson, Paul. *The Birth of the Modern World Society, 1815-1830.* London: Phoenix, 1991.

Kahn, Charles. *Pythagoras and the Pythagorean Way of Life.* Indianapolis: Hackett, 2001.

Kalechofsky, Roberta. "Jewish Law and Tradition on Animal Rights." In Roberta Kalechofsky, ed., *Judaism and Animal Rights,* 46-55. Marblehead, MA: Micah, 1992.

–. "Judaism and Vegetarianism: In the Camp of Kibroth-Hatavah." In Roberta Kalechofsky, ed., *Judaism and Animal Rights,* 195-200. Marblehead, MA: Micah, 1992.

–, ed. *Judaism and Animal Rights.* Marblehead, MA: Micah, 1992.

Kapleau, Philip. *To Cherish All Life.* Rochester, NY: Zen Center, 1986.

Karl, Frederick. *George Eliot: Voice of a Century.* New York: Norton, 1995.

Kean, Hilda. *Animal Rights: Political and Social Change in Britain since 1800.* London: Reaktion, 1998.

Kenyon-Jones, Christine. *Kindred Brutes: Animals in Romantic Period Writing.* Aldershot: Ashgate, 2001.

King, James. *William Blake: His Life.* London: Weidenfeld and Nicholson, 1991.

Kingsford, Anna Bonus. *Perfect Way in Diet: A Treatise Advocating a Return to the Natural and Ancient Food of Our Race.* Kila, MT: Kessinger, n.d.

–, and Edward Maitland. *Addresses and Essays on Vegetarianism.* 1912. Reprint, Kila, MT: Kessinger, n.d.

Kruuk, Hans. *Hunters and Hunted: Relationships between Carnivores and People.* Cambridge: Cambridge University Press, 2002.

Lal, Basant K. "Hindu Perspectives on the Use of Animals." In Tom Regan, ed., *Animal Sacrifices: Religious Perspectives on the Use of Animals in Science,* 199-212. Philadelphia: Temple University Press, 1986.

Lambert, Malcolm. *The Cathars.* Oxford: Blackwell, 1998.

Lamm, Martin. *Emanuel Swedenborg: The Development of His Thought.* 1915. Reprint, Westchester, PA: Swedenborg Foundation, 2000.

Langland, William. *Piers the Ploughman.* Translated into modern English by J.F. Goodridge. Harmondsworth: Penguin, 1959.

Lavington, Margaret. "Rupert Brooke: A Biographical Note." In Rupert Brooke, *The Collected Poems of Rupert Brooke,* 183-92. New York: Dodd, Mead and Company, 1940.

Levi, Peter. *Tennyson.* New York: Charles Scribner's Sons, 1993.

Linzey, Andrew. *Animal Theology.* Urbana: University of Illinois Press, 1995.

–. "Christianity and the Rights of Animals." *Animals' Voice,* August 1989.

–. *Christianity and the Rights of Animals.* New York: Crossroad, 1991.

Locke, John. *An Essay Concerning Human Understanding.* 2 vols. 1690. Reprint, London: H. Hills, 1710.

–. *Some Thoughts Concerning Education* (1693). In John William Adamson, ed., *Educational Writings of John Locke,* 41-152. Cambridge: Cambridge University Press, 1922.

Loomis, Louise Ropes, ed. *Aristotle: On Man in the Universe.* 1943. Reprint, New York: Gramercy, 1971.

Lovejoy, Arthur O. *The Great Chain of Being: A Study in the History of an Idea.* 1933. Reprint, New York: Harper, 1960.

–, and George Boas. *Primitivism and Related Ideas in Antiquity.* 1935. Reprint, Baltimore: Johns Hopkins University Press, 1997.

Lukes, Steven. *Marxism and Morality.* Oxford: Oxford University Press, 1985.

Mack, Maynard. *Alexander Pope: A Life.* New York: Norton, 1988.

Mackenzie, John. *Hindu Ethics: A Historical and Critical Essay.* 1922. Reprint, New Delhi: Oriental Books Reprint Corporation, 1971.

Maitland, Edward. *Anna Kingsford: Her Life, Letters, Diary and Work.* 3rd ed. London: G. Redway, 1913.

Mandeville, Bernard. *The Fable of the Bees, or Private Vices, Publick Benefits.* 1714-28. Reprint, Oxford: Clarendon, 1924.

Map, Walter. *De Nugis Curialium: Courtiers' Trifles.* Ed. and trans. M.R. James. Oxford: Clarendon, 1983.

Marx, Karl, and Friedrich Engels. *Marx and Engels on Religion.* New York: Schocken, 1964.

Mascaró, Juan, ed. and trans. *The Dhammapada.* London: Penguin, 1973.

–, ed. and trans. *The Upanishads.* London: Penguin, 1973.

Mattal, Sushil, and Gene Thursby, eds. *The Hindu World.* New York: Routledge, 2004.

Maxwell, James, ed. *America's Fascinating Indian Heritage.* Pleasantville, NY: Pegasus, 1978.

McCarthy, Mary. *The Group.* 1963. Reprint, Franklin Center, PA: Franklin Library, 1978.

McManners, John, ed. *The Oxford History of Christianity.* Oxford: Oxford University Press, 2002.

Meyers, Jeffrey. *D.H. Lawrence: A Biography.* New York: Vintage, 1992.

Midgley, Mary. *Animals and Why They Matter.* Athens: University of Georgia Press, 1983.

Millington, Barry. *Wagner.* Rev. ed. Princeton: Princeton University Press, 1992.

Minto, William. *Logic: Inductive and Deductive.* London: John Murray, 1909.

Moore, J. Howard. *The New Ethics.* London: E. Bell, 1907.

–. *The Universal Kinship.* Ed. Charles Magel. 1906. Reprint, Fontwell, UK: Centaur, 1992.

–. "Why I am a vegetarian." *Chicago Vegetarian,* September 1897.

More, Thomas. *Utopia: Latin Text and English Translation.* Ed. and trans. George M. Logan, Robert M. Adams, and Clarence H. Miller. Cambridge: Cambridge University Press, 1995.

Morris, Desmond. *The Animal Contract.* London: Virgin, 1990.

Morton, H.V. *Through Lands of the Bible.* London: Methuen, 1938.

Murray, Oswyn. "Life and Society in Classical Greece." In John Boardman, Jasper Griffin, and Oswyn Murray, eds., *The Oxford History of the Classical World,* 204-33. Oxford: Oxford University Press, 1986.

Naganathan, G. *Animal Welfare and Nature: Hindu Scriptural Perspectives.* Washington, DC: Center for Respect of Life and Environment, 1989.

Nash, Roderick Frazier. *The Rights of Nature: A History of Environmental Ethics.* Madison: University of Wisconsin Press, 1984.

Newton, John Frank. *Return to Nature, or A Defence of the Vegetable Regimen; with some account of an experiment made the last three or four years in the author's family.* London: T. Cadell and W. Davies, 1811.

Nicholson, George. *On the Primeval Diet of Man.* Ed. Rod Preece. 1801. Reprint, Lampeter, UK: Mellen, 1999.

Nokes, David. *John Gay: A Profession of Friendship.* Oxford: Oxford University Press, 1995.

O'Meara, Dominic J. *Pythagoras Revived: Mathematics and Philosophy in Late Antiq-uity.* Oxford: Clarendon, 1992.

Ondaatje, Christopher. *Sindh Revisited.* Toronto: HarperCollins, 1996.

Oswald, John. *The Cry of Nature, or An Appeal to Mercy and to Justice on Behalf of the Persecuted Animals.* Ed. Jason Hribal. 1791. Reprint, Lampeter, UK: Mellen, 2000.

Ovid. *Metamorphoses.* Trans. Mary Innes. London: Penguin, 1955.

Paley, William. *The Works of William Paley, D.D., Archdeacon of Carlisle.* 1785. Reprint, Philadelphia: Crissy Markley, 1850.

Plato. *Gorgias: A Revised Text with Introduction and Commentary by E.R. Dodds.* Ox-ford: Clarendon, 1959.

–. *The Great Dialogues of Plato.* Trans. W.H.D. Rouse. New York: Mentor, 1956.

–. *Republic.* Trans. H. Spens. Glasgow: Robert and Andrew Foulis, 1763.

–. *Statesman.* Trans. J.B. Skemp. Indianapolis: Bobbs-Merrill, 1962.

–. *The Trial and Death of Socrates: Four Dialogues.* [1875?]. Reprint, New York: Dover, 1992.

Pliny the Elder. *Natural History: A Selection.* Trans. John F. Healy. London: Penguin, 1991.

Plutarch. *Plutarch's Moralia.* 17 vols. Trans. Harold Cherniss and William Helmblod. 1927. Reprint, London: William Heinemann, 1957.

Porphyry. *On Abstinence from Animal Food.* Ed. E.W. Tyson. Trans. Thomas Taylor. 1793. Reprint, Fontwell, UK: Centaur, 1965.

Preece, Rod. *Awe for the Tiger, Love for the Lamb: A Chronicle of Sensibility to Animals.* Vancouver: UBC Press, 2002.

–. *Animals and Nature: Cultural Myths, Cultural Realities.* Vancouver: UBC Press, 1999.

–. *Brute Souls, Happy Beasts, and Evolution: The Historical Status of Animals.* Vancou-ver: UBC Press, 2005.

–. "The Prodigous Mr. Youatt: Some Unanswered Questions." *Veterinary History* n.s. 12, 3 (2004): 261-72.

–, ed. *Immortal Animal Souls: Joseph Hamilton's Animal Futurity (1877), together with the Debate among Karkeek, Spooner and Manthorp on "The Future Existence of the Brute Creation" (1839-1840).* Lampeter, UK: Mellen, 2005.

–, and David Fraser. "The Status of Animals in Biblical and Christian Thought: A Study in Colliding Values." *Society and Animals: Journal of Human-Animal Studies* 8, 3 (2000): 245-63.

–, and Lorna Chamberlain. *Animal Welfare and Human Values.* Waterloo, ON: Wilfrid Laurier University Press, 1993.

Prine, Ranchor. *Hindu Ecology: Seeds of Truth.* London: Cassell, 1992.

Pucci, Idanna, ed. *Bhima Swarga: The Balinese Journey of the Soul.* Boston: Little, Brown, 1992.

Ray, John. *The Wisdom of God Manifested in the Works of Creation.* 1691. Reprint, New York: Garland, 1979.

Regan, Tom. "Christians Are What Christians Eat." In Steve F. Sapontzis, ed. *Food for Thought: The Debate over Eating Meat,* 177-85. Amherst, NY: Prometheus, 2004.

–. *Liberating Life: Approaches to Ecological Theory,* ed. Jay B. McDaniel. Maryknoll, NY: Orbis, 1990.

–. "McCloskey on Why Animals Cannot Have Rights." *Philosophical Quarterly,* July 1976.

–. *The Three Generations*. Philadelphia: Temple University Press, 1991.

Regenstein, Lewis G. *Replenish the Earth: A History of Organized Religion's Treatment of Animals and Nature – Including the Bible's Message of Conservation and Kindness toward Animals*. New York: Crossroad, 1991.

Richter, Irma A., ed. *Selections from the Notebooks of Leonardo da Vinci*. Oxford: Oxford University Press, 1977.

Richter, Jean Paul, ed. *The Literary Works of Leonardo da Vinci*. 1883. 1st ed. Reprint, London: Phaidon, 1970.

–, and Irma A. Richter, eds. *The Literary Works of Leonardo da Vinci*. 2nd ed. 2 vols. 1883. Reprint, London: Phaidon, 1970.

Ridgway, R.S. *Voltaire and Sensibility*. Montreal and Kingston: McGill-Queen's University Press, 1975.

Ritson, Joseph. *An Essay on Abstinence from Animal Food as a Moral Duty*. London: Richard Phillips, 1802.

Ritvo, Harriet. *The Platypus and the Mermaid and Other Figments of the Classifying Imagination*. Cambridge, MA: Harvard University Press, 1995.

Rolland, Romain. *Jean-Christophe*. Trans. G. Cannan. New York: Random House, 1938.

Rosen, Steven J. *Holy Cow: The Hare Krishna Contribution to Vegetarianism and Animal Rights*. New York: Lantern Books, 2004.

Rousseau, Jean-Jacques. *Discourse on the Origin and Foundations of Inequality among Men in Rousseau's Political Writings*. Ed. Allan Ritter and Julia Conaway Bondanella. Trans. Julia Conaway Bondanella. New York: Norton, 1998.

–. *Eloisa: A Series of Original Letters*. London: John Harding, 1810.

–. *Émile, or on Education*. Ed. and trans. Allan Bloom. New York: Basic, 1979.

Ryder, Richard D. *Animal Revolution: Changing Attitudes towards Speciesism*. London: Blackwell, 1989.

–. *Animal Revolution: Changing Attitudes towards Speciesism*. Rev. ed. Oxford: Berg, 2000.

Sachs, Boria. *Animals in the Third Reich: Pets, Scapegoats, and the Holocaust*. New York: Continuum, 2000.

Saint Athanasius. *The Life of St. Anthony the Great*. 2 vols. Willis, CA: Eastern Orthodox Books, n.d.

Saint Augustine. *Concerning the City of God against the Pagans*. 4th ed. Trans. Henry Betterson. Harmondsworth, UK: Penguin, 1980.

Saint Bonaventure. *Bonaventure: The Soul's Journey into God, The Tree of Life and The Life of St. Francis*. Trans. Ewert Cousins. Malwah, NJ: Paulist Press, 1978.

Saint Francis of Assisi. *Francis and Clare: The Complete Works*. Trans. Regis J. Armstrong and Ignatius C. Brady. New York: Paulist Press, 1982.

Salt, Henry S. *Animals' Rights Considered in Relation to Social Progress*. 1892. Reprint, Clark Summit, PA: Society for Animal Rights, 1980.

–. *The Savour of Salt: A Henry Salt Anthology*. Ed. George Hendrick and Willene Hendrick. Fontwell, UK: Centaur, 1989.

Sambrook, James. *James Thomson, 1700-1748: A Life*. Oxford: Clarendon, 1991.

Sapontzis, Steve F., ed. *Food for Thought: The Debate over Eating Meat*. Amherst, NY: Prometheus, 2004.

Sarna, Vishnu, ed. *The Pancatantra*. Trans. Chandra Rajan. London: Penguin, 1993.

Schaff, Philip, and Henry Wace, eds. *The Church History of Eusebius*. Grand Rapids, MI: William B. Erdmann, 1961.

Schmidt, Hans-Peter. *Mélanges d'Indianisme à la mémoire de Louis Renou.* Paris: Éditions E. Brocard, 1968.

Schochet, Elijah Judah. *Animal Life in Jewish Tradition: Attitudes and Relationships.* New York: KTAV, 1984.

Scholtmeijer, Marian. *Animal Victims in Modern Fiction: From Sanctity to Sacrifice.* Toronto: University of Toronto Press, 1993.

Schopenhauer, Arthur. *On the Basis of Morality.* 2nd ed. Trans E.F.J. Payne. Indianapolis: Bobbs-Merrill, 1965.

Schure, Edouard. *Pythagoras and the Delphic Mysteries.* [1907?]. Reprint, Kila, MT: Kessinger, n.d.

Schwartz, Richard. *Judaism and Vegetarianism.* Rev. ed. New York: Lantern, 2000.

–. "Questions and Answers." In Roberta Kalechofsky, ed., *Judaism and Animal Rights,* 222-45. Marblehead, MA: Micah, 1992.

–. "Tsa'ar Ba'alei Chayim: Judaism and Compassion for Animals." In Roberta Kalechofsky, ed., *Judaism and Animal Rights,* 59-70. Marblehead, MA: Micah, 1992.

Schweitzer, Albert. *Civilization and Ethics.* London: A. & C. Black, 1923.

–. *A Treasury of Albert Schweitzer.* Ed. Thomas Kiernan. New York: Gramercy, 1994.

Scruton, Roger. "The Conscientious Carnivore." In Steve F. Sapontzis, ed., *Food for Thought: The Debate over Eating Meat,* 81-91. Amherst, NY: Prometheus, 2004.

Seidlmayer, Michael. *Currents of Medieval Thought, with Special Reference to Germany.* Oxford: Blackwell, 1960.

Seneca. *Ad Lucillum Epistolae Morales.* 3 vols. Trans. Richard M. Gummere. New York: G.P. Putnam's Sons, 1925.

Serpell, James. *In the Company of Animals: A Study of Human-Animal Relationships.* Oxford: Blackwell, 1988.

Seymour, Miranda. *Mary Shelley.* New York: Grove, 2002.

Shaftesbury, Lord. *Characteristics of Men, Manners, Opinions, Times.* Ed. Lawrence E. Klein. 1711. Reprint, Cambridge: Cambridge University Press, 1999.

Shaw, George Bernard. *The Doctor's Dilemma, Getting Married, and The Shewing-up of Blanco Posnet.* London: Constable, 1911.

–. *Fifteen Self Sketches.* London: Constable, 1949.

–. *Three Plays.* Franklin Center, PA: Franklin Library, 1979.

Shelley, Percy Bysshe. *The Complete Works of Percy Bysshe Shelley.* 10 vols. Ed. Roger Ingpen and Walter E. Peek. New York: Gordian, 1965.

Sherwin, Oscar. *Goldy: The Life and Times of Oliver Goldsmith.* New York: Twayne, 1961.

Shirer, William L. *Love and Hatred: The Stormy Marriage of Leo and Sonya Tolstoy.* New York: Simon and Schuster, 1994.

Siam, Kenneth, ed. *Fourteenth Century Verse and Prose.* 1921. Reprint, Oxford: Oxford University Press, 1985.

Singer, Peter. *Animal Liberation.* 2nd ed. New York: New York Review of Books, 1990.

Sorabji, Richard. *Animal Minds and Human Morals: The Origins of the Western Debate.* Ithaca, NY: Cornell University Press, 1993.

Spencer, Colin. *Vegetarianism: A History.* 2nd ed. New York: Four Walls Eight Windows, 2002.

St. Clair, William. *The Godwins and the Shelleys.* New York: Norton, 1989.

Steiner, Gary. "Descartes on the Moral Status of Animals." *Archiv für Geschichte der Philosophie* 80, 3 (1998): 268-91.

Stuart, Tristram. *Bloodless Revolution: A Cultural History of Vegetarianism from 1600 to the Present Time.* New York and London: Norton, 2007.

Sunnstein, Cass R., and Martha C. Nussbaum, eds. *Animal Rights: Current Debates and New Directions.* Oxford: Oxford University Press, 2004.

Swedenborg, Emanuel. *Angelic Wisdom Concerning the Divine Law and the Divine Wisdom.* New York: Swedenborg Foundation, 1960.

—. *Arcana Coelestia: The Heavenly Arcanes Which Are Contained in the Holy Scripture, or Word of the Lord Disclosed.* London: Swedenborg Society, 1934.

*The Tatler and Guardian.* New York: Bangs Brothers, 1852.

Taylor, Angus. *Magpies, Monkeys and Morals: What Philosophers Say about Animal Liberation.* 1999. Revised as *Animals and Ethics: An Overview of the Ethical Debate.* Peterborough, ON: Broadview, 2003.

Teaford, M., and P. Ungar. "Diet and the Evolution of the Earliest Human Ancestry." *Proceedings of the National Academy of Science* 97 (2000).

Thomas, Keith. "The First Vegetarians." In Kelly Wand, ed., *The Animal Movement,* 27-33. San Diego: Greenhaven Press, 2003.

—. *Man and the Natural World: Changing Attitudes in England, 1500-1800.* London: Penguin, 1984.

Thoreau, Henry David. *Walden, or Life in the Woods, together with Civil Disobedience.* Ed. Philip Van Doren Stern. New York: Barnes and Noble, 1970.

Tolstoy, Leo. *Recollections and Essays by Leo Tolstoy.* 4th ed. Trans. Aylmer Maude. London: Oxford University Press, 1961.

Torrey, Norman L. *The Spirit of Voltaire.* New York: Columbia University Press, 1938.

Tucker, Robert C., ed. *The Marx-Engels Reader.* New York: Norton, 1978.

Vasari, Giorgio. *The Great Masters.* Ed. Michael Sonino. Trans. Gaston C. Du Vere. 1550. Reprint, New York: Park Lane, 1988.

Voltaire. *Candide.* Trans. Tobias Smollett. 1759. Reprint, Franklin Center, PA: Franklin Library, 1978.

—. *Traité sur la tolérance.* 1763. Reprint, Paris: Flammarion, 1989.

Vyvyan, John. *In Pity and in Anger.* Marblehead, MA: Micah, 1988.

Waddell, Helen. *Beasts and Saints.* 1934. Reprint, London: Constable, 1970.

—, ed. and trans. *The Desert Fathers.* New York: Vintage, 1958.

—, ed. and trans. *The Sayings of the Desert Fathers.* New York: Vintage, 1998.

Walters, Kerry S., and Lisa Portmess, eds. *Ethical Vegetarianism: From Pythagoras to Peter Singer.* Albany, NY: State University of New York Press, 1999.

Ward, Benedicta, ed. and trans. *The Sayings of the Desert Fathers.* Kalamazoo: Cistercian, 1975.

Webb, Steven H. *Good Eating.* Grand Rapids, MI: Brazos, 2001.

Ween, Francis. *How Mumbo-Jumbo Conquered the World.* London: HarperPerennial, 2004.

Wei-Hsun Fu, Charles, and Gerard E. Spiegler, eds. *Movements and Issues in World Religions.* New York: Greenwood, 1987.

Weis, René. *The Yellow Cross: The Story of the Last Cathars' Rebellion against the Inquisition.* New York: Vintage, 2002.

Wesley, John. *The Works of John Wesley.* 14 vols. 1872. Reprint, Grand Rapids, MI: Zondervan, n.d.

West, Martin. "Early Greek Philosophy." In John Boardman, Jasper Griffin, and Gwyn

Murray, eds., *The Oxford History of the Classical World*, 113-23. Oxford: Oxford University Press, 1993.

White, Lynn, Jr. "The Historical Roots of Our Ecologic Crisis." *Science* 155 (1967): 1203-7.

Willey, Basil. *The Eighteenth Century Background: Studies in the Idea of Nature in the Thought of the Period*. 1940. Reprint, London: Chatto and Windus, 1946.

Williams, Howard. *The Ethics of Diet: A Catena of Authorities Deprecatory of the Practice of Flesh-Eating*. Ed. Carol J. Adams. 1883. Reprint, Urbana: University of Illinois Press, 2003.

Winston, David, ed. and trans. *Philo of Alexandria: The Contemplative Life*. New York: Paulist Press, 1981.

Wynne-Tyson, Jon, ed. *The Extended Circle: A Commonplace Book of Animal Rights*. New York: Paragon House, 1989.

–, ed. *The Extended Circle: An Anthology of Humane Thought*. London: Cardinal, 1990.

Youatt, William. *The Obligation and Extent of Humanity to Brutes, Principally Considered with Reference to the Domesticated Animals*. Ed. Rod Preece. 1839. Reprint, Lampeter, UK: Mellen, 2003.

Young, Thomas. *An Essay on Humanity to Animals*. Ed. Rod Preece. 1798. Reprint, Lampeter, UK: Mellen, 2001.

Zaehner, R.C., trans. *Hindu Scriptures*. London: J.M. Dent, 1966.

Zimmer, Heinrich. *Philosophies of India*. 1951. Reprint, Princeton: Princeton University Press, 1989.

Zola, Émile. *Nana*. Trans. George Holden. 1880. Reprint, Franklin Center, PA: Franklin Library, 1981.

# Index

Printed and bound in Canada by Friesens

Set in Adobe Garamond by Robert Kroeger, Kroeger Enterprises

Copy editor: Robert Lewis

Proofreader: Joe Zingrone